Roz and Keith,

for 11 December 1999

from,

Lizzie, Neil, Rehan and Ilmir

ILLUMINATIONS

ILLUMINATIONS

THE WRITING TRADITIONS OF INDONESIA

——— FEATURING MANUSCRIPTS FROM ———
THE NATIONAL LIBRARY OF INDONESIA

ANN KUMAR AND JOHN H. MCGLYNN

WITH ESSAYS AND OTHER CONTRIBUTIONS BY
MASTINI HARDJOPRAKOSO, THOMAS M. HUNTER JR.,
SUPOMO SURYOHUDOYO, A.H. JOHNS, HENRI CHAMBERT-LOIR,
IAN PROUDFOOT, VIRGINIA HOOKER, MARK DURIE,
ANNABEL TEH GALLOP, EDI S. EKADJATI,
RAECHELLE RUBINSTEIN, TH. C. VAN DER MEIJ, T.E. BEHREND,
BERNARD ARPS, ROGER TOL, ULI KOZOK,
ALAN FEINSTEIN

THE LONTAR FOUNDATION, JAKARTA
WEATHERHILL, INC., NEW YORK AND TOKYO

Publication of this book
was made possible by a grant from
RAJAWALI CORPORATION

Additional assistance was provided by
THE FORD FOUNDATION
and
GARUDA INDONESIA

First edition, 1996
© Lontar Foundation, 1996

Published by Weatherhill, Inc., 568 Broadway, Suite 705,
New York, NY 10012, in cooperation with the Lontar Foundation.
Protected by copyright under the terms of the
International Copyright Union; all rights reserved.

Printed in Hong Kong

Library of Congress Cataloging-in-publication Data

Kumar, Ann, 1943–
Illuminations: the writing traditions of Indonesia: featuring manuscripts
from the National Library of Indonesia / Ann Kumar and John H. McGlynn;
with essays and other contributions by Mastini Hardjoprakoso . . . [et al.].
p. cm.
Includes bibliographical references.
ISBN 0-8348-0349-6
1. Indonesia—Languages—Writing. 2. Manuscripts—Indonesia.
I. McGlynn, John H. II. Hardjoprakoso, Mastini, 1923–
III. Perpustakaan Nasional (Indonesia) IV. Title.
P381.I54K86 1996
499'.22111—dc20 96-3625
CIP

Opposite page: A decorative textual frame
(*wadana*) from the *Serat Suryaraja*
seen in Figure 216. National Library
of Indonesia, Jakarta.

Contents

ꦗꦮꦶ (Javanese script manuscript text — 7 lines, not legibly transcribable)

FOREWORD

In 1995 we celebrated not only the fiftieth anniversary of Indonesian independence but also the fifteenth anniversary of the National Library of Indonesia. Though the Library traces its roots back to 1778 with the establishment of the Batavian Society for Science and the Arts (Bataviaasch Genootschap van Kunsten en Wetenschappen), it was not until 1990 that the Library actually attained its autonomous status as a non-departmental institution.

Over the years the Batavian Society for Science and the Arts amassed a large number of books and rare manuscripts; today these form the core of the Library's manuscript collection. In 1950, following the establishment of the Republic of Indonesia, when the Society's name was Indonesianized to Lembaga Kebudayaan Indonesia (Institute of Indonesian Culture), the collection remained as one part of the Institute. Similarly, in 1962, when the status of the Institute was changed to that of a government agency—the Central Museum or Museum Pusat—the collection again remained part of the Museum, which is where it stayed until 1991, when it was transferred in its entirety to the newly established National Library.

Building upon this core of manuscripts, the National Library today holds the largest collection of Indonesian manuscripts in the world, some of the finest of which are represented in this volume. In addition to its almost ten thousand original manuscripts, the Library also has in its collection microfilm copies of all Indonesian manuscripts now stored in British collections, as well as a large number of copies of manuscripts from the Netherlands and a good percentage of copies of manuscripts from smaller collections scattered around Indonesia. Ultimately, the Library's hopes to hold copies of all known extant Indonesian manuscripts, thereby making its position as the preeminent source of scholarship in the field of Indonesian manuscripts unsurpassable.

Unfortunately, not all of the Library manuscripts are in pristine condition. Most of the manuscripts in the Library are made from organic materials—paper, *dluwang, lontar,* bark, bamboo, rattan, and the like—which are not, in general, very durable and, unless properly treated and stored, tend to rot and decay. Moreover, because most of the manuscripts are well over a hundred years old, they must be handled with extreme caution and care.

Climatically controlled conditions are crucial to prevent further deterioration of the Library's manuscript collection, and the Library has earmarked a significant share of its financial resources toward improvement of the Library's physical plant and archival work. Even so, it is still a race against time to ensure that either the original manuscripts themselves, or at least copies of them, will be available for generations to come.

Outside the Library, in the many smaller manuscript collections around the archipelago, the situation is even more precarious; pests, unfavorable weather conditions, as well as basic human ignorance threaten the continued existence of thousands if not tens of thousands of manuscripts. Therefore, the goal of this volume is not only to heighten public sensitivity toward the beauty, artistry, and historical and cultural significance of manuscripts, but to raise public awareness of the need for a much larger and more concerted effort on the part of concerned individuals, private institutions, and the government to save Indonesia's manuscripts.

As beautiful as many of the manuscripts represented herein are, it is not their beauty that is the primary reason behind their need for safekeeping. Written in a wide array of languages and scripts and on diverse kinds of materials, Indonesian manuscripts are a rich storehouse of information for researchers from a wide range of disciplines. The kinds of knowledge these manuscripts contain are as diverse as the manuscripts themselves, and both the knowledge and the events

Opposite page: Detail from the manuscript *Serat Punji Jayakusuma* seen in Figure 192. National Library of Indonesia, Jakarta.

that were recorded in these manuscripts by past generations of scholars hold numerous truths for present and future generations of Indonesians. Manuscripts are important not only because they are old and rare, but because they serve as embodied models of thought for the future.

Contributors to *Illuminations* are, one and all, preeminent scholars in the field of Indonesian letters representing a relatively large number of countries, from Indonesia to the Netherlands, Australia, Germany, France, Great Britain, New Zealand, and the United States. Thus, while geographical distance might make it impossible for these scholars to meet frequently or face to face, this volume offers both them and the wider reading public a forum for the exchange of ideas and information about the Indonesian manuscript tradition.

It is our sincere hope that publication of this book will not only act as an impetus for contributing scholars to continue their work on Indonesian manuscripts but will stimulate the growth of a new generation of scholars and a larger, more appreciative audience for the heretofore hidden but wondrous worlds that can be found in Indonesian manuscripts.

The Lontar Foundation is to be commended for the huge amount of effort that has gone into bringing this book into fruition. The National Library is proud to have contributed to that effort. Together we share the hope that this book will provide impressive witness to the writing traditions of Indonesia.

Mastini Hardjoprakoso
Director, National Library of Indonesia

PREFACE AND ACKNOWLEDGMENTS

The Indonesian intellectual heritage recorded on palm leaf, bamboo, bark, and paper is of exceptional significance, and Indonesia is a land with an abundance of priceless manuscripts. However, heat, humidity, pests, and human ignorance imperil nearly every manuscript. Within a few generations many of the manuscripts in Indonesia that are not kept in climatically controlled conditions might very well be lost.

Investment in the preservation and dissemination of knowledge about these manuscripts is essential. However, part of the problem in raising funds to support such a venture is the limited information available on Indonesia's trove of "undiscovered" manuscripts. It was for this reason—to publicize Indonesia's written traditions—that, in 1991, the Lontar Foundation embarked on a campaign to produce a textual and visual record of Indonesia's writing traditions. One result of that campaign is this book; another is its Indonesian edition, *Candi Bahasa: Tradisi Tulis Indonesia.*

In the years that have passed since this project was first conceived, the Lontar Foundation and, more specifically, the editors of this book have relied on the many contributors to this publication, who gave freely of their time and undertook their work with little thought of financial recompense. We must also thank our friends for encouragement and advice, financial sponsors for their unswerving commitment to the project, and the numerous institutions that opened to us their manuscript collections.

The names and addresses of the institutions from which the illustrations in this publication derive are found in the List of Illustrations. Suffice it is to say, without their assistance this book never would have been completed. To the proprietors, curators, and staff of these collections we offer a collective thanks as well as the encouragement to continue to improve their manuscript collections. As this publication shows, these collections are not merely repositories of old books; the paper, metal, bark, palm, and bamboo texts found therein form a significant part of Indonesia's cultural heritage and are an infinite source of inspiration.

The majority of images in this book come from manuscripts in the collection of the National Library of Indonesia. Located in Jakarta, the National Library holds the largest single collection of Indonesian manuscripts in the world, yet this has thus far been insufficiently recognized. In part this is understandable, for until recently the National Library was unable to offer scholars the access and sophisticated amenities that other major collections provide. Fortunately, this situation is changing and the collection is now kept in round-the-clock, climatically controlled conditions. Further, the bulk of the collection has been placed on microfilm and a database developed especially to serve researchers' needs.

In large part the National Library's increased professionalism is due to the vision of one person, Mastini Hardjoprakoso, the library's director, whose years of dedication to the field of library sciences serve as an inspiration for all. Lontar and the editors of *Illuminations* owe a special debt of gratitude to Ibu Mastini. Her unstinting labors to preserve Indonesia's written heritage truly place her in a category occupied by no other.

At the National Library Ibu Mastini is well served by a number of individuals of similar dedication and zeal. In the preparation of this volume W.W. Sayangbati-Dengah, former head of Library Services, Paul Permadi, the section's current chief, Ediyami Bondan Andoko, Head of Deposits and Conservation, and Nindya Nugraha, Head of the Manuscripts Collection, all supplied a measure of assistance above and beyond the call of duty. For their help we are very grateful.

The staff of the National Library's manuscripts collection were always ready to serve our needs. We would like to thank, by name, the following individuals:

Tutinah Banuwati Munawar, Jumsari Yusuf, Sanwani, Fatmi, Sri Sumekar, Woro Wijati Rahmananta, A.A.G. Alit Geria, Sarmiati Seragih, Mariana Ginting, Siti Hasniati, Komari, and Mardiono.

Also at the National Library we would like to to thank, in the Photographic and Microfilm Section, Nurbay Amir, Tarmidi, and Husni Djasara; A. Chaitami in Public Relations; Artikno S., Chief of Conservation; Dady P. Rachmananta, Chief for Bibliographic and Automation Services; Gardjito, Chief of Manuscripts Preparation; M. Razak, and all the secretaries, guards, and other individuals whose assistance made our work at the National Library much easier than it might otherwise have been.

Outside the National Library, Lontar collected photographic materials from numerous other institutions in Indonesia. For assistance in obtaining access to these collections we would like to thank: at the National Museum, Suwati Kartiwa, Intan Mardiana Napitupulu, Suhardini, and Paulina Suitela; at the National Archives, Noerhadi Magetsari and Djoko Utomo; at the Palace of Yogyakarta, Sri Sultan Hamengkubuwono X and G.B.P.H.H. Prabukusumo; at the Sonobudoyo Museum in Yogyakarta, H. Basuki, Saifur Rachman, and Pardiyono; at the Sri Baduga State Museum of West Java, Yetti Heryati; at Museum Bali in Denpasar, I Putu Budiastra; at the Gedong Kirtya manuscripts collection in Singaraja, I Made Nila; and at Yayasan Pemeliharaan Naskah (YAPENA) in Bandung, Viviane Sukanda-Tessier and Haris Sukanda.

Thanks are also due to the family of Liem Khen Yong in Ujung Pandang, especially to his surviving children, Liem Biao Ing and Liem Biao Siong, and his niece, Lucia Suryanti, who gave us access to the family's collection of manuscripts.

During the pre-production stage of this publication the editors had the privilege of working with a number of highly skilled and professional photographers. Special thanks go to Annie Gilbert of the British Library who came to Jakarta to work with the staff of the National Library to photograph most of the manuscripts featured herein. Additional photographic work at the National Library was undertaken by Ferry Ardiyanto. It was a true pleasure to work with both these photographers.

For photographic work outside the National Library, we must also thank, in Indonesia, Johnny Hendarta, Leonardus Agus, Tara Sosrowardoyo, Leonard Lueras, and Ridha N. Kusumabrata. Edwin Rahardjo and his assistant, Hasan, of Edwin's Gallery, deserve a special note of thanks for giving so freely of their time and producing many of the wonderful images that appear in this publication.

To the people of Tunggalis village who demonstrated for us the *daluang* production process we also give our thanks, as we do to the people of the village of Bungaya Kangin in Karangasem who helped to describe the *lontar* production process and to I Dewa Gde Catra and Cokorda Rai Sudharta who helped to arrange the necessary photographic work.

In the Netherlands we have several people to thank for assistance in obtaining photographic materials: at the University of Leiden Library, Jaan Joost Witkam and Hans van der Velde; Roger Tol at KITLV; and Henk Porck at the Royal Library in The Hague. Additional thanks go to Dick van der Meij and René Teygeler. A special note of thanks to H.I.R. Hinzler for her assistance in photographic work of the *lontar* production process and Balinese manuscripts.

For photographs from British collections we have especially to thank, at the British Library, Annabel Gallop, Michael Hoey, and Marjam Foot; at the Bodleian Library, Doris Nicholson; and at the School of Oriental and African Studies, Robert Boyling. In Australia we have to thank Robyn Maxwell at the National Gallery of Australia; in the United States, Mary-Ann Lutzker of Mills College; and in Singapore, John Miksic of the National University of Singapore.

On behalf of Tom Hunter, the editors would also like to thank Randall E. Baier of the University of Michigan for his assistance in finding materials that made possible the writing of "Ancient Beginnings: The Spread of Indic Scripts"; on behalf of Raechelle Rubinstein we would like to thank Peter Worsley for his comments on the Balinese chapter. We are grateful to Claudine Lombard Salmon for permitting the incorporation of material from her work on the literature of the Ujung Pandang Chinese community into the chapter on the Chinese manuscript tradition.

In addition we would like to thank the following persons, for advice, assistance, and other services that proved so vital to this project: Edi Sedyawati, Director General of Cultural Affairs; Haryati Soebadio, the former Minister of Social Affairs; Stephen Roman; Rosemary Shipsey; Maureen Pieters; Janet Boileau; Amir Sidharta; Stephen Grant; Gregory Churchill; W.J. Frost; David Salman; T.E. Behrend; Henri Chambert-Loir; Jennifer Lindsay; Mildred Wagemann; Gai Littler; T.W. Kamil; Karin Johnson; Joesoef Isak; K.R.T. Hardjonegoro; J.G. Vredenbregt; Petrus Voorhoeve; W. Stokhof; Marijke Klokke; John Guy; Daniel Meury; I Kuntara Wiryamartana; and Willem van der Molen.

We also thank Weatherhill, Inc. and its president, Jeffrey Hunter, for sustained support of this project over many years; Liz Trovato and Mariana Canelo, the book designers; and Meg Taylor, the editor.

A final personal note of thanks goes to two individuals without whose consistent backing and support this project might never have gotten off the ground: Mary Zurbuchen, currently the director of the Ford Foundation's Southeast Asia Office, and Alan Feinstein, formerly the cultural program officer at the Ford Foundation.

In terms of funding, *Illuminations* represents, for Lontar, an extraordinarily massive undertaking. Lontar's regular operating costs are underwritten by Friends of Lontar, a loosely organized group of companies and individuals who share Lontar's goals and help to underwrite Lontar's operational expenses. These friends include Yayasan Jaya Raya, PT Kodel, Fikri Jufri, Matra Magazine, PT Danamon, Lippobank, Tempo News weekly, PT HM Sampoerna, The Kresna Group, Nirwan Bakrie, and PT Freeport Indonesia.

The high cost of this publication made it necessary for Lontar to establish a special project fund. A substantial grant from the Ford Foundation was used to offset research and development costs. Additional assistance from the British Council helped to cover part of the cost of photography in Indonesia, and a grant from the Indonesian Linguistics Development Project of the Department of Languages and Cultures of Southeast Asia and Oceania made possible some of the photographic work in the Netherlands. Chedi Hotel in Bandung provided in-kind assistance.

Joop Ave, Minister for Tourism, Post & Telecommunications, gave the project a huge boost by hosting a fund-raising dinner for Lontar. His generosity and kindness is gratefully acknowledged.

Lontar was also fortunate to find a friend in Garuda Indonesia Airways, this publication's official air carrier. For that company's assistance we are especially grateful. The editors extend a special note of thanks to Kussuyono, Senior Vice President of Commercial Affairs, and Soepandi, President.

Finally, Lontar owes a special debt—a *hutang budi* as well as a *hutang emas*— to Rajawali Corporation. Rajawali Corporation has shown an admirable and continuing commitment to the preservation of Indonesia's cultural traditions, which we very much hope other corporations will feel inspired to emulate. Peter Sondakh, President Director of Rajawali, has put great personal effort into the successful completion of the long journey resulting in *Illumminations*. It has been both an honor and a pleasure to work with him.

John H. McGlynn

INTRODUCTION

This book—remarkably enough the first ever to bring together in one volume Indonesia's aesthetically and intellectually rich writing traditions—is intended to be several things. First and most obvious, a source of visual delight, in which the aesthetic sensitivity and ingenuity displayed in the interplay of medium (whether stone, copper, *lontar*, bark, or paper), writing, and decoration enchant the eye of the reader. But it is also more than another art book, however beautiful: it is a revolutionary transformation of the accepted picture of Indonesia's past and of what are usually referred to as the traditional societies of Indonesia's many islands. These societies are often seen as static, somewhat isolated societies where the oral rather than the written was the dominant means of communication, literature, and transmission of learning: societies that were suddenly awakened from rustic somnolence by the arrival of the dynamic West. Yet the contributions to this book reveal written communication going back two millennia, constantly evolving, revealing, and giving rise to major social and intellectual transformations. The geographical spread of these traditions is an exemplification of the national motto, Unity in Diversity. There is diversity in plenty, yet if we survey the whole scene rather than looking at one particular region, there is also a unity that is not due, as often claimed, to the imposition of a harsh colonial yoke, a unity that springs from gentler yet stronger bonds than the conquests of indigenous kings. This unity springs from the role of great indigenous centers of learning, which not only spread their light to the rest of the archipelago but also far beyond it.

Indonesia's writing traditions have a spread in time that is as deep as their geographical spread is wide: in fact the use of writing in Indonesia may have begun much earlier than has previously been recognized. As Thomas M. Hunter Jr. writes, scholars have long suspected that an international trading network linking China and Southeast Asia with India and the Near East had developed by the beginning of the first millennium A.D., and hard evidence has now come to light with recent discoveries on the north coast of Bali. Here, in addition to pottery shards carrying evidence of the Brahmi script common in southern India c. A.D. 100–400, pieces of rouletted pottery nearly identical to samples from southeast India and datable to the period 150 B.C. to A.D. 200 have been unearthed. Another important find at the same site is a fragment of a clay mold used in the manufacture of bronze Dongson drums originating in northern Vietnam and traded widely throughout the archipelago from at least c. 500 B.C. Though the pottery finds reveal only the presence of an Indian script, it is highly likely that Indonesians too had learnt the skill of writing, perhaps before the Christian era, in order to participate in this network.

However, the earliest dated evidence of the use of writing in Indonesia is still the Yupa inscriptions from Kutai, West Kalimantan, of c. A.D. 400. They are related to inscriptions of the South Indian Pallava dynasty and to inscriptions in modern Vietnam dated c. A.D. 350, indicating that Indonesia had extensive connections to the north and to the west by this date.

The use of Sanskrit in these inscriptions is one piece of evidence among many of the overwhelming attraction of Indian civilizations and religions—Hinduism and Buddhism—for the aristocracies of Southeast Asia. This led among other things to the adoption of Indic scripts for the writing of the indigenous languages of the region. In Java, the script that developed is generally called Kawi. This script also became the mother script for many other societies of present-day Indonesia. In its Javanese homeland it underwent a long and inventive evolution, and many different styles were produced, ranging from the simple, elegant, and clear to the highly elaborated.

With the first emergence of Indonesia's history from the mists of unrecorded time—unrecorded, that is, in any surviving writings—we find the Indonesian centers of learning referred to above already in existence. As Supomo Suryohudoyo writes, by the seventh century some of these had gained such a high reputation as centers to study Indic religion that even people from overseas were attracted to visit and study there. The Chinese pilgrim I-Ching, for instance, tells us in his memoirs that the Buddhist priests in Srivijaya studied the whole Indic curriculum. He himself stopped in Srivijaya to study grammar while on his way to India in A.D. 671 and later returned and stayed for another four years to complete a new translation of the scriptures into Chinese. Another Chinese pilgrim, Hui-ning, went to Walaing in Central Java in 664 and translated the Sanskrit texts of the Theravada into Chinese under the guidance of a Javanese monk.

As the spread of literacy reached wider circles of the community, the use of Sanskrit as the language of the inscriptions was gradually replaced by indigenous languages. By the time of I-Ching's visit to Srivijaya, the use of Old Malay must have been more common than the use of Sanskrit, since the inscriptions found in southern Sumatra from this period are all written in Malay. In Java, Old Javanese inscriptions began to appear in the early ninth century and in Bali the Old Balinese language began to be used in the late ninth century. Much of the unifying dynamic referred to above springs from the roles and interaction of these two great written traditions, the Javanese and the Malay, which did so much to draw together the island world into a many-stranded yet somehow enduringly interwoven pattern of civilization, religion, and learning.

We see the central role of Java in two waves or diffusions of the Kawi script developed there. In the first of these, later forms of Kawi were influential outside Java, particularly in Bali, where a large number of copperplate inscriptions reveal both Javanese influence and local characteristics. The Sundanese script and the Malay script of the central Sumatran king Adityavarman (1365–1375) also evolved from forms of Kawi script. The second diffusion of Kawi led to the evolution of simpler core sets of characters in the so-called "ka-ga-nga" syllabaries, found in Bali and other parts of insular Southeast Asia, particularly Sumatra, southern Sulawesi, and the Philippines.

FROM INSCRIPTIONS TO LITERATURE

The earliest evidence we have of the existence of an indigenous literary tradition is an Old Javanese inscription dated 856 A.D.. Like most Javanese inscriptions, it is a legal document—confirming the granting of a freehold by a king to a village official; unlike the others, however, it is written in verse. It is a short poem of twenty-nine stanzas written in a Sanskrit poetical form called *kakawin* in Old Javanese—a derivative of the Sanskrit-derived word *kawi* ("poet"). Within these twenty-nine stanzas the poet demonstrates his ability to use no less than six different meters, as well as his mastery of difficult literary devices from the Indian tradition.

Turning to major literary works, the *Ramayana kakawin* is the only surviving Old Javanese work datable from the Central Javanese period. It is now generally accepted that this poem must have been written before the transfer of the seat of power from Central to East Java, probably in the middle of the ninth century, thus at approximately the same period as the metrical inscription. Its choice of model—a notoriously difficult Sanskrit text intended to illustrate the rules of Sanskrit grammar and poetical embellishments—is testimony to the advanced abilities and ambitions of its author, who succeeded in writing what was without doubt a masterpiece, and has been honored as such throughout the centuries.

The writing of the *Ramayana* based on such a difficult text and the building of the magnificent temples of Borobudur and Prambanan with their thousands of bas-relief sculptures, based on Buddhist texts and a version of the Rama story, reflect the vigorous study of literary texts that had begun at least by the seventh century. This is corroborated by a ninth-century inscription from the mainland kingdom of Champa, which tells us that a high official went on a pilgrimage to Java "to acquire magical science," a reference to Java's reputation for possessing esoteric knowledge.

The Javanization of the Indian Heritage

It is clear that Javanese versions of the Indian classics are not simple translations but have been rewritten in accordance with local norms. One of the most common changes is the elaboration of a character who in the original plays only a minor or an inconspicuous role. In other cases wholly new characters are invented: for instance, the heroic Suwandha in the Javanese *Arjunawijaya*, who became famous among Javanese through the centuries as an exemplary hero, and whose courage and loyalty is held up as a model for those who aspire to enter a ruler's service. Wives are a popular choice when new characters are added, reflecting a typically Indonesian desire to give prominence to women. In the *Bharatayuddha*, for instance, we find Bhanumati, Ksitisundari, and Satyawati as the wives of Duryodhana, Abhimanyu, and Salya respectively; and in the *Arjunawijaya* there is Citrawati, the wife of Arjuna.

Another change is the transposition of what are basically Indian narratives into a Javanese setting. Especially when the narrative moves from the capital city to the countryside, there is little doubt that the poets are describing a Javanese panorama, depicted in a way that springs from the Javanese cult of beauty. It was a landscape with which the poets were familiar, as it was through such scenery that they wandered in search of secluded spots where they could be united with the god of beauty. The scenery is definitely Javanese, complete with all manner of typical Javanese fruits and flowers, birds and fishes, which are still found in Java even today.

In these and other ways Indic materials were thoroughly made Indonesia's own. At this juncture, a second great influence from even further west brought the religious, intellectual, and aesthetic enrichment of one of the world's greatest writing traditions.

The Beginnings of the Islamic Manuscript Tradition

How and when did the Islamic writing tradition take root in the Malay world? A.H. Johns writes that it is not possible to document it further back than the late seventeenth century though these earliest Malay works extant already show evidence of a remarkable symbiosis between Malay and Arabic which bespeaks an interaction between the two languages over centuries. The absorption of a rich Arabic vocabulary into Malay, and the adoption of the Arabic script, may have sprung from the establishment of Muslim quarters in already existing port cities, or the founding of new ones by Muslim traders. We may assume the presence here of Islamic scholars and perhaps also of an educational curriculum that included *tafsir* (Quranic exegesis), *hadith* (prophetic tradition), *tawhid* (dogmatics), *fiqh* (jurisprudence) *kalam* (scholastic theology), *tasawwuf* (mysticism), and *nahu* (grammar). Astronomy, mathematics, history, lexicography, poetry, and rhetoric were presumably also taught.

Basic to the curriculum is a mastery of Arabic, the language of revelation, the language of the Prophet, and the language of the great disciplines which are at the core of training in *madrasa* and *pesantren* and are essential to the functioning of an Islamic community, foremost among them jurisprudence.

The section on the Acehnese Quran school of Tanoh Abee gives us some idea of how such institutions functioned as centers of Islamic literacy and learning.

Every Muslim is required to be able to read correctly the fully vowelled Arabic script of the Quran. A fundamental rite of passage for boys and girls all over Indonesia in schools such as Tanoh Abee is *tammat Quran*, completion of study of the Book. Every Muslim should have a copy of the Quran to be kept with love and reverence. As late as the nineteenth century, Malay scribes were copying Qurans for the East India Company sepoys. Yet the practice is a very old one, and increasing numbers of Qurans would have been needed as soon as there were Muslim communities in the region. A number of beautifully written Qurans from different places in Indonesia are among the highlights of this volume.

The need to make copies of the Quran stimulated general skills in calligraphy. Once these had been acquired, they could be put to a variety of other uses such as copying collections of the Hadith, of credal statements, and other Arabic works on disciplines such as exegesis, devotion, theology, and grammar. From this it was only a short step to use of Arabic script for the writing of Malay as for many other languages, as far west as Spain.

WRITING IN MALAY: DEVELOPING A NEW TRADITION OF UNITY

By the period of the Malay manuscript the historical evidence is somewhat fuller than the tantalizingly patchy records of very early history; and thus we can form some picture of the diverse social world that produced this writing tradition. As Ian Proudfoot and Virginia Hooker note in their chapter, Malay manuscripts come from Sumatra, peninsular Malaya, southern Thailand, Brunei, coastal Sarawak, Kalimantan, the Javanese coastal area, Lombok, Makasar, Bima, Ambon, and other areas of eastern Indonesia. Malay was used along the shipping routes as a lingua franca for people who spoke quite different languages at home. The workaday Malay of sailors and traders prepared the ground for other uses of the language in intraregional and international networks, and the language was also used in the very different social circle of the court, for literary and for religious works. From the courts come also the elaborate royal letters presented in this volume, letters that usually bore the royal seals described and illustrated here.

Court Malay was also used for the composition of dynastic histories centering on the ruling house: these first trace the history of the dynasty, then set the constitution of the state. They provide us with interesting insights into political issues of the time and place. The *Sejarah Melayu*, for instance, deals with problems of distinguishing authority and executive power, in particular of reconciling the Sultan's remit with that of his chief minister; Pasai and Aceh histories lament fratricidal conflict within the state; and those of Pattani and Aceh deal with the problematic nature of female rule for Muslims.

The romance was a very popular genre in both court and village circles, and many Malay romances deal with the rise of a lowly hero, typically a prince abandoned at birth and raised as a commoner. Some, like the *Hang Tuah*, not only deal with the hero's worldly and spiritual advancement but also express a distinctive Malay political ethos, and contain episodes meant to demonstrate Malay guile against the might of the Chinese or Javanese. Other Malay texts of Islamic origin reflect the military aspect of Islam and its enthusiastic reception by local elites, as for instance the epics dealing with Muhammad Hanafiah, Raja Handak, and Amir Hamzah.

Malay interacted over a long period with the other great seminal language of Indonesia, Javanese. It shows much influence from Javanese Panji stories as well as of Hindu-Javanese legends such as that of Rama, and of *wayang* stories. From the Islamic heritage, the Malay *Hikayat Syaikh Abdul Kadir Jilani*, hagiographies of the founders of the Kadiriah, is a translation from Banten Javanese. Conversely, the stories of Islamic heroes were translated from Malay into Javanese, and were popular on the coast. It seems that the two languages developed complementary areas: Malay was the main language of Muslim discourse, while Javanese has a rich devotional and mystical literature. On the other hand Malay was the language generally preferred for translations of Arabic dogmatic texts, and a greater range of commentaries, manuals of law, and orthodox theological works was available in Malay. So even in Java, Malay was a language of the *pesantren*, especially on the cosmopolitan north coast.

A common genre of manuscript in Malay (as in Javanese) was the *primbon*, a sort of personal or family mini-encyclopedia containing notes and diagrams on everything from numerology to aphrodisiacs, once again reflecting the spread of literacy beyond elite circles.

Malay ballads show a fascination with the fluctuations of fortune, hidden identities, the crossing of class boundaries, and the quest. Just as we have seen how Javanese adaptations of Indian works give greater prominence to female characters, so Malay ballads more often than not give a woman the leading role: the eponymous *syairs Ken Tambuhan, Bidasari, Puteri Akal, Saudagar Budiman, Siti Zaiwah, Selindung Delima,* and others bear the names of their leading ladies. Most are women of spirit, and several don disguises to rescue wimpish husbands.

Other ballads relate contemporary events, mostly single events of current interest. The *syair* style was used as an effective means of giving public exposure to the issues of the day as well as to social events, gossip, and even scandal: in other words, we see here the beginning of the journalistic tradition that Malay would later carry forward in print. Subjects range from wars, particularly victories and defeats in engagements with Europeans, to descriptions of receptions, marriages, and deaths. In this connection mention may be made of the gorgeously decorated manuscript of the *Syair Perkawinan Kapitan Tik Sing*, the wealthy head of the Chinese community in Riau. Like his glittering wedding, the manuscript is lavish and designed to impress.

The great significance of the role of the Malay language in developing an intellectual tradition that drew in many different regions of Indonesia goes back much further in time than is generally appreciated. In Bima, for instance, Islamization also meant Malayization. The Bimanese had both a native tongue (*basa* Mbojo) and used Malay as the language of politics and culture. To what extent the Bima (Mbojo) language had been used previously in written form is still a matter of debate, but a local historical text states that in 1645 the second sultan ordered that from then on every official document would be written down "in Malay, in the script prescribed by Allah."

As a result Bima became one of many active centers in a wide network of Malay culture. Malay texts produced in faraway centers were known in Bima, and new original texts were produced locally. Copies of famous texts such as the *Taj us-Salatin, Qisas al-Anbiya,* or *Hikayat Indra Jayakusuma* survive to this day. Inner evidence from other texts proves that the most important works of Malay literature, whether historical, literary, or religious, were familiar to the educated Bimanese. In Sulawesi, too, Malay-Islamic texts were extremely important: the *Lukman al-Hakim,* for instance, and adaptations from Malay of the *Bustan* and *Taj as-Salatin*.

In Aceh, Malay was the language of written communication and scholarship by the seventeenth century, and the political ascendancy of Aceh in the 1600s meant that it was a major literary center for Malay. A number of important early Malay manuscripts originate from Aceh. Religious textbooks, letters, and other documents such as passports, laws, contracts, and seals of authority were traditionally produced in Malay written in Arabic script, though only a minority of people would probably have been proficient in this written Malay. And in South Sumatra, we find that Malay with Javanese influence was used as the high or literary language, while in the Batak area we see again the enormous influence of Kawi as mother script. Uli Kozok notes an interesting anticolonial text written in 1915 and dealing with the Karo Batak leader of Batukaran, who in 1904 tried unsuccessfully to prevent the annexation of the Karo highlands by the colonial army, something of a parallel to the Acehnese *Hikayat Prang Sabil*, which played such an important role in the Aceh War.

REGIONAL RICHES AND INTERREGIONAL LINKS

Within the larger currents and commonalities described above, there was room for much local invention—intellectual, aesthetic, and technical—as the chapters on the different regional writing traditions show. In the chapter on Sulawesi, we see this in the technical sphere in the ingenious roll manuscripts, based on the same principle as videocassettes; and in the literary sphere in the *La Galigo* epic, perhaps the most voluminous work in world literature. Set in a meter of five and in some cases four syllables, it is set in pre-Islamic Luwuq, regarded as the cradle of Bugis culture.

Yet despite these and many other regional achievements, one should not regard these regional writing traditions as hermetically sealed compartments. The Javanese tradition, for instance, shares with Malay the use of *primbon*, the largest group of popular texts, often compiled by individuals over many years, or by families over the space of several generations. Forming the core of this group of texts are the guides to the complex systems for measuring time—the sacral or semantic time of the *pawukon* system—and for dealing with its consequences. In other genres too, the Javanese manuscript tradition overlaps with Malay, for instance in the epics and romances dealing with heroes and heroines, whether indigenous (Panji), Indic (Arjuna, Sembadra), or Islamic (Amir Hamzah, Iskandar, Yusup). There is also some common ground in the chronicles, centering around royal genealogies, wars, and court events, though the political ethos of the Javanese courts differs somewhat from that of the Malay world. The chapter on Sunda provides a strikingly impressive illustration of a society where these interregional linkages led to the development of a multilingual literacy utilizing the vernacular language, Javanese, and Malay.

THE MANUSCRIPT AS ART FORM

The manuscripts presented in this book exhibit an extraordinary variety in medium and in script and illustration, ranging from the visually stunning Batak bast manuscripts through the wonderful detail of the Balinese *lontar* to the illuminated book-form manuscripts in the Islamic tradition. Perhaps the most highly developed aesthetic tradition over a long period is that of the Javanese manuscript. This often reveals a strong link between the written text and the *wayang* theatrical tradition; there are eighteenth-century manuscripts with illustrations in *wayang beber* style, and others in *wayang kulit* style. In a small number of manuscripts a hybrid, three-dimensional style appeared. Here it is not the flat exemplars provided by *wayang kulit* puppets, but the round, wooden *wayang golek* puppets that form the illustrator's models.

Later Javanese manuscripts show some Western aesthetic influence, but T.E. Behrend argues convincingly that the *wayang* tradition appears to have placed limits on the extent to which naturalism could be adopted via Western influence. In this tradition, representational naturalism can be used for ogres, as for flora and fauna. But humans possess culture, behavioral norms, and spiritual wisdom that set them apart from nature. The more refined an individual becomes, the more civilized, the wiser, the more removed that person becomes from the world of nature. Thus in *wayang* iconography the less human a character appears, the more fully human he actually is in moral terms. This aesthetic seems to be at work as well in manuscript illustration, inhibiting the development of human realism. Yet, should we regret this? Surely the *wayang* style, like the Japanese print, should not be regarded as a failure to achieve Western norms but rather as a whole alternative aesthetic.

Other aesthetic features of Javanese manuscripts include illumination and the use of enframing and textual gateways. At times page frames would be elaborated on the opening and closing pages of a manuscript, becoming ornamental frontispieces, called *wadana*, that acted as monumental gateways giving access to the inner pages of the text, then leading out of that sacred textual space at the end. It is in these ornamental gates that Javanese illumination reached its most spectacular heights.

Pictorial calligraphy, where decorative devices or animal figures are created by manipulating and contorting the lettering of a selected text in either Arabic or Javanese script, is relatively rare. In Cirebon, in the early through mid-nineteenth century, there was a full-blown tradition of true figural calligraphy. This is attested not only in a small number of manuscripts, but in numerous ornamental wood carvings and wall panels in the *kraton* of the city.

THE LIVING MANUSCRIPT TRADITION

The section on Bali provides the fullest picture of a living manuscript tradition. Here we see the complicated technical business of production of *lontar*, with its many successive procedures. We also see in Bali the multiple social and learned uses of *lontar* manuscripts: for personal records, village records (membership of village councils, and members' duties), regulations about cockfighting, rice cultivation, irrigation; contracts between kings; letters; esoteric specialist lore, such as the vocational manuals of high priests, temple caretakers, Sudra exorcists, metaphysical treatises on *wayang*, artists' guides, guides for healers. There were also texts not belonging to any one group like the *Tutur Aji Saraswati*, which deals with the philosophical foundations of alphabet mysticism; as well as the *pangayam-ayaman*, which deal with the characteristics of roosters and were consulted when betting at cockfights. *Lontar* texts were thus used for everything from recordkeeping to ritual occasions and religious instruction. They were also used for genealogical and historical writing and belles-lettres, preserving a pre-Islamic heritage composed of Balinese, Javanese, and Indic contributions.

THE END OF THE MANUSCRIPT TRADITION

Chapter 14, "The Decline of the Manuscript Tradition," deals with a revolution in Indonesian communication as transformative as the first introduction of writing two millennia before: the consequences of the mid-nineteenth-century print revolution. From this time, European and Chinese printers printed Malay newspapers and new books in the Dutch script, while Muslims used lithography to multiply faithful copies of Arabic-script manuscripts. In present-day Sulawesi, the art of the manuscript partly survives through the use of lithography in the more Islamic-oriented sections of society.

This revolution is a new story, and owes much to the role of itinerant Muslim religious figures bringing books and literacy from urban to rural areas. It is a story that cannot be fully told here, though it should be noted that the implications of print superseding manuscripts were enormous for literacy, and for the spread both of Western-style education and of Islamic reform.

We cannot regret that in Indonesia as elsewhere the efficiencies of print over manuscript have been appreciated; or ask that Indonesians, who have always been so inventive themselves and so appreciative of the inventions of others, should remain in a time warp, however picturesque, for the delectation of tourists. But the last and perhaps most important purpose of this book is to emphasize that

Indonesia's manuscript heritage is non-renewable, and that every instance of loss or damage is a permanent diminution of that heritage. Alan Feinstein's contribution sends a message that is crucial to the purpose of this book. It clearly reveals the difficult choices that have to be made under funding constraints, and the necessity for stimulating an increased awareness of the role that people generally, not just librarians, can play in conserving, or unwittingly destroying, these regional and national treasures. I hope that we contributors, in paying tribute to the work of the artists, poets, scholars, and scribes who produced these wonderful manuscripts, have shown how important this heritage is: in aesthetic terms, in intellectual terms, for our understanding of Indonesia's history in its own terms, and for our understanding of human civilization as a whole.

Ann Kumar

ILLUMINATIONS

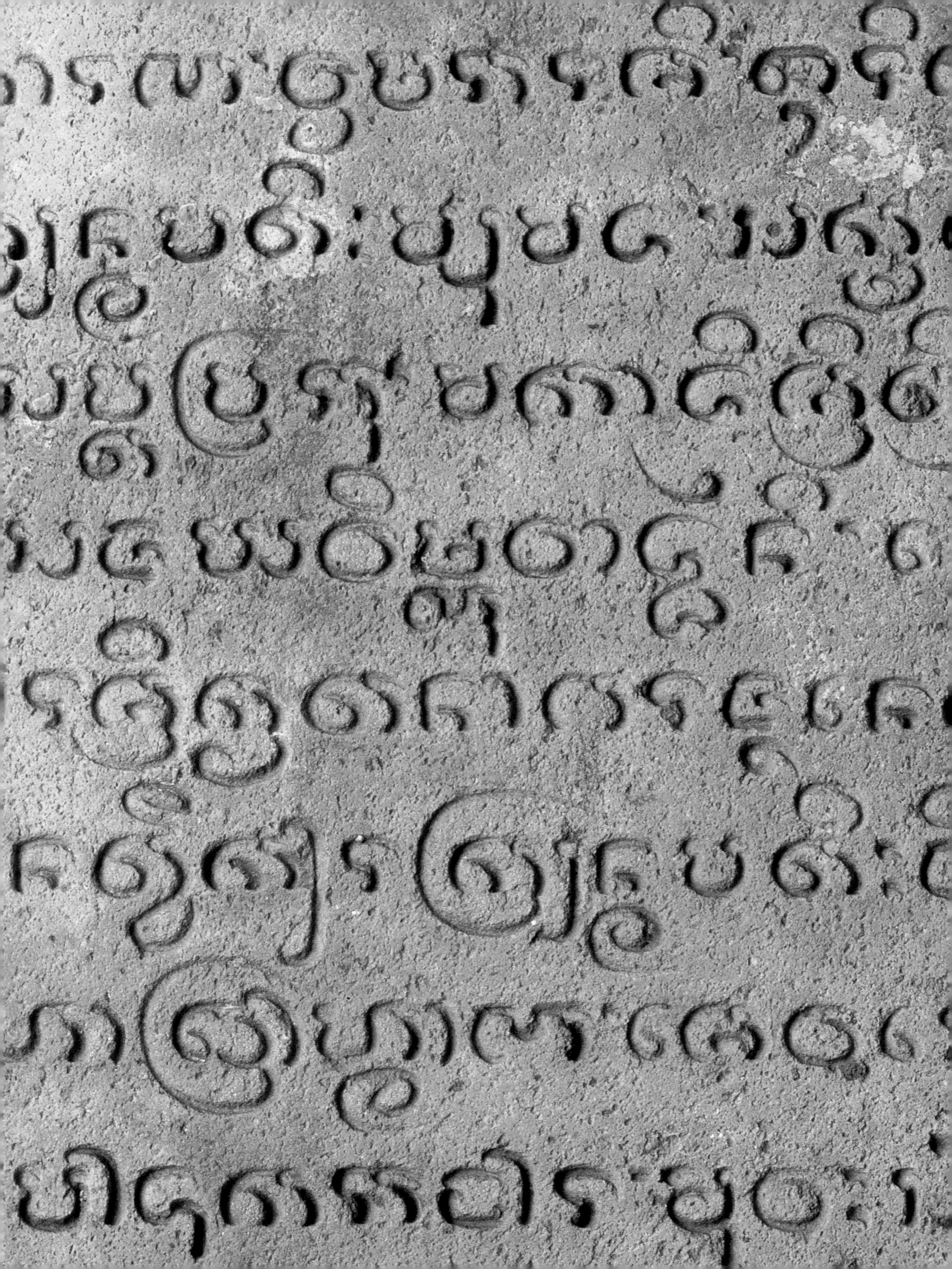

ANCIENT BEGINNINGS:
THE SPREAD OF INDIC SCRIPTS

While today the majority of Indonesian documents are written in the Roman alphabet, a significant number are still produced either in some form of Arabic script or in regional scripts such as Javanese, Sundanese, and Balinese that share a common origin in ancient writing systems of Indian provenance. A rich inheritance of texts in scripts no longer in common use, like Batak and Bugis, also attests to the dissemination of the technology of writing throughout Southeast Asia during an era of maritime trade that brought with it the spread of Hinduism and Buddhism.

The study of the historical evidence recording the early evolution of writing in insular Southeast Asia creates a romance of its own, redolent with the aroma of spices carried on the Indian, Indonesian, and Chinese trading vessels that plied Southeast Asian waters in the first millennium A.D. A brief survey of the inscriptions in stone and copperplate, which are the most visible traces of this evolution, opens a window onto an ancient maritime network that had profound consequences on the development of Southeast Asian political, religious, and cultural forms. It is also a necessary background to any survey of the writing systems that sprang from these ancient roots.

EARLY AND LATER PALLAVA SCRIPT

While scholars have long suspected that an international trade network linking China and Southeast Asia with India and the Near East had developed by the beginning of the first millennium A.D., hard evidence has only recently come to light, with findings reported by Ardika and Bellwood for Sembiran on the north coast of Bali. Here, in addition to pottery shards carrying evidence of the Brahmi script common in South India c. 100–400 A.D., Ardika has unearthed pieces of rouletted pottery ware nearly identical in composition to samples from the Arikamedu site in southeast India, datable to the period 150 B.C. to A.D. 200. Another important find at this site is a fragment of a clay mold used in the manufacture of bronze drums of the Dongson type originating in northern Vietnam and traded widely throughout the archipelago from at least c. 500 B.C. This find pushes the evidence for an international trade network with a port of call on the north coast of Bali back into the first millennium B.C. With these findings in mind, let us turn to the inscriptional evidence.

In 1918 J.P. Vogel in his detailed study of the Yupa inscriptions from Kutai, West Kalimantan (fig. 1), showed that their script was related to inscriptions of the South Indian Pallava dynasty as well as to inscriptions at sites like Vo-canh in modern Vietnam (part of the ancient Cam kingdom that was in existence in the early second century A.D.) and Anuradhapura in Sri Lanka. He also demonstrated that the Southeast Asian examples reflect refinements to the Pallava script that were only later incorporated into Pallava dynasty edicts of the Indian mainland.

Vogel's approximate dating of the Vo-canh inscription at c. A.D. 350, the Yupa inscriptions at c. A.D. 400, and the closely related Ci-Aruten inscription of West Java at c. A.D. 450 provides a rough chronology of the earliest development of what we now know as the Early Pallava script of Southeast Asia. This was a script particularly suited for monumental purposes. A combination of characters of different length, one twice the length of the other, produces a strong sense of contrast, while the bold "box-headed" serifs attached to many of the vertical strokes accentuates the heroic character of the script. A fine example of Early

Opposite page: Detail from the Singsosari stone seen in Figure 20. National Museum, Jakarta.

FIGURE 1

Yupa posts in Pallava script from Kutai.
National Museum, Jakarta.

Pallava script, still in good condition, is to be found in the third Yupa inscription (fig. 2). The inscription may be translated as follows:

> Let the foremost of priests and pious men hear of the meritorious deed of Mulavarman, the illustrious king of resplendent fame—let them hear of his great gift, of cattle, a wonder-tree, and land. For these multitudes of pious deeds this sacrificial post has been set up by the priests.

Like other writing systems of Indian descent, the Pallava script is correctly termed a syllabary rather than an alphabet, since each sign, rather than representing a discrete unit that can be used to "spell out" larger units, represents instead a syllable, either a single vowel or a combination of a vowel with a consonant or consonants. Indian analysts from as early as the Pratishakya texts (c. 700 B.C.) had noted that the syllable, as the minimal pronounceable unit of language, is the natural unit of linguistic segmentation. They termed these units *aksara*, "unsplittable(s)," later applying the term to the written symbols that began to appear in India with the development of Brahmi script. The term *aksara* has lived on in Indian and Southeast Asian paleography as the preferred term for the written units of scripts of Indian descent. The first line of the Yupa inscription thus reads, syllable by syllable: *Sri-ma-dvi-ra-ja-ki-rttih*.

FIGURE 2

A Yupa post from Kutai. National
Museum, Jakarta.

While a number of other scripts of Indian provenance exerted influence on the evolution of letters in mainland Southeast Asia, Pallava script gained a firm foothold in insular Southeast Asia. This is attested to by inscriptions in the "Later Pallava" script. We owe this term to de Casparis, whose *Indonesian Paleography* represents the first complete account of the history of Indonesian writing after nearly a century of collection and commentary on individual inscriptions or sets of inscriptions. De Casparis notes that this script style represents a decisive step in the development of later Indonesian writing systems:

> The basic difference of this script in comparison with Early Pallava is what may be described as the "equal height" principle: the tendency to write all letters equally high, as though they were held in position between invisible base and top lines. . . . The great significance of this principle is that it draws a clear dividing line between the basic system of signs and the derivative or accessory symbols. It entails a separation of functions which facilitates reading and contributes to an orderly aspect of the written texts. (De Casparis: 1975, 20–21.)

While a few inscriptions in Later Pallava script have been found in Java, the most important examples are inscriptions of the great maritime kingdom of Srivijaya written in the Old Malay language (fig. 3). Srivijaya's power and wealth were based on its ability to link the outward flow of raw materials from the river basins of Sumatra and Malaysia with the inward flow of trade goods from China and India. Buddhist in religion, it was known as a center of learning from at least A.D. 671, when the Chinese pilgrim I-ching stopped at a Srivijayan port to study Sanskrit grammar in preparation for his onward trip to India. He records (fig. 4) that there were more than a thousand Buddhist priests in the city, and advises Chinese priests who wish to go to India to first study in Srivijaya for a year or two.

FIGURE 3

The "Talang Tuwo" stone, inscribed in the Old Malay language for Sri Jayanasa on the gift of the "Shriksetra garden" and dated 606 Saka (A.D. 684), illustrates the main characteristics of the Later Pallava script. National Museum, Jakarta.

FIGURE 4

One of a set of gold plates that contain
Buddhist texts. Although the script is
very difficult to see, it illustrates the close
association of Later Pallava script with
Buddhist scholarship fostered under
Sriwijaya in the late eighth century.
National Museum, Jakarta.

EARLY AND LATER KAWI SCRIPT

By the middle of the eighth century, the interior of Java had begun to develop as a center of religious activity and state formation. This was also a period when written literacy had developed to a point where a cursive style of writing began to replace the monumental style of the Early and Later Pallava scripts. Scholars like Kern termed this new writing style "Kawi script" because of its frequent association with documents written in the Old Javanese, or Kawi, language. De Casparis, in *Indonesian Paleography*, summarizes the main points that distinguish this new form of writing from the types that preceded it:

> Pallava script . . . is clearly a lithic script used for monumental purposes. Its most striking feature is the presence of long "sculptured" verticals with distinct headmarks, elaborate and elegant curves, rounded-off angles and often notched horizontals. The Early Kawi script, on the other hand, is apparently a script used for writing on palm leaf (*lontar*) and thus shows a cursive hand, but "translated" into shapes appropriate to the stone. The technique of writing on *lontar* involves the use of a sharp-pointed stylus, with which it is not easy to draw long vertical strokes, whereas a round and slightly sloping style comes almost natural. (De Casparis: 1975, 28.)

De Casparis distinguishes "archaic" and "standard" forms of the Early Kawi script. The archaic phase is represented by Javanese examples beginning with the inscribed linga of Dinoyo (fig. 5). Dated A.D. 760, this inscription was produced just thirty years after the last example of Pallava script on Java, the Sanskrit inscription of Canggal, which relates the early history of the Hindu Sanjaya dynasty that was later to rise to a position of political ascendancy in Central Java.

By the middle of the ninth century, use of Standard Early Kawi was well established in Java. This is a simple, functional script, well suited to its primary purpose of recording the details of land grants composed in the Old Javanese language, which were published in significant numbers during the reigns of Kayuwangi (856–882) and Balitung (899–910). A set of copperplates from the reign of Balitung illustrates the unembellished simplicity that marked the form of Standard Early Kawi (fig. 6).

Toward the end of the first millennium, as Old Javanese was developing from a language of the chancery into a literary language of great flexibility and subtlety, political power shifted from Central to East Java. This brought about a

further evolution of Kawi script. The first stage in this evolution was the development of a handsome inscriptional style based on Early Kawi, but once again inclining to a more monumental style, in this case marked by a tendency to squareness modulated by the rounding-off of corners through the use of acute-angle connections between vertical and horizontal strokes. This script, termed Later Kawi by de Casparis, is also notable for the development of concise means for distinguishing characters that in the past had looked very similar.

The earliest phase of the Later Kawi script is represented by rock-cut inscriptions from the reign of Daksa (910–919). Inscriptions in a more ornamental style, noted for what de Casparis terms its "painted serifs" are well represented by inscriptions of the charismatic King Airlangga (1019–1042), who reunited East Java after a period of chaos during the mid-tenth century. According to legend, Airlangga retired from the throne in his later years to pursue a path of asceticism, dividing the kingdom between two of his sons and so ushering in the Kadiri period (c. 1100–1220). Figure 7 shows an edict of Mpu Sindok. Dated 851 Saka (A.D. 929), this elegant inscription illustrates the fine balance between decorative and functional characteristics that were hallmarks of the Later Kawi script.

We know from the evidence of the great poetic works of the *kakawin* genre that literacy in the Kawi script was widespread, at least among the nobility who were the patrons of the *kakawin*. Wandering poet-princes, as well as the court ladies who evoked their praises, or laments, were frequently portrayed in the *kakawin* as fond of inscribing their sentiments in short verses on such ephemeral media as the blossoms of the pandanus flower.

_____ FIGURE 5 _____

Left: The Dinoyo stone inscription, an example of Standard Early Kawi script. National Museum, Jakarta.

_____ FIGURE 6 _____

Right: Another example of Standard Early Kawi script: the "Taji" plates, dated 823 Saka (A.D. 901). National Museum, Jakarta.

A similar concern for the aesthetic elements of the art of writing can be seen in the development of the Kadiri Quadrate script, a highly ornamental form of the Later Kawi script in which the block-like characters of the script are filled in to create a puzzle-like effect. Frequently represented above the entrances to rock-cut temples from sites as distant from the East Javanese heartland as Gunung Kawi in the Pejeng-Bedahulu region of Bali, the Kadiri Quadrate script is also well known from Javanese examples such as the frequently illustrated *kentongan* bell of the National Museum collection (fig. 8).

By the beginning of the twelfth century the power of Kadiri had waned. It was replaced first in 1222 by the Singosari dynasty, and in 1294 by the politically

FIGURE 7
An example of Later Kawi script, dated 851 Saka (A.D. 929), showing an edict of Mpu Sindok. National Museum, Jakarta.

expansive Majapahit kingdom, which remained powerful until the latter part of the fifteenth century. There are a significant number of both copperplate and stone inscriptions from this period. Regional variation in the arts is characteristic of this period, and is also seen in the calligraphy of the inscriptions.

In copperplate inscriptions of the Majapahit period the influence of a cursive technique appropriate to writing on *lontar* palm is evident, with a tendency to embellishment that does not diminish the clarity of the written characters (fig. 9). In this type of Majapahit calligraphy (fig. 10) the serifs are regularized into horizontal strokes, so that the effect is of an invisible line running along the top, broken only by the curving circular forms of the character *r*, called *cakra* ("wheel").

On the other hand, the style of Majapahit stone inscriptions exemplified by the inscription of Candi Singosari, issued by Kertanagara in 1351, reveals the Later Kawi style stripped to its bare essentials, its graceful rounded forms contrasting sharply to the sharp, linear effect created by the calligraphy of the copperplates (see fig. 21).

REGIONAL VARIATIONS OF KAWI SCRIPT

The archaic phase of Early Kawi script had a wide provenance, largely due to its use by the Shailendra and Srivijaya dynasties. Later forms of Kawi that evolved in Central and East Java were also influential elsewhere, particularly in Bali, where a large number of copperplate inscriptions reveal both Javanese influence and local characteristics.

Inscriptions in the Old Balinese language are found for the period 882 to 1016. From 996 the language of royal edicts and land grants was a mixture of Old Balinese and Old Javanese; after 1016 the language of the Balinese chancery shifted exclusively to Old Javanese. This shift can be related to the marriage alliance of the Balinese king Udayana with a higher-ranking Javanese princess, Gunapriyadharmapatni, or Mahendratta, a direct descendant of Sindok, founder of the East Javanese Uttungadeva dynasty.

Considering that this royal union had as its fruit the birth of Airlangga, it is not surprising that a good many Balinese edicts written in Old Javanese after 996 were inscribed in Later Kawi script of the kinds current in East Java beginning in the early tenth century. The history of Kawi script in Bali appears to have many anomalies, with an apparent mismatching between the date indicated by the content of some inscriptions and the period of the script (Early or Later Kawi) in which they were written. Some of these anomalies in the history of Kawi script on Bali can be explained in terms of an independent Balinese scribal tradition drawing inspiration from Javanese models, others are to be understood in terms of the frequent reproduction of older inscriptions in the calligraphy of later periods. Thus three sets of Old Javanese copperplates in the Pura Pamrajan Raja Purana in Klungkung are dated 994 Saka (A.D. 1072), yet are all written in hands reminiscent of Majapahit-era calligraphy and use the distinctive form of the character *ra* known only from Majapahit inscriptions (1294–c. 1450).

A similar situation exists for inscriptions in Later Kawi found in Sunda (West Java) and Sumatra, perhaps due to local development from earlier forms of the Kawi script. Thus, for the Ci Catih inscription of Sunda, dated 1030, de Casparis notes a resemblance to the Central Javanese Kawi of the end of the ninth century and suggests that the Ci Catih scripts were borrowed from Central Java and thereafter underwent few changes, a conservatism natural to an area where script was not in common use.

The Sundanese kingdom of Pajajaran arose when Majapahit was at its height, but it used a quite different script, which probably evolved from the Ci Catih type. The characteristics of this form of Old Sundanese script are illustrated in the "Kebantenan" copperplates (fig. 11) in the collection of the National Museum, Jakarta.

FIGURE 8

A bell showing an example of Kadiri Quadrate script. National Museum, Jakarta.

FIGURE 9

Above: One of the Manuk I copperplates illustrating the cursive Later Kawi script of the Majapahit dynasty. Issued by Rajasanagara, identified in the inscription by his well-known pen name Hayam Wuruk, thus dating to his reign (1272–1296 Saka, or A.D. 1350–1374). National Museum, Jakarta.

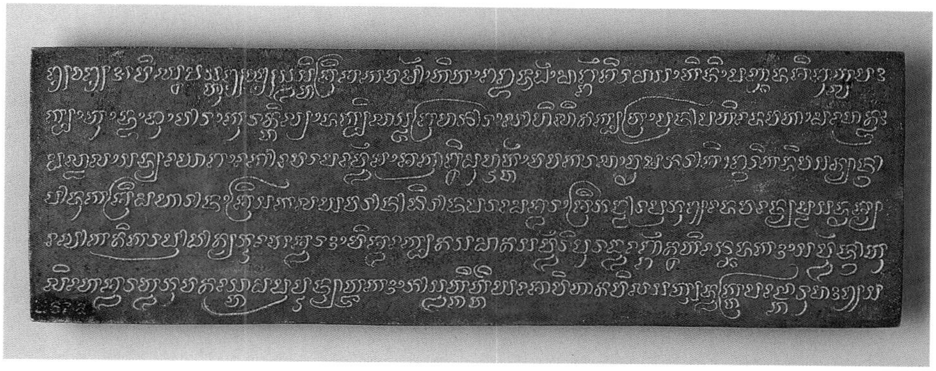

FIGURE 10

Middle: Waringin Pitu, copperplate dated 1369 Saka (on November 22, 1447); inscribed for Krawijaya. National Museum, Jakarta.

FIGURE 11

Below: One of the "Kebantenan" plates, an example of Old Sundanese script (dated c. 1340–1400), inscribed for Sri Baduga Maharaja. National Museum, Jakarta.

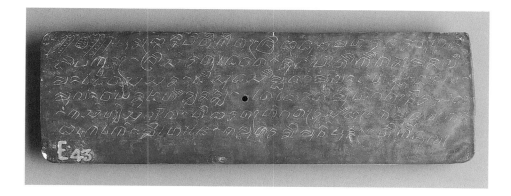

For the Malay script of the Central Sumatran king Adityavarman (1365–1375) de Casparis proposes a similar evolution from local variants of Early Kawi, suggesting that future discoveries may bring to light evidence of earlier stages in this evolution.

Inscriptions found on the island of Madura and in Bima on Sumbawa island are more positively identifiable as variants of Majapahit script, thus attesting to the political expansion of this dynasty, which is also revealed in the fourteenth-century *Nagarakertagama,* a panegyric in the *kakawin* poetic form that records historical details, including the annexation of Bali in 1342 and a campaign against Sumbawa in 1357.

INFLUENCE ON LOCAL KA-GA-NGA SYLLABARIES

While Early Kawi syllabaries were presumably still set up along the phonetic lines favored by Indian analysts, the simpler sound systems of western Austronesian languages led to the evolution of simpler core sets of characters, with characters of Indian origin without a local phonetic equivalent relegated to a secondary set of characters. In Bali this core set of characters is referred to as the *ha-na-ca-ra-ka* syllabary after the first of four sets of five characters that make up the core set of consonants, while the secondary characters are termed the *wayah,* or "ancient" set. These syllabaries are direct descendants from Javanese and Balinese varieties of Later Kawi script. In other parts of insular Southeast Asia, especially Sumatra, southern Sulawesi, and the Philippines, similar syllabaries are found whose existence must have predated the introduction of the Arabic and Roman alphabets. De Casparis notes the difficulty of dating the development of writing in areas of Southeast Asia with no tradition of issuing royal edicts in stone or copperplate, and points out that in such areas as the southern Celebes and the Philippines, where script was used in the sixteenth and seventeenth centuries, writing may have been in use on perishable materials, such as palm leaf, that have not survived.

Reid, in his comments on the high rate of literacy observed by Spanish and Portuguese travelers of the sixteenth century to Indonesia and the Philippines, concludes that this could in part be attributed to a "domestic literacy" that existed alongside a "restricted literacy" devoted to preserving a sacred literature whose potency was accentuated by its relative inaccessibility.

Both these types of literacy are represented in syllabaries of the *ka-ga-nga* type that developed in areas peripheral to the main centers of activity of the Hindu-Buddhist kingdoms of the seventh to fifteenth centuries. While the ephemeral nature of the materials used for writing in these alphabets makes possible an argument that at least some of them may have predated the introduction of Indic modes of writing, there is enough evidence of the influence of Kawi script on *ka-ga-nga* syllabaries of Sumatra to make a case for at least a degree of influence that would obscure the supposed form of any pre-existing script. The strongest similarities are with the Early Standard form of Kawi.

It seems probable that the Sumatran *ka-ga-nga* syllabaries were among the first to appear, and that the development of such scripts in southern Sulawesi and the Philippines may have been stimulated by interaction with Malay traders using variants of the *ka-ga-nga* syllabaries developed in coastal Sumatra and Malaysia. A thorough study of this fascinating subject would surely broaden our understanding of the flow of information through the trade networks of precolonial insular Southeast Asia, in addition to providing a more accurate picture of the spread of the technology of writing.

Thomas M. Hunter, Jr.

THE SOVEREIGNTY OF BEAUTY: CLASSICAL JAVANESE WRITINGS

Literacy and written literature, like Hinduism and Buddhism, entered the Indonesian world through the gates of the royal compounds. Merchants may have first introduced the Indian script, perhaps inadvertently, when they brought merchandise to the region, but the more systematic dissemination of literacy and literature must have been carried out by the Hindu Brahmans and the Buddhist monks for whom the study of books was always a significant part of daily life. These men of religion may have come to the region driven by missionary zeal, but we know from some inscriptions from Kutai (fig. 12), eastern Kalimantan, that many were there by the invitation of a local ruler to perform gift-giving ceremonies involving rewards of huge numbers of cattle and plenty of gold. It was a mutually beneficial arrangement: by displaying his munificence in a traditional ceremony conducted in accordance with the new faith, the ruler was able to increase his prestige in the eyes of his subjects and the neighboring tribes, and the Brahmans gained material rewards. Some probably stayed on in Kutai after the ceremony was over, and others moved again to other areas, such as Sumatra and Java.

It was around such Brahmans that people would gather to hear the message of the new religion and to learn new skills, including literacy. In the beginning, disciples must have been limited to a small number, drawn mainly from members of the royal courts and from those among the local elite who aspired to become Brahmans. This constituted the nucleus of the local learned men. Proficiency in the Sanskrit language must have been one of the primary requirements for those wishing to be allowed into these elite groups. This is evident from the earliest inscriptions found in the archipelago—Kutai (around A.D. 400), West Java (fifth century), and Central and East Java (seventh and eighth centuries)—all of which are written in Sanskrit, using Sanskrit meters, and are either religious or eulogistic in nature. It is reasonable to assume that in such Sanskritized kingdoms, Sanskrit literature must have been introduced by Brahmans at the earliest opportunity—in particular the *Mahabharata* and the *Ramayana* epics and the Puranas, which have played such an important role in the spread of Sanskrit civilization throughout the ages. In fact, the name Yudhisthira, the eldest of the Pandawas, is found in one of the earliest inscriptions from Kutai, probably referring to an episode from the *Sabhaparvan*, the second book of the *Mahabharata*.

These seeds of literacy apparently found such fertile ground that by the seventh century some places in the Indonesian archipelago had gained such a high reputation as centers of learning that even people from overseas were attracted to visit and study there. I-ching, a well-known Chinese pilgrim, for instance, tells us in his memoirs that the Buddhist priests in Sriwijaya "examine and study all possible subjects exactly as in Madhyadesa India." He himself stopped in Sriwijaya to study grammar while on his way to India in A.D. 671 and later returned and stayed for another four years to complete new translations of sutras and shastras into Chinese. Another Chinese pilgrim, Hui-ning, went to Walaing in Central Java in 664 and translated the Sanskrit texts of the Theravada into Chinese under the guidance of a Javanese monk called Jnanabhadra.

At the same time, as the spread of literacy reached wider circles of the community, the use of Sanskrit as the language of the inscriptions was gradually replaced by the indigenous language. By the time of I-ching's visit to Sriwijaya, the use of Old Malay must have become more common than the use of Sanskrit, since the inscriptions found in southern Sumatra from this period are all written in Malay. In Java, Old Javanese inscriptions began to appear in the early ninth century—the earliest one dated A.D. 804, and in Bali the Old Balinese language began to be used in the late ninth century.

In such circumstances it seems reasonable to assume that some sort of indigenous literature must have developed in those centers of learning. If Chinese scholars were able to translate Sanskrit works into Chinese during their stay in those countries—one even expressly stated that he had worked under the guidance of a local scholar—then it would be expected that the indigenous scholars would have been able to do the same into the vernaculars, or even to produce original literary works in their languages. However, no evidence of the existence of such literature from that time has been found. In fact, apart from a few inscriptions, there are no other writings from the whole Sriwijaya period, or from ancient Bali, that have come down to us.

THE FIRST *KAKAWIN*

It is from Central Java that we find such evidence, although it is dated about two centuries after Hui-ning's visit to Walaing. The first is an Old Javanese inscription of A.D. 856. Like most Javanese inscriptions, it is a legal document, in this case confirming the granting of a freehold by a king to a village official; unlike the others, it is written in verse. Admittedly, it is only a short poem—the inscription contains no more than twenty-nine stanzas—but it is clear from these verses that it is not written in an indigenous form of poetry, for its metrical rules are the same as those of Sanskrit prosody: each stanza consists of four lines; each line has a fixed number of syllables and a fixed metrical pattern based on the quantity of the syllable—that is, whether a syllable is long or short. This poetic form is called *kakawin* in Old Javanese a derivative of the word *kawi,* "poet" which no doubt is a rendering of the Sanskrit *kavya* "court poetry."

As a document that contains the earliest specimen of Old Javanese poetry, this metrical inscription therefore is of great significance for Javanese literary history. The fact that the inscription was written in *kakawin* form rather than in the indigenous form of poetry or song called *kidung*—which must have existed at that time, though probably not in the sense of a genre as it was considered to be later—is an indication that although Old Javanese had replaced Sanskrit as the language of the inscription, the poet, and no doubt literary men in general, continued to have a high regard for Sanskrit literature. By then, writing in *kakawin* form had probably already been practiced for a long period of time. In this particular inscription, even in the limited space that was available to him, the author was able to demonstrate his ability to write a valuable document in a poetic form until then used only in Sanskrit inscriptions. In it we find at least six different meters and, as de Casparis has pointed out, the inscription also shows that the author was skillful in the use of *alangkara,* "poetical embellishments," including the difficult *yamaka,* which is a common feature in *kavya* literature.

That *kavya* literature was known and studied in those days is evident from the *Ramayana kakawin,* the only surviving Old Javanese work datable from the Central Javanese period. Unfortunately, like the great majority of Old Javanese writings, neither its author nor the exact date of its composition are known to us. In some *kakawin* from the East-Javanese period, we find the names of royal patrons who may be known from dated inscriptions or other sources. No such name, however, occurs in the *Ramayana.* Accordingly, the dating can only be based on the language, especially its vocabulary and grammatical peculiarities. Such dating is always fraught with difficulties. It is not surprising, therefore, that different dates have been suggested by a number of scholars, ranging from the

FIGURE 12

Yupa post from Kutai. National Museum, Jakarta.

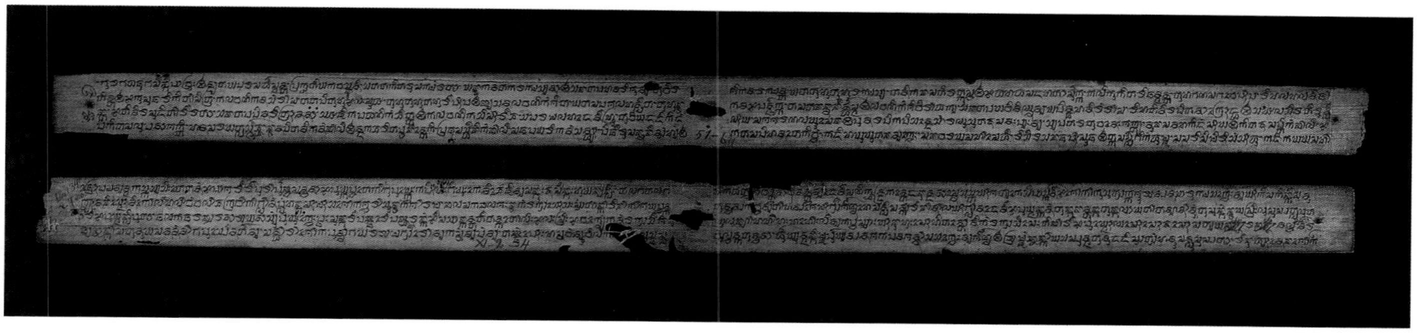

FIGURE 13

Two leaves from a *Ramayana* manuscript
from the Merapi-Merbabu Collection.
National Library of Indonesia, Jakarta.

tenth to the fourteenth century. It is now generally accepted that the poem must have been written before the transfer of the seat of power from Central to East Java, probably during the reign of King Balitung (A.D. 898–910). More recently, Stuart Robson has ascribed it to the middle of the ninth century, dating it to approximately the same period as the aforementioned metrical inscription.

Although both the *Ramayana* and the inscription are written in *kakawin* form, the two works differ enormously in size and the subject matter they deal with (fig. 13). With its 2,770-odd stanzas—more than ninety times longer than the inscription—the *Ramayana kakawin* is the lengthiest of Old Javanese works, and while the inscription is describing a contemporary event relating to the granting of a freehold, the *Ramayana*, like most *kakawin*, is basically a narrative poem depicting the great deeds of a mythical epic hero of yore—in this case the well-known story of Rama. There are, however, numerous versions of the Rama stories in India, and the *Ramayana kakawin*, surprisingly, is mainly based on the *Ravanavadha*, also called *Bhattikavya*, a sixth- or seventh-century Sanskrit *mahakavya*, "great poem," written by Bhatti. The choice of the *Bhattikavya* rather than, say, the *Ramayana* of Valmiki to serve as the model of the *Ramayana kakawin* is remarkable, for the latter is not only the best-known version of the Rama saga, but the language of the former is notoriously much more difficult than any other Sanskrit texts, because apart from dealing with the story of Rama, Bhatti's principal aim was to use his work as a means to illustrate the rules of Sanskrit grammar and poetic embellishments. Whatever reason prompted the choice, the finished product was without doubt a masterpiece, a gem among all that has been produced by Old Javanese poets. To later generations it became the *adikakawin*— that is, first and the foremost among the *kakawin*.

The writing of the *Ramayana kakawin* and the building of the magnificent temples of Borobudur and Prambanan with their thousands of bas-relief sculptures (figs. 14, 15), based respectively on various Buddhist texts and on a version of the Rama saga, are clear testimony to the continued study of literary texts that had begun in Walaing at least by the seventh century. This is corroborated further by a ninth-century inscription from Champa, which tells us that a high official from what is today the central coast of Vietnam went on a pilgrimage to Java "to acquire magical science"—which, as O.W. Wolters comments, may epitomize Java's reputation for possessing esoteric knowledge. Except for a single *kakawin*, the *Ramayana*, and perhaps one religious text called the *Sang Hyang Kamahayanikan*, however, no other works on "magical science" from the Central Javanese period have survived the passage of time. In the case of the *Ramayana kakawin*, it is obviously a case of the survival of the finest.

THE *PARWA* AND THEIR ROYAL PATRONS

Further evidence of the existence of literary and other cultural activities during the Central Javanese period is provided by a copperplate inscription known as the Sangsang inscription (fig. 16). A charter was issued by King Balitung in A.D. 907 to confirm the granting of freeholds to the Buddhist monasteries of Hujung Galuh

FIGURE 14

Above: A relief of a bodhisattva attending the school of Vicvamitra, located on the principal wall on the first terrace at Borobudur. The students are holding writing boards (*lontar*).

FIGURE 15

Below: "The Abduction of Sita by Rawana in the guise of a priest," a scene from the Rama saga as depicted at Prambanan (built c. A.D. 825–850).

and Dalinan. To celebrate what must have been an important event for the whole region, a variety of performances were given. Apart from entertainment such as singing and play-acting, the inscription also mentions a *wayang* performance (*mawayang*) of the story of Bhima(ya)-kumara, a *Kicaka* dance performance (*mangigal*), and a recital (*macarita*) of the *Bhima-kumara* by a certain Nalu, as well as a recital of the *Ramayana* by Jaluk. Both *Kicaka* and *Bhima-kumara* most likely refer to a certain episode from the *Wirataparwa*, the fourth book of the *Mahabharata*. What is less obvious is whether "*Ramayana*" here refers to the *Ramayana kakawin* or to the Sanskrit epic of Valmiki. Although one should not discount the possibility that it was the former—or any other version, for that matter—the fact that it is mentioned together with an episode from the epic *Mahabharata* seems to suggest that it was the *Ramayana* of Valmiki. Since there is no evidence that an Old Javanese translation or adaptation of these epics existed at that time, it is not possible to say with certainty whether the narrators read Old Javanese texts—subsequently lost along with most literary products of the Central Javanese period—or whether they recited Sanskrit texts, and then, as in an Indian *harikatha*, explained them to their audience in Javanese. (A *harikatha* is a public reading of the epics and the Puranas by a trained master of the art. In a *harikatha,* the priest reads and explains a religious story to his audience. Each story takes a few weeks to complete, the audience meeting for a few hours every evening in a temple. The faithful believe that such listening leads to the acquisition of spiritual merit. It is perhaps not too farfetched to suggest that the *mabasan* in present-day Bali, in which people gather to listen to a recital of an Old Javanese poem and its interpretation in Balinese, has its origin in this kind of *macarita.*)

FIGURE 16

An example of Standard Early Kawi
script. An edict of Dyah Balitung.
National Museum, Jakarta.

In any case, the earliest-surviving Javanese renderings of the *Mahabharata* and the *Ramayana* epics hailed not from Central Java but from the eastern part of the island and dated from some ninety years after the recitals at the monastery of Dalinan. Unlike the Old Javanese *Ramayana*, which is written in a poetic form, these renderings of the epics are all written in prose. Regardless of whether it is a rendering of a *parvan* (part of the *Mahabharata*) or of a *kanda* (part of the *Ramayana*), such a prose rendering is called *parwa*.

Not all parts of the two epics are available in Old Javanese. Of the eighteen books (*parwa*) of the *Mahabharata,* we have only nine, and of the seven books of the *Ramayana,* only one—namely, its last *kanda*, the *Uttarakanda.* In the latter case, this is perhaps not a coincidence. The *Ramayana kakawin*, like its prototype, the *Bhattikavya*, ends with the return of Rama to Ayodhya. In other words, it ends with the sixth *kanda* of the *Ramayana* of Valmiki. It is possible, therefore, that the Old Javanese *Uttarakanda* came into existence as a response to a demand for a supplement to make the story of Rama as recounted in the *kakawin* "more complete."

In the case of the *Mahabharata*, the matter is somewhat more complicated. The extant nine *parwa* are the *Adiparwa* (1), *Sabhaparwa* (2), *Wirataparwa* (4), *Udyogaparwa* (5), *Bhismaparwa* (6), *Asramawasaparwa* (15), *Mosalaparwa* (16), *Prasthanikaparwa* (17), and *Swargarohanaparwa* (18). The number in parentheses indicates the sequential number of the *parvan* of the Sanskrit *Mahabharata*: the *Bhismaparwa*, for instance, is the sixth book of the *Mahabharata*. In addition, four other *parwa*—namely, the *Dronaparwa* (7), *Karnaparwa* (8), *Salyaparwa* (9), and *Sauptikaparwa* (10)—may also have been completed but were lost sometime after the composition of the *Bharatayuddha kakawin* in 1157. Considering the sequential order of the completed *parwa*, it seems more likely that, as P.J. Zoetmulder says, those *parwa* were part of a comprehensive project intended to embrace the whole epic. But whether the project was later discontinued—probably because of the sudden death of Dharmawangsa Teguh, the patron of the whole undertaking, in 1016—or whether the undertaking had been successfully completed but half of them were subsequently lost is another question that cannot be answered with any certainty.

A most important event in relation to the rendering of these epics was a *macarita* held at the court of Dharmawangsa Teguh, where people gathered to listen to a recital of the *Wirataparwa* for "one month minus one evening"—commencing on October 14 and ending on November 12, 996. The importance of the occasion is evident from the fact that the king himself attended all the sessions except for one, when he "was prevented by other affairs." It is very likely, therefore, that this was the first recital of a Javanese rendering of the *Mahabharata*—some kind of a premiere, as Zoetmulder suggests. It is true that the *Wirataparwa* is not the first book of the *Mahabharata*, but, as in India, the reciters perhaps began their sessions with the *Wirataparwa* and not with the *Adiparwa*, because the *Wirataparwa* was apparently regarded as the *manggala* (introduction) by *Mahabharata* reciters. This gives us a firm date for the writing of the *Wirataparwa*. Of the other surviving *parwa*, three—namely, the *Adiparwa, Bhismaparwa,* and the *Uttarakanda*—also bear the name of Dharmawangsa Teguh as patron, so they must have been written during his reign. Since by 996 at least one of these four *parwa* had been completed, the decision to undertake the rendering of the epics itself must have been made not long after his accession to the throne (that is, 991 at the latest).

Dharmawangsa Teguh, then, undoubtedly had a great interest in the cultivation of literature in his kingdom. His sudden death during the attack and the destruction of his *kraton* (royal compound), therefore, must have been a great loss for the cultivation of Old Javanese literature. His meritorious deeds in sponsoring the rendering of the *Mahabharata* and the *Ramayana*, however, were not in vain. The importance of the *parwa* for the development of Old Javanese literature and Javanese culture in general is obvious from the fact that they had become the most important sources from which poets borrowed themes for their *kakawin*—more than half of the narrative *kakawin* surveyed by Zoetmulder have heroes and heroines from the epics, or somehow related to the epic heroes, as their main characters. Moreover, the very success of this undertaking apparently also had become the impetus for the rendering of other Sanskrit works into Old Javanese. It is very likely that the rendering of a number of the Puranas (such as the *Brahmandapurana* and the *Agastyaparwa*), the compilation of didactic Sanskrit verses with Old Javanese paraphrases (such as the *Sara Samuccaya* and the *Slokantara*), and the writing of philosophical texts (such as the *Wrhaspatitattwa* and the *Ganapatitattwa*) took place at about the same time as the writing of the *parwa* or not long after. It must have been owing to the popularity of these renderings of the *Mahabharata* and the *Uttarakanda* throughout the centuries that the term *parwa* in Old Javanese is often used as a generic term for "tale" from the epic and Puranic tradition in general, regardless of whether it is in oral or in written form.

CHRONOLOGY OF EAST JAVANESE *KAKAWIN*

Considering the great personal interest that Dharmawangsa Teguh had in the writing of the *parwa*, it is somewhat surprising to find that there is not a single *kakawin* that can be ascribed to the period of his reign. The earliest extant *kakawin* from the East Javanese period, the *Arjunawiwaha*, was not written until some fifteen years after Teguh's death. There is thus a hiatus of about one and a half centuries between the writing of the *Ramayana kakawin* and the *Arjunawiwaha* (figs. 17, 18). Nevertheless, it is clear from these two earliest *kakawin* that there must have been a continuity in the *kakawin* writing tradition during this period, since both follow the same basic principles of metrical rules and poetic requirements. It seems reasonable to assume that even if no other *kakawin* were written during this period, the *Ramayana kakawin* must have continued to be copied by the scribes and to be read on *macarita* occasions—otherwise, it could not have survived and come down to us in its entirety.

On the other hand, significant differences do exist between the *Ramayana* and the *Arjunawiwaha*, which clearly indicate that the author of the *Arjunawiwaha* did not always look to the *adikakawin Ramayana* as the model of his poem—and in this regard all the later poets conformed more to the *Arjunawiwaha* than to the *Ramayana*. One of the most obvious departures from the *Ramayana* is the division into smaller units. Like its prototype the *Bhattikavya*, the *Ramayana* is divided into polymetric *sarga* (cantos)—that is, each *sarga* consists of a number of stanzas written in at least two, sometimes even ten, different

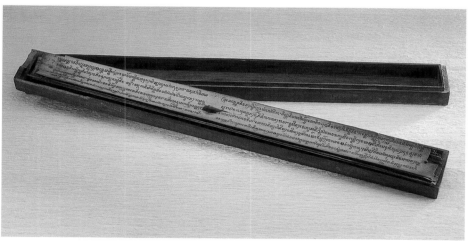

meters, whereas the *Arjunawiwaha* and the rest of the *kakawin* are divided into monometric cantos.

Another fundamental difference concerns the commencement of the poem. The *Ramayana*, again like its prototype, plunges at once into the story with the very first line of the verse. The *Arjunawiwaha* and the other *kakawin*, on the other hand, begin with a kind of introduction consisting of a number of stanzas. This introductory section is commonly called *manggala*. The *manggala* of the East Javanese *kakawin* usually, but not always, contains three elements, namely, an invocation of the *istadewata* (deity of one's choice), a glorification of the patron (also called *manggala* or *manggalya*), and self-deprecatory remarks by the poet. Most *kakawin*, including the *Ramayana*, also have a concluding section consisting of a few stanzas in which we also find self-deprecatory remarks or an apology by the poet for his shortcomings, and sometimes also another few lines in praise of the patron's generosity.

Based on data from the *manggala* and the epilogues, the dating of some *kakawin* can be done with a certain degree of confidence. The information could be in the form of a *sakakala* (chronogram) or the name of the royal patron. In the former case, the exact date of composition can be determined without much difficulty. The best-known example is from the *manggala* of the *Bharatayuddha*, in which we find not only a chronogram—*sang akuda suddha candrama* (he who has horses as white as the moon) with the numerical value of 9-7-0-1—but also other calendrical data, such as the day, the *wuku,* and the month, so that we can give its exact date, namely, September 6, 1157. In the latter case, on the other hand, we may have to rely on data from dated inscriptions or other sources, in which the name of the patron occurs—often in somewhat different form (for example, Pamekas ing Tusta in the *Arjunawijaya* but Wekas ing Sukha in the *Pararaton*, or Rajasarajya in the *Sutasoma* but Rajasanagara in the *Nagarakertagama*).

Unfortunately, most of the extant *kakawin* do not have such data, so that we have to rely on the language to establish an approximate date. As we have pointed out earlier, dating an Old Javanese work based on linguistic evidence alone is fraught with difficulties. The latest example is the case of the *Subhadrawiwaha*. According to Zoetmulder, the foremost expert on the language of the *kakawin*, so far as the language is concerned there seem to be no convincing arguments against dating the work at the end of the fifteenth or the beginning of the sixteenth century. Helen Creese, however, has convincingly argued that Sri Surawirya, the royal patron of the *Parthayana A*, which is the prototype of the *Parthayana B* (that is, *Subhadrawiwaha*), was the ruler of Klungkung, Bali, who reigned from sometime after 1722 until 1736. The *Subhadrawiwaha*, which was dedicated to Sri Surawiryawangsaja, that is, a "descendant of Surawirya," therefore, must have been written much later, perhaps even as recently as the nineteenth century. Though apparently contradicting Zoetmulder's opinion on this particular poem, Creese's findings merely confirm Zoetmulder's main thesis that *kakawin* literature was highly conservative, with new poems written on the pattern of old ones. In the use of language in particular, the author exerted himself to follow his models as closely as possible in both vocabulary and modes of expression, so that in dating these works we have to allow a margin of error not just of decades but of centuries.

Allowing for such uncertainties, it is now generally accepted that out of some one hundred extant *kakawin*, about twenty can be ascribed to one of three periods covering the whole East Javanese period, which extends from the eleventh to the late fifteenth century. Unless specified otherwise, the dates of the following *kakawin* are based on Zoetmulder's *Kalangwan: A Survey of Old Javanese Literature*.

1. The early East Javanese period (c. 996–eleventh century), from which we have a number of *parwa* (c. 996–1016) and one *kakawin*, the *Arjunawiwaha* by Mpu Kanwa (1028–1035).
2. The Kadiri period (c. 1135–1222), which is often called the "golden age" of Old Javanese literature. There are six or seven *kakawin* ascribed to this period, namely, the *Hariwangsa* by Mpu Panuluh (before 1157), *Bharatayuddha* by Mpu Sedah and Mpu Panuluh (1157), *Smaradahana* by Mpu Dharmaja (c. 1182–1185), *Sumanasantaka* by Mpu Monaguna (c. 1204), *Krsnayana* by Mpu Triguna (c. 1204), *Ghatotkacasraya* by Mpu Panuluh (after 1194), and *Bhomantaka*.
3. The Majapahit period (1293–late fifteenth century). Three *kakawin* were written in the second half of the fourteenth century, namely, the *Desawarnana* (*Nagarakertagama*) (fig. 20) by Mpu Prapanca (1365), and the *Arjunawijaya* and *Porusadasanta* (*Sutasoma*), both by Mpu Tantular (1367–1389). Two *kakawin*, namely, the *Wrttasancaya* (*Cakrawaka-duta*) and *Siwaratrikalpa* (*Lubdhaka*) were written by Mpu Tanakung in the second half of the fifteenth century. A number of short poems are also ascribed to Mpu Tanakung, among others, the *Banawa Sekar* and a didactic *kakawin Sutasasana*.

A number of *kakawin* with strong didactic and philosophical or religious elements may also come from the later part of the East Javanese period, such as the *Parthayajna*, *Kunjarakarna* (fig. 19), *Nitisastra*, *Nirartha-prakrtha*, and *Dharmasunya*—in fact, the last two *kakawin* are datable from 1459 and 1460 respectively. It is interesting to note that in this type of *kakawin* we do not usually find the names of the patrons. Since it seems unlikely that a poet would have missed out on the opportunity to praise his royal patron had there been one, the

FIGURE 20

Above right: The Singosari stone, an example of the monumental style of Later Kawi script, dating from the Majapahit dynasty (1273 Saka, A.D. 1351). The history of Singosari forms part of the text of *Nagarakertagama*. National Museum, Jakarta.

absence of such names in these *kakawin* seems to suggest that they were products of literary activities from outside the royal courts—probably from religious establishments at some distance from the *kraton*. In fact, one of the authors of such works, the *Kunjarakarna*, admits to being "rustic" (*kadi ngwang adusun*) and calls himself "Master Yokel" (Mpu Dusun)—which, unless it is just another form of self-deprecation, seems to indicate that he came from or lived in a rural area.

Like the *Ramayana*, almost all *kakawin* directly or indirectly borrowed the themes of their narratives from Indian sources, mostly from the epics (such as the *Bharatayuddha, Arjunawijaya,* and most of the Balinese *kakawin*) and the Puranas (such as the *Hariwangsa* and the *Siwaratrikalpa*), as well as from *kavya,* namely, the *Smaradahana* and the *Sumanasantaka.* Unique among *kakawin* as far as its sources are concerned is the *Desawarnana*. The poem, which since its discovery in

Lombok in 1894 has been known by the name of *Nagarakertagama*, is a depiction of contemporary life at the court of Majapahit during the reign of King Rajasanagara and of the countryside through which the king traveled during his frequent visits to various parts of the realm; hence, its title "Description of the Country." In passing, the poet also gives us a brief account of the king's ancestors. A similar *kakawin*, but on a much smaller scale, is the *Banawa Sekar* by Mpu Tanakung, which tells us of a *sraddha* festival that took place in fifteenth-century Majapahit. Together with a number of inscriptions and a chronicle called *Pararaton*, these constitute useful sources to determine the chronological order of the *kakawin*.

KIDUNG

In the last part of the *Nagarakertagama/Desawarnana*, we read that besides this work Prapanca also had completed, or was about to complete, a number of other works, namely, the *Sakabda, Lambang, Parwasagara, Bhismasarana,* and *Sugataparwa.* Then in the next stanza the poet tells us that it was because of his devotion and his love for the king that he, Prapanca, joined others who praised the king by writing *sloka, kakawin,* and *kidung* (fig. 21). According to Theodore Pigeaud, these three categories of poems refer to "Sanskrit verses," "poems in Indian meters," and "Javanese poetry" respectively. Apart from the *Nagarakertagama*, however, none of the other works are found among the Old Javanese manuscripts that have come down to us, so that it is not clear which of the five is a *sloka, kakawin,* and *kidung.* In fact, what Prapanca meant by the term *kidung* itself is not very clear here. In Modern Javanese, *kidung* refers to a particular kind of incantation poem in *macapat* form for the purpose of warding off evil spirits. In Bali, on the other hand, it refers to a particular genre of narrative poems that is distinguished from *kakawin* in three respects: it is written in a language now usually called Middle Javanese; it uses indigenous prosody called *cilik* (which is similar to Modern Javanese *macapat*) and *tengahan* (which is unknown in Java); and its narratives are mainly based on events that are supposed to have happened in eastern Javanese kingdoms—Majapahit and Kadiri in particular.

Did Prapanca write in three different languages, then—Sanskrit for the *sloka*, Old Javanese for the *kakawin*, and Middle Javanese for the *kidung*? Although perhaps we should not discount the possibility that poets in those days were able to write in these three languages, it seems more likely that Prapanca's works were all written in one language, namely, Old Javanese. By *sloka,* Prapanca probably meant works such as the *Slokantara* and *Sara Samuccaya,* that is, compilations of Sanskrit moralistic and didactic verses with Old Javanese translations or paraphrases. That *kidung* at one stage of its development may have been written in Old Javanese can be deduced from the fact that the word *kidung* and its derivatives, such as *mangidung* and *angidungaken,* already occur in some inscriptions from the earliest period as well as in the earliest-surviving literary products, the *Ramayana kakawin* and the *parwa*. In all these places, *kidung* and its derivatives seem to have the meaning "song" and "to sing" respectively. In many East Javanese *kakawin* from the Kadiri period onward, however, we find passages in which the word *kidung* is mentioned alongside *kakawin* or other poems written in *kakawin* meter, such as *bhasa* "lyrical poems," which seems to indicate that the word *kidung* was used not only in the sense of song but also in the sense of a genre different from *kakawin*. In *Bharatayuddha*, for instance, Mpu Panuluh tells us that when Satyawati was deeply worried that her husband, King Salya, who was about to fight the Pandawas, might be killed in battle, he comforted her "with loving words, interspersed with *bhasa* and *kidung,* as well as jokes and passionate words of endearment." In the *Ghatotkacasraya,* the same poet tells us that among the female attendants of Ksitisundari who were amusing themselves on the seashore, there were some who "sang *bhasa*, while others recited [prose] stories and *kidung*, which they had composed themselves." It is not surprising, therefore, that the oldest *kidung* known by its name is said to have been composed in the Kadiri period. According to the *Pararaton*, it was called *Wukir Polaman* and was written by Jayakatwang, the last ruler of Kadiri, while he was in captivity in Junggaluh (in 1293), shortly before his death. It is obvious, then, that there was a certain degree of continuity in the writing of *kidung* in ancient Java, at least from 1157 when the *Bharatayuddha* was written to 1365 when the *Nagarakertagama* was composed.

Unfortunately, like Prapanca's *kidung*, the *Wukir Polaman* and other *kidung* that were written in ancient Java seem to have been lost. To be sure, there are a considerable number of *kidung* found in Bali, but all of them were probably written in Bali. Unlike East Javanese *kakawin*, most of which mention the names of the royal patrons either in the *manggala* or in the epilogues, *kidung* do not have such names. Accordingly, we cannot say with any certainty that any of the extant *kidung* came from Java. Moreover, unlike *kakawin, kidung* seem to have been continually rewritten, not just copied, throughout their transmission, so that even if a *kidung* happens to have calendrical data indicating that its original was written during, say, the Majapahit period, we are not sure whether that particular *kidung* is basically the same as when it was written on that date, or whether it was completely rewritten, becoming in effect a new work. The *Kidung Ranggalawe*, for instance, has some calendrical elements in canto 1, stanza 2, which indicate that it was written in 1334—only some thirty years before Prapanca wrote his *Kidung*. However, the frequent mention of firearms in battle scenes in the text makes it very likely that in its present form the *kidung* dates from a much later period. In fact, according to Robson, the style is rather reminiscent of the *Kidung Pamancangah,* which seems to have been written after 1700. The second instance is the *Kidung Panji Margasmara*. It contains a chronogram indicating that it was composed in the Saka year of 1380, that is, 1458. Since eight or nine other *kidung* are mentioned in the text, if the extant *Panji Margasmara* was really written in 1458, then it gives us valuable information about *kidung* that may have existed in Java before that date. The text, however, also mentions the *Subhadrawiwaha*, and because, as we have noted before, this *kakawin* was a product of literary activities in eighteenth- or nineteenth-century Bali, we are forced to conclude that the *Panji Margasmara* as we now have it must have been written in Bali, at least three centuries after 1458. Indeed, as Zoetmulder points out, on the basis of the works have come down to us, it would be possible to argue that all Middle Javanese literature as known at present was of Balinese origin.

THE SIGNIFICANCE OF *KAKAWIN* WRITING

Besides chronograms and names of patrons—which are most useful for dating the *kakawin*—*manggala* also contain other data that provide us with clues for understanding the *kakawin* and the functions of *kakawin* writing. As we have noted earlier, one of the three elements occurring in a complete *manggala* is an invoca-

FIGURE 21

Kidung Subrata (Merapi-Merbabu Collection). National Library of Indonesia, Jakarta.

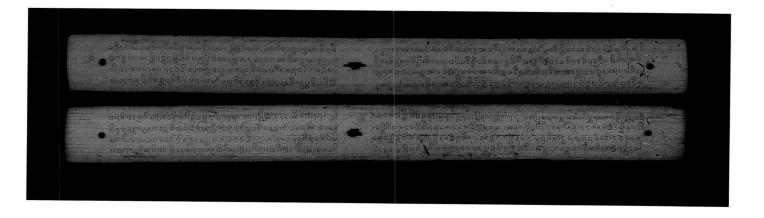

tion of a deity—and the fact that most *manggala* begin with this invocation rather than with praise of the royal patron indicates the importance of the religious aspect of *kakawin* writing.

KAKAWIN AS TEMPLE

Depending on the poet's—or perhaps his patron's—personal devotion to a particular deity, this *istadewata* could be any god or goddess: Siwa, Wisnu, Kama, Lord of the Mountains, Buddha, Saraswati, or the nameless *hyang ning hyang* "god of gods." But, as Zoetmulder's study has clearly shown, despite the variety of names, the god concerned is always worshipped by the poet as the god of beauty—who is present and manifest in everything that can be described as *lango*, that is, "beauty" in its widest sense. The term *lango* also refers to the kind of swooning sensation when one is completely absorbed by such beauty and lost in it, so that "everything else sinks into nothingness and oblivion." *Lango* is of course present everywhere, and the poet could become *alango*, that is, entranced or enraptured by the manifestations of *lango*, in all kinds of surroundings—in a charming garden bathed in moonlight, in a lovely artificial pond under the bright morning sun, in a splendid bedchamber where a lover deflowers his beloved, or on a gruesome battlefield. The most favored place to experience *lango*, however, is a solitary spot where the poet could meditate—such as in a cave on an inaccessible mountain, or near a roaring waterfall crashing down into a deep ravine in the heart of a great forest. It was in such a place that he hoped to be *alango* for an extended period of time in order to create a *kalangwan*, that is, a thing of beauty or poetry, for only then could he achieve his ultimate goal, namely, the union with the *lango*. To reach this place, the *kawi* would have had to travel a great distance, carrying his "dark-colored case" (*kasang wulung*) with all his writing implements through the beautiful countryside, along the shore, crossing many rivers, traversing frightening wildernesses and wooded mountains. These wanderings, as Zoetmulder has pointed out, were often described in terms normally used for ascetics in quest of saintliness or supernatural power: *awukiran* ("to retire to the mountains to devote oneself to religious observance"), *athirta* ("to visit holy bathing places on a pilgrimage"), and *abrata* ("to perform ascetic practices").

Clearly, we are dealing here with a form of religious practice and experience in which striving after union with the deity is central. It is a kind of yoga that—as it involves the writing of *kakawin* as a medium into which the deity with whom the poet seeks the union descends—may be called a literary yoga. And whatever his religious persuasion, the *kawi* was primarily a devotee of *lango* and an adept of its cult. For such a poet, composing *kakawin* is obviously a religious devotion. This act of worship is sometimes likened to building a temple, and the fruit of his devotion, the *kakawin*, is described as a *candi bhasa* or "language temple" (fig. 22). This is beautifully expressed by Mpu Tantular in the *manggala* of the *Arjunawijaya*, when, after invoking Lord Parwataraja, he says:

> The purpose of my praise is to implore Him to pay heed to the homage of one who devotes himself to poetry. . . . This is what I ask as I build my temple of language on my writing board.

With its successful completion, the *kakawin* then became the receptacle of the god of beauty, into which he was called down and wherein he dwelt as in his temple. It also served as a means of meditation in seeking union with the deity in his *niskala* (immaterial) state. For the devotee of *lango*, both the poet and the audience, the *kakawin*—in both its visible form as it appeared on *lontar* and in its audible form as it was chanted aloud before an audience—provided the most appropriate way of achieving the ultimate goal of literary yoga, namely, the union with the divine Absolute.

FIGURE 22
Detail from the *Dampati Lelangon*.
National Library of Indonesia, Jakarta.

Kakawin As Allegory

The glorification of the royal patron in the *manggala* suggests another function of the *kakawin*. It is evident from reading the *manggala* that the praise of the king is more than just an attempt by the poet to win the favor of his patron. It has a great deal to do with the widespread belief that a word has the power to effect what it expresses because there is a kind of identity between the word and what it stands for. Accordingly, a *kakawin* is also believed to be imbued with extraordinary magical power, because it was written by a practitioner of a particular craft in which mastery of words must have been the single most important prerequisite. It was a skill that could be achieved only by serving a long apprenticeship with a "teacher" (*guru*), under whose personal guidance an aspirant to *kawi*-hood had to study all the secrets of the words and to learn how to arrange them in the right order so as to achieve the most perfect combination or, one might say, the highest concentration of their magical power. He also had to master the sacred scripts, which were equally imbued with magical power, and to learn how to inscribe them. And only then, after mastering all these and other necessary skills, would he be admitted to the service of the king as a *kawi*, and be allowed to use the title Mpu as an indication of his status as a priest—a special kind of priest whom Berg called "a priest of literary magic." As such, he had the duty to write a *kakawin*, which, as Mpu Panuluh put it in his poem *Hariwangsa*, "at least may help promote the invincibility of the king and the prosperity of the world." This could be done by selecting the right story and choosing the right words to recount it, alluding to the relationship between what happened in the poem and what was taking place at the court, so that through the power of verbal magic he could influence the course of events. The *Arjunawiwaha*, according to Berg, is such a *kakawin*. The story of the poem was perhaps deliberately chosen by the poet, Mpu Kanwa, as it was considered to have strong similarity with the life story of Erlangga—Arjuna's penance on Mount Indrakila is similar to Erlangga's years spent in a hermitage, Arjuna's victory against the demon king Niwatakawaca who wished to destroy heaven has its counterpart in Erlangga's triumph against all his adversaries, and Arjuna's "wedding" (*wiwaha*) in heaven may stand for Erlangga's union with his queen. In the same manner, Berg argues that the *Bharatayuddha* (fig. 23) is an allusion to the war between Jayabhaya, the patron of the poets Sedah and Panuluh, and his brother.

Arguing from the possible connection between the Old Javanese term *palambang,* which is often used to indicate certain *kakawin*, and the Modern Javanese *pralambang* "allegory," and noting the identification of historical personages with ones from the epics in the Indian *kavya* literature, Robson suggests that Rama of the *Ramayana kakawin* can be equated with the historical King Rakai Pikatan and the demonic King Rawana of Langka with Balaputra, the last Shailendra king of Java who fled to Sumatra. Similarly, Krishna of the *Hariwangsa* and King Jayabhaya are to be equated; the god Kama of the *Smaradahana* should be identified with King Kameswara of Kadiri, and Kama's wife with the queen; and Indumati of the *Sumanasantaka* might have been a Kadiri princess who married a prince at Jayawarsa's court, the Aja of the story.

Kakawin As Didactic Poems

This hypothesis no doubt supports our attempt to understand the meaning of *kakawin* literature. One should not, however, be too carried away by an assumption that there are buried treasures of historical facts behind the narrative of every *kakawin*. For it is the opposite that is evidently true: unless we know the historical facts underlying the narrative, it would not be prudent even to hazard a guess as to what or whom is alluded to in a particular *kakawin*. Indeed, Robson himself appears to have cautioned us against such possible excess of enthusiasm when he suggests that Lubdhaka of the *Siwaratrikalpa* should not be seen as standing for a

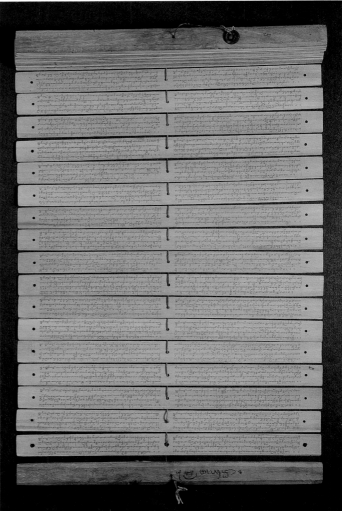

FIGURE 23

A "language-temple" on a palm-leaf
manuscript of the *Bharatayuddha*, a
kakawin written by Mpu Sedah and Mpu
Panuluh in 1157. Sonobudoyo Museum,
Yogyakarta.

certain person who once lived, but rather "as standing for all sinful mankind who
have little hope of reaching Heaven unless they make use of the opportunity to
win salvation offered by the Night of Siwa ritual." In other words, the poem has
a didactic message: it reminds the readers that one should not neglect the observance of the holy Night of Siwa.

It is customary for us to divide *kakawin* into different categories, such as religious, moralistic-didactic, and belletristic *kakawin*. For the poets of ancient Java,
such distinctions were probably irrelevant. Mpu Tanakung, for instance, as we
have noted earlier, not only wrote the *Siwaratrikalpa* (a narrative *kakawin* with
strong didactic elements) but also the *Sutasasana* (a didactic *kakawin* containing
precepts for children), the *Cakrawakaduta* or *Wrttasancaya* (a simple narrative
kakawin cum handbook on prosody), and the *Banawa Sekar* (a short account of a
sraddha festival that he himself was perhaps witnessing). Apart from the
Sutasasana, which Pigeaud lists in a group of "lyric poems," Pigeaud also mentions eight other didactic *kakawin*, including the aforementioned *Nitisastra* and
Nirarthaprakrta. Moreover, a great number of didactic passages are also found in
the so-called belletristic *kakawin*, scattered in various places throughout the
poem. Passages that expound the "three aims of human life"—*dharma* (religion
and ethics), *artha* (material progress), and *kama* (the pleasures of the senses)—are
as common as those that contain the depiction of all kinds of *lango*. Through the
mouth of a sage, god, or the hero of the story, for instance (such as in the
Kunjarakarna and the *Sutasoma*), the poet may impart the teachings on *dharma*;
from Rama's instructions to Bharata and Wibhisana in the *Ramayana,* kings and
princes may acquaint themselves with *niti* (royal political wisdom); from

Suwandha's harsh words to his warriors in the *Arjunawijaya*, ministers may learn what loyalty to the king means in the *ranayajna* (battle-sacrifice); and even the lowly female attendants' remarks in numerous *kakawin* teach a future bride what to expect from the first encounter with the groom on her wedding night. Such passages clearly indicate that providing all manner of guidance to the audience was one of the main functions of *kakawin* writing that the poets of ancient Java took very seriously.

KAKAWIN AS PANGLIPUR

Another function of the *kakawin* is what I have called *panglipur*, that is, as "a means of soothing or comforting." The yogic, the magico-political, and the didactic aspects of *kakawin* may have been of great significance for the *kawi* and other religious men and for kings and princes, but for a great majority of the audience this *panglipur* aspect must have been no less—if not more—important. This function of *kakawin* writing is of course not uniquely Javanese. As Warder has pointed out, in the theoretical works on Sanskrit dramaturgy and poetics, producing "joy or delight" is also regarded as the primary function of *kavya*.

Poets often tell us that they wrote *kakawin* to comfort themselves. This is apparent, for instance, from *Siwaratrikalpa* in which Mpu Tanakung says, "There would be no comfort for my confusion (*nora ng panglipura prapanca*), and the darkness of my mind is so deep as to lead to torment, if I did not take my refuge in beauty as a means of soothing cares (*panghilanga sungkawa*) in the manner of one who occupies himself with poetry." The poet's main concern, however, is to bring joy to the audience—as the anonymous author of the *Arisraya* (A) says in the epilogue, "It would be impossible for me to imitate the accomplished great poets of the past, for I am foolish and crazy, but I hope that this poem will bring great happiness and joyous laughter to those willing to read." Again and again we read in *kakawin* of a lover (usually the hero of the story) singing a *kakawin* in an attempt to comfort or to mollify his beloved. We read in *Arjunawijaya*, for instance, that in the king's effort to "soothe the irritation" (*anglipuraken turida wuyung*) of the queen, "He praised her breast, sang a *kidung* and a *kakawin*, and kissed her cheeks. And coaxed in this way, her heart softened like a night lotus opening its petals to the moonlight." In *Kalangwan*, Zoetmulder presents many other similar quotations. In fact, among the main worries that a *kawi* had after completing his work—besides his concern that his work might not "bring contentment to his master's mind" (*manginakana ri buddhi ning tuhan*), that it would "constantly be censured, reproved, and laughed at by the great poets" (*titir winada cinacad ginuyu-guyu tekap sang kawiswara*) or that it would become "an object of derision by the general public" (*paninda ning para*)—was that, to quote a colorful expression used by Mpu Tantular in *Arjunawijaya*, his verses "cannot even be used to comfort a sullen lady in the bedchamber" (*tan kena panglipura wuyung ing adyah ing tilam.*)

As a consequence of this commitment to bring joy and comfort to the audience, it is not surprising, then, that in most *kakawin* the story ends with a happy conclusion: the virtuous hero triumphs over the evil adversaries and after all those tribulations he and the heroine will lead a most happy life together in this world—or in the rare cases when one of them dies first, the poet would not fail to mention that the other will soon follow and that they will be reunited in heaven where an even happier life awaits.

THE JAVANIZATION OF THE INDIAN SOURCES

In the *manggala* of the *Wirataparwa*, we find an expression used by the anonymous writer to indicate the aim of his undertaking, namely, *mangjawaken Byasamata*—literally, "to Javanize Byasa's thought." Another expression of similar meaning occurs in its concluding section, namely, *pinrakrta*, a passive form of *mrakrta,* "to render [the story] into the vernacular." It is apparent from its occurrence in a number of *kakawin,* that the term *mrakrta* may apply to composition both in prose and in poetical form. In the concluding section of the *Sumanasantaka,* for instance, we find the following lines: "In the Nandana grove ends the *Sumanasantaka* story in Raghu's book [*aji Raghu*]. It was rendered into the vernacular in *kakawin* form [*pinrakrta rasa kakawin*] and offered to His Majesty as a gift of holy water." There seems to be little doubt that by *aji Raghu* the poet, Mpu Monaguna, here meant the *Raghuvamsa,* a *mahakavya* written by the famous Indian poet Kalidasa.

There is a big difference, however, in the way the Sanskrit sources were handled in the *parwa* and in the *kakawin.* It is clear from comparing the *parwa* with their Sanskrit originals that it was not the intention of the authors of these *parwa* to provide a full rendering of the latter. It is true that many passages in the *parwa* are literal translations from the Sanskrit texts, but the omission of elements deemed as nonessential to the narrative is very common. On the other hand, no attempt seems to have been made to insert any additions—except for a few lines in the introductory and the concluding passages—or to make significant changes that would point to an independent attitude on the part of the *parwa* writer. In fact, if there are changes or new characters in the *parwa* at all, they seem to have been the result of a misunderstanding of the Sanskrit text on the part of the author.

In the *kakawin* the "vernacularization" was more than just a substitution of Javanese words for Sanskrit. Here, changes and additions are as common as omissions. While the Aja episode of the *mahakavya Raghuvamsa,* for instance, covers no more than 293 stanzas, in the *Sumanasantaka* it covers 1,154. One of the most common changes is an elaboration of a character that in the Indian sources plays only a minor or an inconspicuous role. Sweta is such a figure in the *Bharatayuddha kakawin.* In the *Mahabharata,* he plays only a minor role in the war between the Pandawas and the Korawas, but in the *kakawin* he becomes the leader of the Pandawa army at the start of the war, and his fight against Bhisma occupies one whole canto of eleven stanzas in this *kakawin* of fifty-two cantos. Another example is the appearance in the *Ramayana kakawin* of Trijata, who, according to Khanna and Saran, surpasses all her Indian forebears, emerging as an important, fully developed character who greatly enhances the dramatic effect of the scenes in which she appears. While both Sweta and Trijata are known in the Indian sources, the heroic Suwandha is an important new character in the *Arjunawijaya* unknown in its Indian sources. From a nameless minister in a passage occurring in the *parwa,* the *Uttarakanda,* he became a well-defined character in the *kakawin.* In fact, as Arjuna Kartawirya's first minister, Suwandha, has become famous among the Javanese as an exemplary hero, whose courage and loyalty are set as a model for those who aspire to enter a ruler's service. Wives seem to be a popular choice when new characters are added. In the *Bharatayuddha,* for instance, we find Bhanumati, Ksitisundari, and Satyawati as the wives of Duryodhana, Abhimanyu, and Salya respectively; and in the *Arjunawijaya,* there is Citrawati, the wife of Arjuna. Companions and confidantes are also favorite additional characters. In the *Bharatayuddha,* we have Sugandhika, the faithful lady-in-waiting of Satyawati; in the *Sumanasantaka,* we have Jayawaspa, Indumati's attendant, and Kawidosa, Aja's companion; and in the *Hariwangsa,* there are Kesari, Rukmini's confidante, and Priyambada, Krishna's companion. Their presence may not affect the predestined outcome of the narratives, but there is no doubt that they differ greatly from their Sanskrit originals.

Another change more fundamental than the introduction of new characters into the *kakawin* is the transposition of what are basically Indian narratives into a Javanese setting. All the names of the kingdoms and places where the stories are set and those of the heroes and the heroines of the stories are, to be sure, Indian, and a great many of them, in particular the principal heroes and their kingdoms, are known from the Indian sources. In the *Kakawin Bharatayuddha*, for instance, the Pandawas and the Korawas are fighting their fraternal war for the kingdom of Hastina on the battlefield at Kuruksetra—just as related in the *Mahabharata*; and in the *Arjunawijaya,* Arjuna Kartawirya is fighting a fierce battle against Rawana on the banks of the Narmada River—just as in the last *kanda* of the *Ramayana* of Valmiki (fig. 24). Yet when we come to the description of the environment where the actions took place, the scenery depicted is far removed from what we find in their Sanskrit originals. This may not be so obvious when the poets describe the battlefields and the *kraton*, where they are obviously prone to exaggeration, but when the narrative moves from the capital city to the countryside, there seems to be little doubt that the poets are describing Javanese scenery. While the depiction of the mountains and the valleys, of the rivers and the shores, of the sunset and the moonrise, and of all other scenery that is beautiful may have its origin in the need to satisfy the requirements of Sanskrit poetics, the great zeal that the Javanese poets appeared to have shown whenever there was a chance for them to insert such depictions into the Sanskrit-based narrative may have had to do with the Javanese cult of beauty. It was a landscape with which the poets were familiar, as it was through such scenery that they wandered in search of secluded spots where they could be united with the god of beauty. And so, regardless of whether a mountain is called Indrakila or Meru, a river is called Narmada or Gangga, or whether the nameless villages and forests are situated in the kingdom of Hastina or in Ayodhya, the scenery is definitely Javanese, similar to that described by Prapanca in the *Nagarakertagama*, complete with all manner of typical Javanese fruits and flowers, birds and fishes, many if not most of which are still found in Java even today.

With all the *kakawin* stories set in such an environment, it is not surprising to find that people eventually believed that all those events narrated in the *kakawin* actually took place in Java and that those places with Indian names were situated in Java. The story of the removal of Mount Mahameru from India to Java, which is found in various Old Javanese works, such as the *Tantu Panggelaran* and the *Korawasrama*, may have been created to justify such beliefs. As recounted in the *Tantu Panggelaran*, Lord Guru gave orders to all the deities to move Mount Mahameru from India to Java so that the island of Java would stop swaying up and down. After much effort and hardship, including the death of the gods and their restoration to life by Guru, the peak of the mountain was eventually brought to Java, so that the island of Java ceased moving. Once the mountain was in Java, the Lord ordered all the deities to worship it. Although both the *Tantu Panggelaran* and the *Korawasrama* were probably written sometime after the fall of Majapahit—the terminus ante quem of both works is 1635—the contents could be from a much earlier period. As I have argued previously, such a story may also have had to do with the indigenous cult of a mountain deity, which seems to have been in vogue throughout Javanese history.

In this long process of Javanization of the Indian sources, the ultimate stage was eventually reached in which the epic heroes were fully accepted as Javanese. We find in various Javanese chronicles, for instance, that Arjuna becomes the ancestor of the rulers of Mataram, while according to the early-nineteenth-century *Serat Cabolang*, Yudistira (Sanskrit: Yudhisthira) is said to have performed asceticism in a forest in the region of Majapahit in search of a way to die, which he eventually found and was subsequently buried in the mosque of Demak. Ironically, this stage was only reached long after the Javanese had embraced Islam.

As mentioned at the beginning of this chapter, written literature was introduced into the Indonesian world by Indian men of religion through the local aristocracy. That this special relationship between kingship and religious establishment

FIGURE 26
Kakawin Bharatayuddha. Sonobudoyo Museum, Yogyakarta.

FIGURE 24

Opposite page, above: The Pandawa forces arrayed for battle on the field of Kurusetra, from a sumptuously illustrated *Serat Bratayudha* produced in the palace of the Yogyakarta sultan, Hamengku Buwana VII. Kraton Kasultanan Yogyakarta; copied in Yogyakarta 1902–1903; European paper.

FIGURE 25

Opposite page, below: Serat Arjunawijaya, also known as Arjuna Widya Budaya. Collection of the Kraton Yogyakarta.

was also the most crucial factor in the development of literature in ancient Java is evident from the surviving Old Javanese works that against heavy odds have come down to us. As we have seen from the preceding discussion, this is most apparent in the writing of *kakawin*—arguably the most important part of Old Javanese literature—which was mainly cultivated within the confines of the royal compounds, by poets who belonged to a group of religious functionaries working under the patronage of the reigning kings and princes.

It is not surprising, therefore, that with the demise of the last Hindu-Buddhist kingdom of Majapahit in the late fifteenth or early sixteenth century, followed by the emergence of Islam as the dominant religion in Java, the kind of literary activities in ancient Java that had produced Old Javanese literature also came to an end. With constant warfare in both Central and East Java before the seat of power was again firmly established in Central Java—the birthplace of Old Javanese literature—not only were new works no longer written, but the old ones were fast disappearing as well. The survival of the old works, written as they were on fragile *lontar* leaves, must have required great care and frequent copying of the manuscripts. And so, even though there was never any policy of a deliberate burning of the so-called Buddha books—as asserted, for instance, in the modern Javanese *Serat Dermagandul*—the destruction and the burning of the *kraton* and many other smaller centers of power would inevitably have caused the loss of such literary heritage. Accordingly, had our knowledge of Old Javanese literature been based only on the extant manuscripts hailing from Java and works that had been rendered into Modern Javanese, we would have to conclude that the six centuries of literary activities in ancient Java yielded no more than seven *kakawin*, namely the *Ramayana, Arjunawiwaha* (fig. 25), *Bharatayuddha* (fig. 26) *Arjunawijaya, Nitisastra, Dharmasunya* and *Dewaruci.*

It is from Bali, where a form of Hindu religion continues to be practiced to the present day, that we are able to gain a fuller picture—still far from complete though it is—of the literary achievements of the Javanese writers of the past. It was in this "sanctuary" that quite a few literary products of ancient Java found refuge after the collapse of Majapahit, and no doubt it was mainly due to the skill and diligence of many generations of Balinese scribes that we still have a considerable number of manuscripts of those works—many of them in excellent condition, generally much better than the few that have survived in Java. The field covered by these writings may not be quite as extensive as Javanese civilization itself, as Pigeaud claims, but they certainly encompass a wide variety of topics, such as

FIGURE 27

Detail from the *Bhomakawya*. National
Library of Indonesia, Jakarta.

religion and ethics, history and mythology, medicine and law, dictionaries and treatises on prosody as well as belles-lettres.

Moreover, while the Javanese authors ceased to write the kind of material their ancestors produced and began to use a greatly different form of language to write new literary works, the Balinese continued to write new works modeled on the finest tradition from ancient Java and using the same form of linguistic expressions and idioms employed by the Javanese poets of the past. Yet, despite the existence of new *kakawin* that had been produced in Bali by the Balinese themselves, it is the *kakawin* from ancient Java that apparently continue to be held in greatest esteem by the Balinese. Thus, while Creese reports that no Balinese she has met is familiar with the eighteenth-century *Parthayana*, for instance, Raechelle Rubinstein attests that the *Ramayana, Arjunawiwaha, Bharatayuddha, Bhomakawya* (fig. 27), and *Sutasoma* are still the five most popular *kakawin*. As Rubinstein has clearly shown in the present volume, these literary works from ninth- to fifteenth-century Java are still very much part of the living tradition in contemporary Bali.

Supomo Suryohudoyo

In the Language of the Divine:
The Contribution of Arabic

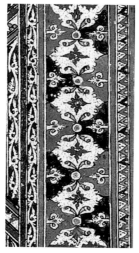

Arabic manuscripts are an important part of the documentary heritage of the Malay world. They have not, up to the present, received much academic attention. In this respect, the situation is little different from that in most other areas of the non-Arabic-speaking Islamic world. As G. W. J. Drewes remarked in a 1971 article on the study of Arabic in Indonesia, "Almost nowhere in the non-Arabic Islamic world, apart perhaps from Turkey and Iran, does the spread of Arabic and Islamic learning and religious lore written in Arabic seem to have been explored in detail." There are a number of possible reasons for this neglect. On the one hand, Arabists in general do not find the Arabic works written in geographically peripheral areas of the Muslim world such as Southeast Asia sufficiently distinctive to merit attention. On the other, few scholars of Southeast Asia have a direct concern with the specifically Islamic jurisprudential norms and principles that lie behind the diverse patterns of social life of local Muslim communities or with the primary sources of spiritual and intellectual life that inform their world outlook. Thus the importance of both Arabic and Arabic manuscripts is largely overlooked.

Van Ronkel's *Supplementary Catalogue of Arabic Manuscripts in Indonesia* and Voorhoeve's *Catalogue of Arabic Manuscripts in the Netherlands*, which list many manuscripts of Indonesian provenance, including the Snouck Hurgronje collection, give a general idea of the wide range of Arabic learning established in the archipelago. Even so, the works listed represent a sampling of Arabic in the region. They include only information concerning manuscripts that by one means or another, and often by chance, have found their way into libraries and museums. And there are many in the National Library of Indonesia in Jakarta, for example, that have not even been described. They are the tip of the proverbial ice-berg. Manuscripts might belong to individuals, to be passed down as heirlooms in families. They might belong to religious schools (fig. 28), or to court libraries (figs. 29, 30). In a damp climate manuscripts quickly decay, and in times of political instability libraries are burnt or broken up or plundered. In his book *Directions for Travellers on the Mystic Path,* Drewes has given a graphic account of the breakup of the library of the Palembang Sultanate in the early nineteenth century, some of its contents finding their way to Batavia, others being lost.

Yet these Arabic manuscripts are not simply relics, of interest only to specialists and of tangential relevance at best to social or even intellectual history. They reflect the texture of Muslim life and thought, and are an important component of the documentation of the Islamization of the region, and the processes by which Indonesia came to have the largest Muslim population of any country in the world.

Arabic is the language of the Quran (fig. 31), of all the liturgical actions of Muslims, both public and private, and likewise the language of the great traditions of Muslim learning, in which are explained and codified the jurisprudential norms that govern human relationships with God *'Ibadat*, and with one's fellow Muslims (*mu'amalat*).

Rashid Rida (d. 1935), the Egyptian leader of the Islamic reformist movement pioneered by Muhammad 'Abduh (d. 1905) was known to many Jawi students in Cairo in the 1920s and early 1930s. In the *Tafsir al-Manar*, in an excursus under the rubric "Arabic, the language of Islam" he writes:

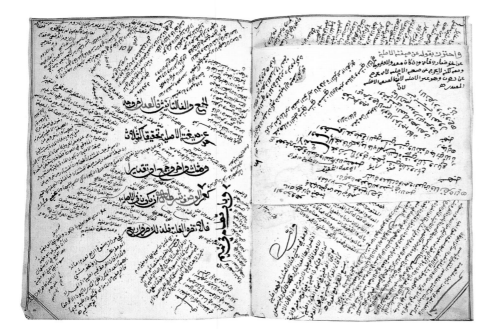

FIGURE 28

Audahu l-Masaliki Ila Alfiyyati Ibn Malik. National Library of Indonesia, Jakarta.

Among the studies that Muslims should undertake is that of the language of Muhammad. It is the language of the Divine Book which God revealed to him. It commands all who follow him, and profess his religion to worship God by means of it, to recite it both within the ritual prayer and on other occasions, and to meditate on its content. To do this requires a mastery of his language, which is Arabic. It is in this [sacred] language of theirs that Muslims make known the Call to every people, teaching the precepts of Islam to those whom God's good pleasure has set on the right path, and made to enter Islam.

He quotes the *Usul al-Fiqh* (Principles of jurisprudence) of al-Shafi'i' (d. 830), founder of the school of Law dominant in Indonesia, to the effect that the Quran was revealed in Arabic, and that all humankind should learn this language, or at least as much of it as is possible, in order to testify in this language that there is no god but Allah, that He is One, that He has no partner, and that Muhammad is His servant and His messenger, and in order to be able to recite in it the Book of God and to utter the expressions of praise and glorification of God's greatness that are incumbent on Muslims.

It is against this background that the following facts need to be understood: all Malay manuscripts were written in Arabic script, and between 15 and 18 percent of the vocabulary of Malay is of Arabic derivation. While a number of these loan words have entered Malay indirectly, that is, as loan words already present in the languages of non-Arab peoples with whom the Malays had trade or social contact, a high proportion of them are direct borrowings from literary Arabic. Although many are from religious works, not all are directly to do with religion. The days of the week, for example, with the partial exception of Sunday, for which a Portuguese-derived word is also common, are from Arabic. A comprehensive account of such loan words is given in a book by Muhammad Abdul Jabbar Beg entitled *Arabic Loan-Words in Malay: A Comparative Study.*

THE ROLE OF *MADRASA* AND *PESANTREN*

Arabic manuscripts are among the oldest manuscripts to have survived in the region, although there are few that date from before the early seventeenth century. It is clear from the catalogues that some were copied in Arabia, some in the Indian subcontinent, and others locally. Although the documentation they provide of the spread and distribution of tendencies in the Islamic intellectual heritage may

FIGURE 29

Opposite page, above: A Quran copied at the Kraton Surakarta in 1797–1798 by Ki Atmaparwita. Widya Budaya Collection of the Kraton Yogyakarta.

FIGURE 30

Opposite page, below: Two more pages from the same manuscript. Widya Budaya Collection of the Kraton Yogyakarta.

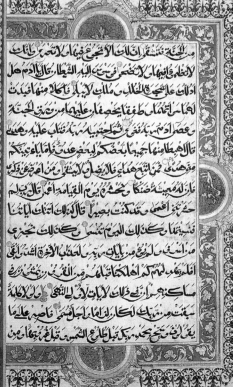

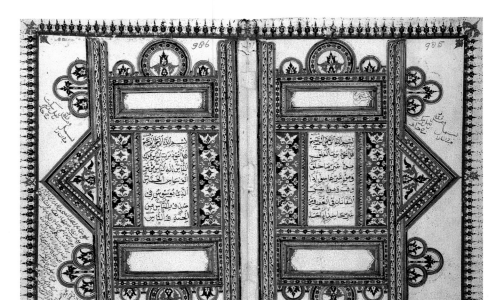

FIGURE 31

The *Quran l-Karim.* National Library
of Indonesia, Jakarta.

appear incomplete and perhaps even arbitrary, they add up to a critical mass sufficient to indicate the existence of *madrasa*—religious schools—in which they
were used. As elsewhere in the Muslim world, some of these institutions were supported by the courts, others had an autonomous urban quarter or even village
base. Foreign *ulama,* whether from Arabia or the Indian subcontinent, came to
court-sponsored and independent *madrasa* alike, and local teachers spent many
years, if not their entire working lives, at Mecca or Medina.

It is clear that by the seventeenth century a significant stage in the establishment of an Islamic literary and intellectual culture had been reached. Arabic
works were known and studied; Arabic was well known, in professional religious
circles at least; a form of the Arabic script was widely accepted as the vehicle of
literary cultures in Malay over a wide area of the Malay world; Arabic loan words
together with phrases and verses from the Quran and the Hadith, as well as a
number of Arabic formulaic expressions for particular occasions were perceived
as an integral part of Malay-speaking cultures; and there were a number of vernacular works on Islamic topics.

The writing of Arabic manuscripts did not only take place *in situ*. Religious
scholars from the area of present-day Indonesia traveled to the holy cities of Mecca
and Medina and other centers of learning from at least the 1500s. In 1640 it is possible to identify two individuals from widely separate areas of the region, 'Abd al-
Ra'uf of Singkel (Aceh) and Yusuf from Makasar. They were in Medina together
for an extended period, and must have known each other there. While in Arabia,
both studied *tasawwuf* (mysticism) from the same shaikhs, Ahmad Qushashi and
Ibrahim al-Kurani. Part of their apprenticeship was the copying of Arabic manuscripts. Ibrahim set Yusuf to make a copy of *al-Durra al-Fakhira* (The precious
jewel), one of the works of the great mystic Jami, and this copy, now in Princeton
University Library, is the best existing manuscript of this work and was used by
Nicholas Heer as the basis of his edition. Yusuf also wrote a number of works in
Arabic on mystical topics, manuscripts of which are listed in Voorhoeve's catalogue. 'Abd al-Ra'uf remained in Arabia for twenty years, returning to Aceh in
1661, Yusuf for six or seven. Back in Java, he took a prominent role as a leader of
resistance to the Dutch East India Company. He was captured and exiled to the
Cape where he died in 1695.

'Abd al-Ra'uf and Yusuf were not the first Jawi to make the pilgrimage or to
spend years studying in Mecca and Medina. The Acehnese Sufi poet Hamzah

FIGURE 32

Marginal detail from the *Quran l-Karim.*
National Library of Indonesia, Jakarta.

Fansuri, who died around 1598, also made the pilgrimage. In all probability so too did Shams al-Din of Pasai (d. 1630). Hamzah is famous as a brilliant religious poet in Malay. Shams al-Din is an important figure for other reasons: he is the first Sumatran known to have written original works in Arabic in the Ibn 'Arabi tradition on the Unity of Being. A number of manuscripts of his works are extant, two of them published by C.A.O. Van Nieuwenhuijzen. He popularized an Arabic tract by the North Indian scholar Muhammad b. Fadl Allah al-Burhanpuri (d. 1590), *al-Tuhfa al-mursala ila ruh al-nabi* (The gift addressed to the spirit of the Prophet). This work was to become known in many parts of the Muslim world, in the Hijaz, Syria, and the Indian subcontinent as well as Sumatra and Java. Its popularity derives in part from its skillful summation of the essential principles of monistic Sufism, and its reduction of the exuberant theosophical mysticism of Ibn 'Arabi to a manageable schema of seven Grades of Being. There are many Indonesian manuscripts of this Arabic work and a number of Arabic commentaries on it. In addition, Shams al-Din played an important role in the court of the Acehnese Sultan Iskandar Muda (r. 1607–1636) who gave him the Ottoman title Shaikh al-Islam.

How and when did this intellectual tradition begin? It is not possible to document it further back than, say, 1580. Yet the earliest Malay works extant, in particular the poems of Hamzah Fansuri, show evidence, even by that date, of a remarkable symbiosis between Malay and Arabic that must be the fruit of cohabitation of the two languages over centuries. What could have been the circumstances and motivations that led both to the absorption of such a rich Arabic vocabulary, and the adoption of the Arabic script, developments that served to transform existing written cultures, and to generate new ones where none had been before?

It may well have been in response to the establishment of Muslim quarters in already existing port cities, or the founding of new ones by Muslim traders. The origins of such Muslim communities are obscure. The earliest evidence of Islam in the region with a political profile is provided by the tombstone of Sultan Malik al-Saleh of Pasai (d. 1297 or 1307). This does not exclude the possibility, the likelihood, even, of Muslim communities of a certain size and stability existing either before the establishment of that sultanate or at other focal points in the archipelago.

The presence of *ulama* in such communities is virtually certain. Can one say the same of *madrasa*, the institutions in which they taught? The first *madrasa* and the curricula that were to become standard for many centuries throughout the Muslim world were established in Nisapur and Baghdad by the end of the tenth century. The curricula included *tafsir* (Quranic exegesis), *hadith* (the prophetic tradition), *tawhid* (dogmatics), *fiqh* (jurisprudence), *kalam* (scholastic theology), *tasawwuf* (mysticism), and *nahu* (Arabic grammar). (See figs. 33, 34). Astronomy (for calendrical calculations and establishing the direction of Mecca), mathematics (for the calculation of fixed shares of an estate), history, lexicography, poetry, and rhetoric were often taught as well.

It is not possible to establish that any such *madrasa* existed anywhere in the Indonesian archipelago in the fourteenth century, even though there is abundant evidence of Muslim communities in the region. Yet any *'alim* worth his salt in these communities would have had some training in a *madrasa*, and would know at first hand the many years of study these disciplines demanded. Basic to all study in *madrasa* is a mastery of Arabic. Knowledge of it is essential to make possible a genuine encounter with the Divine through the Quran. But Arabic is not simply the language of revelation, it is the language of the prophet, of his *ipsissima verba* preserved in prophetic tradition, words sacred beyond those of any other human being. It is also the language of the great disciplines that are at the core of training in a *madrasa* and are essential to the functioning of an Islamic community, foremost among them jurisprudence, in its two great branches of *'Ibadat* and *mu'amalat*.

FIGURE 33

Above: Marginal detail from the *Quran l-Karim*. National Library of Indonesia, Jakarta.

FIGURE 34

Below: Marginal detail from the *Quran l-Karim*. National Library of Indonesia, Jakarta.

In Tanoh Abee, a hamlet some 50 kilometers to the southeast of Banda Aceh in the province of Aceh, is a famous Quranic school, called a *dayah*, from the Arabic *zawiya,* "prayer room." In 1980 the Dayah Tanoh Abee had about 130 pupils between the ages of seven and eighteen, with girls outnumbering boys. As is usual in *pondok* and *pesantren* all around the Malay world, the principal teacher is the director of the school himself, and he is assisted by senior pupils. More than half the pupils live on the *dayah* premises, and all of them also attend a public school.

The teaching is divided into various stages. Each pupil has to fully master one stage, however long it may take, before he or she is allowed to go on to the next one. The first stage is the reading of the Quran, beginning with the last chapter. Then comes the study of three short treatises on the basic Islamic duties, one after the other. These three texts are usually credited to Acehnese authors. Next comes the study of a popular collection of tracts also credited to local *pondok*, called *Kitab Delapan* (The Book of Eight) or *Kitab Majmu* (The Compilation). When the pupil has reached this last stage, he or she is oriented toward a specialized field such as law (*fiqh*), theology (*tawhid*), exegesis (*tafsir*), mysticism (*tasawwuf*), and so on. Here again the teaching consists mostly of the study of treatises by local authors, such as the famous Nuruddin ar-Raniri or Abdurrauf of Singkel. In other words, this traditional teaching, transmitted from generation to generation over more than a century, has a very strong local component. Teaching is done in Acehnese, though the texts are written in Malay or Arabic, as is usual in Quranic schools in Sumatra and Java as well.

The collection of manuscripts inherited from the present director's father, which provides the core of the school's teaching, is relatively large (about seven hundred items) and consists exclusively of Islamic texts. It thus provides a quite exceptional picture of the character of instruction in an Acehnese Quranic school, from the end of the last century to the present day. In earlier times the *dayah* was also a scriptorium, a place where manuscripts are copied, so it is also an example of one type of scriptuary tradition in an Indonesian village setting.

According to the family tradition, the *dayah* was created in the second half of the seventeenth century by the son of a Baghdad judge (*qadi*), Syeikh Fairus al-Bagdadi, who had migrated to Aceh in the time of Sultan Iskandar Muda. The story goes that Syeikh Fairus' descendants created four *dayah* in Aceh: three in the Seulimeum area (at Tanoh Abee, Klut, and Leupung Ngoum), and one at Lampucuk in the Indrapuri area. The founder of Dayah Tanoh Abee, Syeikh Nayan, was reputedly a disciple of Syeikh Baba Daud, who was himself a disciple of Abdurrauf of Singkel.

The *dayah* became particularly famous on the eve of the Aceh War (1873–1913), when it was directed by Syeikh Abdul Wahab, who is still known as Teungku Chik Tanoh Abee. This *ulama* was very active both in collecting and in copying manuscripts, and enjoyed the reputation of being able to write in no less than seven different styles of Arabic calligraphy. In his time, the collection contained more than two thousand manuscripts.

However, half this library disappeared during the Aceh War and its aftermath: some books were burnt, others were lost or simply decayed for lack of proper preservation. It is indeed a continuing paradox that the very cultural environment which has nourished the production and use of valuable books can also be responsible for totally neglecting them. In the 1950s, the manuscripts were still in piles in the various rooms of the *dayah*. When there was an occasion to sort them out, those which were considered too dilapidated were thrown into a special basket, to be burnt: in other words, the only curatorial efforts were not to preserve the manuscripts (from ants, fire, floods, humidity, and so on) but to dispose of them. The present director, Teungku Muhammad Dahlan, however, takes great care of the remaining collection, and every manuscript has been wrapped and labeled, to be stored on shelves in glass cabinets. More remarkable is that over the years he has made a systematic Malay-language catalogue of the collection, an abridged version of which was published by the provincial government in 1980.

The seven-hundred-odd manuscripts are in fact seven hundred volumes or library items, each of them either one text, part of a text (one chapter, or what is left of a damaged book), or a collection of texts. One item can easily comprise two, five, or ten short tracts. For this reason, people often speak of the library having two thousand rather than seven hundred manuscripts.

All the manuscripts are related to Islamic matters, and more precisely to Islam as a religion and a field of study. There is no text for instance on hagiography (no story of the Prophet's miracles, no "Life of Abdulkadir al-Jaelani"), and there is not a single one that could be classified under the broad category of *hikayat* (epics and romances), even Muslim ones (no *Hikayat Muhammad Hanafiah*, no *Hikayat Amir Hamzah*).

An Islamic student. Detail from Nasehat, *a book of advice. National Library of Indonesia, Jakarta.*

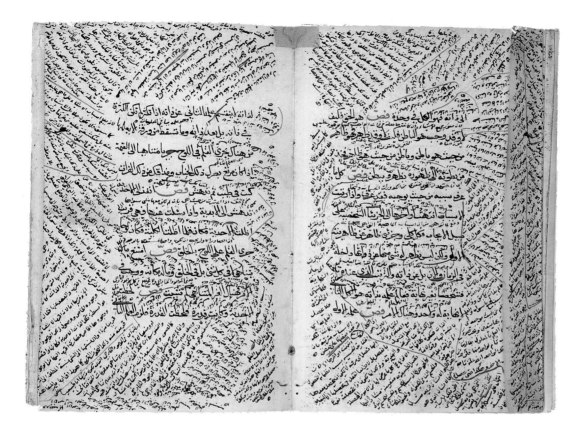

There are no historical texts either. One manuscript, however, deserves special mention for its particular relevance to Aceh's history. This is a code of law compiled in the middle of the eighteenth century. This text, entitled *Safinat ul-Hukkam* (The Ship of the Judges), was written by Syeikh Jalaluddin bin Muhammad Kamaluddin al-Tursani in Bandar Aceh in A.H. 1153 (1741) at the request of Sultan Alaiddin Johan Syah. It is a kind of legal treatise arranged according to six topics: terminology, duties of rulers and high dignitaries, commercial law, law on marriage, criminal law, and law on inheritance. At least two other manuscripts of this text existed in Aceh in 1980, and it certainly deserves to be edited and published.

Among the 700 items only about 120 are in Malay, all the others being in Arabic. Of the roughly 580 Arabic manuscripts more than 150 are works or fragments of works by al-Ghazali, "the greatest theologian of Islam" who lived from 1058 to 1111. This exceptional number is a testimony to al-Ghazali's fame and popularity in Indonesia. Some of his works have been translated into Malay by the Sumatran *ulama* Abdussamad al-Palimbani: the most important is the translation, entitled *Sair us-Salikin*, carried out in the 1780s, of the abridged version of al-Ghazali's masterpiece, *Lubab ihya 'ulum al-din*. Chapters from this work and others by the same author are found by the dozens in the *dayah* collection, perhaps as the result of copying exercises by its pupils. One of these manuscripts gives an insight into the process of text diffusion. This manuscript (no. 30 in Teungku Muhammad Dahlan's catalogue) was copied in A.H. 1270 (1853) at Tanoh Abee, perhaps by Teungku Abdul Wahab himself. It was copied from another manuscript which had been copied by one Muhammad al-Jawi al-Asyi ("The Acehnese") in Mecca in A.H. 1233 (1818). In other words, an Acehnese who was making

the pilgrimage to Mecca or studying there took the opportunity to copy Abdussamad's work. Then he brought back his manuscript to Aceh, where it was copied again at Tanoh Abee, and no doubt used in the *dayah* curriculum.

Works by Abdussamad al-Palimbani are to be found in many other libraries in Indonesia. The Tanoh Abee collection also holds manuscripts which are of special interest in that they are works by Acehnese authors, some of them very well known, others still obscure or unpublished. Well known, for instance, are the works by Hamzah Fansuri (there is a copy of the *Sharab al-ashiqin*), by Nuruddin ar-Raniri (these include fragments of the *Bustan us-Salatin*, a rare copy of *Durrat ul-fara'id*, and an apparently unique yet incomplete copy of *Lata'if al-asrar*), by Syamsuddin as-Samatreani, or by Abdurrauf of Singkel. Less known but no less interesting are tracts, treatises, and translations by local *ulamas*, including Abdurrauf ibn Ali Fansuri, Syeikh Baba Daud (Daud bin Ismail Rumi, also called Teungku Chik di Leupeu), Muhammad bin Khatib Langien, Muhammad Zain bin Jalaluddin, and Zainuddin al-Ma'ruf. Some of these men were local *ulamas* popular enough to have their works reproduced in the *Kitab al-Majmu*, some opened new schools, some were judges (*qadi*) at the court of a sultan.

Other collections of Indonesian manuscripts, the result of collecting manuscripts from a large area over a long period of time, are more voluminous. The Dayah Tanoh Abee collection is extremely valuable because it has always been and still is the library of a Quranic school. As such it deserves to be studied, not just for the value of one particular manuscript, but as a reflection of religious teaching in Aceh over more than a century.

Henri Chambert-Loir

FIGURE 35

Doa Chatam Koer'an containing prayers to follow Koranic lessons. National Library of Indonesia, Jakarta.

The coherence of any stable Muslim community, then, by definition almost, depends on a knowledge of Arabic. The Quran is an Arabic revelation. Every Muslim, even if not an Arab, is required to be able to read correctly the fully voweled Arabic script of the Book. A fundamental rite of passage for boys and girls all over the Islamic world is *tammat Quran*, completion of study of the Quran (fig. 35). Every Muslim should have a copy of it to be kept with love and reverence. Numerous copies of the Quran are necessary, if not of the whole at least of chapters associated with particular occasions, such as *Ya Sin* (*sura* 36) to be recited to the dying.

This being so, it is not unreasonable to suggest that the Arabic manuscripts tradition began with the copying of the Quran. As late as the nineteenth century, Munsyi Abdullah earned money by copying Qurans for East India Company sepoys. Yet the practice is a very old one, and increasing numbers of Qurans would have been needed as soon as there were Muslim communities in the region. The copies made by Abdullah were probably not of aesthetic significance (fig. 36). Nor, in all probability, would have been those made for early Muslim communities. They were to meet a practical need. This is the case with the greater part of the Arabic manuscripts now extant, whether of the Quran or other works. They were for daily use, to serve the community. And though a small proportion of Quran manuscripts are decorated with artistic motifs, none approach the artistic refinement of the Iranian tradition.

The need to make copies of the Quran stimulated at least rudimentary skills in calligraphy. Once these had been acquired, they could be put to a variety of other uses—copying collections of *hadith*, of credal statements, and other Arabic works on the disciplines mentioned above. From this it was only a short step to use of the script for the writing of Malay, just as for many other languages, from Spanish when Spain was under Muslim rule, to Afrikaans in the Cape.

The copying of the Quran, word-by-word glosses of its meaning, explanation of credal statements such as the *Umm al-Barahin* using the same technique, extracts from works of *fiqh*, similarly explained to give additional authority to legal decisions, brought local individuals into intimate contact with Arabic. Memorization played the important role that it does in traditional Muslim education, and the process generated consistently used Malay equivalents for Arabic words and phrases. In the course of time, these words included increasing numbers of the Arabic words so explained that attained a diffusion outside the religious context. Drewes, in his study of Arabic grammar referred to above, has drawn attention to the possibility of establishing a stratigraphy of such borrow-

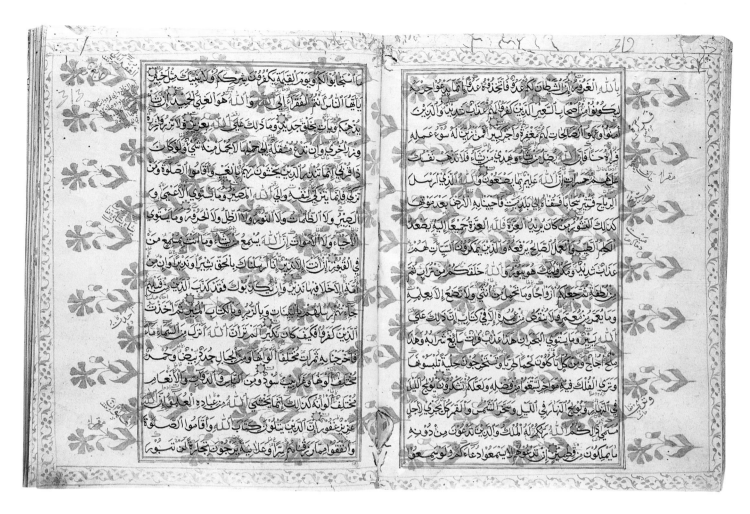

FIGURE 36

An elaborate copy of *Quran l-Karim* with gold leaf throughout. National Library of Indonesia, Jakarta.

ings, pointing out, for example, that in many cases the time came when a word of Arabic derivation was so much felt to be a part of the language that it was used to gloss or explain another Arabic word. Examples are *qiyamat* (or *kiamat*) for *ma'ad* (Day of Resurrection), or *murid* for *talib* (student).

This would be a natural consequence of what Snouck Hurgronje described as the "native method" of teaching such texts: putting before the pupil a simple Arabic manual of jurisprudence or dogmatics and proceeding immediately to interpret it in Malay or Javanese without any preliminary grammatical instruction. (The script of course would have been known from study of the Quran.) Drewes concedes that remarkable results were sometimes attained by the use of this "deplorable method." It is a method that has had a long life. Muhammad Radjab in his autobiography *Semasa Kecil di Kampung* (A village childhood) gives a vivid account of how in 1917 he was taught Arabic grammar in this way.

How long this process continued before one can speak of a corpus of Arabic manuscripts cannot be determined. We need to realize that it was continuous, and duplicated in numerous centers, albeit of varying levels of importance, influence, and intellectual standing. It included the study of basic texts of religion, compilations of *hadith*, works on jurisprudence, collections of prayers (figs. 37, 38), and works on Arabic grammar (figs. 39, 40) as soon as such traditional activities of life in a Muslim community became established. A similar mode of the generation of Arabic manuscripts can be observed in many parts of the Islamic world from Lagos in West Africa to Marawi in the Philippines. Such teaching activities generated the production of more copies of key works, and the creation of a manuscript tradition multiplied in Quran schools, *madrasa* and *pesantren,* all over the area that is now Indonesia.

Thus looking back from the vantage point of the seventeenth century, when the Arabic script was almost universally accepted, and a rich stratum of words of

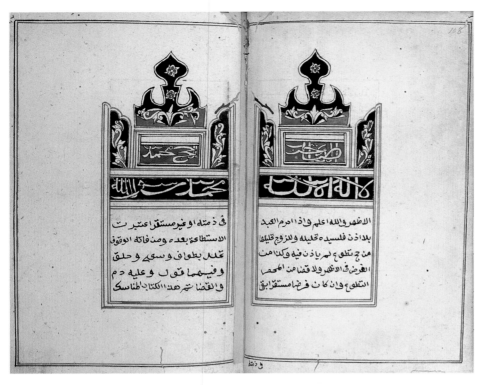

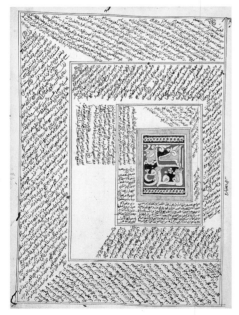 

Arabic derivation had become part of the Malay language, we see that the distance covered from the time—say, five hundred years earlier when Islam was scarcely known in the archipelago—is extraordinary. And it is difficult to account for this achievement other than as the outcome of a growing use of and familiarity with basic Arabic texts over the range of the Islamic disciplines in some kind of institutional, whether *madrasa* or proto-*madrasa*, context, in which they had a place and a function, although details of the processes involved are inaccessible to us. An 1886 study by L.W.C. van den Berg of the catalogues then shows how from the seventeenth century on, the bases of Islamic learning were spread throughout the archipelago, although there is little direct information until the nineteenth century about the context in which they were used, how they fitted into an education system, what students used them, or who were the *ulama* who taught from them.

At all events, it is only in the framework of such institutions, however little we know of them, that the range of Arabic manuscripts preserved can be seen to have any sense as representing fragments of a corpus of learning.

FIGURE 41

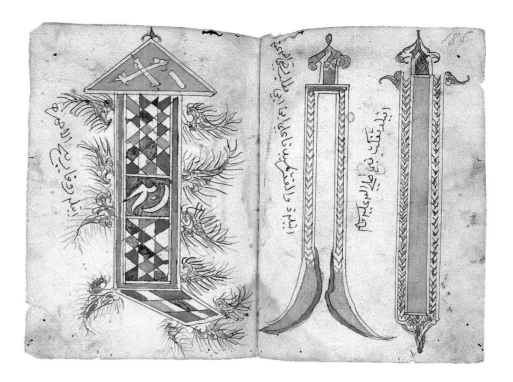

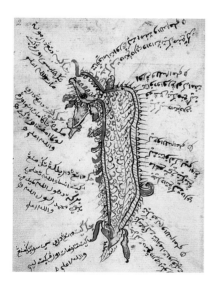

FIGURE 42

A page from *Umm l-Barahin.* National
Library of Indonesia, Jakarta.

SURVIVING MANUSCRIPTS

Arabic works surviving in manuscript may be compared to pieces of a jigsaw puzzle. There is little that is totally ad hoc in traditional Islamic education, which is tightly networked and family based, although the listing of manuscripts in the catalogues might not give this impression. Thus we know in broad outline the big picture of which they are part. They come together in clusters, the clusters representing the various disciplines, some better and more fully represented than others. This of course does not mean that the *ulama* teaching in such institutions did not know or have access to a far wider range of sources or authorities than are listed in the catalogues. Moreover, it does not follow that the works so listed were necessarily the most popular. Paradoxically, works on *wujudiyya* mysticism may have found their way into collections because they were rare and perceived as being of special value. Since they were for an elite, they would have been kept with special care. It is highly unlikely, for example, that in early seventeenth century Aceh the *Tuhfa* of Muhammad b. Fadl Allah would have been studied, and that Shams al-Din would have written on *Wahda al-Wujud* (The unity of being) without there also being available works on *tafsir, hadith,* dogmatics, *fiqh,* and Arabic grammar, all of which had to be mastered before students graduated to mysticism, even if manuscripts of works on these foundation subjects have not survived from this time (figs. 41, 42). (The study of *tasawwuf* was demanding, intellectually and spiritually. It had nothing of the twentieth-century dilettantism associated with the writings of Idries Shah.) By the seventeenth century, then, it is clear that these disciplines were studied at points all over the Indonesian archipelago, even though the survival of Arabic works is sporadic in its distribution. In addition, alongside the accumulation of works in Arabic, a vernacularization of Islamic learning in various fields is observable (fig. 43). This has some remarkable achievements. Foremost among them is 'Abd al-Ra'uf's *Tarjuman al-Mustafid,* a rendering of the *Tafsir al-Jalalayn,* the only commentary of the Quran as a whole existing in Malay until the 1930s! Only fragments of earlier Malay renderings of other commentaries such as that of Khazin survive. The *Jalalayn* is probably the most-used Arabic commentary throughout the Muslim world. This is certainly the case in Indonesia and Malaysia, as the manuscripts catalogues testify. 'Abd al-Ra'uf's Malay rendering, which probably began its life as an interlinear translation, is a

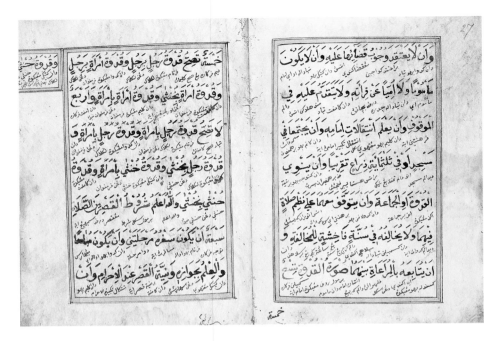

—————— FIGURE 43 ——————

Above: Mogadamah, a mixed-text
manuscript that includes Islamic laws and
their interpretation in Malay; the first step
in the vernacularization process. National
Library of Indonesia, Jakarta.

—————— FIGURE 44 ——————

*Below: Syarhu Fi Bayani l-Majazi
Wa t-Tasybih.* National Library of
Indonesia, Jakarta.

skillful, reliable guide to the Arabic text, and was clearly written with this in mind—to lead students into the Arabic original.

The same principles guided the compilation of works of *fiqh*, whether al-Raniri's *Sirat al-Mustaqim* on *'ibadat*, or Abd al-Ra'uf's *Mir'at al-Talibin* on *mu'amalat*. The point is that authority resides in the Arabic text. The authority can certainly be followed and explained through the medium of a local language, although this explanation in many cases was not written. Nothing can replace the authority of the Arabic text, or that of the person with access to the Arabic text (fig. 44).

In fact, given the authority of Arabic, and the fact that the Malay literary tradition did not have the strength of, say, Parsi, Turkish, or some of the Indian vernaculars, the sense of the Arabic texts was largely carried in vernacular languages by the oral tradition. It is thus not surprising that the first commentary on the Quran by a Southeast Asian, *Marah Labid* by Nawawi al-Bantani, is written in Arabic. There is an irony in the fact that this work was first published in 1885–1886 on the recently established Makkan Press. This represented a milestone in the acceptance of the legitimacy of the use of printing technology for the dissemination of religious works, and thus marks the beginning of the end of the manuscript tradition.

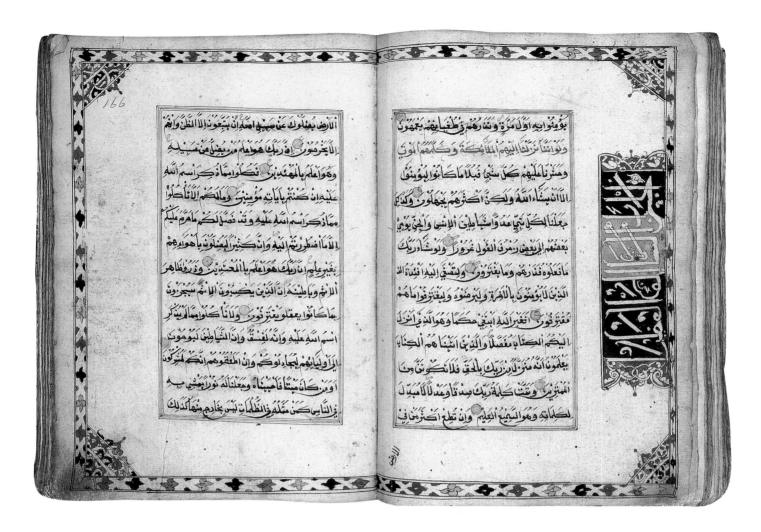

FIGURE 45

Al-Quran l-Karim. National Library of Indonesia, Jakarta.

THE CENTRALITY OF THE QURAN AND QURANIC EXEGESIS

The illustrations selected give some idea of the character of Arabic manuscripts of Southeast Asia. It should be noted once again that the use of Arabic and the production of Arabic manuscripts was functional. They include working copies for students to make annotations in the margins, or to use the available space to copy selections from commentaries or other works. They were written to meet the needs of communities of Muslims who needed copies of the Quran, commentaries on the Quran, compilations of sayings of the prophet, reference works on Shafi'ite *fiqh*, works on Arabic grammar, works on *kalam*, works on mathematics and astronomy, and so on.

There are many manuscripts of the Quran both as a whole and of individual chapters or verses for devotional purposes. Some are attractively decorated (figs. 45, 46, 47).

Quranic exegesis is a field of extraordinary richness and diversity with a wide range of emphases. These range from those such as the *Jalalayn*, which provide for the most part word-by-word glosses, to those that expand and draw out the sense of Quranic narratives and make clear the moral lessons to be drawn from them; those that have most concern with the legal passages of the Quran and their application; and those concerned to explain the mystical dimension of the Book. This area of Islamic learning is not widely represented in manuscripts of Indonesian provenance. There are, however, manuscripts of complete commentaries and fragments from a variety of works. The most popular, as was mentioned earlier, is that of the *Jalalayn*, which does not go much further than word-by-word glosses, but there are also a number of copies of al-Baydawi, who is comprehensive in his concerns, and includes spiritual insights, haggadic expansions, treat-

———— FIGURE 46 ————
Above: Al-Quran l-Karim. National
Library of Indonesia, Jakarta.

———— FIGURE 47 ————
Below: Al-Quran l-Karim. National Library
of Indonesia, Jakarta.

———— FIGURE 49 ————
Opposite page, above: Maulid Syaraf l Anam,
spiritual counsels attributed to Sufi sages.
National Library of Indonesia, Jakarta.

———— FIGURE 50 ————
*Opposite page, below: Maulid Syaraf
l-Anam,* exordium to a mystical work in
the tradition of Ibn Arabi. National
Library of Indonesia, Jakarta.

ment of legal issues and some detailed grammatical analysis in addition to word-
by-word glosses (fig. 48).

DEVOTIONAL AND THEOLOGICAL WORKS

There is a variety of devotional works, in praise of the Prophet (fig. 51).

The theosophy of Ibn 'Arabi, whether stemming directly from Ibn 'Arabi or
other exponents of the tradition he created, was studied in different areas of the
archipelago, although it should be stressed that this was by no means the only tradition of Islamic spirituality in the region (figs.49, 50).

Fiqh (jurisprudence) deals with an abundance of practical matters (fig. 53).

The mainstream Sunni Ash'arite tradition, which saw the divine omnipotence
as best expressed through an occasionalist philosophy, regularly attacked the views
of its enemies the Mu'tazilites who believed in free will, and in the necessity of God
to treat His creatures with justice. Statements of Mu'tazilite views and refutations
of them were part of the stock in trade of *madrasa* training for many centuries.

———— FIGURE 48 ————
Tafsir Al-Quran. National Library of
Indonesia, Jakarta.

بسم الله الرحمن الرحيم الحمد لله العلي
العظيم الولي الكريم الذي زاد
لأنسابها زكاة وكمالية كما غاية
ومع هذا نرجم منجنيا اذ لها المجد
الى الامهات نذرع ارباب الغلبة
المنصور عليها في الكتاب
احكم بقوله مهوا الأول

والآخر والظاهر هو الباطن
وهو بكل شيء عليم والصلاة
والسلام على سيدنا محمد مجمع من
ايسر بيار النبوة وتمام المرا
وعلى أله واصحابه ارباب الغنوة
وأهل ولايته وخلفاءه الراشدين
القائمين مقام الحق يوم الدين

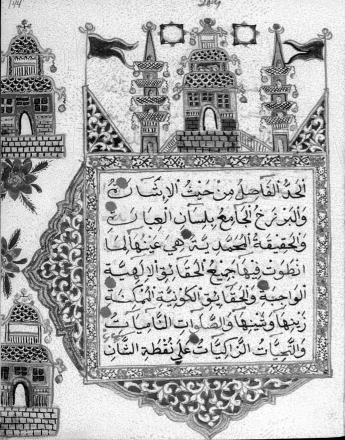

بسم الله الرحمن الرحيم
الحمد بلا حد ولا نهاية والشكر
بلا عد ولا غاية للوجود الله الذي
وحد ته منشأ أحديّته وواحديّته
وسرّ أزليّته وابديّته ورابطة
باطنيّته وظاهريّته وواسطة
أوليّته وآخريّته للّتي يقال لها

الحد الفاصل من حيث الانثان
والبدء خرج الجامع بلسان العباد
والحقيقة المحمديّة هي عينها لما
انطوت فيها جميع الحقايق والالهية
الواجبة والحقايق الكونية الممكنة
زبدها وثنيها والصلوات الناميات
والتسبيات الزاكيات على نقطة الثان

ARABIC GRAMMAR

Arabic grammar is a remarkable achievement of Islamic learning. It was fully fledged by the ninth century with a complete descriptive grammar of the language by Sibawayhi. There are numerous works on Arabic grammar, some in verse to facilitate memorization. Drewes's paper referred to earlier gives a survey of Arabic works on grammar and syntax known in Indonesia between the seventeenth and nineteenth centuries. The number of works that he mentions shows how seriously the study of Arabic grammar was taken (fig. 52).

THE STATE OF SCHOLARSHIP

The study of Arabic in Southeast Asia is still an open field. As Drewes puts it, "a wide field of enquiry still lies fallow." Manuscripts of works on all these topics are scattered across the archipelago. Unfortunately, the descriptions of the manuscripts given in the catalogue are not sufficient to exempt the researcher from actually reading the manuscripts. Van Ronkel's catalogue, although it gives some idea of how well Arabic was known among the *ulama*, and the depth to which traditional issues were studied at the various *madrasa* in the archipelago, often does not give a full account of the content of the manuscripts it lists, and pays little regard to provenance, often making do with such comments as "taken from pirates." Much work remains to be done before it can be used to good effect, and there still remain the uncharted waters of manuscripts not described at all.

What is necessary is a careful study of the manuscripts themselves, together with a listing of place of origin, age, and frequency of occurrence of particular titles. By this means it may be possible to reconstruct curricula and the contents of libraries. Drewes has done some pioneering work in this direction with his paper on the study of Arabic grammar. He has done similar work in describing the manuscripts associated with the Palembang sultanate in *Directions for Travellers on the Mystic Path*. A paper by Matheson and Hooker has done important work toward the study of the tradition of Arabic learning in Patani.

The art of copying Arabic manuscripts in Southeast Asia has gone the way of all flesh. Manuscript copying is labor intensive, and printing renders it superfluous. Yet the tradition of "love of learning and the desire for God" to which these manuscripts bear witness is still alive. A colleague specializing in Yemeni studies showed me a collection of basic texts on *fiqh* and Arabic grammar that he had acquired in the Hadramaut. It was published in Surabaya.

A.H. Johns

MEDIATING TIME AND SPACE: THE MALAY WRITING TRADITION

In most major public collections of manuscripts from the present-day nations of Malaysia, Indonesia, and Brunei, there are many thousands of manuscripts in the Malay language. With very few exceptions, these Malay manuscripts were written in modified Arabic script.

The great number of Malay-language manuscripts is significant, for it indicates that the Malay language played a special role in the Malayo-Indonesian world. The places of origin of these manuscripts and their style help explain what this role may have been. There are examples of Malay-language manuscripts from Sumatra, peninsular Malaya, southern Thailand, Brunei, coastal Sarawak, and Kalimantan, the north coastal areas (Pasisir) of Java, Lombok, Makasar, Bima, Ambon, and other areas of eastern Indonesia (figs. 54, 55).

The currency of the Malay language across this wide area, among peoples who spoke quite different languages at home, stems from its use as a lingua franca along the shipping routes that bound the coasts of island Southeast Asia together and linked them to the outside world (fig. 56). The workaday Malay of sailors and merchants prepared the ground for other uses of the language in intraregional and international networks. The colloquial forms of the harbor and the marketplace thus found parallels in the literary forms of the court and the scholarly forms of the religious conclave (fig. 57).

LETTERS

In courts and chanceries across island Southeast Asia, a literary register of Malay served as the language of diplomacy. It played a key role in the status maneuvering that consumed Southeast Asia's elites. The effect and reception of a letter was inextricably linked with its sender. A royal letter was regarded as representing the ruler himself, and it was received with the same respect as if the sender were present in person. According to the early Malay history of Malacca, *Sejarah Melayu*:

> If it was a letter from Pasai it was received with full ceremonial equipment, trumpet, kettledrums and two white umbrellas side by side and the elephant (bearing the letter) was brought alongside one end of the audience hall.

As Annabel Gallop points out in "Seals and Signatures," great care was taken over the composition of such letters and their calligraphy. The language of their texts, the forms of salutation, the terms of address all had to be carefully weighed for their effect. This language delights in formulaic phrases of the utmost politesse. The impression created by the words of the letter could be magnified, or diminished, by the physical form of the letter. In some beautiful examples, the text was elaborately framed and embellished in gold (the color reserved to royalty) and traditional floral motifs. Such letters were wrapped in envelopes of gold cloth (figs. 58, 60, 61). A letter could bear the full standing of its author. On the other hand, Abdullah bin Abdul Kadir relates an occasion when Raffles received a letter in Malay from the ruler of Siam that had a torn corner, a way of subtly diminishing the polite tone of the text.

Not all letters were addressed to kings and governors, though most of those that have been preserved were. Care over terms of address and formal salutations was important even in commercial and personal correspondence. To help the uninitiated navigate the shoals of propriety, collections of model letters were compiled,

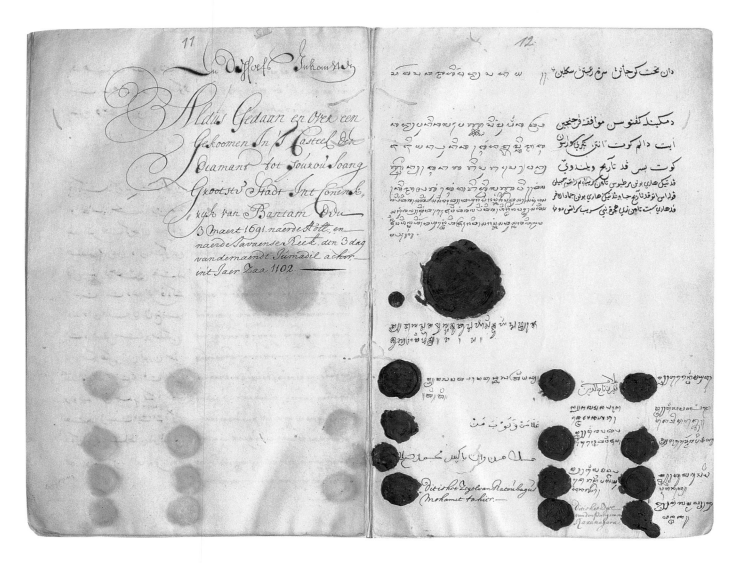

and copied in manuscript form. These *tarasul* offer model terms of address and elaborate salutations appropriate for all occasions: subjects writing to rajas, commoners to courtiers, grandchildren to grandparents, pupils to teachers, mothers to children, lovers to lovers, friends to friends, Malays to Chinese, and so on in all imaginable variations. *Tarasul* could be used in somewhat the same spirit as the English "Letter Writers" of the Victorian Age, which instructed the lower middle classes in how to address their betters, and the rest of society in how to cloak spontaneity in proper form (fig. 59).

DYNASTIC HISTORIES

Dynastic histories were also products of the chancery. Like the letters, these important political texts are highly patterned and formulaic. They invoke the name of Allah in opening and closing passages, refer to rulers as God's representatives on earth, and acknowledge Allah as the ultimate arbiter in all matters. The confident, stately, and predictable style of these manuscripts marked them as formal documents whose contents were weighty.

The focus of these local histories was on the descent of the ruling house. They typically describe the supernatural origins of the dynasty and link it to legendary founding heroes, including Iskandar (Alexander), who was co-opted for this role across the Muslim world as well as in Christendom and Hindu India. The wider Muslim historical tradition, on which the local histories draw, is represented by the widely copied *Bustan al-Salatin* (Garden of kings) (fig. 62). This universal moral history was written by the Muslim scholar Nuruddin al-Raniri in Aceh about 1640. It begins with the creation of the seven layers of heaven and of earth, and gives the histories of the prophets and of the kings and ministers who ruled before

——— FIGURE 54 ———

A 1684 agreement signed by Sultan Abul Mahassin Muhammad Zainal Abidin of Bantam to pay the East Indies Trading Company 100,000 guilders. National Archives of Indonesia, Jakarta.

——— FIGURE 55 ———

A seal affixed to the Ternate Agreement. National Library of Indonesia, Jakarta.

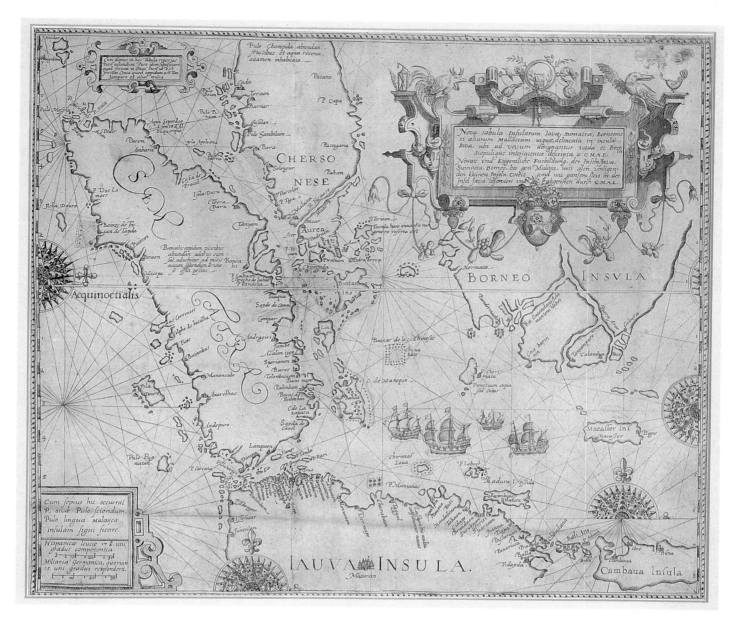

───── FIGURE 56 ─────

"Nova Tabula Insularum Lavae, Sumatrae,
Borneonis et aliarum Mallacam, delineata
in insula lava," a sixteenth-century map of
Southern Malaya, Sumatra, Northern Java,
and part of Borneo by Lodewijcksz,
printed by De Bry of Frankfurt.

───── FIGURE 57 ─────

"A person who can speak Malay can be
understood from Persia to the
Philippines," said François Valentijn, a
cleric and historian, in 1725. Map of
the Malay archipelago, from the first
Malay-English dictionary, Thomas
Bowrey, editor (London, 1701). British
Library, London.

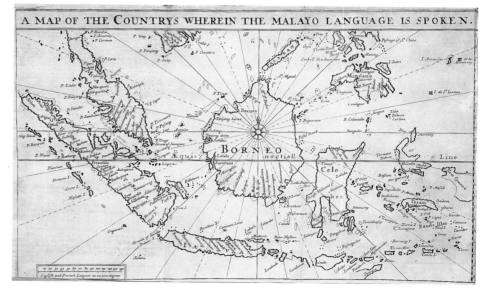

and after Muhammad. The account spans time and place from Pharaonic Egypt to contemporary Malacca, Pahang, and Aceh. Its later chapters offer lessons from history by distinguishing those who ruled justly, wisely, and generously from those who were oppressive, cruel, and treacherous.

The local histories, having traced the origins of the dynasty, typically proceed to set out the constitution of the state. This is done by describing the establishment of the first court, the institution of its ceremonies, and the adoption of Islam. Setting out the bases of royal authority, these histories follow a genealogical structure, recording the fate of the royal house through successive generations.

Naturally these narratives capture local preoccupations, often involving relations with external powers. The *History of Patani* shows a court that survives by playing off the competing claims of Siam to the north and Johor to the south. The latter part of the *History of Pasai*, in north Sumatra, is similarly preoccupied with defining its independence vis-à-vis the expansionary Javanese power of Majapahit. In Banjar, in southeastern Borneo, the issue was how to reconcile Javanese political influence with the economic pull of Malay maritime trade. The court, preferring to bask in reflected Javanese glory, railed against the Malay lifestyle, which it saw as corrupting the Banjarese. It seems ironic that these views were promoted in a court text written in the Malay language, until we recall that the Javanese also used Malay to communicate with those abroad.

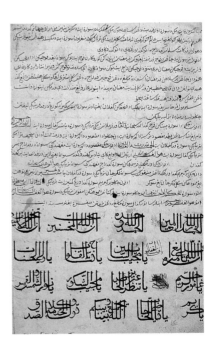

FIGURE 59

Surat Terasul, by Encik Jurutulis Abdul Kadir ibn al-Khatib Dendang of Palembang, dating from the late eighteenth century. Leiden University, Leiden.

In other cases, the preoccupations are internal. The histories of the north
Sumatran kingdoms, Pasai and Aceh, agonize over fratricidal conflicts in the ruling house. The *History of Cirebon*, in north Java, stresses the religious authority of
a line of rulers descended from an early Muslim saint said to be a descendant of
the Prophet. The Malaccan history, *Sejarah Melayu*, is built around the problems
of distinguishing authority and executive power, in particular of reconciling the
sultan's prerogatives and powers with those of his chief minister. The later histories of the Riau kingdom, including the *Tuhfat al-Nafis*, rationalize power sharing
between Malay and Bugis dynasties. Both Patani and Aceh were ruled on several
occasions by queens, and their histories take up the problematic nature of female
leadership in the public sphere. In short, these texts are not mere chronicles. They
have a didactic purpose, which is often quite explicit. It may be spelled out in a
preface to the text, or in deathbed scenes in which a dying ruler vouchsafes per-
tinent advice to his successor. This was a favorite device of royal historians eager
to drive a point home (fig. 63).

Texts of histories reflect the fluctuating fortunes of their courts. Some dwin-
dle away into genealogical jottings as the court, too, faded into insignificance.
Others were written up after a golden age seemed to have passed. Manuscripts of
such texts might become heirlooms and items of regalia. The possession of such
a text helped to stake a political claim. *Silsilah Raja-Raja Pagaruyung*, a Malay-
language manuscript sprinkled with Minangkabau words, traces the genealogy of
the rulers of West Sumatra (fig. 65). *Salasila Kutai*, the account of the genealogy
of the rulers of Kutai in East Kalimantan, contains an account of the birth of the
ancestress of the dynasty. This story was ritually reenacted each year to sustain
the spirit of the royal line. A manuscript of *Sejarah Melayu*, which recorded the
history of the Malacca dynasty from which the Riau princes claimed descent, was

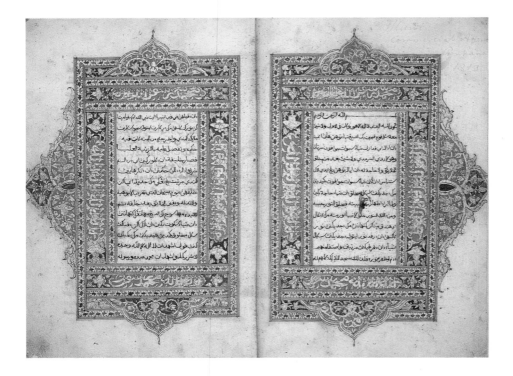

——————— FIGURE 62 ———————

Bustan al-Salatin (Garden of kings), by Nuruddin al-Raniri. Also contains *Taj al-Salatin*. Malay in Jawi script; black ink with red rubrics on English paper "GR," endpapers "1814." Royal Asiatic Society, London.

kept in the Riau palace wrapped in golden silk. On ceremonial occasions it was taken out and read to the accompaniment of cannon salutes (fig. 64).

The societies that produced these works revered the spoken, and even more the written, word as instruments of power and potential power. The word for language, *bahasa,* also meant manners, and implied the adept negotiating of interpersonal relations. In a society driven by status, words defined events. Indeed, words were events. The mystique of writing in a largely illiterate society lent special potency to the written words of manuscript texts. The manuscripts abound with fine-grained descriptions of royal splendor, rich costumes and precious jewels, the beauty of women and of men, the lavishness of banquets, the prosperity of ports and trade, and the scale and skill of heroic battles. While most Malay courts were in reality quite modest, the word-world of the manuscripts was alive with color, luxury, bounteous wealth, and fantastic accomplishments.

HEROIC LEGENDS

Although local histories were a prestigious use of writing, invested with political meaning, they do not form a numerous or even an important category of manuscripts. Knowledge and use of them tended to be restricted to court coteries. Histories are greatly outnumbered by recreational manuscripts that entertained audiences in court and *kampung* alike. Some of these are in fact rather akin to the dynastic histories, and written in the same stylized prose. These are the heroic legends. Mostly they are set in the imaginary never-never land of Anta Beranta, and in some undefined past era. Some recount the stories of Indian legendary heroes, thoroughly acclimatized to the Southeast Asian environment. A great favorite has always been *Hikayat Seri Rama*, the story of Rama, which happens to be found in one of the oldest surviving Malay manuscripts (fig. 66). The Rama legend is the mainstay of the shadow puppet theater, which the northern Malay states share with Thailand. The shadow puppet theater of Java has also provided numerous stories. *Hikayat Cekel Waneng Pati*, on a *wayang* theme, is actually put into the mouth of a puppet-master (*dalang*). It is, we are told, the tale he composed to capture the heart of a princess he loved. He succeeded, using his story to soothe her cares. All who heard it were transported to a world beyond consciousness. Like its many counterparts, it is a story of gods and men in the traditional setting of long-ago Java kingdoms.

Above: Hikayat Raja Handik, copied by Encik Usman in Semarang on 8 Syaban 1211 (February 6, 1797), and *Hikayat Raja Pasai* (incomplete). Malay in Jawi script; ink on Dutch paper, "C & I Honing." British Library, London.

FIGURE 64

Below: Sejarah Melayu. National Library of Indonesia, Jakarta.

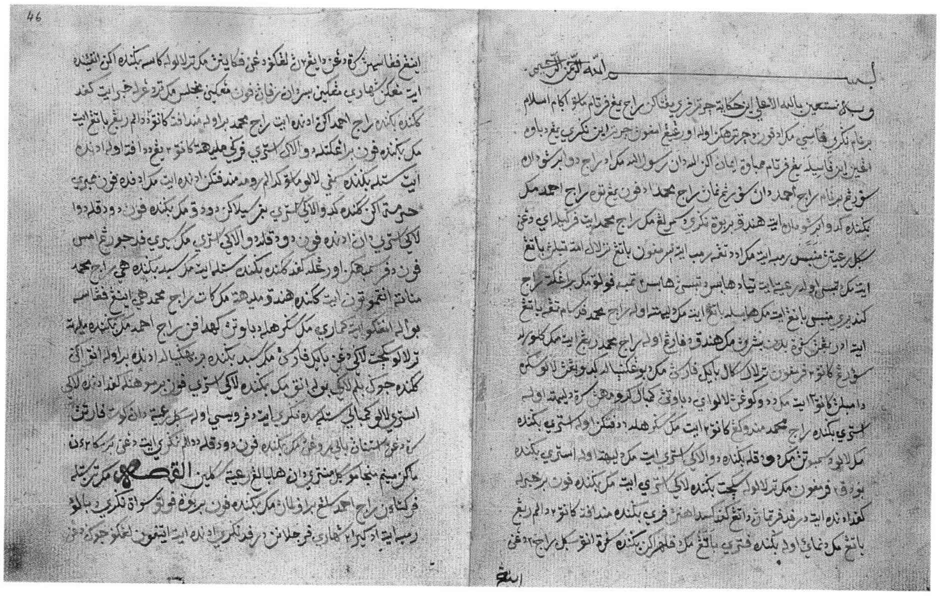

FIGURE 65

The "family tree" of the kings of Pagaruyung: *Silsilah Raja-Raja Pagaruyung.* National Library of Indonesia, Jakarta.

At court these long stories provided an uplifting form of entertainment. In the villages they might be read aloud in the evening hours or presented professionally by itinerant storytellers. Amin Sweeney describes the style of delivery thus: "The reciter did not dramatize his text, but intoned it in a rhythmic monotone, not unlike the chant used in some forms of professional (oral) storytelling." Malay *hikayat* are still read aloud in this style in Lombok. All-night readings of appropriate stories are held on the occasion of circumcisions, weddings, and funerals.

The themes of these written stories have affinities with those of oral storytelling. In this literature there is little concern with character development, but a fascination with exploring alternative social roles. Themes of disguise, hidden status, and changing fortunes provide endless interest, often played out against an archetypal theme of separation, search, and reunion. The stories of Malim Deman, for instance, pick up some favorite storytellers' themes. The prince, abandoned at birth and raised by a poor village couple, leaves home to seek his fortune, is adopted by a fairy godmother, and after heroic deeds wins the heart and hand of the princess—at which point his true identity is recognized. The hero, raised as a commoner, wins entrée to the palace, and carries the audience with him—onlookers in awe of the splendors of a fairyland court. These adventure tales, always involving romances at court, belong to a genre that is widespread throughout Southeast Asia. They have counterparts in the Panji tales of Java and the Inao cycle of Thailand.

The great Malay epic, *Hikayat Hang Tuah*, is somewhat in this vein too (fig. 67) It combines qualities of the dynastic histories with heroic adventure and the great quest. It follows the career of Hang Tuah, a loyal servant of the ruler of Malacca. Hang Tuah and his four companions are shadows of the Pandawa brothers, heroes of the *Mahabharata*. But these Malay adventurers are humbly born, and seek their fortune in the sultan's service. The story of Hang Tuah entwines several themes of progress toward perfection. On the personal level, the hero moves through youth to maturity, growing in stature and status in the service of the king. Spiritually, the story follows him from his childhood Quran school and induction into the secrets of the martial arts, on a great voyage to the West. His journey retraces the sources of Malay religious identity, through southern India and on to the holy lands of Islam. And politically the story depicts Hang Tuah outfoxing the Malay's old rivals, the Javanese, with mousedeer-like guile. He then faces the new threat of the Portuguese Franks. But finally the epic takes a tragic turn. Hang Tuah's loyal service cannot save the kingdom, which falls to Portuguese attacks. Hang Tuah withdraws to the jungle where he waits, it is said, to assist Malays in times of danger. This long text was a favorite of Malay audiences, who could enjoy it as a vigorous adventure as well as an exploration of deep issues of Malay civilization.

Such tales are not only a celebration of the high culture of the courts, but they are also allegorical voyages of self-discovery. In *Hikayat Inderaputera,* the career of the hero, Inderaputera, provides the frame for a succession of fantastic and magically charged adventures. As the story begins, the audience's appetite is whetted by the storyteller, who intones:

> This is the story of Inderaputera, who was famous in the world of men and jinns. He was the one who was carried away by the golden peacock, the one who walked on his own through great forests, the one who met Princess Kemala Ratnasari, the one who was given the magic stone, the one who was carried through the air by the jinn, the one who saw mountains of gold, silver, diamonds and fire, the one who journeyed through a cave for a month, the one who killed the powerful snake. He was the one who was cast in the sea for three years, the one who was given a silken cloth as fine as dew, the one who was given the magic bow.

It is impossible to convey briefly the enchanting fantasy that follows. One episode, though, is even more vivid than the rest. In it, the hero pursues the almost unattainable goal of union with the princess's Candralela Nurlela, who is kept in a magically defended castle. The stairs to the princess's chamber are alternately steps of gold and sharp swords. Already thirty-nine princely suitors, overcome by a glimpse of the princess's radiance, have lost their footing and perished. Inderaputera alone holds fast until he has reached her lofty chamber, where, finally in her presence, he too is overcome. It has been supposed that this episode is an allegory of the Sufis' mystic quest, which mounts the seven stages of the mystic path to the Godhead.

More overtly didactic is the popular story of Shah-i Mardan, alias Inderajaya, a story that looks very much like a Panji tale recast as a vehicle for Islamic instruction. It provides what may seem today a queer amalgam of Muslim metaphysics in a pre-Muslim setting. The hero wins three princesses as his wives in a series of

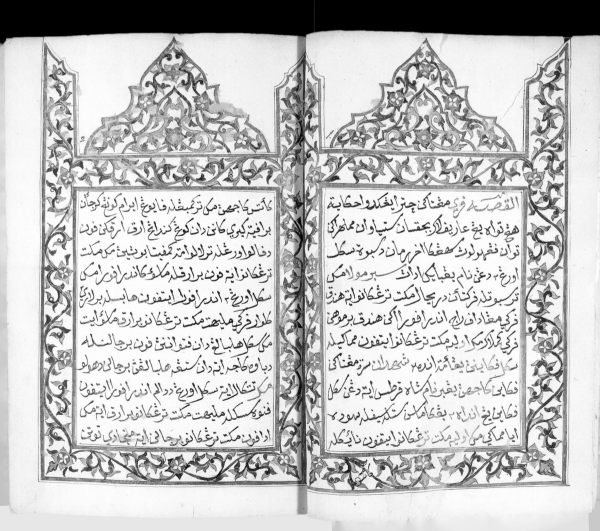

complicated adventures. Along the way, the hero answers a number of riddles alluding to religious truths that are put to him by Lukman the Wise, and by his second and third wives. His answers culminate in an explanation of the seven stages of the mystic path. All this while he has been accompanied by his Brahman teacher, who now joins him in displays of spirit projection.

Other heroic tales belong to the folk tradition of Islamic history. They are the semihistorical tales of the early defenders of Islam. One is *Hikayat Raja Handak*, the story of the siege of Medina, which was ended by Ali, the Prophet's son-in-law (fig. 70). *Hikayat Amir Hamzah* describes the exploits of the uncle of the Prophet, a great warrior for Islam, in ninety-two episodes, making it surely the longest Malay manuscript text. *Hikayat Muhammad Hanafiah* is a popular account of early Islam, from the life of the Prophet Muhammad to the violent and tragic story of Ali and his sons Hassan, Hussain, and Muhammad Hanafiah, who faced Yazid in a furious climactic conflict. These stories provided inspirational role models for Malay warriors, and the Sejarah Melayu records that on the eve of the storming of Malacca by the Portuguese, the Malay commanders planned to nerve themselves for the coming fray by listening to a reading of *Hikayat Muhammad Hanafiah*. The sultan cleverly sent them *Hikayat Amir Hamzah* instead, saying he feared they might not match the more exalted model. Stung, his commanders strengthened their resolve, and asked again. "The king smiled, and gave them the story of Muhammad Hanafiah instead." But to no avail (fig. 68).

Inspiration shaded into devotion, for reading and listening to the accounts of these heroes brought blessing and dissolved sins. *Hikayat Muhammad Hanafiah*, which begins with the birth and life of the Prophet, was read publicly as an act of devotion during the first ten days of the Muslim new year. Biographies of the prophets and accounts of significant events of the Prophet Muhammad's life were also read devotionally. Short narrative accounts described how the Prophet was shaved miraculously, how he performed miracles, how he split the moon in two, how he ascended to heaven from Jerusalem, and how he died. The power of blessing also resided in the lives of Muslim saints. A popular text, of which there are numerous manuscripts, was the *Hikayat Syaikh Abdul Kadir Jilani*. This text, which was translated from Banten Javanese into Malay, gives hagiographies of the founders of the Kadiriah mystical order. Those who used this text for devotions have almost invariably added to its manuscripts readings from the Quran or prayers in Malay, Javanese, or Arabic (fig. 71).

MALAY AS A LANGUAGE OF ISLAM

The stories of Islamic heroes were popular along the Pasisir, the north coast regions of Java. Javanese versions of the stories have been adapted from Malay models, indicating the important role of Malay in disseminating Islam through the archipelago. Islam's first footholds were gained in the maritime trading world and it continued to flourish with greater intensity and orthodoxy in that environment. The widespread currency of colloquial and literary Malay in that environment made the language an ideal vehicle for the transmission of Islam.

Thus Malay and Javanese emerged as the two preeminent languages of Islam in Southeast Asia—that is, among what Arabic speakers in the Middle East and Muslims in Southeast Asia alike termed the Jawi people (*ahl al-jawi, orang jawi*). It is worth pausing over this name. In Mecca it was applied indifferently to pilgrims from all over Southeast Asia regardless of their mother tongue or place of origin, though its etymology reflects the reality that the Javanese were most numerous among them. Yet in both Arabic and older Malay, *jawi* is also the name of the Malay language (*al-lughat al-jawiyyah, bahasa jawi*). This reflects the reality that Malay, which was written in the Arabic script (unlike most Javanese), was the main language of Muslim discourse among Southeast Asians. While Javanese has

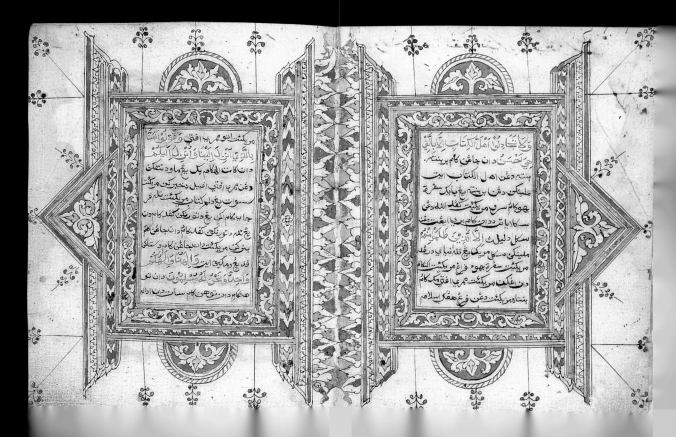

a rich devotional and mystical literature, Malay was the language generally preferred for scholarly translations and adaptations of Arabic dogmatic texts. A greater range of commentaries, manuals of law, and orthodox works of theology was available in Malay. This meant that even in Java, Malay was a language of the *pesantren* (schools for Quranic study), particularly in the more cosmopolitan north coastal regions. The Dutch scholar Lodewijk van den Berg inspected *pesantren* in North Java in the mid-nineteenth century and remarked with surprise when he came across one teacher who had no command of Malay: it was as if a Dutch scholar knew no French! (Actually it is just as likely that the teacher feigned ignorance of Malay in order to be spared this colonial busybody.) Writing about Aceh, the great orientalist C. Snouck Hurgronje remarked that "an Acehnese who desires to learn something beyond the first elements of doctrine and law finds Malay indispensable."

Contributions to this literature have come from scholars right across the archipelago. Their scholarly religious works belong to the class of manuscripts called *kitab* in Malay and other Indonesian languages. *Kitab* is of course the common word for book in Arabic, with sacred connotations only in reference to the Book, the Quran. In Southeast Asia this Arabic word has taken on the more specific meaning of "book on [religious] science." Some of the finest of all Malay manuscripts are *kitab*. Naturally, the highest care and artistry were lavished on copies of the Quran and its commentaries. The beautiful example illustrated is distinguished by the elaborate but controlled adornment of its frame and its strong lines of clear script (fig. 69). It uses color to separate the canonical text of the Quran, given in red, from its interpretation, in black. Elements of its interpretation are the vowel marks added to the Arabic text to fix its pronunciation and the Malay paraphrase that follows the Quranic text verse by verse.

Many *kitab* are direct translations of scholarly Arabic texts or commentaries on them. Commonly the text is arranged on the page in alternating lines of Arabic followed by Malay. A good example of this form is a short bilingual text in verse that was commonly recited in the first stages of religious education, and known to teachers and pupils as the *Abda'u*, after the Arabic word with which it began. The text is Marzuki's *Aqidat al-Awamm* (Catechism for laymen) (fig. 72). In its Malay incarnation, each line of Arabic verse is followed by a line of Malay verse that translates it and imitates its meter. This text was memorized and recited line by line, the verses of Arabic alternating with their Malay counterparts.

In bilingual texts intended for higher study, the interlinear Malay may not really attempt a continuous translation of the Arabic so much as provide Malay glosses for its words and phrases. In manuscripts of this kind, the glosses are strung along in alternate lines, hanging diagonally beneath the relevant Arabic words. A distinctive pattern was thus created. This led to such texts being referred to as "bearded," which was not only an apt description of the shape of the text, but also a sly dig at those who used them, whose pretensions to a smattering of Arabic encouraged them to affect wispy beards of just that style (fig. 73).

The practice of glossing Arabic texts in Malay has had a marked effect on the style of language used in Malay *kitab*. It has created a kind of translationese. The practice of giving each word of Arabic a counterpart in Malay and of tending to make the Malay word order conform to that of the Arabic produced a style so distinctive that it is sometimes hard to follow the drift of such Malay without having a notion of what the Arabic original might be. But of course that is what makes this variety of Malay so redolent of learning. To enhance the effect, some Malay *kitab* were given titles in rhyming Arabic, in imitation of the showy practice of classical Arabic literati. So we find *Masa'il al-Muhtadi li Ikhwan al-Mubtadi* (Guided inquiring for students aspiring), *Hidayat al-Salikin fi Suluk Maslak al-Muttakkin* (Travelers' guide along the path well tried), and so on.

——— FIGURE 70 ———

Above: Hikayat Raja Handak. National Library of Indonesia, Jakarta.

——— FIGURE 71 ———

Below: A manuscript containing stories of the Prophet's life, including *Hikayat Raja Khaibar* (about a king who rejected the Prophet and was crushed by Ali), *Hikayat Bulan Belah* (Splitting the moon), *Hikayat Nabi Bercukur* (The shaving of the Prophet), and *Hikayat Nabi Wafat* (The death of the Prophet). National Library of Indonesia, Jakarta.

FIGURE 72

Aquidat al Awamm. National Library of Indonesia, Jakarta.

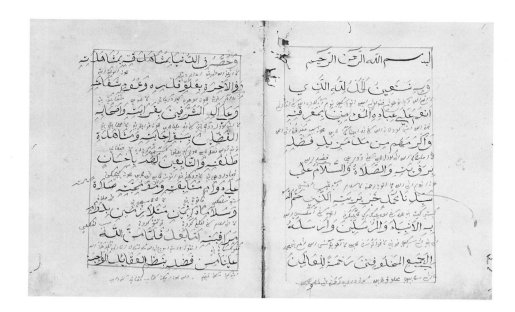

FIGURE 73

Right: A page from a "bearded" text, *Fathu r-Rahman li Syarhi l-Waliyyi Ruslan.* National Library of Indonesia, Jakarta.

FIGURE 74

Far right: Bidayat Al-Muhtadi. Pages of a carefully copied compilation of useful texts: prayers for various occasions, especially burials; two pieces on the four elements; symbols of the names of God; and verses on the seven stages of the mystic path. National Library of Indonesia, Jakarta.

The most numerous manuscript copies were, of course, of texts used for elementary religious instruction. Two widely used primers were *Masa'il al-Muhtadi,* which is a catechism on basic tenets of the faith and the pillars of Islam, and *Bidayah al-Muhtadi,* which gives a brief introduction to the meaning of Islam, faith, the unity of God, and knowledge of God, and then leads its students through the minimal ritual requirements of Islam in prayer and fasting (fig. 74).

At more advanced levels are the more comprehensive digests of law. The most widely current was the venerable *Sirat al-Mustakim* (The Right Way) (fig. 75) compiled in Malay in 1644 by Nuruddin al-Raniri, a scholar of mixed Gujerati and Malay birth, who taught in Aceh and Pahang. He drew together material from several renowned digests of the Shafi'i school to provide an accessible compendium of the prescriptions of Islamic law. His digest covers the topics of purification, prayer, alms, fasting, the pilgrimage, sacrifices, and clean and unclean foods. In short, it provided the essence of what an *ulama* (scholar) needed to know in order to guide the faithful in the outward requirements of religion. It consequently served as one of the foremost objects of study in the advanced levels of *pesantren.* There were more specialized studies of marriage and inheritance law.

As elsewhere in the Muslim world, there was a longstanding tension between legalist and mystical emphases in religious life. This has left abundant traces in the Malay manuscript tradition. The metaphysical stream goes back to works put into Malay in Aceh in the sixteenth century, notably *Asrar al-Insan*, written by Nuruddin al-Raniri's uncle, and the widely copied *Umdat al-Muhtajin*, by Abdul Rauf Fansuri of Singkel near Barus in northern Sumatra. Abdul Rauf's work is divided into seven sections, corresponding to the seven stages on the path to mystical enlightenment, and focuses on the use of *zikir*—that is, rhythmically patterned repetition of the confession of faith—as a means of achieving higher states of consciousness.

A great many later texts spoke to those of a mystical bent. Their subjects include the deeper meanings of the letters and syllables of holy phrases and of the prayer ritual, texts of prayers, mystically suggestive questions, and diagrams that depict the correspondences between levels of perception, conditions of being, qualities, and so forth. These were powerfully charged texts. *Hikayat Nur Muhammad* (Story of the light of the Prophet), which deals with creation and cosmology, promises that the owner of the text and its reader will acquire the merit of a pilgrimage to Mecca. More, that one who reads it day and night gains the blessing of the martyr for the faith—that is, an assured place in heaven. Very popular in this genre was the hagiography of Shaikh Muhammad Saman. Full of his miraculous deeds and wondrous virtues, peppered with Arabic phrases and pious admonitions, it was read to ward off evil. Those who fell sick or incurred misfortune might make a vow to sponsor readings of this text if they were delivered from suffering.

G.W.J. Drewes has made an interesting study of eighteenth-century religious texts from Palembang, entitled *Directions to Travellers on the Mystic Path*, which shows the continuing tension between the teachings of the mystical orders and the need to ensure faithful adherence to the external requirements of the faith prescribed by law. Only later in the eighteenth century did the works of al-Ghazali, the great synthesizer of mystical and legalist tendencies, become accessible to Malay-reading audiences through translations by a Palembang scholar resident in Mecca, Abdul Samad Jawi. His works *Hidayat al-Salikin* and *Siyar al-Salikin* are still used today.

Such *kitab* were dictated, memorized, discussed, translated, and explicated in the centers of learning across the archipelago, at the courts of pious rulers and in rural cloisters, where disciples gathered to study under an eminent scholar. The manner of their use in study is often evident from the notes added by later scholars or pupils in the margins of the manuscript page or snaking around the lines of text.

This makes *kitab* the most visually varied and complex of manuscripts. That is not to say they are always the most beautiful, for that is sometimes far from the case. They are often quite unlike the beautifully calligraphed and embellished chancery letters or the plain but orderly literary texts. Their untidiness is clearly functional. It extends beyond the appearance of the page, to the content of the manuscript. *Kitab* manuscripts are more likely than others to be incomplete. They are also more likely to conclude with fragments from other sources. Here is a contradiction. *Kitab* texts are typically highly structured, with logically arranged sections or chapters, clearly marked and labeled. Yet the manuscripts containing them are more likely than others to be disorderly. The reason is of course that these texts were used in a way that others were not. They were often copies made by students under instruction from a teacher. This was both an intellectual and a vocational action. The pupil's copying was a step to his own possession of the text, both in memory and in manuscript. Students used their personal copies for practice in memorization. The process of copying, and annotating, was thus an aid to

FIGURE 75

Above: Detail from *Sirat al-Mustakim* (The Right Way). National Library of Indonesia, Jakarta.

FIGURE 76

Below: Bidayah al-Hidayah, a Malay version of al-Sunusi's *Umm al-Barahin*. National Library of Indonesia, Jakarta.

FIGURE 77

Kitab Bintang. National Library of Indonesia, Jakarta.

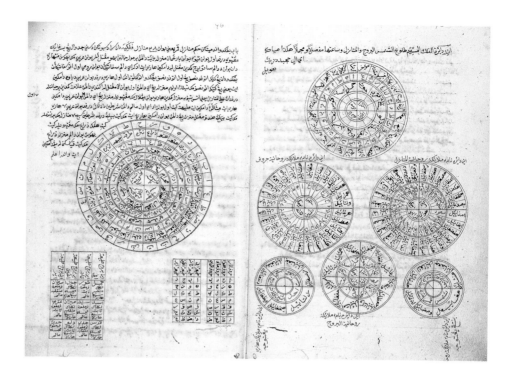

FIGURE 78

Above: Detail from *Kutika*, a divination table showing the procession of well- and ill-omened days through the Muslim year. National Library of Indonesia, Jakarta.

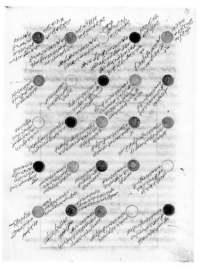

FIGURE 79

Below: Bilangan Takwin. National Library of Indonesia, Jakarta.

study. And in the future, the manuscript would remain with the student as an *aide-mémoire* and reference work.

Consider in this light some manuscripts now kept in the National Library's collection in Jakarta. This collection has some seven manuscripts of the *Bidayah al-Hidayah*, a Malay version of al-Sanusi's *Umm al-Barahin* (fig. 76). This famous book summarizes religious doctrine. It was put into Malay by an Acehnese, Muhammad Zain, in Mecca in the eighteenth century. Of the seven manuscripts containing this work, only one is no more and no less than a complete text of the work. The other six all depart from the ideal in one way or another. Several are incomplete copies of the main text, but have added material of other kinds. One complete copy has added notes on the duties of the *kadi* (jurist) in Arabic, a poem on God's attributes in Acehnese, recipes for *jimat* (charms), notes on Islamic law, an account of the Twenty Attributes of God, prayers and charms. In short, we are looking either at students' workbooks, or the handbooks of practicing *ulama*.

The untidy manuscripts that are the raw products of the *pesantren* never let us lose sight of the practice of religion. They are the everyday tools of religious life. Alongside them must be placed the religious tools of everyday life. These are not works of literature in any sense but manuscripts with diverse practical uses. Leaflets and booklets show how to fix auspicious times and days of the month. Others list and explain signs and omens. One such is the *Takbir Mimpi* (Interpretation of dreams), which is the Malay translation of a well-regarded Arabic work. From it we learn, for instance, that a woman who dreams of a snake will soon marry. All such practical information, and more, was gathered into compendia called *primbon*. These contain notes and diagrams on everything from numerology to recipes for aphrodisiacs (figs. 77, 78, 79).

Other manuscripts have the character of charms themselves. A single sheet in manuscript could be a *jimat*: its possession alone would confer blessings, even invulnerability (fig. 80). It could be worn on the body as an amulet. A potent verse from the Quran, or the name of God, or the confession of faith—these have inherent powers. The effect is enhanced if the text is calligraphed in the hand of a revered religious teacher, and perhaps bestowed in the course of initiation into a brotherhood of disciples. Collections of such potent texts and efficacious prayers and spells were put into manuscript booklets that, if we are to judge by the state of surviving copies, were very well used.

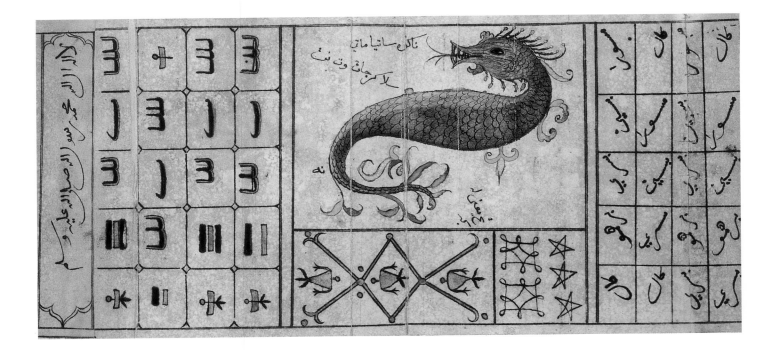

Verse for Every Purpose

The form of literature that was closest to everyday life was verse. Quite contrary to modern notions, in the days of the manuscript it was verse, not prose, that was easier for authors to compose, for performers to read and recite, and for listeners to follow. Compared to verse, texts put in prose had a somewhat intimidating air of authority or sanctity. Prose painted in oils, verse in watercolor. Verse was closer to common Malay speech. Its grammatical forms were more colloquial, its syntax was simple, and its sense units were short and predictable. The universal meter is called *syair* (fig. 82). The *syair* line consists ideally of ten to twelve syllables, four of which are given rhythmic stress, with a weak midline caesura. Each cluster of four lines shares an end-rhyme. On the manuscript page, pairs of lines were conventionally arranged across two columns running down the page. Each line was thus clearly separated, and ended in a predictable rhyme. This format made *syair* the easiest of all literature to read from the manuscript page. It was certainly easier to read than unpunctuated prose. The same predictable repetition of simple rhythm and rhyme aided listeners too. Put into verse of this kind, information became digestible. This accessible form was favored both for texts of instruction and for amusement.

The oldest known *syair* fall in the first category. They are the short poems of Hamzah of Barus, composed in the late sixteenth century. Hamzah's verses are inspirational meditations on the Sufi doctrine of the unity of being. The insights are expressed simply, but often with ingenious rhymes. By using verse, Hamzah could reach a wider audience with a text that was more easily memorized. His example was followed in later centuries by other authors of popular religious handbooks. Less intricate *syair* gave instruction on the pilgrimage to Mecca and Medina, on prayer, on the basic teachings and duties of Islam, on marriage law, on the Twenty Attributes of God, on doomsday, on divination, on the interpretation of dreams, and on character development. Most popular were a few that took a more whimsical approach. The *Syair Burung* (The birds' ballad), for instance, has two birds discussing points of dogma (fig. 81). The imaginative use of nonhuman protagonists was an idea adopted from a more popular genre of Malay verse.

The second and larger category of *syair* is the ballad, or verse romance. These ballads took full advantage of the exceedingly simple form of the *syair*. In performance, the hypnotic rhythm of the text was enhanced by a melodic line that

FIGURE 80

Detail of a Malay *jimat*, this one originating from Aceh. National Library of Indonesia, Jakarta.

accentuated its regularity. The simple combination of rhythm, rhyme, and melody was chanted over and over again. In the longer ballad texts, it propelled the audience over several thousand lines of narrative.

The metrical shape of the *syair* is closely related to the more complex oral art of the *pantun*. A *pantun* comprises a pair of couplets with alternating rhymes and assonances. An admired social skill was the witty swapping of *pantun* among those gathered for some social occasion, or in courting groups. Each contributor builds on the second part of the previous couplet. If a nimble-tongued Malay youth could spin an allusive *pantun* to tease a lover, then he or she would have no trouble turning out a few verses in *syair* form. There was thus an irresistible temptation to use *syair* for the same kind of fun and games that the *pantun* deal in. We find nice examples of this kind in the "flower and animal" ballads, described by Hans Overbeck. The suggestive title of one, *Syair Kumbang dan Melati* (Ballad of the bee and the jasmine), sets the mood (fig. 83). These little tales deal with unrequited love, illicit flirting by those separated by social class, and the goings-on in one or another royal house, which, then as now, were greatly relished by gossips. These flower and animal ballads apply the *pantun* principle of using nature to disguise allusions to human behavior. In the *pantun*, the allusion is foreplay. In the ballad it becomes allegory (fig. 84).

——— FIGURE 81 ———

Syair Berang-Berang, copied in Kampung Tembura on 14 Rabiulawal, Wednesday (no year given, probably late eighteenth century). Malay in Jawi script; ink on European paper, sheets sewn and pasted together to form a scroll. Bodleian Library, Oxford.

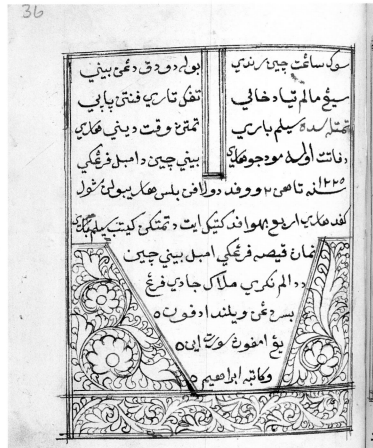

Some *syair* are on a more ambitious scale. They are verse counterparts of the prose adventure romances. In a few cases, prose originals have been put into verse. *Syair Bidasari* (Ballad of Bidasari) opens in Cambay, a stock setting for these verse adventures. After the queen of Cambay becomes pregnant, the kingdom is annihilated by a *garuda*, and the queen, fleeing to the land of Inderapura, gives birth to a baby girl who is cast adrift in a boat. The baby is raised by a merchant couple and given the name Bidasari. The queen of Inderapura, seeing Bidasari as a rival, entices her to the palace, imprisons, and tortures her. Bidasari escapes to live in a secret palace in the jungle, until one day the prince of Inderapura discovers and wins her and they leave to found a new kingdom. Meanwhile Bidasari's father has regained the kingdom of Cambay, and his wife has given birth to a boy, Bidasari's brother. He goes in search of Bidasari, and with the help of her adoptive mother, they are brought together. Bidasari's mother and father, the king and queen of Cambay, are invited to Inderapura, where all are happily reunited and live in peace and prosperity. All, that is, except the evil queen who, now repentant, lives on in misery or, in other versions, dies.

Like the prose adventure tales, these ballads share a fascination with the fluctuations of fortune, hidden identities, the crossing of class barriers, and the quest. Princess Bidasari's solitary forest palace recalls the eyrie of Princess Candralela Nurlela in *Hikayat Inderaputera*. But these ballads also differ from their prose counterparts in some interesting ways. They relate wondrous and magical happenings, including the obligatory intervention of a *nenek kebayan* ("fairy godmother"), but are more down to earth in developing their principal characters. The plots give plenty of scope for melodrama, and the emotional level is pumped up by the extensive use of direct speech. In performance, this produces an effect somewhat like recitative. These ballads more often than not give a woman the leading role. *Syair Ken Tambuhan* (fig. 85), *Syair Bidasari, Syair Puteri Akal, Syair Saudagar Budiman, Syair Sitti Zawiah, Syair Selindung Delima*, and others all bear the names of their leading ladies. Most are more feisty than Bidasari. Several don disguises to rescue their wimpish husbands rather than waiting to be rescued themselves. The language of these ballads, and their melodramatic treatments of love and family life, suggest a popular audience. Certain ballads of this kind were indeed performed as folk theater, among them *Syair Abdul Muluk* and *Syair Ken Tambuhan.*

Other ballads were neither romantic fantasies nor the adventures of strong-willed women. Rather, they relate contemporary events. They tell mostly of single events of passing importance, and thus lack the sweep of the court histories. In these cases the *syair* style was chosen to produce, as it were, the journalism of the manuscript age. Subjects range from wars, particularly victories and defeats in engagements with European forces, to recent local history, biographies of rulers and governors, descriptions of receptions, marriages, and deaths.

The manuscript of *Syair Perkawinan Kapitan Tik Sing* (Commissioner Tik Sing's wedding ballad) nicely illustrates this publicity function (see fig. 226). The manuscript is gorgeously decorated and has a striking form, its pages being pasted together into a single strip measuring 10 meters long. Tik Sing was the wealthy head of the Chinese community in Riau. Like his glittering son's wedding, the manuscript is both lavish and designed to impress. In another case, *Syair Perang Siak* (Ballad of the Siak War), the *syair* took on something of the role of a court history, being read aloud on ceremonial occasions.

The counterpoint to these public-relations exercises are *syair* composed in reaction to certain events, and they often take the form of allegorical sketches of court scandals mentioned earlier. For obvious reasons such texts were of mainly local and ephemeral interest. But there was a wider audience for the new kind of human-interest reportage represented by *Syair Sinyor Kosta* (Ballad of Senhor

Costa). This is the tale of the scandalous elopement of a Chinese merchant's wife with the Portuguese merchant Costa, only to be pursued by her husband with five ships before escaping to Europe. This genre was to develop in print rather than manuscript, its outstanding example being the famous account of events leading to the murder of an Englishman's mistress, Nyai Dasima, in Batavia.

Syair were popular in Java, and once Muslim printing got under way in Singapore in the middle of the century, they became a staple of the book trade and were printed in considerable numbers. It would be rash to suppose that folk of older days enjoyed this adaptable form any less. It may be just that manuscripts of these usually frivolous and often ephemeral texts are the least likely to survive from earlier centuries. Indeed, this is a salutary reminder that our picture of the world of manuscripts depends on what has survived, and that means it reflects the interests of those who have collected and preserved them.

THE MANUSCRIPT TRADITION

Our dependence upon what has survived clouds our understanding of the early history of the manuscript tradition. Internal evidence from the contents of Malay texts establishes that manuscripts were being written in the fourteenth century. The *Hikayat Raja-Raja Pasai* (Story of the rulers of Pasai) concludes with events that took place in the early fourteenth century, indicating that the text was authored quite soon afterwards; however, there are no surviving manuscripts from that period.

Among the earliest manuscripts that we can date with certainty are letters from Malay rulers to European courts. Two of these are letters from the Sultanate of Ternate to the King of Portugal and they bear the dates 1521 and 1522 (figs. 86, 87). They are now in the Lisbon archives. From Aceh there is a contract made in 1602 between the *syahbandar* (port controller) and captains of Dutch vessels who were negotiating to trade in pepper (see fig. 98). From 1615 there is an impressive letter, now in the Bodleian Library, Oxford, from Sultan Iskandar Muda of Aceh to King James I of England (see fig. 97). The earliest manuscript on a religious topic is a copy of the *'Aqa'id* of al-Nasafi, a concise theological credo, which bears a copyist's date of 1590. As for literature, the earliest datable manuscript is a beautiful copy of *Hikayat Seri Rama*, also in the Bodleian. It was acquired by Archbishop Laud in 1633, and thus the date of its copying should be put some years earlier.

It must have been soon after 1612 that the first manuscript version of *Sejarah Melayu*, the record of the rulers of Malacca and their descendants, was completed. This important and influential Malay history has been frequently recopied, and often revised by local court historians for rulers who claimed descent from the old Malacca ruling house. Some years ago the Dutch scholar Roelof Roolvink studied the available manuscripts in European and Southeast Asian collections. He found no fewer than twenty-nine copies; however, not one of them could be dated earlier than the nineteenth century. This pattern is generally true.

It is consequently very difficult to unravel the history of the manuscript tradition. We have no direct evidence of the physical form of Malay literary culture before the first Malay manuscripts fell into European hands. In fact, we have no evidence of the tradition before the profound impact of Islam in Southeast Asian maritime societies. Old Malay inscriptions dating from the seventh to tenth centuries in southern Sumatra and central Java are written in an Indic script, in common with traditional Javanese, Balinese, and mainland Southeast Asian languages. But these inscriptions give no inkling of the form of any literary tradition. It is possible that Malay was incised upon treated palm leaves in the Indian manner, or written on bark like the divination books of the non-Muslim Batak of inland north Sumatra. Perhaps early Malay literature was written in a Sumatran script like

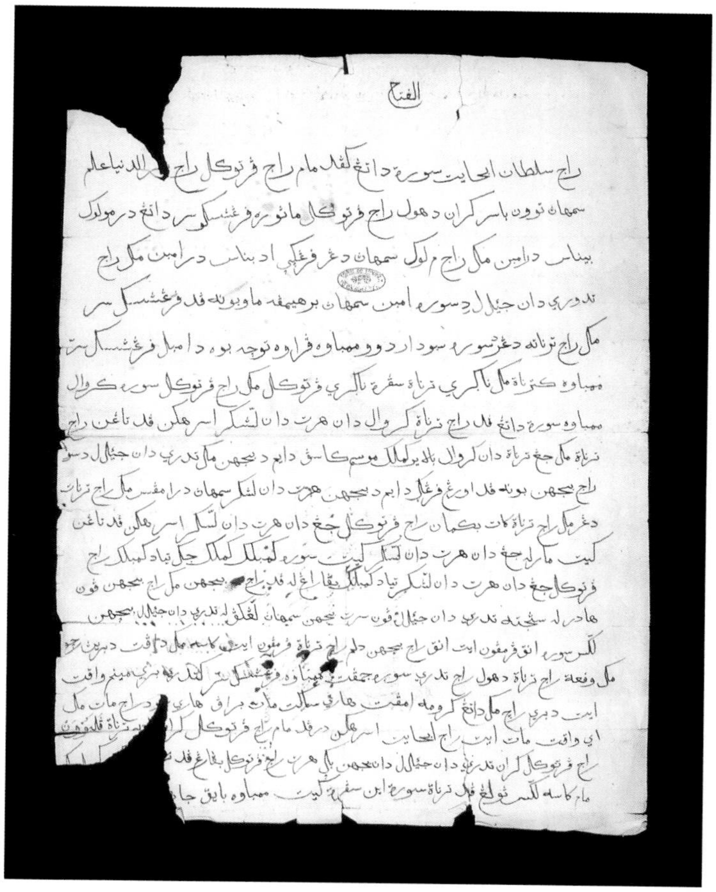

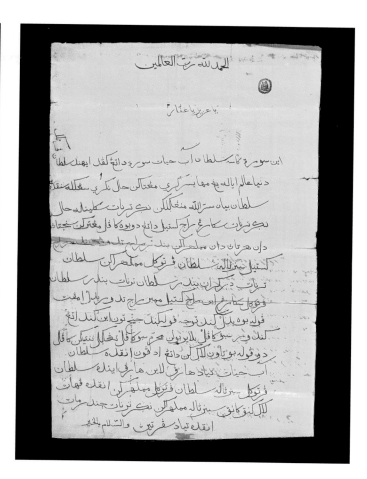

FIGURE 86

The earliest Malay letter known (front side). A letter from Sultan Abu Hayat of Ternate to King John III of Portugal dated 1521. Ink on European paper. Arquivos Nacionais Torre do Tombo Gavetas, Lisbon.

FIGURE 87

The second-earliest Malay letter known (front side). Letter from Sultan Abu Hayat of Ternate to King John III of Portugal dated 1521. Ink on European paper. Arquivos Nacionais Torre do Tombo Gavetas, Lisbon.

those that have survived in inland pockets, or it may even be that there was no written literary tradition in Malay. Whatever the case, the coming of Islam revolutionized the technologies of written communication. Traces of this revolution are embedded in the vocabulary of classical Malay. There is no general word for book, but a pair of terms for books of spiritual knowledge, one of Indian origin (*pustaka*) for books of divination, and one from Arabic (*kitab*) for books of religion. The words for writing are indigenous (*tulis, surat*), while terms for the implements of manuscript writing—paper, ink, and pen—are Arabic in origin (*kertas, dawat, kalam*). This linguistic archeology suggests that Islam brought, along with its new doctrine and new script, a new technology of writing, which together made a clean sweep of earlier literary practices over all of maritime Southeast Asia (excepting south Sulawesi, where a Sumatran-type script was retained alongside the new Arabic script).

The subsequent history of this manuscript tradition also remains problematic. Rather few manuscripts include information on when or where they were copied. When such information is given, it usually appears in a colophon on the final page. There is always an element of doubt over whether the date and other details refer to the copying that produced the manuscript, or whether the latest copyist has simply taken over the information he found at the end of the older manuscript that he was copying. Dating is a particular problem with *kitab* manuscripts. Retaining information about the date and circumstances in which the eminent author completed his work has rightly been seen as more important for the authority of the text than information about any later copy. With only sporadic information about the dates and provenance of manuscripts, it is hard to piece together a picture of variations in the practice of copying over time or from place to place (fig. 88).

Indirect means of dating and locating manuscripts can help here. All the physical properties of the manuscript are potentially useful for this. What ink was

FIGURE 88

Colophon of *Mawa'iz al-Badi'ah*
(Wondrous counsels), fifty lessons in
mystical doctrine. The colophon gives the
date of translation as A.H. 1250 (1835),
but this must in fact be the date of copying, as the text is a seventeenth-century
composition. National Library of
Indonesia, Jakarta.

used? Local ink was manufactured variously from soot, resin from the *ketereh* tree
(*Anacardium occidentale*), and from the purple liquid from the petals of the
senduduk flower (*Melastoma polyanthum*). What paper was used? Is there a dis-
cernible style of writing, and are there characteristic spellings, peculiarities of layout? If the manuscript is decorated, what are the motifs, and where are they
applied? What of the bindings, if any? All these could help fill out a picture of this
manuscript tradition. Timothy Behrend has begun some interesting work on
Javanese manuscript traditions using some of these indicators. Work on the Malay
side has not advanced as far.

Most progress has been made through the dating of paper. Although Malay was
written on other materials—tree bark (*jeluwang*), bamboo strips, wooden panels,

and vellum as well as the hide of goats and sheep—these were exceptions. Most extant Jawi manuscripts are written on imported European paper. This can be examined for identifying characteristics such as watermarks and chain lines. These can then be compared with published descriptions of European papers, and dates for the paper established. Russell Jones has studied the papers used in dated manuscripts and concluded that generally no more than twenty years separates manufacture of the paper and its use. This rule of thumb makes it feasible to date a manuscript from its paper. Papers from China and India, which were not watermarked, are not amenable to dating in this way.

VARIATIONS

Hand in hand with the difficulties of getting a clear picture of the manuscript tradition across time is the problem of local variations. Malay manuscripts were current across a wide geographic area among people speaking Malay dialects and other languages. Naturally some of this diversity is reflected in the manuscript tradition.

Some distinctive forms are found at the margins of the tradition. There are a small number of manuscripts in Malay written in Sumatran scripts, on bark and paper. There are also a few written in Roman script (or Dutch letters, as it was known in the Dutch East Indies). One is the copy of *Syair Darma Adil*, in Jakarta, illustrated here (fig. 89). For several centuries, copies of Bible extracts circulated in the Moluccas in manuscript, copied from the early Malay translation of the Bible printed by the Dutch East India Company.

By and large, however, the mainstream Malayo-Muslim Jawi manuscript tradition has been successful in filtering out local differences. William Marsden, an officer of the English East India Company who wrote an early grammar of Malay, remarked on the "striking consistency in the style of writing, not only of the books in prose and verse, but also of epistolary correspondence." As an outsider, Marsden was perhaps not aware of the subtler variations, and had in mind the stylized chancery letters. But there is some truth in his comment.

Some of the reasons for this have already been mentioned. The written Malay of Jawi manuscripts is a highly contrived artifact, which overlay a variety of local Malay dialects and other first languages. Even in areas renowned for a fine literary style, like Riau, this written language is far removed from the spoken tongue. The consistency of this written superstratum was maintained by the intensity of regional networks. These were not just political relations, though these were intimate enough. More important were commercial and above all religious networks, with pilgrims, advanced students, and scholars moving about the archipelago and

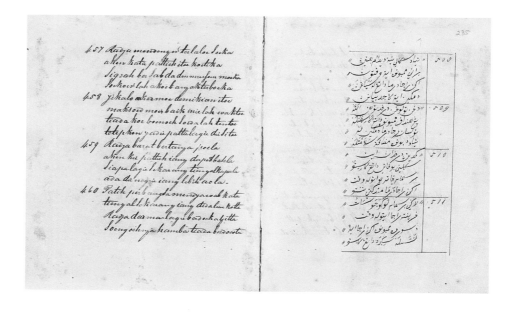

FIGURE 89
Syair Darma Adil. National Library of Indonesia, Jakarta.

traveling to Mecca. The tenacity of these linkages is well illustrated by the history of the Malays of Sri Lanka. These descendants of Javanese and other Indonesians exiled to Ceylon by the Dutch in the seventeenth century came to speak a Malay creole heavily laced with Tamil while maintaining a manuscript literature in standard written Malay.

A second reason for uniformity is that Malay manuscript writing was a local eddy in the ocean of Arabic scribal practice. Malay texts are written in *naskhi* script, the practical hand of clerks all over the Muslim world. There was great stability over time and place in this large, dispersed, interacting network. The most evident variations in the use of the Jawi script are in precisely those features not kept standard by reference to the Muslim great tradition. They include the choice of etymological or phonemic spellings, and the manner of indicating vowels.

The influence of local dialects and languages also seeps into the manuscript tradition, though the degree to which this occurs is dampened by the nature of the Jawi script. Jawi script is actually quite ill adapted to writing Malay, certainly very much inferior to either the Indic alphabets that probably preceded it or the Roman script that has followed it. Its main weakness for writing Malay stems from the reluctance of Arabic to indicate vowels, and then to indicate them with only three vowel signs. Classical Malay has eight vowels and diphthongs, and so is poorly served. There is, however, one advantage in this inadequate script. A prominent element of dialect variation among Malay speakers is vowel change. This has plagued the reformers of Roman script spelling, but it is quite hidden in the Arabic script.

Regional variations of spoken Malay do show through now and then in the area of vocabulary. Not surprisingly, such variation tends to be more evident in the style closest to speech, the *syair*. It is less commonly evident, but not absent, from the more cultivated registers of Malay. The *History of Banjar* is a case in point. This text starts out in standard literary Malay, but in its later parts shows increasing influence of colloquial Banjarese, a Malay dialect influenced by Dayak and Javanese. This shows up in nonstandard spellings, but more significantly in the area of vocabulary, with an infusion of Javanese and local Banjarese words. This is not true of another Banjar example, this time a religious text. Muhammad Arsyad al-Banjari (of Banjar) wrote a book entitled *Sabil al-Muhtadin*, on the pillars of Islam (fig. 90). He compiled this digest in 1779 on the model of the older standard work by Nuruddin al-Raniri, the *Sirat al-Mustakim*. In his preface, he justified writing a new book by pointing out that the *Sirat* was too difficult for Malay readers to understand because of the Acehnese expressions it contained. Or as he put it, in the *kitab* argot, "in that instance it was the case that certain exemplifications were obscure in respect of certain of those who were drawing benefit from it because it consisted in Acehnese and that which was removed from their own language was not understood by those who pursued study of it." His new work would remedy any lack of clarity by using good Malay. Better understanding of the historical and regional shape of the tradition will make more of these variations recognizable.

AESTHETIC EFFECTS

The Jawi world has no great art of calligraphy like that of India or Persia. In the Muslim scheme of things, the Malay maritime world was civilization on a small scale, and its manuscripts are comparatively rather plain. Their common *naskhi* script puts them in the realm of the scholar and the clerk rather than the calligrapher. It is true that Abdul Rauf of Singkel once spoke of the metaphysics of calligraphy. But fragments of the drafting sheets of celebrated calligraphers were not for sale in Southeast Asian marketplaces. There seem not to have been brotherhoods of initiates in the calligraphic art tracing descent from the early caliphs. In Persia or

FIGURE 90

Sabil al-Muhtadin. National Library of Indonesia, Jakarta.

FIGURE 91

The opening pages of *Hikayat Raja Budak*
in a polished manuscript with decorated
head-pieces, key words in red ink.
National Library of Indonesia, Jakarta.

India, a caliph or a king might be a calligrapher, but no ruler in maritime Southeast
Asia was known for his fair hand. Nor indeed could many write at all, or read.

That is not to say that there are no examples of good penmanship and hand-
somely decorated manuscripts. The elegance of letters of state is rarely matched
in books. The text on the first double page of a book was conventionally set in
extrawide margins. In some impressive examples, these margins are filled with
elaborate colored borders, intricately decorated, usually with motifs of curling
tendrils. Gold paint is sometimes used. This first opening has the decorative function of the dust jacket on modern books. It was, if you like, a way of dressing up
a text, rather as fine clothes marked status at court and in society.

The script itself is naturally decorative, lending itself to flourishes and ornament. Its features can be highlighted to put emphasis on key words and phrases,
by writing them in thicker strokes, or sometimes in red ink. These key words
might be Arabic quotations, especially quotations from the Quran, or royal names
and titles, or most commonly "punctuation words." Punctuation marks rarely
appear in Jawi manuscripts, but pauses, new sections, and changes of topic in the
texts are indicated by words whose function is to indicate a turning point. As is
shown in the pages of the mystic's handbook illustrated on this page, punctuation
words are sometimes picked out in red ink.

At the same time, it is not unusual to turn the decorated first pages of a manuscript and find that the rest is plain text. Narrative prose may fill page after page
with solid text, sometimes in a frame ruled in colored ink, sometimes not. There
are no titles, no title pages, no chapter headings, no paragraphs, none of the para-
phernalia that make modern books more accessible to the eye. Even the colophon
runs directly on from the end of the text on a conventionally tapered final page.
The colophon of *Mawa'iz al-Badi'ah* in figure 88 is one such example. The
colophon begins in the middle of the fourth line. More often than not even the
margins of the opening pages are left blank (fig. 91).

Comparison with the Javanese tradition is telling. This was an independent
manuscript tradition using its own script, the product of a civilization with a more
developed high culture than any of the Malayo-Muslim trading ports. The visual
sophistication of the better Javanese manuscripts is striking. Illustration is not
unusual in Javanese manuscripts, but exceedingly rare in Jawi Malay manuscripts,

Today the small port of Bima is the chief town of a district (*kabupaten*) far from Jakarta and the economic and intellectual turmoil of the capital. It is difficult therefore to imagine that it was once an autonomous and prosperous sultanate, a busy stopping place on the trade route from the western to the eastern part of the archipelago. Already in the second decade of the seventeenth century, the Portuguese traveler Tome Pires lists the commercial goods—brazil wood, cloth, horses, slaves, tamarind, meat, and fish—for which native merchants called in at Bima on their way from Malacca to the Moluccas. Many centuries before this period, the trade route had brought Hinduism to Bima: a Shaivite site across the bay, complete with an eleventh-century Pallava inscription, bears testimony to this religious influence. In the same way, trade brought Islam to Bima at the beginning of the seventeenth century. Bima was actually Islamized as the result of military campaigns sent in 1618 and 1619 by Makasar, the main kingdom of South Sulawesi, which had converted in 1605. But traders, travelers, and missionaries had already paved the way. The "heathen king" of Bima, as Tome Pires has it, converted to Islam and took the name of Sultan Abdul Kahir in 1621. From then on, Islam was to become a predominant feature of Bimanese culture.

Islamization also meant Malayization. It is well known that Malay was the lingua franca of the whole archipelago, and also the language of Islamization. It is less recognized, however, that written Malay became a kind of official language in many a sultanate outside the Malay-speaking area, so that Malay literature was not only produced in the Malay peninsula and the Riau region but from Aceh to Ternate, and in Bima as well.

Just as the Acehnese used their native tongue in everyday spoken language and adopted Malay as the official language of the court, the Bimanese too had both a native tongue (*basa Mbojo*) and also used Malay as the language of politics and culture. To what extent the Bima (Mbojo) language had been used previously in written form is still a matter of debate. In the last century, three foreign scholars (Raffles, Zollinger, and Matthes) were shown what were supposed to be Bimanese native alphabets, but the three alphabets differ from one another, and we do not have a single text written in any of them. The Bimanese language was certainly used now and then in a script adapted from the Makasarese. A local historical text states that in 1645 the second sultan ordered that from then on every official document would be written down "in Malay, in the script prescribed by Allah."

As a result, Bima became one of the active centers in a wide network of Malay culture. Malay texts produced in faraway centers were known in Bima, and new original texts were produced locally. We know, for instance, that in the time of Sultan Abdul Hamid, at the end of the eighteenth century, *hikayat* (epics and romances) were read at the palace. A few remains of this literary wealth still exist, and copies of famous texts such as the *Taj us-Salatin, Qisas al-Anbiya* or *Hikayat Indra Jayakusuma* survive to this day. Inner evidence from other texts prove that the most important works (historical, literary, or religious) of Malay liter-

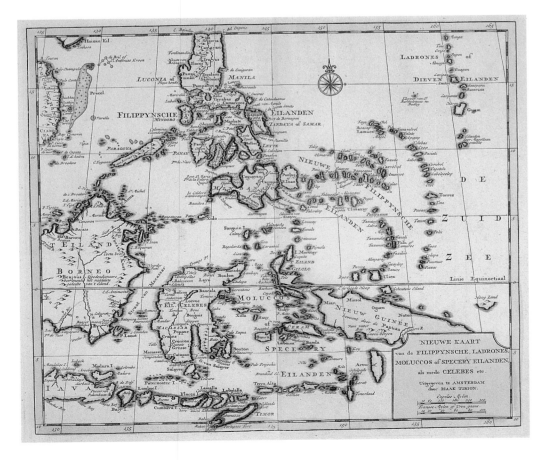

A small speck in a sea of islands: the regency of "Biema" (Bima) is located on the island of Cumbava (Sumbawa) between Lomboc (Lombok) and Flores to the east of Iava (Java) and Baly (Bali). This map was produced by Isaak Tirion in Amsterdam in the mid-eighteenth century.

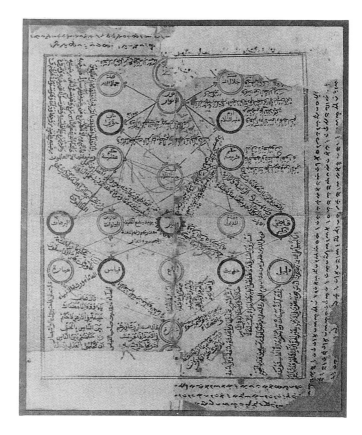

A genealogy from a Malay manuscript. Museum Kebudayaan Samparaja, Bima.

ature were familiar to the educated Bimanese. Of the original texts produced in Bima, most were of a historical nature, and extremely valuable for a knowledge of Bima society during the seventeenth, eighteenth, and nineteenth centuries. These texts started to be unearthed some twelve years ago, and to date only a few of them have been edited. A catalogue of the manuscripts still available in Bima, prepared by the late S.W. Rujiati Mulyadi and H.S. Maryam R. Salahuddin, gives an idea of the state of the art. Thousands of pages, many of them loose or torn off, await analysis. This is a long and difficult task but a very rewarding one, as the manuscripts contain information found nowhere else.

Like other sultanates in Indonesia, Bima has produced its own dynastic history. The text entitled *Ceritera Asal Bangsa Jin dan Segala Dewa-Dewa* (The story of the origins of the jinn and the devas) gives a brief account of the story of humanity from the creation of the first female jinn and the first man down to the foundation of the kingdom of Bima through episodes borrowed from various sources, including the Javanese versions of the *Mahabharata.* This complex tale was based on a genuine Bimanese kernel (common in fact to many Indonesian primitive societies) explaining the organization of society by the union of the forces of the upper, middle, and nether worlds. Subsequently this original myth was modified and expanded under Hindu-Javanese influence: via the central figure of Bima, the Bimanese kings were related to the superhuman heroes of the *Mahabharata.* With the coming of Islam, the myth was extended and elaborated once more in order to give it a new dynamic: all the characters became part of the jinn genealogy, and the jinn were all Islamized by Alexander the Great.

The last version of this dynastic history was probably written down shortly after Islamization. A century later, at the beginning of the eighteenth century, an epic, the *Hikayat Sang Bima,* was based on it, disregarding its historical and mythological elements. We know of another historical text that was composed yet a century later—around 1830—in Bima, by one Khatib Lukman. It is a *syair* (a narrative poem made up of monorhyme quatrains) relating four recent events that the author had himself witnessed: the devastating eruption of Mount Tambora in 1815, the death and burial of Sultan Abdul Hamid in early 1819, the attack of Bima by pirates, and the enthronement of Sultan Ismail in late 1819.

Bima has produced yet another kind of historical text still awaiting proper study. These texts, generically called *bo'* (probably from the Dutch *boek* for "book"), are diaries written from the middle of the seventeenth century to the end of the nineteenth century at the sultan's palace as well as at the residences of several high dignitaries. This habit of keeping diaries was undoubtedly inherited from Makasar, and was linked to the Islamization of the kingdom. All the diaries were written in Malay, most of them by specially appointed secretaries. Those belonging to the prime minister (*raja bicara*) and to the royal

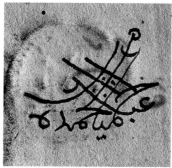

Signature of the Sultan of Bima. Detail from a contract between the Kingdom of Bima and the Dutch government dated May 26, 1792. National Archives of Indonesia, Jakarta.

judge (*qadi*) were destroyed in a fire in 1918. Many others simply decayed or disappeared in the course of time. The few that remain today are extremely valuable, containing very diverse information written down in the most concise way. They have been copied again and again (and perhaps transformed in this process) and are arranged without chronological or thematic order. We find for instance political notes (wars, peace treaties, contracts with the Dutch East India Company, diplomatic correspondence with Batavia and Makasar), information about the royal family (genealogies, dates of births, marriages and deaths, travels), administrative acts (appointments, lists of villages administrated by the sultan, decisions of the state council), religious information (accounts of the conversion of the kingdom, descriptions of ceremonies, calls for people to carry out the prescriptions of Islam), and judicial notes (texts of laws, court verdicts, lists of private property of individuals, acts of manumission of slaves).

Henri Chambert-Loir

reflecting Muslim inhibitions at depicting living forms. Rarely does a Jawi scribe overcome this reluctance, and Malay manuscripts hold to geometric and natural motifs. The scribe of one manuscript of *Hikayat Hang Tuah,* copying the famous story of how Hang Jebat placed platters on the palace floor so he could not be speared from below, wrote the text in spiral lines on the page. But this is hardly illustration. It is no coincidence that those rare Jawi manuscripts that contain illustrations have been produced in Java, and thus under the influence of the more libertarian Javanese manuscript tradition. There is no parallel in the Jawi tradition for the Javanese manuals of manuscript illumination.

It is fair to say that in the Malay world, the manuscript was always secondary to the text. Even when manuscripts were kept for ceremonial purposes, as heirlooms, it was the text, not the physical manuscript, that was treasured. A manuscript was most importantly the locus of a text.

MAINTAINING THE TRADITION

Few old manuscripts have survived in Southeast Asia for this very reason. All the earliest manuscripts are ones that fell into European hands and survive in European collections. The great majority of extant Malay manuscripts were collected by Europeans during the nineteenth century, and mainly date from that century as well. It must seem at first glance that Southeast Asians have been careless of their manuscripts, while Europeans have preserved these cultural treasures, even though they were not their own. While there is an element of truth in this, the moral judgment it implies is misplaced.

A governing factor is climate. Humidity, heat, and voracious insects do irrevocable damage to paper and ink. To keep the text in good order, manuscripts need to be recopied at least every few generations. There is thus a choice to be made: retain the text by renovating its manuscripts, or retain the manuscript while losing the use of the text. In the Malay tradition, the choice has always been for the text. (By contrast, for early European collectors the reverse was the case. They collected manuscripts as scientific specimens in the same way that plant and insect samples were gathered from the four corners of the earth. Torn from their cultural moorings, these manuscripts became objects in catalogued European collections.)

The function of Malay manuscript copying was thus not to reproduce manuscripts but to preserve meaningful texts. Western scholars have noticed the great variations among manuscript texts of both histories and tales. Episodes are added, wording changed. To print-conditioned Europeans, this seemed a sign of woolly-mindedness among inferior native intellects. Rather, it shows that the texts were in use in a living manuscript tradition. Those who copied out works of fiction acted as editors. They felt no compunction in making stylistic changes, extending descriptive passages, and smoothing out any infelicitous turns of phrase. Why should they? These were anonymous works without any single authoritative version. Each copyist, in making a copy, was an interpreter of the text—rather as a *dalang*, in each performance, was the interpreter of a Rama episode. Historical texts grew through the regular updating of events. Local versions of *Sejarah Melayu* are found up and down the coast of eastern Sumatra, and in the islands of the Riau archipelago. These versions maintain the early parts of *Sejarah Melayu* but focus on local events in the later parts of the text. It is even possible to trace a dialogue between groups of these local texts as they react and respond to each other's claims. Here the use of the text positively stimulated the recreating of its manuscripts. But when the meaning of the text required accurate verbatim copying, that is what we find. Works of religious scholarship were accurately copied, for they depended upon the authority of an eminent author, in whose name the text was presented. These texts, which were aids to verbatim memorization, were copied verbatim.

TRAFFIC IN MANUSCRIPTS

Manuscripts were never easy to come by. Europeans and Malays alike complained about the difficulty of locating texts. Recent estimates by leading Malay scholars suggest that the number of Malay manuscript books in use in Southeast Asia early in the nineteenth century was six or seven thousand at most. This means that they were fairly thin on the ground. Abdullah bin Abdul Kadir was ready to look for a book he could not find in Singapore as far afield as Kelantan, still without success. A manuscript of the Muslim heroic legend *Hikayat Raja Handak* reveals that one Kari Telolo in Makasar arranged for a Malay scribe to travel to Semarang to make a copy of the manuscript there in 1797. The great collector Hillebrandus Klinkert, on Riau, when he got a request for a particular title, could only send messengers to scout around the villages in the vain hope of finding what was required.

Up to this time, manuscripts were not objects of commerce. Most manuscripts were of texts embedded in the social relations of court or cloister, and access to them was consequently governed by those relationships. The texts of dynastic histories or potent religious knowledge could be handled only by experts whose knowledge matched the contents. Owners of manuscripts of recreational literature did lend them, but not apparently for pecuniary reward. We know from the notes added to the end of some manuscripts that owners were anxious that manuscripts they lent would be treated with care and returned promptly. Social proprieties made it difficult to press for the return of property. Typical is a nineteenth-century copy of *Hikayat Hang Tuah*, which has a note in a hand different from that of the text's scribe on one of the blank front pages of the manuscript, noting that it belongs to the Sultan of Pahang (who reigned in the 1890s), and asking whoever might borrow it to return it quickly.

This began to change in the course of the nineteenth century. Perhaps it started in 1808 when Raffles began collecting manuscripts in earnest from his base at Malacca. He was willing to pay a good price for manuscripts, and Abdullah bin Abdul Kadir saw him collect some 360 Malay prose works. A subsequent Dutch manuscript-hunting expedition in 1821, led by Abdullah's father, was equipped with letters of introduction from the Dutch governor of Malacca, a ship flying the Dutch flag, and a war chest of five hundred dollars. Sixty to seventy books were acquired. Abdullah was fearful of the impact this collecting would have, anguishing over the loss of texts and manuscripts to the Malay community.

The manuscript tradition was tenuous, and texts have undoubtedly been lost in the past. Ruling houses have been deposed; new religious movements have gained strength. Through several centuries, this has meant flux in the continuing tradition: Pasai making way for Aceh, Malacca spawning a handful of successor states, the Shattariah *tarekat* losing ground to Nakshbandiah, not to mention the changing fashions in literature. Many manuscripts had just been put to the torch in Terengganu early in the nineteenth century in the wake of a *fatwa* forbidding the reading of the old romances. In this continuing flux, some texts have been lost, and others composed and copied in their place.

Abdullah's worst fears were confirmed with news that the ship carrying Raffles's magnificent collection of Malay manuscripts and other specimens had been lost off Sumatra.

> When I heard this my imagination reeled to think of all the works in Malay and other languages, centuries old, which he had collected from many countries, all utterly lost. Had they been printed in many copies, there would still be a record of them.

But the main effect was not that feared by Abdullah. Rather, European intervention stimulated manuscript production. Some of Raffles's 360 lost works were new copies made specially for him. He had employed five clerks for this purpose during his time in Malacca, and later during the occupation of Java did the same in Bogor. The idea was taken up by the returning Dutch, and clerks of the general secretariat in Batavia were put to work copying manuscripts to be sent to Holland.

The deeper effect was that manuscripts gained a commercial value, becoming objects for which European collectors would pay high prices. It is no accident that the manuscripts in the great collections of Jakarta, Leiden, and other European centers overwhelmingly date from the nineteenth century. This was the age of the extension of colonial power across maritime Southeast Asia. Ding Choo Ming has sketched some of the transactions that filled the shelves of European libraries. A combination of political assertion and scholarly interest was at work. From Malacca, Raffles went on to seize the library of the court of Yogyakarta in 1812. Taking the hint, at Raffles's instigation, the Sultan of Pontianak had the *History of Banjar* copied as a gift for him in 1816. The returning Dutch went on to purchase the royal library of Banten in a job lot about 1830. Later, other rulers followed the example of the Sultan of Pontianak. Copies of *Syair Pangeran Syarif Hasyim*, describing Dutch wars against "rebels" (local Dayaks) in southern Kalimantan, were appropriately dedicated to the local Dutch commissioner and to the Dutch resident. Those manuscripts are currently held in the National Library in Jakarta and the Leiden University Library. In a similar gesture, the ruler of Riau presented a copy of his local history, *Tuhfat al-Nafis*, to the retiring Dutch resident in 1896, who in turn bequeathed it to the Royal Institute (KITLV) in the Netherlands, where the manuscript is now found (fig. 92).

In the latter part of the nineteenth century, the Dutch administration employed scholars like Von Dewall, Snouck Hurgronje, Klinkert, and, later, Kern, who were active collectors. Von Dewall alone collected more than three hundred manuscripts. The geographic areas where these scholars were active were determined by the extending tentacles of colonial power. The National Library collection in Jakarta is unusually strong in religious manuscripts from Aceh. These were deposited in the National Library's colonial predecessor, the Batavian Society of Arts and Sciences, during the course of the Aceh war, the long war of resistance to Dutch rule mobilized by Muslim scholars. Some of these manuscripts come from mosque libraries seized as booty in this war. By contrast, Terengganu and Patani were reputed to be literary centers but escaped European attention. They have not been well represented in public collections. Thus, ironically, as colonial intervention wreaked havoc in the social environment that gave meaning to texts, it salvaged the manuscripts. Colonial libraries became mortuaries, their manuscript cabinets filled with the corpses of dead texts.

The nineteenth century saw further commercialization of manuscripts in the new social environments that developed under European rule. Lending libraries that made manuscripts available at the princely rate of ten cents a night (or a similar charge) appeared in Palembang, Batavia, and perhaps other growing urban centers. In the mid-nineteenth century, a family of scribes in Batavia began an enterprise of copying manuscripts, which lasted for fifty years and formed the basis of a lending library. More than seventy manuscripts have been identified as belonging to their lending system (fig. 93). These libraries lent recreational Jawi manuscripts to Malay and Chinese readers alike. As book-hiring shops and peddlers were well known in China, it seems likely this innovation was Chinese inspired. It signifies the dissolution of traditional networks in fast-growing urban centers.

Time was not on the side of manuscript lending libraries. The increasing availability of printed books meant that one could buy a book for the cost of borrowing a manuscript for several nights. By the turn of the century, the stock of both Palembang and Batavian libraries had been sold to European collectors.

Ian Proudfoot and Virginia Hooker

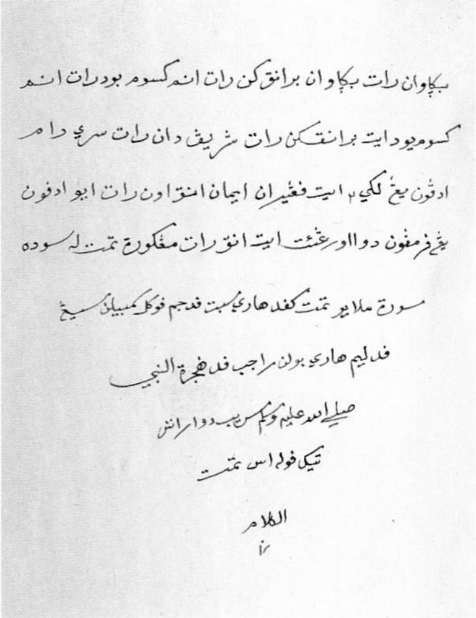

FIGURE 92

Above: Hikayat Raja-Raja Banjar dan Kotaringin (Chronicle of the Kings of Banjar and Kotaringin), also called *Hikayat Lambu Mangkurat*, dated 5 Rejab 1231 (June 1, 1815). Malay in Jawi script; ink on Chinese paper. British Library, London.

FIGURE 93

Below: Hikayat Merpati Emas dan Merpati Perak, one of the manuscripts from the lending library of Muhammad Bakri. Chambert-Loir comments that the insertion of illustrations was "a striking idiosyncrasy of Muhammad Bakir as a scribe." National Library of Indonesia, Jakarta.

POETRY AND WORSHIP:
MANUSCRIPTS FROM ACEH

Acehnese traditional literature is one of the major achievements of Indonesian literary culture, and its creations are relatively well represented in manuscript collections, both inside and outside Indonesia (fig. 94). It is therefore regrettable that only a small handful of scholars outside of Aceh can read Acehnese texts, and at no institution in the world is there a program that provides a systematic introduction to Acehnese language and literature.

Our understanding of Acehnese literature owes much to the path-breaking work of C. Snouck Hurgronje, who surveyed and described the literature as he found it in the late nineteenth century. Since then his contemporaries and students have added much to our knowledge of Acehnese manuscripts and literary texts; however, the Dutch tradition of scholarship in this field has not been continued, and today the only center that has an ongoing tradition of work on Acehnese manuscripts and literature is Banda Aceh, the provincial capital of the Special Region of Aceh. Some important work is also being done by Acehnese native speakers employed outside of Aceh.

THE EARLIEST EVIDENCE

The earliest date for which there is evidence of an Acehnese manuscript tradition in the Acehnese language is the year A.H. 1069 (A.D. 1658–1659). According to the lists of manuscripts in the Museum of Aceh, this year is mentioned in a manuscript of the *Hikayat Sema'un.* Coming soon after this is the date A.H. 1074 (1663–1664), given in the text of a *Hikayat Tujoh Kisah* (Tale of seven stories) as the time when the author began his work. The source mentioned is the Malay eschatological work *Akhbar al-akhira,* composed in Aceh twenty-two years earlier (A.H. 1052) by Nur al-Din al-Raniri. Another more literal rendering of this Malay text was apparently composed some sixteen years later in A.H. 1090 (1679) by a Raseuni Khan, who reports that because "so few people know the Jawi language" (that is, Malay written using Arabic letters), he "gave it a composition in the manner of our recitation" (fig. 96). This remark is interesting from a number of perspectives. Since Raseuni Khan's text is written in Arabic letters, using spelling conventions significantly derivative from Malay, and since Malay was at that time the language of written communication and scholarship in Aceh, it seems quite implausible that anyone could have had the ability to read Raseuni Khan's Acehnese text unless he could also read Malay (fig. 97). It seems therefore that Raseuni Khan made an Acehnese version of al-Raniri's text for the purpose of recitation by someone who would have known both Malay and Acehnese, to Acehnese speakers who were much less familiar with Malay.

The particular Acehnese form that Raseuni Khan uses is what is now known as *sanjak,* a form of verse is recited with the aid of a melody. Indeed *sanjak* is the form in which virtually all Acehnese poetry, including the large majority of all manuscript texts, is composed, and these remarks of Raseuni Khan, now over three hundred years old, reflect the enduring function of Acehnese manuscripts as an aid to the oral performance of *sanjak* texts.

Another early Acehnese text is composed in praise of the holy cities of Mecca and Medina. It was written in Mecca, and concludes with a letter to relatives of the author in Aceh, expressing his longings for Aceh, which he sees in his dreams. The author is apparently named Tuan Ahmad and the text is dated Tuesday, 13 Rabi' II, 1125 (May 9, 1713). In one line he addresses his letter to "those who are

FIGURE 94

Hikayat Pocut Muhammad, the most complete manuscript of an Acehnese literary masterwork. This manuscript is a copy made for Djajadiningrat, who used it in compiling his dictionary of Acehnese. It is also the manuscript used by G.W.J. Drewes for his published edition of this *hikayat* in 1979. National Library of Indonesia, Jakarta.

present listening to the *hikayat* [poetic performance], the owner of the letter, and the one who is reading it out" (*ngon nyang hal/ ngo hikayat, ngon po surat ngon nyang baca*)."

Although we cannot with any certainty project the history of Acehnese-language manuscript production any further back than the middle of the 1600s, it is clear that Malay has been the dominant language of scholarship, governance, and trade in north Sumatra from at least as far back as the early 1400s and probably much earlier (figs. 98, 99). A Chinese delegation to the kingdom of Sumatra (present-day Syamtalira in North Aceh) reported in 1416 that its language and customs were that of Malacca, that is, Malay. The history of Aceh, as written by Western scholars, is virtually indistinguishable from that of a Malay port state. The political ascendancy of Aceh in the 1600s meant that it was a major literary center for Malay in the region, and indeed a number of important early Malay manuscripts derive from Aceh (fig. 100). Malay has been, and remains in its modern guise of Indonesian, the standard language of written communication. Acehnese manuscripts fit into a multilingual matrix of literacy in Malay and Arabic (fig. 101).

It is intriguing to speculate whether Acehnese was a written language before the advent of Islam in Sumatra. If so, it would almost certainly have used an Indic script of some kind. Acehnese is clearly a close sister to Cham, spoken in southern Vietnam, for which we have written inscriptions dating back 1,600 years to the end of the fourth century. These Chamic inscriptions actually predate the earliest written materials from Indonesia. It seems quite plausible that in ancient times the first Acehnese speakers came to Sumatra and made it a trading outpost or a refugee colony from the empire of Champa. After Champa declined in power from c. A.D. 1000, the connection between it and Aceh would have gradually faded from memory. It is interesting that Chamic people in Vietnam and Cambodia today use both the Arabic script as well as the more ancient Devanagari-derived script to write their language, those Chams who converted to Islam some centuries ago having transferred to an Arabic-based script as part of the process of Islamization. We can also mention here the existence in modern times in Sumatra of Devanagari-based scripts for other languages, notably the Batak script and the south Sumatran scripts.

COLLECTIONS AND COLLECTORS

Manuscripts of the three texts referred to above and another containing Acehnese language materials, all religious texts, are found today in the library of the School of Oriental and African Studies in London. They come from William Marsden's

FIGURE 95

A rare late-seventeenth-century map of Sumatra, the Malay peninsula, and Cambodia, showing Aceh on the northern tip of Sumatra. Vincenzo Coronelli–Jean Baptiste Niolin, 1687.

FIGURE 96

Rawiatôn Saabeu'ah, one of several renderings into Acehnese poetry of Al-Raniri's Malay eschatological work *Akhbar al-akira*. The Acehnese poet is named as Raseuni Khan. The lines of poetry are written continuously, without any signs to mark the verses. This is one of a small number of manuscripts from the Marsden collection. School of Oriental and African Studies, London.

FIGURE 97

A letter written in Malay from Sultan Iskandar Muda of Aceh to King James I of England. Bodleian Library, Oxford.

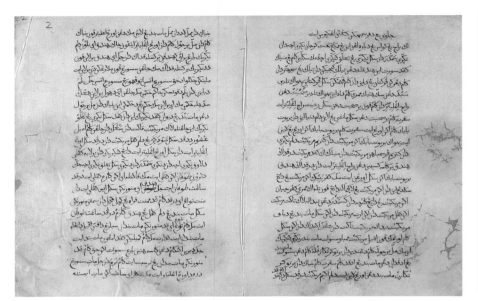

private collection, acquired by him in the early 1800s, and are probably the oldest Acehnese manuscripts in existence.

The next European after Marsden to collect a number of Acehnese manuscripts was K.F.H. van Langen, who acquired several in 1882. He employed two Acehnese scribes (*krani*) to copy texts, Haji Mohammat and Krani Ismail. Excerpts from some of these texts are reproduced in Van Langen's introduction to the Acehnese language, *Handleiding voor de beoefening der Atjehsche taal,* and presumably provided material for his dictionary, *Woordenboek der Atjehsche taal*, the only one to use the traditional Arabic-derived script. Van Langen's collection was subsequently given to Snouck Hurgronje, who enlarged upon it partly by purchasing texts, but mainly by borrowing texts and having them copied. Much of this copying work was done by L.B. Teungku Mohamad Noerdin, himself an accomplished poet, who worked on the materials into the 1930s at the Balai Poestaka publishing house in Batavia (Jakarta). It is difficult to overestimate the importance of Teungku M. Noerdin's contribution in copying, cataloguing, and transliterating Acehnese manuscripts, a task to which he devoted the greater part of his life. It was his labors over many years that made Djajadiningrat's great dictionary of Acehnese possible. M. Noerdin also made a crucial contribution to Snouck Hurgronje's important ethnography of the Acehnese, *De Atjèhers* (*The Achehnese*), which includes what still stands today as the most important overview of Acehnese literature. No doubt one of the reasons for the phenomenally short time in which Snouck Hurgronje produced this work, apart from his own personal qualities and deep familiarity with Islam in Indonesia, was the support he received from his assistant, Teungku M. Noerdin, and from other scribes, such as Nyak

FIGURE 98

Far left: A copy of a trading permit issued to an English sea captain in Aceh c. 1602. Bodleian Library, Oxford.

FIGURE 99

Left: A letter of authority to trade given to Captain Harry Middleton by Sultan Alauddin Riayat Syah of Aceh in 1602. Bodleian Library, Oxford.

FIGURE 100

An Acehnese *jimat* manuscript, written in Malay. This example illustrates one aspect of the role of Malay in Acehnese society. Note the beauty of the *jimat* in comparison to the often rather plain Acehnese-language manuscripts. A *jimat* had intrinsic magical or mystical value. National Library of Indonesia, Jakarta.

Musa, who is named as the copyist in one of the manuscripts dating from the time of Snouck Hurgronje's stay in Aceh from July 1891 to February 1892.

From the first part of this century, three non-Acehnese individuals—Snouck Hurgronje, Hoesein Djajadiningrat, and H.T. Damsté—acquired significant private collections of Acehnese manuscripts (fig. 102). Snouck Hurgronje's collection was given to the Leiden University Library after his death, and Djajadiningrat's collection was given on loan to the Museum of the Batavia Society of Arts and Sciences in 1948. At some point, apparently, it was incorporated into the collection of the society's successor, the National Museum. I say "apparently" because much of the Djajadiningrat collection cannot be located. Fifteen years ago, the manuscript collection of the National Museum was moved to the newly established National Library. An inventory of the collection revealed a number of "holes." However, as is attested by the two Djajadiningrat manuscripts illustrated here, some of the confusion over the whereabouts of certain manuscripts might be attributed to the assigning of new catalogue numbers for them. *Hikayat Malém Diwa*, for example, whose former catalogue number was D (for Djajadiningrat) 4, now goes under the number VT 267. And *Hikayat Pocut Muhammad*, whose catalogue number was once Dj 48 was given the new number NB 98.

Manuscripts taken as "official booty" by the Dutch during the Dutch-Acehnese war now belong to the National Library, which today has one of the largest collections of Acehnese manuscripts.

The Leiden University Library holdings of Acehnese manuscripts increased in size considerably by the acquisition of Damsté's private collection of Acehnese manuscripts. Damsté had been a controleur in Aceh (1901–1903, 1908–1912), and enjoyed a deep appreciation of Acehnese literature. He made a special study of war literature and, in an article he published in 1928, described some of his manuscripts as follows: "They could not be called fresh study materials! Written in Acehnese-Arabic letters, often by a clumsy hand, using a kind of sooty water as ink, filthy from many thumbs, smeared with betel and sometimes with blood, these scraps of paper did not awaken any love on first sight! But they had caught my interest, and I found that they deserved the interest of others too." Damsté's large collection was presented to the library by his widow in 1955. While Snouck Hurgronje's collection focused on *hikayat*, many of which were commissioned copies, Damsté collected many original manuscripts of a rather diverse nature, including numerous religious texts, and some printed booklets.

Today, the Leiden University Library and the National Library of Indonesia have the two largest collections of Acehnese-language manuscripts. The legacies of Damsté and Snouck Hurgronje have made the Leiden University Library collection the largest single collection of Acehnese-language manuscript materials in the world. Around eight hundred separate texts are preserved there, although the actual number of codices (physical bundles of papers or writing books) is rather smaller.

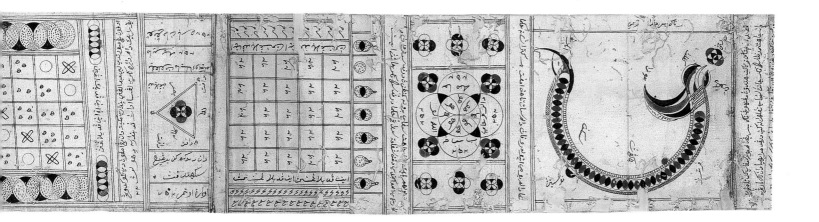

——— FIGURE 101 ———

Above: Within the covers of this one manuscript are three Acehnese texts: *Hikayat Nubuet Nabi, Hikayat Meucukô,* and a fragment of the *Hikayat Hayaké Tujuôh.* The mixed status of the languages in this manuscript is characteristic of Acehnese literacy. National Library of Indonesia, Jakarta.

——— FIGURE 102 ———

Left: A mystical text, one of a collection of booklets from the 1898 collection of Snouck Hurgronje. Leiden University Library, Leiden.

There are also several much smaller collections in the Netherlands, most notably in the Royal Institute for the Tropics in Amsterdam, and at the Royal Institute for Linguistics and Anthropology in Leiden. Some manuscripts are also housed in the Amsterdam Municipal University Library, the Antwerp Ethnographical Museum, the Breda Ethnographical Museum, the Breda Royal Military Academy, the Leiden National Museum of Ethnography, the Rotterdam Museum, and the Utrecht University Library. The School of Oriental and African Studies in London has the four Marsden manuscripts mentioned above, and a manuscript also exists in the Musée de l'Homme, Paris, acquired in 1886.

None of the above collections have grown much, if at all, since the mid 1950s. The institutions have no special enduring commitment to collecting Acehnese materials. In recent years, by far the most important public collector has been the Museum of Aceh itself, which bears the major responsibility for collecting Acehnese manuscript materials in the future. Significant cataloguing work has been done at the Museum of Aceh over the past twenty years. The Syiah Kuala University in Banda Aceh has also collected some manuscripts in recent years.

The documentation and cataloguing of public collections of Acehnese manuscripts owes most to the labors and persistence over a period of about forty-five years of P. Voorhoeve, a scholar well known for his work on Batak, Malay, and Arabic manuscripts. Before the Second World War, Voorhoeve had studied Acehnese in Leiden under Snouck Hurgronje. In 1949 Voorhoeve produced a typewritten catalogue of the two Jakarta collections, and another of the Leiden

WAR-BOOTY MANUSCRIPTS

These religious manuscripts of mixed-language contents were taken as war booty in the Gayo hinterland during the first few years of this century. By this stage the war against the Acehnese guerrillas was being pursued deep into the mountains. These manuscripts were kept in pouches, with long straps so that they could be carried around from place to place, on the run. Normally manuscripts would be stored in a safe place in a house, and would not need such a pouch. A number of the National Library manuscripts were booty confiscated from Acehnese resistance fighters by the soldiers who pursued them far from their homes. Other war-booty manuscripts found their way into private collections of Dutch officials and from there into public collections in the Netherlands. These "guerrilla texts" must have been very precious to the resistors to have been carried so far, under such adverse circumstances. We can assume that manuscripts were an important source of encouragement to Acehnese fighters in their struggle against the Dutch: the religious inspiration of the Acehnese resistance has been well documented. Acehnese writers have themselves testified to the important role that particular texts played in stirring enthusiasm for the Holy War. Indeed war-booty texts were mostly of a religious nature, often containing a mixture of Arabic, Malay, and Acehnese.

Library manuscripts were among the booty confiscated from Acehnese resistance fighters. National Library of Indonesia, Jakarta.

collection as it was at that time, including the incorporated manuscripts of Snouck Hurgronje. Damsté had already catalogued the Acehnese manuscripts in the Royal Institute for the Tropics in Amsterdam. Voorhoeve's hope of combining these three catalogues into a single catalogue of what would have been all manuscripts in public collections was frustrated by Leiden University Library's acquisition of the large Damsté collection after Damsté's death in 1955. The collection included manuscripts of diverse contents that were very time-consuming to catalogue, and also a number of new works that were not represented in other collections and whose contents were not summarized in Snouck Hurgronje's survey of Acehnese literary works. From 1954 to 1959 the Acehnese scholar Teungku Iskandar, then a student at Leiden University, worked on the Damsté collection. He prepared summaries of the contents of manuscripts, and continued cataloguing the Leiden collection. He carried on with this work during 1974, and by 1984 Voorhoeve had himself completed the final cataloguing work during his retirement. The whole catalogue was translated into English, updated with the addition of information on recent acquisitions by the Museum of Aceh in Banda Aceh, and edited for publication. It is Voorhoeve's catalogue that has provided the primary source material for this article, as it is the basic reference work on Acehnese manuscripts.

The situation in private collections is less well understood and is much more precarious. There still seem to be large numbers of manuscripts in the private collections of Acehnese people throughout Aceh. Many individuals have just one or two Acehnese-language manuscripts, but a working paper published by U.U. Hamidy in 1974 shows that some private collections are of major importance, that of the late Teungku Anzib Lam Nyong, to name just one. It also seems likely that significant collections exist or have existed with well-known poets or performers, such as Syeh Rih Krueng Raya, Teungku Adeunan (more popularly known as PMTOH, pronounced "pèmtoh," a spoonerism for *poh tèm,* meaning "beat the drum" and also the name of a popular bus line!), the poet Teungku Nyak Tihawa Arsyady of Jeunieb, the late poet Abdullah Arif, and also with some scholars at Syiah Kuala University. The Tanoh Abée *pesantren* library is described by Henri Chambert-Loir elsewhere in this volume.

There is an urgent need to survey and catalogue manuscripts in private collections. Some of these texts are extremely rare, in the sense that no public collection has a manuscript copy. One danger is that after a collector's death, private collections are not usually developed further, and can easily be dispersed, or even locked away from use by understandably protective relatives until they decay or are eaten by insects. Texts in private collections are often guarded very closely by their owners, which can make it difficult even to determine whether someone possesses a copy of a manuscript.

WRITING SYSTEMS

Most manuscripts and some printed books are in the Arabic-derived script. This more traditional script was never standardized, and it is distant from the ideal of a phonemic orthography.

The ability to read and write Acehnese in the traditional script is acquired in a rather indirect way. The first stage begins in childhood, when groups of children learn to recite the Quran. The word for "read" in Acehnese is *beuet,* and refers primarily to the recitation of the Quran, but also to reading Acehnese manuscripts (figs. 103, 104). Children learn to pronounce the Arabic alphabet and to recite a few short but important passages from the Quran in the village classroom. The meaning of the passages is explained to them, but they do not learn to understand the Arabic directly: the important thing is to be able to recite correctly. This skill is valued most highly, and the teacher who imparts it is spoken of as making the children into people (*peujeuet keu ureueng*).

FIGURE 103

Two pages from the *Al-Qur'an l-Karim*, the *sura* al-Kahf, starting with first half of verse 78 from the story of Moses meeting with Khidr and accompanying him in search of spiritual wisdom. This Quran was copied in Aceh. National Library of Indonesia, Jakarta.

The next stage in the traditional acquisition of literacy involves learning *basa jawoe* (Jawi), that is, Malay written in the Arabic script. This is the usual language of written prose in traditional Acehnese society. Religious textbooks, letters, and other documents such as passports, laws, contracts, and seals of authority were traditionally produced in Jawi, and today continue to be produced in Indonesian, Malay's offspring (fig. 105). Traditionally only a minority of people, but a significant one, would have achieved some proficiency in this written Malay. For a young man, learning it would normally mean attending a *pesantren*, a religious school, for a period of perhaps two or three years.

Through an ability to read Arabic and Jawi, an Acehnese person could acquire the skill of reciting Acehnese from written texts. There appears to have been no recognized formal process of instruction in reading and writing Acehnese. Rather, it depended heavily upon pre-existing literacy skills in Jawi. The Acehnese writing system was itself much less regular than Jawi. That this must necessarily be the case will be grasped when one understands that Acehnese has twenty-five or more distinct vowel sounds, while the Jawi script inherits from Arabic only three vowel distinctions. At the same time, the same sound may be represented by more than one letter. This means that there is a many-to-many relationship between sounds and letters in Acehnese. It is therefore only really possible to learn to read traditional Acehnese manuscripts if one already possesses a good working knowledge of Acehnese, in addition to a sound knowledge of Malay and some Arabic.

Although the traditional Acehnese writing system is far from transparent, it is nevertheless quite an effective system for native Acehnese speakers who are also schooled in Jawi and the fundamentals of Arabic. A good number of Acehnese words have easily recognizable cognates in Malay, both borrowings and inherited

FIGURE 104

Final page of the *Al-Qur'an l-Karim* showing the *sura* al-Ikhlas. Curiously, the copyist says that this is the conclusion of the Quran, whereas in fact there are two additional chapters. Some very early "readers" of the Quran regard these last two chapters, each beginning with the invocation "I take refuge," as prayers, not part of the Quran proper. National Library of Indonesia, Jakarta.

forms from early stages of the languages. There are also many borrowings from Arabic. The tendency is to simply spell all these words in their easily recognizable Malay or original Arabic form.

It is significant that with very rare exceptions, written Acehnese is in verse, in the *sanjak* form mentioned above, being chanted with the aid of a melody. In most Acehnese poetry, three out of every sixteen syllables rhyme, and these syllables fall on the stressed, most prominent words in the line. This contributes greatly to comprehension, and many Acehnese people have made the observation that without the assistance of the rhyme, prose written in the traditional script is hard to

FIGURE 105
A cleverly folded letter. National Library
of Indonesia, Jakarta.

read. If something must be written in prose, then Malay is used (fig. 106). There
are virtually no Acehnese manuscripts or published texts set in prose, and most of
these are written for children or language learners. My own personal experience
is that the vast majority of personal letters I have received from Acehnese people,
if written in Acehnese, have been composed in verse. This also seems typical of
Acehnese texts found in the small number of letters preserved from the turn of the
century in public manuscript collections. It is true too of the letter, mentioned
above, that was written from Mecca to Aceh in 1713. And note that the very early
translations of the al-Raniri Malay text into Acehnese involved transferring it from
prose to verse.

In this century, the use of a Romanized script for Acehnese has become much
more widespread, and in recent years Acehnese-language publications have tended
more frequently to be in a Romanized form. For Romanized scripts there is even
less standardization than for the traditional script: despite efforts of leading scholars in Banda Aceh, it has not been possible to impose a recommended standard
spelling. There is considerable individual variation in spelling conventions, and
dialect differences tend to affect the written form more readily in the Romanized
spelling systems.

Earlier in the century, Snouck Hurgronje's Romanized spelling system was in
use, and this is the system in Hoesein Djajadiningrat's great Acehnese-Dutch dictionary. A good number of Acehnese manuscripts were transliterated by Teungku
M. Noerdin using this system, and these transliterations are noted as manuscripts
in the catalogue. Since then, reforms of Indonesian spelling have had their impact
on Acehnese spelling too, and so even in its modern Romanized form, Acehnese
spelling continues to be dependent upon spelling conventions of the non-
Acehnese standard written language. Writers tend to adapt their Indonesian
spelling conventions in a creative way to the spelling of Acehnese. The influence
of Arabic spellings can also be observed in Romanizations, with, for example,

This manuscript, from the estate of Snouck Hurgronje, begins and ends with the usual self-deprecatory remarks on the poor skills and misfortune of the writer. But it is also interesting for what it says about the way the writer approached his work and his relationship to the person who had commissioned the manuscript. An excerpt from the first page:

> I teach about twelve matters;
> at the end I will explain them.
> Out of sympathy and love as well
> I transmit it onto the white paper.
> On white paper I lay out rows of red together with black.
> For red I use *sidalinggam**; for black, resin soot.
> Would that I might use gold and silver,
> but where could I get that, I am so poor?

And from the coda:

> I am not yet clever like the others;
> I have never copied from a manuscript before.
> Though it be to my shame, the text is finished:

indeed the harbor master ordered it.
And so, to my shame, I studied the parables and tales;
If you happen to recite this,
my friends, sin not lest you burn.
Ruined paper I will replace, my friend the owner.
There is no need for doubt or suspicion;
all which you provided will be returned, brother.
I had a packet of paper,
one hundred and ten sheets, my brother.
The paper has become damp and a little limp;
I have moistened it all:
That way the paper becomes stiff.
Some sheets are extremely fine on one side.
One side is good, the other bad;
the rows are not of an even length.
It is not my fault, my brother;
Your manuscript is ready.
In the year A.H. 1264 this humble writer's work is finished.

* *sidalinggam* (Malay: *sadalinggam*) is described in dictionaries as vermilion (red mercuric sulfide) or red lead (lead oxide).

Kisah dua blah peukara (*Tale of twelve matters*), *the first eleven of which are vices, while the twelfth is the virtue of faith. Leiden University Library, Leiden.*

One page of a Malay mystical text. This manuscript contains Acehnese religious poetry. National Library of Indonesia, Jakarta.

Arabic loans tending to be spelled as if they were pronounced in their Arabic form rather than in their actual Acehnese form. This applies even when the rhyme clearly demands an Acehnese pronunciation.

Despite all the variation, certain key features deriving from Snouck Hurgronje's original system, such as the use of the digraph *eu* to represent a single vowel, have proved remarkably persistent across the various Romanized orthographies.

ACEHNESE VERSE

Because of the preeminent use of verse in Acehnese manuscripts, it is useful to describe briefly the main features of Acehnese *sanjak*. It rhymes in two ways, having an end rhyme and a line-internal rhyme. The end rhyme pattern is perhaps borrowed from Malay over the centuries of contact with that language. The internal rhyme follows a pattern generic to mainland Southeast Asia, and goes back to the origins of Acehnese on the mainland. The basic pattern of the internal rhyme is that a syllable at the end of a certain length of verse rhymes with a syllable in the middle of the following segment of verse of the same length. The following is an Acehnese example, with a line of sixteen feet. The syllable at the end of the first half-line (after eight feet) rhymes into the middle of the next half-line (after another four feet). In addition the syllable at the end of the whole line (the second syllable of *mata* here) will be held constant over many verses, forming the end rhyme.

Gah ban gajah, sie ban tulô,	Fame like an elephant, flesh like a sparrow,
jitueng judô di nap mata.	he is cuckolded, before his very eyes.

This kind of internal rhyme is not linked to having lines of a particular length, either in Acehnese or in mainland Southeast Asia generally. The following Acehnese verses display two independent internal rhymes: foot number four rhymes with the syllable two feet later, and foot number eight rhymes with the syllable four feet later. Note in this particular example the second internal rhyme is held constant from line to line, and the line end rhyme here is -*a*.

Droe jipeugah susah lagoe ék,	He said he was in the greatest difficulty:
haté mubalék cirét pih raya.	his heart in turmoil, his bowels in commotion.
meunan bak kamoe bunoe jibisék,	Thus he whispered to us earlier:
jipeugah h'an ék keunoe jiteuka.	he said he could not come.

The internal rhyme pattern appears in minute scale in a nursery rhyme:

T'um beudé, blé kilat.	A rifle fires: lightning flashes.
Reubah alèe, asèe lumpat.	A rice pounder topples over: a dog jumps.

This accelerating internal rhyme gives a characteristic pace and turn to the sound of the verse.

In Acehnese manuscripts, *sanjak* verses may be laid out in different ways. Some manuscripts have one verse per line. Others have them continuously, but with a symbol (such as three dots) separating lines, and some manuscripts give no indication of verse boundaries.

In order to understand the composition and use of Acehnese manuscripts, it is important to realize that *sanjak* is not just a written form of Acehnese. It is the verse form used for virtually all forms of oral and traditional folk poetry, from the cradle to the grave, including *pantôn*, riddles, songs, nursery rhymes, recitations accompanying dance and music, and many proverbial sayings. Every Acehnese-speaking person will have at least some facility, however limited, in composing *sanjak* verse, and will be able to recall or recognize a large number of sayings that are expressed in it. Often just a few words can instantly call to the hearer's mind the rest of a poetic sequence. For many individuals, including skilled reciters and composers of manuscripts, the poetic art is very highly developed. Some have the ability to produce verse impromptu, and certain traditional types of competitive poetic performances, including the famous *seudati* dance, depend upon this. Each *seudati* troop has an expert singer of poetry, the *aneuk seudati*. In recent years the governor of Aceh was accompanied by the famous professional poet Teungku Adeunan (alias PMTOH) during his election campaign travels. After the governor had presented his prose speech, the poet would sing a summary of it in verse. The widespread mastery of such skill is important for understanding the use of manuscripts: many readers are adept in the conventions of the poetic art. If people reading a manuscript come across something obscure in the written text, they will very often make something up on the spot to fit in with the verse. The copyist may easily make changes to a manuscript to improve the sense, or replace a reading that seemed uninterpretable.

PERFORMANCE STYLES

Acehnese manuscripts are designed to be sung, or rather chanted, to a repeated melody of one or two lines' duration. There are numerous melodies available, although certain ones are particularly popular. Melodies are held constant over a long sequence of verses. Texts are performed in private or in public; solo, and in groups; by professionals and amateurs; for entertainment and for worship; with and without musical accompaniment; in village huts and royal courts. There is enormous variety in performance context and style. One should also keep in mind that not all performers actually use manuscripts: there are well-known cases of blind performers, illiterate poet-performers, and those who can read but choose instead to recite from memory. Indeed sometimes manuscripts are written from memory (fig. 107). Manuscripts can in some sense be seen as an aid to performance, rather than an indispensable component of it.

Melodies and performance styles can be divided into two types: the slow, melodic style closely associated with historical epics and romances, and the quick style most closely associated with religious works. At one extreme is a very languorous, sensual style, which can send shivers up your spine; at the other a fast, rhythmic style reminiscent of religious *ratép* performances. The slow style I have only heard chanted by a solo performer. The fast style may be performed by groups, sometimes with flute, violin, and drum.

If the aim of the slow style is to transport the listener with the fluid sweetness of melody and rhyme, that of the fast style is to mesmerize by transporting the listener with the rhythm. Often, this mesmerizing effect is helped along by mismatching the melody to the lines (for example, starting the melody in the middle of a line), so that the main rhyming syllables do not fall on the main musical beats. Either way, the intent is to sweep the listener away in the sound. This is a common strategy of Acehnese poetry in general, from *dabôh* (Malay: *dabus*), where the effect of the poetry is to encourage young men to stab themselves, believing they will not be harmed, through the dance recitations of *seudati*, to the incantations of the *ratép*.

The fact that manuscripts are meant to be performed often has clear effects on the texts themselves: most texts seem to assume a group audience. One may find versified comments in the texts, such as "I am thirsty, I need to take a break," "Hey, my friends," or "Listen to my story," which reflect the perspective of a performer-hearer relationship rather than that of an author-reader.

LITERATURE SURVEY

A standard reference for an overview of Acehnese written literature is still *The Achehnese* by Snouck Hurgronje. This has been supplemented and filled out in Voorhoeve and Iskandar's catalogue of Acehnese manuscripts, mentioned above. For the sake of completeness, we should also incorporate into this framework

FIGURE 107

Hikayat Ahmat Beureumalilé, a romantic
work set in Khorasan. This coda reports
that the manuscript has been written from
memory; the writer is not the author; and
the *hikayat* was written by two people.
The manuscript is dated A.H. 1337, and
then vertically, in a different ink: *Hijrat
Belanda 1919 tamat surat*. Leiden
University Library, Leiden.

about two hundred or so Acehnese-language publications, most of which have
come out in the past thirty to forty years. Many of these are now extremely rare
(indeed, a few important ones are probably lost altogether). However, here our
focus is necessarily on the manuscript tradition.

Most Acehnese written texts can be described as *hikayat*. This term is also
used in Malay for long works in the epic style. The Acehnese use of the term is
similar to the Malay in that *hikayat* are intended for an extended oral performance
using a melody, and typically written down. The Acehnese manuscripts differ
from the Malay in that the Malay *hikayat* are in prose. The Acehnese *hikayat*
themselves are best classified in terms of the nature of their subject matter. The
categories I mention here—abusive texts, versified folk tales, mythic folk epics,
war epics, romances, moral epics, texts for religious edification and instruction,
personal tales, and cautionary and hortatory tales—are rather different from those
proposed by Snouck Hurgronje and incorporated into Voorhoeve and Iskandar's
catalogue.

Abusive texts form a relatively small and rare group. These are dedicated to
abuse and are quite short. They perhaps find their origins in oral competitive
poetic performances, in which poets take turns in denigrating each other.

Versified folk tales form another fairly rare category of manuscript: they consist of material that is usually passed on orally, but that an author has rendered into
verse. *Hikayat si Miseukin*, for example, concerns the activities of a rascal figure.

Our knowledge of Indonesian seals is largely based on the thousands of seals on manuscript documents from the eighteenth and nineteenth centuries. Most of these documents are letters, but they also include contracts, treaties, travel permits, ships' passes, and harbor documents; and very occasionally, seals are impressed in books either as signs of ownership or to verify authorship.

But seals have been used in Indonesian society for well over a thousand years. The kings of Sriwijaya were said to stamp their letters with seals inscribed in Sanskrit; large numbers of gold signet rings with Kawi inscriptions dating from the seventh to tenth centuries have been excavated in Java; and Chinese court archives in the fifteenth century record the presentation of silver seals to the rulers of the Sumatran kingdoms of Pasai and Haru. From the beginning of the seventeenth century, seals on documents began to survive, and from these we can gradually form an idea of how, where, and when seals were used. The oldest-known Indonesian seal on a manuscript is the remarkable royal seal of Sultan Alauddin Riayat Syah of Aceh, found on a trading permit of 1602, whose strikingly sophisticated calligraphy, workmanship, and choice of inscription hint at a tradition of

Indonesian Islamic seals that had already developed over some considerable time.

Seals are obviously a mark of officialdom, and in Indonesia the documents on which they are found are naturally most often written in Malay, the language of diplomacy and trade throughout the archipelago. These Malay seals are normally inscribed in Arabic or Malay in the Jawi script, occasionally in conjunction with Roman script or regional ones such as Javanese, Bugis, and Batak, while seals on court documents or letters in Javanese are often wholly in the Javanese script. The information found in the seals themselves is usually a combination of personal name, title, place, date, and a religious phrase such as *al-wathiq bi-Allah* (He who places his trust in Allah). Even their position on the document was determined by protocol: in general, the higher the position of the seal on a letter, the greater the status of the sender vis-à-vis the recipient. Yet in addition to their use on important diplomatic documents, seals could be required for the most mundane purposes as well. According to one Malay legal code, sealed permits were necessary in order to authorize journeys from one village to the next, or to export rice, or even in order to slaughter a buffalo.

Three gold seal rings with Old Javanese inscriptions, seventh to tenth centuries. National Museum, Jakarta.

Four silver seals from Aceh, late nineteenth century. National Museum, Jakarta.

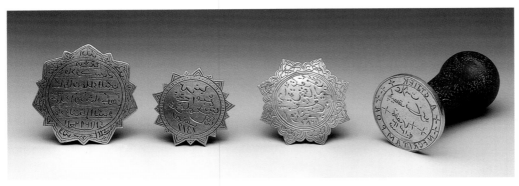

The seals of Sultan Alauddin Riayat Syah of Aceh, c. 1602, left: Bodleian Library, Oxford; right: National Library of Indonesia, Jakarta.

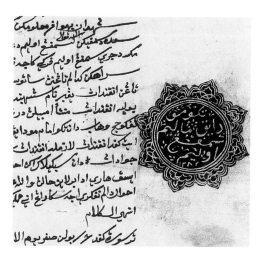

The seal on this letter has been impressed with the silver seal matrix shown second from right in the figure on page 94. National Library of Indonesia, Jakarta.

The "real" seal of the Sultan of Boné, Sulawesi, late eighteenth century. British Library, London.

Though there is no great Malay tradition of calligraphy or book illumination comparable to the art of the Islamic book in India, Persia, or Turkey, Malay seals surprisingly turn out to be among the most beautiful of all Islamic seals. Larger than those from other Muslim cultures, they exhibit a remarkable degree of ornamentation and give one an idea of the high level of craftsmanship of Malay seal makers.

The most popular shapes are circles and petaled circles that draw their inspiration from the lotus blossom. The seal matrices themselves were usually made of silver or brass, and were large—3 to 5 cm in diameter on average, but sometimes as much as 8 or 9 cm—providing a broad canvas for master silversmiths to show off the skills of their craft. Malay seals often bear elaborate domed petals and beautiful borders filled with arabesques and foliate or floral meander patterns. By contrast, however, while the finer Javanese manuscripts bear witness to a tradition of book decoration infinitely more sophisticated than that of Malay manuscripts, Javanese seals tend to be smaller and plainer than Malay seals, the most common Javanese shapes being octagons, circles, and ovals, with dotted or notched borders as the only decorative elements.

The color and medium of a seal, too, were also likely to be influenced by its provenance. Malay seals were usually stamped in lamp black, a method whereby the metal seal matrix was held above a candle or lamp until its surface was covered in soot. It was then stamped on the document, and a small flap of paper was sometimes fixed above the seal impression to protect it from smudging. Occasionally, inks of various colors—red, black, green, blue—were also used. Seals from Java, Madura, and Bali were most commonly stamped in wax, which can be attributed to European influence. Wax seals are usually red or maroon, but the sultan of Banjar—a Malay sultanate under strong Javanese influence—sported a wax seal in yellow, the color of Malay royalty.

Alongside these broad generalizations, however, there is also infinite variety. Nearly all Indonesian manuscripts bearing seals are made of paper, but on Balinese *lontar* letters and documents, seals are impressed directly onto the pliable palm leaf. Unusual seal shapes include potent symbols of Islam: in Aceh, the harbormaster of Lhok Seumawe stamped all shipping permits with a seal in the shape of the crescent moon, while a Bugis seal from Sulawesi is carved in the shape of Dzulfikar, the double-edged sword of 'Ali. One generally accepted prohibition was on the representation of living creatures, and where this was contravened, as in the exceptional case of Sultan Masud Badaruddin of Jambi—whose seal includes images of a lion, tiger, elephant, and buffalo on four of its eight petals—retribution followed swiftly: in 1811 the sultan was deposed, for, it was said, "He did not uphold the customary and religious laws."

Seal matrix of Sultan Alauddin Muhammad Daud Syah of Aceh, A.H. 1296 (1878). National Museum, Jakarta.

Like father, like son: seals of the first three sultans of Pontianak. From top to bottom: 1) the seal of Pengiran Abdul Rahman of Kuala Landak, founder of the Pontianak dynasty, and those of his sons: 2) Sultan Syarif Kasim (British Library, London) and 3) Sultan Syarif Uthman (National Library of Indonesia, Jakarta.

Regional and dynastic characteristics can also be discerned in Indonesian seals, often so distinctively as to enable immediate identification of the actual document. Many royal seals from Bima are vertical ovals, a rare shape for Malay seals, while the seals of the first three sultans of Pontianak are all concentric octagons, the borders filled with an apparently obscure selection of letters. Yet similar shapes could also mask very differing personal characteristics: one of the most beautiful Indonesian seals is that of the sultans of Siak, a large twelve-petaled circle, whose petals and border are densely filled with floral motifs. The humble inscription written in simple Malay chosen by one sultan, "The poor worthless servant of Allah, Sultan Abdul Jalil Saifuddin," contrasts dramatically with the grandiose inscription in Arabic of his son and heir "The King who has achieved Oneness with Allah, Sultan Abdul Jalil Khaliluddin," although their seals are identical in shape and size. Most Malay seals in the shape of petaled circles bear eight petals; only occasionally are four, twelve, or sixteen petals found, while exclusively in Aceh, apparently, seals with odd numbers of petals such as seven or nine were regularly used. From Aceh, too, originates the most distinctive of all Indonesian seals, copies of which all sultans of Aceh have possessed since at least the seventeenth century, and whose basic design has remained unaltered though the size, shape, and medium may have varied. The great seal of state of Aceh, containing a central circle bearing the name of the reigning sultan, surrounded by eight circles with the names of previous rulers of Aceh, was directly inspired by the seal of the Mogul emperors of India.

As all these examples show, while Indonesian seals are primarily highly symbolic representations of status, kingship, religion, and culture, at the same time, seals can impart refreshing flashes of character and idiosyncrasy into the sometimes dauntingly impersonal and conformist world of Indonesian formal letters. This dualism is perhaps best illustraed by a sketch for a seal dated 1780, scribbled on a piece of paper found inside

"Imagined" seals of the same sultan. British Library, London.

a royal diary from South Sulawesi. The inscription in Arabic reads:

> The sultan who has knowledge of Allah, Ahmad al-Salih, the proclaimer of the religion in the city of Goa and its people.

These grandiloquently pious epithets for the sultan make this just another typical example of an Indonesian Islamic seal inscription—until we discover that Ahmad al-Salih was not the ruler of the Makasarese kingdom of Goa at all. He was in fact the *arumponé*, the ruler of the Bugis kingdom of Boné, Goa's neighbor and arch-rival. Now the sketch found inside the *arumponé's* personal diary assumes an entirely new significance, for we are suddenly afforded an extraordinarily voyeuristic glimpse into the most private thoughts and ambitions of an eighteenth-century Indonesian ruler.

The literary leanings of the *arumponé* were not typical, for, as in many contemporaneous courts throughout the world, the literacy of Indonesian rulers was by no means assured. Letters were usually written by a professional scribe, whose name is sometimes mentioned at the end of the letter. Seals were thus an important means of authenticating a document, and personal signatures are not a traditional feature of Malay letters. When signatures are found, these are generally on documents that are nontraditional in format, such as contractual agreements with Europeans. Often, such signatures are awkward and gauche, reflecting a lack of familiarity with the pen, although the beautiful calligraphy of others, such as the signature of Sultan Abdul Hamid Muhammad Syah of Bima, indicate a ruler with artistic and cultured tastes.

Annabel Teh Gallop

The Giyanti Agreement, 1755. National Archives of Indonesia, Jakarta.

Mythic folk epics deal with holy or spiritually powerful personages from Aceh's past. The most famous is *Hikayat Malém Diwa*, which describes the activities of a mythical figure in North Aceh, who is now known under the Islamic title of Teungku Malém (fig. 108). This *hikayat* cannot be performed lightly, and is regarded as holy, both in its manuscript form and in its performance. Before a performance, a *khanduri*, a ritual meal, must be eaten, and I have been told of dire consequences (such as a plague of mice destroying a village's crop) due to inadequate preparation for the performance. Other examples in this class are *Hikayat Putroe Ijô* and *Hikayat Jugi Tapa*, also set in North Aceh. This type of *hikayat* owes much to pre-Islamic mythical material.

War epics describe battles and campaigns from history. About a dozen or more texts, both manuscript and printed books, exist in this genre. Some deal with the period of the Dutch war and later skirmishes during the colonial period. A well-known example of this genre is the *Hikayat Prang Gômpeuni* that Snouck Hurgronje describes in considerable detail. It was Snouck Hurgronje himself who arranged for this text to be written down from the recitation of its illiterate author and performer. Other texts deal with battles at the time of the Second World War, including the civil war known as the *Prang Cumbôk*. The *Hikayat Éseutamu*, which deals with the Crimean war, should probably be included in this class.

In this group, the older war epics, harking back to Aceh's more remote past, form a small but highly significant group. They have been much studied and constitute something of a high point in Acehnese literature. The two great exemplars are *Hikayat Meukuta Alam*, which describes events in the time of Iskandar Muda, and *Hikayat Pocut Muhammat*.

Romances, with strong mythical elements, form a very large and quite diverse group. Some are set in Aceh and have historical content. These may be called historical romances, and include *Hikayat Nun Parisi*, set in the old port kingdom of Samudra, and *Hikayat Raja Jeumpa*, set in the region of Bireuen in North Aceh. Most romances are set in mythical or far distant times and places: many place names have no real location (fig. 109). Others are set in places such as Abyssinia, India, Yemen, Hindustan, Persia, Siam, Syria, Ceylon, the kingdom of the Jéns (Siam), and China. Such figures as the emperor of China or his daughter(s) make regular appearances. A common theme is the overcoming of supernatural difficulties, often by supernatural power or the aid of supernatural beings. The cate-

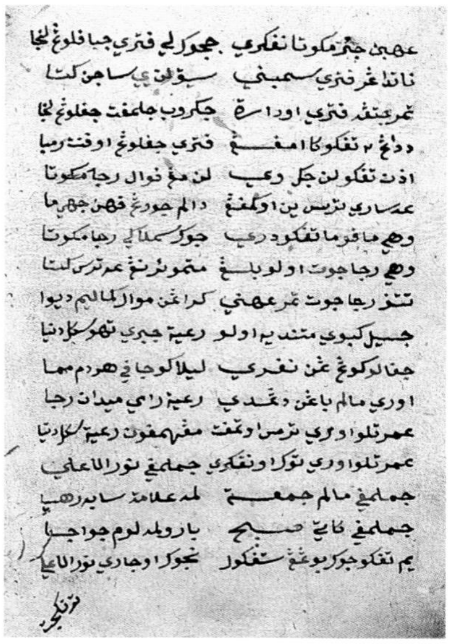

FIGURE 108

Hikayat Malém Diwa, from the Djajadiningrat collection. National Library of Indonesia, Jakarta.

FIGURE 109

Hikayat Putroe Baka'uli, a romance also known in Malay, Persian, and Hindustani versions. National Library of Indonesia, Jakarta.

FIGURE 110

Above: Hikayat Abeukô Karim, a text for instruction, describing the principal truths of Islamic faith together with laws of purification and prayer. In some versions the author is named Teungku Seumatang. National Library of Indonesia, Jakarta.

FIGURE 111

Below: Another exemplar of *Hikayat Akeubô Karim.* National Library of Indonesia, Jakarta.

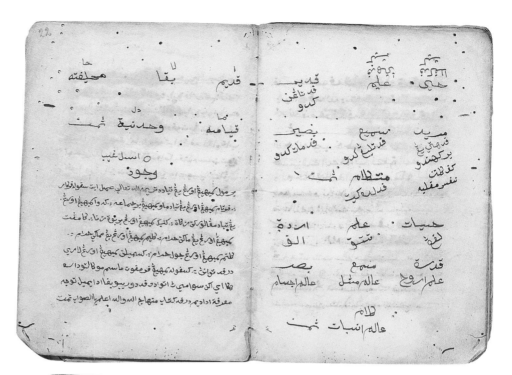

gory of folk epics described above may be considered a subset of this group. These romances seem to be much less popular today than they were a hundred years ago. Much of the narrative material has been borrowed via Malay from other literatures, including a significant amount from Persia. Some of the romances are set in the general region of Aceh, but do not correspond to historical events. Of these some, such as *Hikayat Putroe Ijô,* have parallels in the oral literatures of other ethnic groups in Sumatra.

Holy and moral epics also form a large and popular group. They are not located in Aceh and typically involve Islamic saints and holy figures from an older Islamic heritage (including the period before Muhammad), such as the *Hikayat Nabi Usôh,* the story of Joseph, and the *Hikayat Hasan Husén,* concerning the story of the martyrdom of the Prophet's grandsons, Hasan and Husein.

Texts for religious edification and instruction are a rather diverse category. They include the eschatological *Hikayat Tujôh Kisah* mentioned in the introduction, and the *Hikayat Akeubô Karim* (figs. 110, 111).

Personal tales form a small but interesting group. These are less well represented in public collections. An example is an autobiographical *hikayat*, written by Teungku Hasan of Bireuen, and now in the possession of his son Mawardi Hasan, who is employed at Syiah Kuala University. Mawardi Hasan had been an *aneuk seudati*, a reciter in the famous *seudati* dance during his youth, when he would have gained a good facility with Acehnese verse. A published account of the well-known poet Abdullah Arif's trip around the world in his *Seumangat Acèh* series also belongs in this category. An older example is *Hikayat Ranto*, a cautionary account of misery and depravity on travels away from home, on the west coast of Aceh, which has been edited and published by the Dutch scholar G.W.J. Drewes.

Cautionary and hortatory tales also have a strong religious and political content. They include, for example, Teungku Tiro's lessons on the Holy War and the famous *Hikayat Prang Sabi,* which urges listeners to take part in the Holy War. This latter piece was important in inciting enthusiasm for resistance against the Dutch, and also enjoyed something of a revival in Aceh during the late 1950s and early 1960s. Brief works of cautionary fiction have provided much material for poetic publications in the past thirty or so years, presumably because they have met a market need among the pious Acehnese, and are readily contextualized to contemporary society.

Mark Durie

CULTURAL PLURALITY:
THE SUNDANESE OF WEST JAVA

This chapter on the Sundanese writing tradition limits itself to manuscripts written on such materials as palm leaf, bamboo, and paper. Stone and metal inscriptions are not considered here except to elucidate the manuscript tradition. In geographic terms "Sunda" refers to that part of western Java that now encompasses the province of West Java and the Special Municipal Region of Jakarta (fig. 112). Sundanese manuscripts are defined as manuscripts either written in Sundanese, by Sundanese authors, or pertaining to Sundanese culture.

ORIGINS

The Sundanese writing tradition can be traced back to the middle of the fifth century A.D. Seven stone inscriptions dating from that period provide evidence of the existence of a Sundanese community in the reign of King Purnawarman of the Tarumanagara kingdom. These inscriptions were written in Sanskrit using Palawa script.

A number of stone and copperplate inscriptions from the period of the Sunda and Galuh kingdoms, covering the eighth to the sixteenth centuries, have also been found. These inscriptions, which were found in Bogor, Sukabumi, Garut, Tasikmalaya, Ciamis, Cirebon, and Bekasi, use three different languages (Old Malay, Old Javanese, and Old Sundanese) and two types of script (Old Javanese and Old Sundanese).

The inscriptions themselves are fairly short, some consisting of only one line, and include royal decrees and announcements and the commemoration of events that were apparently considered to be of great importance. Contrasting with inscriptions are manuscripts which, in general, are much longer and cover a wider range of subjects.

In 1914 N.J. Krom obtained from a former regent of Bandung a number of *lontar* manuscripts that had been found in Cilegon (fig. 113). These he later presented to the Batavia Society for the Arts and Sciences (Bataviaasch Genootschap van Kunsten en Wetenschappen). Two of the manuscripts are dated 1256 Saka and 1357 Saka, respectively A.D. 1334 and 1435. As neither of the manuscripts has been thoroughly studied, the question remains whether these years signify the time the texts were composed or the events mentioned in them.

The oldest datable Sundanese manuscripts, written on palm leaf, originate from the fifteenth and sixteenth centuries and include such titles as *Kunjarakarna, Sanghiyang Hayu, Sanghiyang Siksakandang Keresian, Amanat dari Galunggung, Sewaka Darma, Carita Parahiyangan, Bujangga Manik,* and *Pantun Ramayana* (fig. 114). Many more old Sundanese manuscripts exist but have yet to be properly studied.

THE TREASURY OF MANUSCRIPTS

Based on a survey conducted in West Java in 1988, fewer than 1,500 copies of Sundanese manuscripts exist today. Because one can assume that numerous manuscripts remain in the hands of individuals and, generally speaking, outside the realm of researchers, a more exact number would be difficult to establish. One can also assume that the total was at one time much larger.

Sundanese manuscripts can be found in collections both in Indonesia and abroad. The reasons behind their dissemination vary, but the presence of Sundanese manuscripts in public institutions is, in large part, the result of the scholarly pursuits of three gentlemen, namely, K.F. Holle, J.L.A. Brandes, and C.M. Pleyte, who collected Sundanese manuscripts during the second half of the

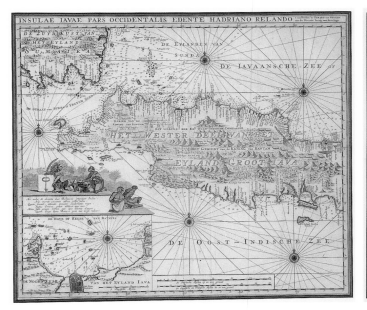

nineteenth century and first part of the twentieth century. Their collections were later given to the Batavia Society for the Arts and Sciences, some before and some after their deaths. Another notable collection of Sundanese manuscripts, that of C. Snouck Hurgronje, was given to the Leiden University Library.

Various factors have led to the decrease in the number of Sundanese manuscripts. In this regard one can cite the damage and destruction of manuscripts resulting from age, accidents (floods, fire, insects, and so on), and poor maintenance. One can also point to the loss and disappearance of manuscripts following the death of their owners. Then, too, manuscripts have been deliberately destroyed because of misunderstandings or on religious grounds. But the main reason for the decrease in the number of extant manuscripts is the cessation of manuscript-copying activities resulting from the diminishment of the manuscripts' function and lack of public demand.

Sundanese manuscripts, like other Indonesian manuscripts, once had many functions. Manuscripts containing family genealogy and ancestral and regional histories were used to improve the social standing of their owners and their families. For the owner's family, the genealogical manuscript served as a guide or a manual of sorts, especially among the nobility. Manuscripts containing religious teachings, ethics, and the like functioned as tools for education (fig. 115). Manuscripts on literature and other arts provided entertainment. Manuscripts on subjects such as agriculture, the calculation of time (fig. 116), history, and customs (fig. 117) served to add to the general pool of knowledge and as a means for the cultural socialization of the young. Then, too, there are manuscripts containing magical formulae and mythological stories as well as manuscripts that are believed to be able to transmit magical strength to their owners (fig. 118).

Unlike in the past, most Sundanese manuscripts are to be found in public or semipublic institutions: libraries, museums, research centers, and the like. Institutions holding Sundanese manuscripts include the Sri Baduga State Museum of West Java and Yayasan Pemeliharaan Naskah in Bandung; the Pangeran Geusan Ulun Museum in Sumedang (16 mss.); the Kasepuhan and Kacrebonan Palaces in Cirebon (fig. 119); the Old Banten Archaeological Museum in Serang; the National Library in Jakarta (493 mss.); the Kuningan Cigugur Museum (18 mss.); Leiden University Library (785 mss.) and KITLV in the Netherlands; and the British Library and Bodleian Library in Great Britain. Sundanese manuscripts can also be found in former capitals of kingdoms and regencies, and in old *pesantren* compounds, which were traditional cultural centers.

FIGURE 112

A map of the island of Java, including the West Java Sundanese region, by van Keulen.

Above: Jatiraga, a *lontar* manuscript.
National Library of Indonesia, Jakarta.

Right: Pantun Ramayana, one of the oldest
Sundanese-language manuscripts, written
in poetic verse. Sri Baduga State Museum
of West Java, Bandung.

Kitab Doa dan Ayat-Ayat Suci, a book
of prayers for religious edification,
YAPENA, Bandung.

WRITING MATERIALS AND SCRIPTS

Sundanese manuscripts were written on palm leaves and bamboo, and paper. Five kinds of palm leaves were used for the production of manuscripts: palmyra (*lontar*), sugar palm (*enau*), coconut palm (*kelapa*), pandanus (*pandan*), and thatch palm (*nipah*). While there is an abundance of sugar, coconut, pandanus and *nipah* trees in West Java, *lontar* trees, which thrive in dry regions, are not to be found in the high-rainfall area of West Java, and it is thought that even in the past, *lontar* leaves for manuscripts were brought into the area from more eastern parts of Indonesia.

The two kinds of paper used for manuscripts were manufactured paper and *daluang*, the latter of which is made from the bark of the *saeh* tree (see box below). Beginning in the thirteenth century, manufactured paper was imported by Muslim

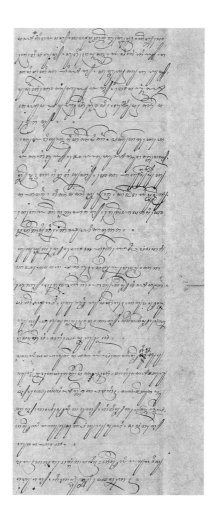

traders and later by the Dutch East India Company from Arabia, China, and European countries. *Daluang* paper was coarse; often the bark fibers were still visible. Manufactured paper was relatively smooth; some carried watermarks.

Generally speaking, manuscripts written on leaves are older than those written on paper. The production of Sundanese manuscripts on leaves ended long ago, probably in the eighteenth century. The production of manuscripts from manufactured paper has also long since come to an end.

Sundanese manuscripts contain a mixture of languages: Sundanese, Javanese, and Malay. Sundanese and Javanese can be divided into old and modern languages. From the end of the seventeenth century until the middle of the nineteenth century, Javanese was the language most used in Sundanese manuscripts. Sundanese itself was relegated to the position of a spoken language and it was not until the mid-nineteenth century that Sundanese came into its own again as a written language, primarily due to the instigation of the colonial government.

Four kinds of scripts are found in Sundanese manuscripts: Old Sundanese, Javanese-Sundanese (*Cacarakan*), Arabic, and Roman, their order reflecting the chronological sequence of their usage. The Old Sundanese script is found in manuscripts written before the eighteenth century. The Javanese-Sundanese script began to be used around the end of seventeenth century, the Arabic script came into use in the early nineteenth century, and the Roman script began to be used in the late nineteenth century.

The emergence and use of a new script, however, does not imply that use of the older ones was completely discontinued. There are periods of overlapping use. During the nineteenth century, for instance, the Javanese-Sundanese, Arabic, and Roman scripts were all being used in the writing of Sundanese manuscripts.

FIGURE 118

Above: Manuscripts like this one, the *Kitab Takrib,* are frequently believed to be endowed with supernatural powers. YAPENA, Bandung.

FIGURE 119

Below: Primbon. National Library of Indonesia, Jakarta.

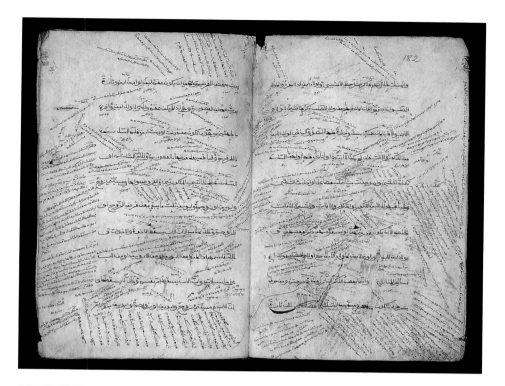

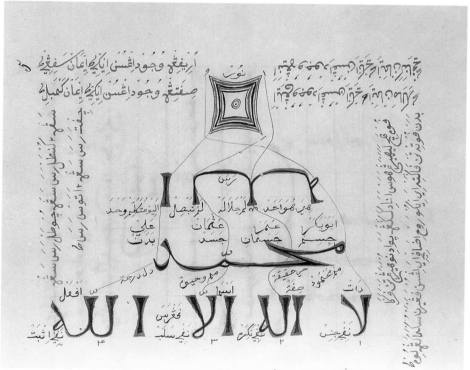

Based on the time of production and characteristics of the manuscript and its text, Sundanese manuscripts can be grouped into one of three periods: ancient, transitional, or modern. The ancient period covers manuscripts written up to the seventeenth century; the transitional period covers manuscripts produced between the eighteenth and nineteenth centuries; and the modern period covers manuscripts from the middle of the nineteenth century until the twentieth century.

Manuscripts of the ancient period were written on leaves and include the titles mentioned in the first section. The transitional period produced such manuscripts as *Carita Waruga Guru, Cariosan Prabu Siliwangi, Carita Purwaka Caruban Nagari, Sajarah Banten,* while the modern period is represented by such manuscripts as *Wawacan Sajarah Galuh, Sajarah Sukapura, Wawacan Carios Munada, Wawacan Nabi Paras* (fig. 120), *Babad Cerbon,* and *Wawacan Ahmad Muhamad.*

THE ANCIENT PERIOD

We mentioned above that the oldest Sundanese manuscripts date from the fifteenth and sixteenth centuries—namely, from the last period of the Sunda kingdom. The Sunda kingdom, including also the Galuh kingdom, existed for around 850 years, from the early eighth century to the end of the sixteenth century, and was characterized by Hinduized culture, dry field agriculture, and the rotation of the capital from place to place. Centers of religious activity called *kabuyutan* were honored and protected by the state. *Kabuyutan* also served as centers of intellectual pursuit. Three of these *kabuyutan*, namely, Gunung Kumbang, Ciburury, and Gunung Larang, are noted as sites where ancient Sundanese manuscripts were created.

Manuscripts of this period were made from the leaves of palm trees. Writing was done either by incising the leaf with a *péso pangot*, a kind of knife (fig. 121), or using pen and ink (fig. 122). The pen that was used was made from the rib of an *enau* leaf or from bamboo and the ink was made from soot. The scripts used were Old Sundanese and Old Javanese, both being Palawa-based scripts. There are two basic shapes of letters in old Sundanese manuscripts, square and rounded, which can be attributed to different writing techniques. Square-shaped letters were incised, while rounded letters were written with pen and ink. Variations on these basic shapes are also apparent, depending on the period of writing.

The languages used were Old Javanese and Old Sundanese. The latter has many Sanskrit and Old Javanese borrowings and is in general unintelligible to contemporary speakers of Sundanese. Here we will discuss only Old Sundanese language manuscripts.

SANGHIYANG SIKSAKANDANG KERESIAN

One of the most important Old Sundanese language manuscripts is *Sanghiyang Siksakandang Karesian* (fig. 123), which, according to its colophon, was finished in the year 1440 Saka (A.D. 1518). The colophon reads, "The writing of this manuscript began on a day bright and clear and was finished in the month of *katiga*. The year the manuscript was finished is thus: *nora* (0) *catur* (4) *sagara* (4) *wulan* (1)." The year the manuscript was finished, 1440 Saka, falls under the reign of Sri Baduga Maharaja, who ruled between A.D. 1482 and 1521.

Sanghiyang Siksakandang Keresian was written with pen and ink on *nipah* leaves, thirty in total. The status of the manuscript is as yet unclear, that is, whether it is a copy or an original, though it has drawn the attention of researchers since the early 1960s.

FIGURE 120

Wawacan Nabi Paras, the tale of the Prophet Muhammad when he first shaved. YAPENA, Bandung.

FIGURE 121

Donga Paningkah Kakawin. A *lontar* manuscript incised with a *péso pangot*. National Library of Indonesia, Jakarta.

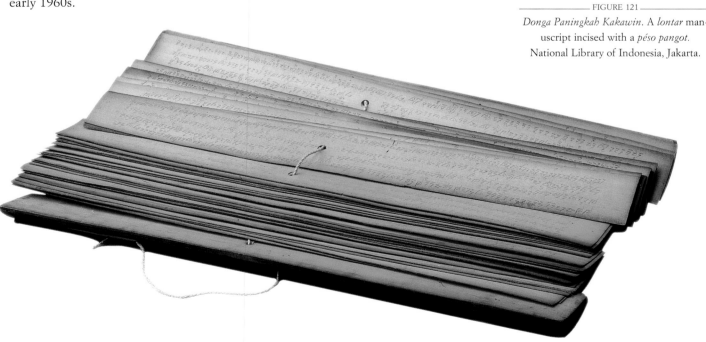

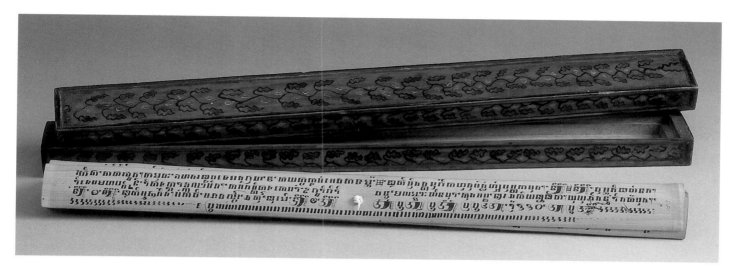

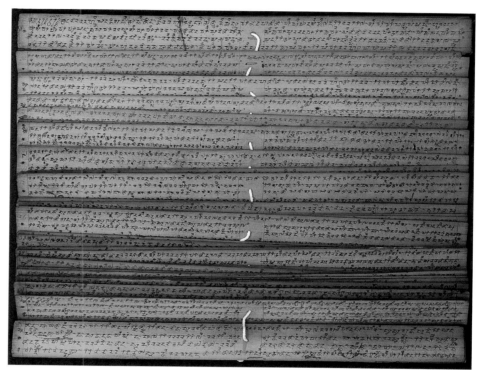

Suhamir, in his study of the manuscript, concluded that *Sanghiyang
Siksakandang Keresian* may be said to be a kind of encyclopedia of Sundanese culture, as it contains various bits of information about Sundanese culture of the
time. In 1973 Atja transliterated the text of this manuscript into Roman script and
it was published nine years later, along with an Indonesian translation and a short
introduction.

According to the manuscript's anonymous compiler, the contents consist
of lessons from the ancestors (*sang rumuhun*), which are called *Sanghiyang
Siksakandang Keresian.* The lessons form a general moral guideline and are based
on Hindu principles (*dharma*) of state and community life. The manuscript provides lessons on how one might achieve happiness and a life of wisdom. The
majority of these lessons are intended for the common people (*hulun, urang réa*),
whatever religion they be (Hindu, Buddhist, etc.). Only a few are intended for the
religious *pendeta* or *resi* class.

According to the manuscript, people will achieve prosperity in life on earth if
each one understands and implements his own *dharma.* And once all the requirements of the *dharma* are fulfilled, world prosperity (*kreta*) will be achieved. This situation will provide an opportunity for *moksa*, for everyone to enter nirvana without

first having to become a priest. The child of a shepherd has the same opportunity as a king to achieve *moksa*, if he succeeds in performing his duties as a shepherd.

What is meant by a life of prosperity is a long life, success in animal husbandry and agriculture, victory in war, abundant harvest, sufficient clothing, a well-tended garden, a well-stocked larder, a full rice barn, a pen filled with chickens, neat fields, healthy plants, good personal health, and more. A person can find this level of prosperity by guarding against the ten sources of desire, which originate from the ears (hearing), the eyes (sight), the skin (touch), the tongue (taste), the nose (smell), the mouth (speech), the hands (taking), the feet (walking), the anus (homosexuality), and the genitals (adultery). If one exercises careful control over these sources of desire, one will achieve the ten ways of prosperity, *Sanghiyang Dasa Kreta*.

The pursuit of knowledge was of great importance for the Sundanese community at that time. But knowledge was to be obtained not only from formal education, through study at a *kabuyutan* or with a priest. It could be found in numerous other ways: from other people's bad experiences, *wayang* performances, public readings, art, travel, and from the mouths of children and old people as well.

Through knowledge and experience one will find contentment and enjoyment, but in that pursuit one should heed the following:

The swan speaks of the lake,
The elephant of the forest,
The fish of the sea,
The flower by the bee.

This means of course that in seeking knowledge of a particular field one should seek the expert in that field and not be afraid to ask questions. The manuscript even tells the reader to whom one might address particular questions: the *dalang* for knowledge of *wayang* stories, the *gamelan* player (*paraguna*) for knowledge of songs, the painter for knowledge of painting, the weaver (*pangeuyeuk*) for knowledge of textiles, the military leader (*sang hulujurit*) for knowledge of the protocol and science of war, the sea captain (*puhawang*) for knowledge of seaports, and the linguist (*sang jurubasa dharma murcaya*) for knowledge of foreign languages.

The *Sanghiyang Siksakandang Keresian* also lists what it terms five antidotes (*panca parisuda*) to criticism. A person must be willing to accept the criticism of others. Criticism, the *Sanghiyang Siksakandang Keresian* says, is water to cleanse dirty skin; oil to soften dry skin; rice to cure hunger pangs; water to quench one's thirst; a quid of betel to calm one's temper.

AMANAT DARI GALUNGGUNG

Another Old Sundanese manuscript is *Amanat dari Galunggung*, which originated from the Ciburuy *kabuyutan* (in South Garut) and is now kept at the National Library (fig. 124). This manuscript, written on thirteen *nipah* leaves in Old Sundanese language and script, was first studied by Holle in the late 1800s. Later studies by Pleyte with R. Ng. Poerbatjaraka, and Atja and Saleh Danasasmita further contributed to the knowledge of its contents.

The manuscript was written by an anonymous author and has no actual title. It was Saleh Danasasmita who assigned the title *Amanat dari Galunggung* to the manuscript, based on the consideration that it contains messages of advice from the Sundanese king Rakeyan Darmasiksa (1157–1297), whose seat was in Saunggalah, part of the Galunggung region. The contents of this manuscript explicitly constitute advice from Rakeyan Darmasiksa to his son, Sang Lumahing Taman, his grandchildren, and their descendants, who are listed down to the ninth generation, together with their relatives.

FIGURE 124

Leaves from an old *lontar* manuscript originating from the *kabuyutan* in Ciburuy. National Library of Indonesia, Jakarta.

Looking at the text, we see that the king's advice is intended to ensure that his offspring maintain their authority, power, and wisdom, prerequisites for a prosperous kingdom and obedience on the part of their subjects. The nuggets of ancestral advice he offers include the following:

Do not be hostile to difference,
show no harshness toward others,
live in harmony, in behavior and aims,
and cling not to your wishes only . . .

Heed the prohibitions set down for you,
take not the lives of those without sin,
scold not those who have done no wrong,
and pay homage to priests and ancestors . . .

Obedience on the part of the people
is the key for a safe and prosperous land,
with that the king will reign in peace,
will enjoy the food he eats,
will win the battles he fights.

The significance of *bertapa* or meditation is also discussed. Meditation, we are told, enables one to perform good deeds. And similarly, if one does not perform good deeds one will not be able to meditate well. It is good deeds that make us rich, good deeds that permit success. Thus, meditation is not something only for priests but for all people. Each person has the same rights and duties, commensurate with his or her work.

Also of interest in the manuscript is its mention of *agamaning paré*, the wisdom of the rice plant. The text tells of the beauty and magnificence of the rice plant and then proffers the advice that man, if he is to obtain benefit from this life, should follow the teachings of the rice plant. We should not be conceited, arrogant, or haughty. Such attitudes reflect the hearts of people poor in experience and empty in the head. We must be polite, well mannered, and modest, for it is these traits that indicate richness of experience and an abundance of knowledge and wealth.

SEWAKA DARMA

Another manuscript of this period is the *Sewaka Darma* (Devotion to the dharma) (fig. 125). This manuscript, which originates from the Ciburuy *kabuyutan*, was written on *nipah* leaves, thirty-seven in total, in Old Sundanese language and script. According to its colophon, the manuscript was compiled by a certain Buyut Ni Dawit in the *kabuyutan* of Ni Teja Puru Bancana in Gunung Kumbang. This particular *kabuyutan* was probably located in the eastern part of the Sunda region,

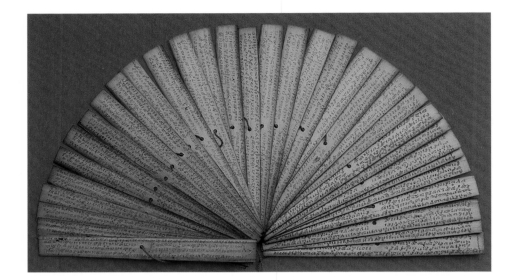

FIGURE 125

A Sundanese-language *Sewaka Darma*
manuscript from the hand of the female
writer, Buyut Ni Dawit. National Library
of Indonesia, Jakarta.

given that the manuscript mentions a number of East Priangan place names, such as Kendan, Medang, and Menir.

Because the shape of letters in the script closely resembles those of the *Ratu Pakuan* manuscript and the *Carita Waruga Guru,* it is likely that this copy of the manuscript originates from sometime in the eighteenth century. However, because the text itself shows no sign of Muslim influence but rather reflects Hindu thought, the original manuscript could very well date from the early sixteenth century. Judging from a number of spelling errors, the manuscript is most likely a copy and not the original. The last line of the manuscript (*nanu namas haba jaja*) might be, in *candrasangkala* form, the year in which the manuscript was written, namely, 1021 Saka (A.D. 1099), even though that would be too far back in time. The text itself ends with two words "Kuta Wawatan," which might be the name of the place the manuscript was written or copied. Kuta Wawatan is in the eastern part of Sunda.

The *Sewaka Darma* manuscript contains a poetic description of *kaleupasan* (*moksa* or "redemption"), which, in accordance with the teachings of dharma, stresses the use of *bayu* (energy), *sabda* (speech), and *hêdap* (resolution). It describes how one must prepare the soul to view death as a gateway to the unseen world. In order to attain eternal happiness, one must heed the advice of priests and such teachings as *Dasa Sila* (the ten prohibitions that form the cornerstone of Buddhist thought) and *Panca Sakit* (the five spiritual diseases: greed, stupidity, evil, presumption, and conceit).

The text describes the journey of the soul after it has left the body and worldly life. During the journey through heaven, the soul witnesses beautiful landscapes on each level, which reflect the regions of Sunda, complete with animal life, trees, arts, clothing, and architecture.

The highest level of heaven is the Golden World or *Bumi Kencana*, where lies eternity and the unseen truth (*jati niskala*). It is there that the soul experiences genuine happiness:

> Joy without sorrow,
> satiety without hunger,
> life without death,
> happiness without misery,
> good without bad,
> certainty without coincidence,
> redemption without reincarnation.

In its description of religious teachings, the *Sewaka Darma* constitutes a blending of Hinduism, Buddhism, and local or indigenous beliefs. Because the text is written in the form of personal advice, the author stresses the importance of understanding the text's message. He also notes for the reader the wrongfulness of anyone plagiarizing his work. Even so, he does not object to—in fact he fully expects—constructive criticism of his work:

> Whosoever reads this seriously
> should bridge no hesitation;
> listen well, absorb the words,
> adhere to its advice.
>
> To plagiarize this work is to do wrong toward me.
> He has not enough words;
> these are mixed up and confused,
> like the tracks of a Chinese crab.
> If a story is not long enough, it should be complemented;
> but if it is overly long, it should be reduced.
> If the result of one's ability is high in value
> it can be used as a remedy if somebody does not get one.

Almost more than anything else, the above quotation reflects the fact that the writing of literary compositions had become a custom by that time.

Carita Parahiyangan

The *Carita Parahiyangan*, an untitled and anonymous text, written in narrative form in Old Sundanese language and script, originated from the Ciamis region (fig. 126). Because of its interesting historical aspects, this manuscript has received considerable attention from researchers. Holle, Pleyte, Poerbatjaraka, and Dam investigated this manuscript in the framework of studies of the Batutulis inscription and the history of Sundanese kingdoms. Meanwhile Noorduyn and Atja looked at this manuscript from a philological point of view in order to compose an edition as well as to interpret the meaning of the whole text.

The manuscript is made up of thirty-five *lontar* leaves. It is inscribed on both sides of the leaves and includes, in addition to the *Carita Parahiyangan*, a number of other texts.

The *Carita Parahiyangan* contains stories of Sundanese kings, beginning with Wretikandayun of Galuh and ending with Nusiya Mulya, the last Sundanese king. Other fragments of text found in the same manuscript contain stories of Sundanese kings but emphasize their genealogical descent from Maharaja Tarusbawa, who established the palace of Sri Bima Punta Narayana Madura Suradipati in the capital of Pakuan Pajajaran.

Based on both the order and the characteristics of the stories, *Carita Parahiyangan* can be divided into two parts. The first part, in narrative form, contains legends and numerous bits of dialogue among the main characters, thereby making each story relatively long. The second part contains a summary description of the various kings. Each king is mentioned chronologically, accompanied by a short description of the duration of his reign and the events and problems that arose during his reign, thereby making this part appear to be more historical than legendary.

Checking the dates given in the manuscript against events whose historical date has been established—for example, the *Bubat* battle in 1357, and also the destruction of the capital, Pakuan Pajajaran, by Bantenese troops in 1579—one can identify each reign and its significant events. One can also establish the identities of the most important Sundanese kings and the relation of their kingdoms to other realms during the same period. The two most important Sundanese kings were Prabu Niskalawastu Kancana, who resided at Kawali, and Sri Baduga Maharaja, whose seat was Pakuan Pajajaran.

——— FIGURE 126 ———

Carita Parahiyangan, a text of great
historical value for the people of Sunda,
composed in the late sixteenth century.
National Library of Indonesia, Jakarta.

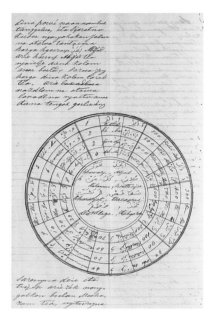

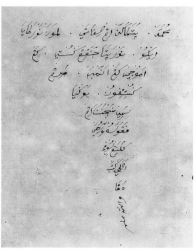

——— FIGURE 127 ———

Above: Tatalining Hirup, a guide for a
healthy and happy life. National Library of
Indonesia, Jakarta.

——— FIGURE 128 ———

Below: Suluk Daka, a manuscript showing
the influence of Arabic and Javanese on
Sundanese culture. National Library of
Indonesia, Jakarta.

As was mentioned above, the *Carita Parahiyangan* end with the last Sundanese king, Nusiya Mulya, who reigned for twelve years and during whose reign the Sundanese armies were defeated by Muslim forces from Demak and Cirebon:

> And then came change: morality sank in a world of unrestrained desire. Disaster came with the Muslims. War broke out at Rajagaluh and the king of Rajagaluh was beaten; war came to Kalapa and the king of Kalapa was defeated; war came to Pakuan, to Galuh, to Datar, to Madiri, and to the Portuguese; war came to Jawakapala and the king of Jawakapala was defeated; war came to Gegelang. Then the war broke out at Salajo. All were defeated by the Muslims and everything came to be occupied by Demak and Cirebon.

This composition must have been made after 1579 or near the end of the sixteenth century, because the conquest of the capital of the Sundanese kingdom by the troops of Banten and Cirebon took place in 1579.

THE PERIOD OF TRANSITION

The main feature of Sundanese manuscripts originating from the period of transition is the appearance of Islamic and Javanese cultural elements. Elements of both cultures sometimes appeared simultaneously in manuscripts because, logically enough, Islam had already been absorbed into Javanese culture by that time.

The spread of Islam through West Java, beginning in the fourteenth century, showed its influence in many ways: in language, alphabet, religious teachings, literature, history, the calendar system, daily living (fig. 127), the social system, science, and technology.

As was the case in Arabia, the Arabic language and script became the identifying features of Islamic culture. We know that by the sixteenth century, Arabic terms had already entered the Sundanese vocabulary, as is evident from the *Carita Parahiyangan*, which contains two Arabic words, *dunya* and *niat*. Furthermore, in keeping with the tradition of Islamic life, a number of Arabic expressions were used in the Sundanese manuscripts, such as *Bismillahirrahmanirrahim, Alhamdulillahirrabil'alamin, wallahu'alam bissawab* (fig. 128). In manuscripts

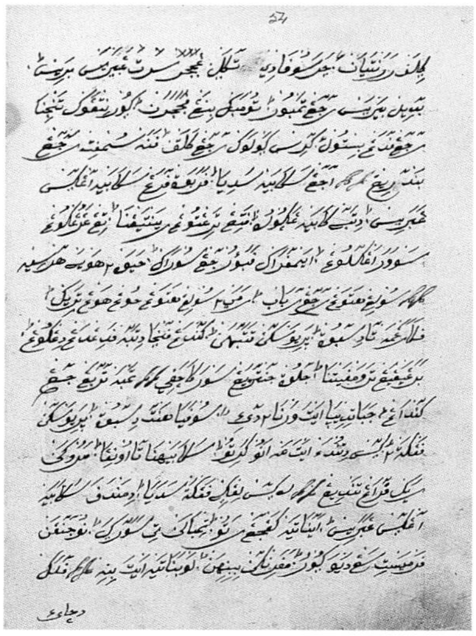

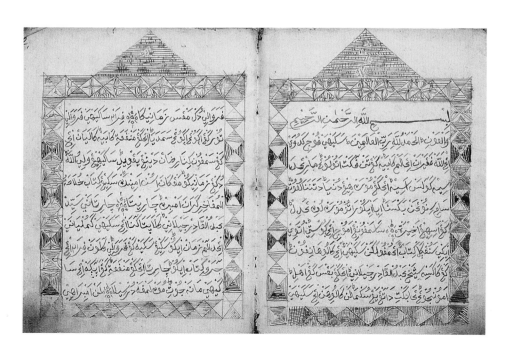

FIGURE 129

Wawacan Nyi Pohaci Sanghyang Sri, a Sundanese manuscript in Arabic script. YAPENA, Bandung.

containing Islamic teachings, we often come across quotations taken from the Quran, the traditions of the Prophet, and other Arabic books (fig. 131). Complete manuscripts of a number of Arabic works found their way into the treasury of Sundanese manuscripts.

Though at first manuscripts containing Islamic religious teachings and Islamic culture were written in Sundanese and Javanese script, as the influence of Islam on Sundanese culture deepened, these scripts were subsequently replaced by the Arabic script. In time Arabic script was used not only for the writing of religious manuscripts but it came to be used for the writing of Sundanese language as well (fig. 129).

In many Sundanese manuscripts, the date given by the scribe for the writing or copying of the manuscript is one based on the Islamic calendar. The year is the Hejira year and the time (when the manuscript was finished) was often one of the five compulsory prayer times. Thus, the *Sajarah Sukapura* was composed on a Saturday evening, the fifth day of the *Haj* month, in A.H. 1303.

A number of Sundanese manuscripts have their basis in Islamic literature and history: *Wawacan Babar Nabi, Layang Seh* (fig. 130), *Carita Samaun,* and *Sajarah Nabi,* to name just a few. Some manuscripts contain Islamic teachings: *Serat Tasauf, Serat Pakih, Kitab Pupujian* (Praises) (fig. 133), and *Rukun-rukunan* (The principles of Islamic teachings).

Javanese cultural elements that appear in the Sundanese manuscripts include language, script, calendrical system, literature, patterns of living, and the like. As was noted by Tome Pires, who visited Cirebon and Cimanuk (Indramayu) in 1513, Javanese language had already begun to make inroads on the north coast of the Sunda region as early as the the beginning of the sixteenth century. Behind this trend was the establishment of trade relations and other links between the Sundanese ports of Cirebon and Banten with the Sultanate of Demak and other seaports on the north coast of eastern Java. The spread of Javanese culture took place simultaneously with Islamization, as both cultures were introduced by the same people (fig. 134).

The Javanese language was also introduced into the interior of Sunda through the process of Islamization, particularly through religious teachings at *pesantren.* But the most profound influence of Javanese culture came in the period after the power of Mataram had penetrated into this region in the early seventeenth century. Although Mataram's power over West Java had ended by 1705,

FIGURE 130

Wawacan Abdul Kadir Jaelani (The biography of Seh Abdulqadir Jaelani, another name for Layang Seh), an adaptation of an Islamic literary work. YAPENA, Bandung.

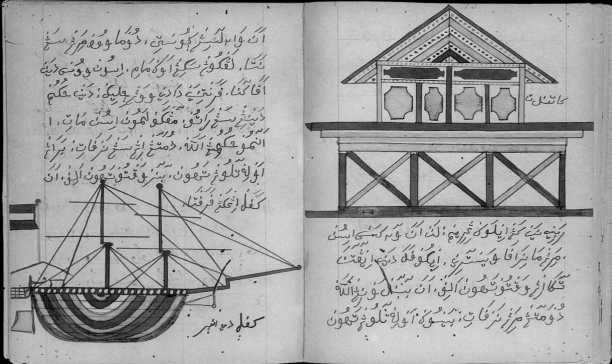

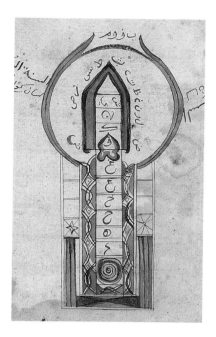

Javanese cultural influence did not stop but in fact expanded: Javanese became the language of government and Javanese language and script were used in official correspondence, decrees of appointments, records, and reports.

The influence was not only one way, of course, and the Javanese script was later modified to better fit the Sundanese sound system, thereby producing the Sunda-Javanese script called *Cacarakan*. *Cacarakan* was taught at schools in West Java from the end of the nineteenth century until the 1950s.

In Sundanese manuscripts from this period and even afterward, the Javanese eight-year cycle is often used in dates. For example, one of the manuscripts of the *Sajarah Banten* has the date Monday, the twenty-sixth of *Sya'ban Ehe* year (fig. 132).

As was noted above, changes in the writing tradition paralleled the Islamization process and the spread of Javanese culture in West Java, first in the northern coastal regions and then in the inlands (Priangan). In the seventeenth century Islamic elements began to appear in manuscripts originating from the north coast. Subsequently Javanese features began to appear as well. At the same time, however, in the interior of Sunda, the older Hindu tradition survived even as late as the early eighteenth century.

SAJARAH BANTEN

The *Sajarah Banten* (The Banten chronicles) is one of the most important Sundanese manuscripts. According to Djajadiningrat, the *Sajarah Banten* was first written in the capital of the Banten Sultanate in 1662–1663. The chronicle was written in the form of a conversation between two characters, Sandisastra and Sandimaya. Sandisastra asked questions that were then answered by Sandimaya in story form.

Sandimaya is not, it appears, the name of the author, but a pen name. The real name of the author is unknown, but it is clear that he was a Bantenese nobleman domiciled in the capital of Banten.

The *Sajarah Banten* was first written in Javanese in *tembang* poetic form. Eight of the ten copies of the manuscripts that Djajadiningrat studied were written in Arabic or *pegon* script and two in Javanese and Roman scripts. But because the eight manuscripts were copies and because in two of them it was mentioned manuscripts that the original text was written in Javanese script, it seems likely that the original *Sajarah Banten* was written in Javanese script.

Djajadiningrat himself makes no mention of the materials from which the manuscripts were made, but evidently they were written on paper. This appears

DALUANG: TRADITIONAL PAPER PRODUCTION

Prior to the seventeenth century, the most common form of writing material in West Java was the palm leaf. The coming of Islam, followed by a rise in literacy and greater demand for ready-made writing material soon changed the situation. While palm leaf continued to fill some writing needs, it could not compete with paper.

Two kinds of paper were used: manufactured (or imported) and a local invention called *daluang,* which is made from the bark of the *saeh* tree (*Broussonetia papyfera*).

The production process for *daluang* is labor intensive, and by the late nineteenth century most manuscripts were being made with factory-produced paper. Today *daluang* production is virtually nonexistent and limited consumer demand, a dwindling supply of materials, and lack of tools have combined to ensure that without a drastic change in the situation, by the end of this century both the practice and the skill of making *daluang* will have become a memory.

THE PRODUCTION PROCESS

After a branch of the *saeh* tree has been chosen (the choice being determined by the size of the sheet of "paper" one needs) and hacked from the tree, a *pisau* is used to cut into the bark, circling the branch at its upper and lower ends.

The bark is then split lengthwise with the assistance of a sharpened stick. Once the bark has been split from top to bottom, the stick is laid aside and removal of the bark continues with the use of one's fingers. After the strip of bark has been removed from the branch, it is then rolled up, against the grain, which causes the outer layer to split, thus making it easier to separate it from the softer, inner layer with a knife or even one's fingers. The inner layer of bark is then cleaned in water and left to soak, generally overnight.

After soaking, the bark strip is then placed on a flat hardwood board and beaten, from top to bottom, with a grooved mallet. The beating continues, up and down the length of the strip, until it gradually begins to widen. The pounding process continues until the desired thinness and width of paper are reached. The greater the width, the greater number of times the strip must be folded and beaten again. In order to prevent cracking, the strip is periodically drenched with water. For very large pieces of paper, several layers can be added and pounded together. Once the desired dimensions have been achieved, the strip is unfolded and washed. After the excess water has been wrung from the limp strip, the strip is wound around a banana trunk whose outer leaves have been removed and then rubbed until smooth and flat with Ki Kandel leaves. In the rubbing process, the leaves exude a sap that helps to align the fibers and fix them in place.

The future *daluang* paper is then placed in a basket lined and covered with banana leaves and left to dry overnight. The following day, the paper is cleaned and left in the sun to dry. Once the paper has dried, it is cut into the desired size and rolled up for future use.

Edi S. Ekadjati & John H. McGlynn

A saeh *tree.*

Splitting the bark.

Removing the bark from the branch.

Rolling the bark against the grain.

Separating the outer layer of bark from the inner layer.

Starting to pound the bark.

The strip grows wider...

...and wider...

...and wider...

Washing the pounded bark.

Wringing excess water from the strip.

Winding the strip around a banana trunk.

Rubbing the strip with Ki Kandel leaves.

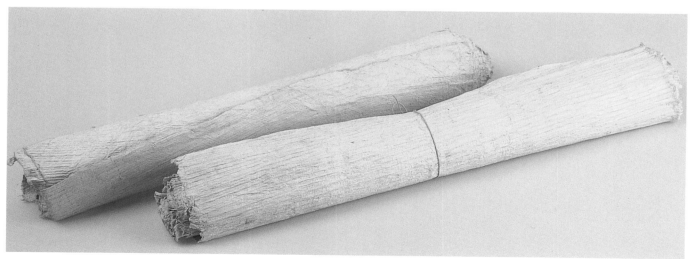

Rolls of daluang *ready for cutting and use.*

to be true of both the copies and the original manuscript, because in the final part of the text we are told that Sandisastra was ready with pen and ink to write down the story told by Sandimaya about the holy war.

That the *Sajarah Banten* was compiled on the basis of a chronicle is stated by the author himself:

> And then Ki Sandisastra asked:
> "Elder brother, please tell me again
> of the events that followed the Jakarta war!
> How does this story go?
> Dear elder brother, please tell me once again!"
> And Sandimaya then answered politely,
> "Enough, younger brother, enough,
> at present I am tired of thinking,
> but perhaps another time.
>
> Family and friends
> often wish to sing about them,
> to reveal the tales therein,
> I have notes on these things, younger brother,
> but have not yet been able to find the time
> to put them down in verse,
> and as they are still in note form,
> I have stored them in a chest,
> together with my books on mysticism,
> which I am wont to read.

The above quotation tells us that writing was common in Banten at the time and that writing was undertaken for the sake of religious teaching. Note the author's reference to his books on mysticism. Indeed the Banten Sultanate, besides being a trade center, also became the center for Islamic teaching and religious propagation, mainly to the western inland regions of West Java and the southern part of Sumatra. At the same time, however, elements of Javanese culture were also being absorbed, such as *tembang* poetry, Javanese language and script, and the use of symbols for names.

The *Sajarah Banten* was intended by the its author to function as a guide to behavioral norms for the royal family and the nobility of Banten as well as a reference book for their duties and rights. In this regard the text informs them that they must know and understand the history of their country and their ancestors.

The contents of *Sajarah Banten* can be divided into two parts. The first part tells about the Hindu kingdoms of Java (Medang Kemulan, Pajajaran, Majapahit), but with an Islamic orientation. The second part contains the story of the Banten Sultanate from its origins until 1659, when the sultanate went to war against the Dutch East India Company located in Jakarta. The story's first part is legendary while the second is more historical. Using a historical approach, Husein Djajadiningrat succeeded in reconstructing the history of the sultanate and in formulating the main characteristics of (traditional) Javanese historical writing. His study has influenced the writing of Indonesian history, particularly in its identification of Sunan Gunung Jati with Falatehan, and their role as religious proselytizers and upholders of Islamic authority in Cirebon and Banten.

A document dated 1681 in the form of a trade agreement between the Cirebon authorities and the Dutch East India Company indicates that written records were in common use in Cirebon at that time. This agreement gave the company permission to establish a fortress in Cirebon. It was written in three languages—Javanese, Malay, and Dutch—and uses three kinds of scripts: Javanese,

FIGURE 135

Tarekat, a manuscript from Cirebon, a large percentage of which contains Islamic teachings. Sri Baduga State Museum of West Java, Bandung.

Arabic, and Roman. Malay, which was usually written in Arabic script, was typically used as the language of communication among coastal communities in the archipelago. While the the official language of the Cirebon palace was Javanese written in Javanese script, this does not exclude the possibility that Arabic script was used for the writing of Islamic-related texts (fig. 135). This premise is supported by later documents dating from the late seventeenth and early eighteenth centuries.

CARITA PURWAKA CARUBAN NAGARI

Carita Purwaka Caruban Nagari (The origins of the country of Cirebon) is a manuscript that was found in the Indramayu region in 1970. Unique elements of this manuscript include its use of "Dutch" or Christian years (*warsaning Walandi*), the distinction it makes between Sunan Gunung Jati and Falatehan as two separate individuals, and the mention of its source. While on the one hand the text of the manuscript offers clarification on certain historical matters, the use of language and even the paper on which the text was written have raised doubts among researchers about its authenticity.

Carita Purwaka Caruban Nagari, the title of which manuscript is based on information provided in its colophon, depicts in prose style the origins and early development of the Cirebon Sultanate with Sunan Gunung Jati as its main figure. The manuscript is said to have been written in 1720 by Pangeran Arya Carbon, a member of the Cirebon Kasepuhan Palace, who himself based his work on the well-known *Nagarakretabumi* (*sinanggurit miturut kitab nagarakretabumi*).

Pangeran Arya Carbon was one of the sons of Sultan Sepuh I who reigned over Cirebon from 1678 to 1697. Based on a decree of the governor general of the Dutch East India Company, issued on August 10, 1699, Pangeran Arya Carbon inherited power over Cirebon, together with his brother, Pangeran Dipati Anom. The region was then divided into two parts: the Kasepuhan under the authority of Pangeran Dipati Anom, and the Kacrebonan under Pangeran Arya Carbon. After power over the Priangan and Cirebon regions was transferred by Mataram to the Dutch East India Company as remuneration for their assistance in settling the crisis in the Mataram Palace (1705), Pangeran Arya Carbon was appointed by a decree of the governor general of the Dutch East India Company dated February 9, 1706, to serve as supervisor of these two regions.

Pangeran Arya Carbon's position provided frequent opportunities to meet with Dutch East India Company functionaries. One of his closest friends was Vaandrig Lippius, who was considered an expert on the language and inhabitants

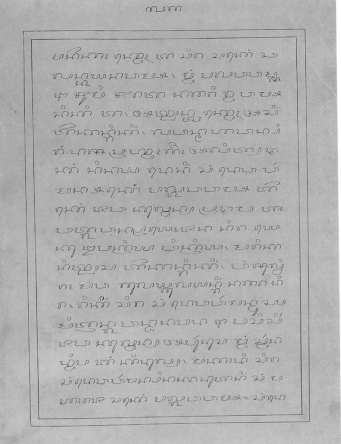

of the Sunda highlands and Priangan region. Through his association with the Dutch, Pangeran Arya Carbon obtained an education and was influenced by their culture. He was an intelligent man who was trusted by the Dutch.

According to the *Carita Purwaka Caruban Nagari*, the development of Cirebon paralleled the the Islamization of the area. Pioneers of Cirebon as a center for the propagation of Islam and the enforcement of Islamic authority were Susuhunan Jati (another name for Sunan Gunung Jati) and his uncle, Pangeran Walangsungsang. Through the maternal line, Susuhunan Jati descended from Prabu Siliwangi, the famous ruler of Pajajaran; through the paternal line he descended from Molana Sultan Mahmud, an Egyptian ruler who himself was descended from the Prophet Muhammad. Susuhunan Jati was the progenitor of the sultans of Cirebon and Banten.

Fadhilah Khan (or Falatehan) was the son of Makhdar Ibrahim, a Muslim scholar who hailed from Gujarat, India. He was born and raised in Pasai but then traveled to Demak, whose sultan ordered him to go to Banten and then straight to Jayakarta to lead the Demak fleet. His troops, supported by Cirebonese soldiers, succeeded in occupying Banten and Jayakarta. He later married Ratu Ayu, the daughter of Susuhunan Jati. He represented (1552–1568) and later succeeded (1568–1570) Susuhunan Jati as the ruler of Cirebon. He was buried east of his father-in-law's grave at the top of the Mount Sembung graveyard in Cirebon.

As was mentioned above, the *Carita Purwaka Caruban Nagari* is said to have been based on the *Nagarakretabumi*, a text whose origins are not in question. Five volumes of this text (from a total of twelve volumes) came to light between 1977 and 1978 (fig. 136). According to information found therein, these five volumes were copied in Cirebon by Pangeran Wangsakerta, uncle of Pangeran Arya Carbon, together with his assistants, between 1692 and 1695 (fig. 137).

_____ FIGURE 136 _____

Left: Pustaka Nagara Kreta Bhumi, the source of information for *Carita Purwaka Caruban Nagari*. Sri Baduga State Museum of West Java, Bandung.

_____ FIGURE 137 _____

Right: Pustaka Rajya-Rajya I Bhumi Nusantara, an unfinished polemical work in Javanese language and script. Sri Baduga State Museum of West Java, Bandung.

The Ciburuy Manuscripts

In 1904, C.M. Pleyte acquired information from the chief of Ciburuy, at the foot of Mount Cikuray (South Garut), on the location of Srimanganti, the name of a hamlet mentioned in a number of *lontar* manuscripts. Srimanganti, this man said, was situated on the western slope of Mount Cikuray, which is why the mountain was also called Srimanganti. G.F.K. van Huls van Taxis, assistant resident of Garut at that time, confirmed this information in a letter to Pleyte, dated March 9, 1904. He also informed him that Srimanganti had once been a part of the village of Cigedug but in 1874 had been abandoned by its inhabitants. Thus, by Pleyte's time, the local people had no recollection of hermit who was reported to have once lived there.

The *lontar* manuscripts that cite Srimanganti (or Mount Larang Srimanganti in full) as a place name are ones collected by Raden Saleh in Priangan in 1856. Now part of the National Library's collection, these manuscripts were written in the Old Sundanese language and script. The colophone of two of the manuscripts is very similar and mentions the author's name as well as the time and place of their writing:

> Accept my apologies,
> and delete extra letters I may have added,
> while adding ones I have forgotten,
> as I complete this manuscript on *Wagé* Friday,
> on Mount Larang Srimanganti,
> the scribe Kai Raga.

Carita Purnawijaya, the title of another one of the manuscripts, ends with the words: "*Beunang diajar nulis kai raga di gunung larang srimanganti*," which translates as: This is the product of Kai Raga who is learning to write at Mount Larang Srimanganti. The colophon of yet another manuscript reads: "*Ini kang nulis kai raga nu keur tapa di sutanangtung*," meaning This is written by Kai Raga who is meditating at Sutanangtung. Sutanangtung is the name of a place at the peak of Mount Cikuray where, as was noted by C.A. van Lange in 1855, a plain encircled by a fortresses (*kuta*) is found and in the middle of is a terraced mound. Raden Saleh noted on manuscript numbers 410 and 411 that the scribe Kai Raga was the grandchild of the hermit at Mount Cikuray.

Judging from the shape of the letters, which resemble those of the *Kunjarakarna* manuscript from Java dated 1635 Saka or A.D. 1713, the Ciburuy manuscripts, including the *Carita Purnawijaya*, are thought to originate from the same period.

The *Carita Ratu Pakuan* begins with the phrase "*Ini carita ratu pakuan ti gunung kumbang*" or This is the story of Ratu Pakuan of Kumbang Mountain. The manuscript is made up of twenty-nine *lontar* leaves, each around 20 centimeters long and containing four lines, except for leaf no. 29, which has only three lines.

The text of *Carita Ratu Pakuan* can be divided into two parts. The first part tells about the *puhaci* (fairies) and the gods and the mountains where they meditate. Their offspring are the princesses who become the wives of Ratu Pakuan and their brothers heroes during Ratu Pakuan's reign. The second part of the text tells the story of the migration of Princess Ngabetkasih, who becomes consort of Ratu Pakuan and moves from a court in the east to Pakuan in the west. When she leaves, it is in a grand procession and she is escorted by her co-wives (*selir*), including Kentring Manik Maya Suda Bok Janur Larang Bacana.

Carita Ratu Pakuan is replete with the spirit of Hindu culture; there is not a Muslim element in it. This is not surprising as it was composed by a hermit in a hermitage (*kabuyutan, mandala*). The same is true of the *Carita Purnawijaya*.

CARITA WARUGA GURU

From almost the same period (the early eighteenth century) another work appeared, the *Carita Waruga Guru*. This manuscript uses the same language and script as the previously mentioned manuscripts but exhibits a number of significant differences. The first is the material on which the text is written, that being European paper instead of *lontar*, and the second is the presence of Islamic elements.

The *Carita Waruga Guru*, a prose manuscript, is written in black ink, measures 20 x 15 centimeters, and is twenty-four pages long. The manuscript was found at the *kabuyutan* in Kawali (North Ciamis), which was the capital of the Galuh kingdom in the fourteenth and fifteenth centuries. Prabu Niskala Wastukancana was its most famous king, and the Surawisesa court was built there.

The Islamic features of *Carita Waruga Guru* include Arabic vocabulary (*alam, gaib, nabi, dunya*), the names of the Islamic prophets (Adam, Isis, Enoh), and other proper names (Mesir, Jabalkap, Seh Majusi, Susunan Puger). At the same time, however, the story and orientation of the text are definitely pre-Islamic Sunda and the influence of Hinduism is very strong. The genealogical table revealed in the text stops at the figure of Susunan Puger, a ruler of the Mataram dynasty in the early eighteenth century. Based on this information, Pleyte guessed that the *Carita Waruga Guru* was written between 1705 and 1709.

KITAB WARUGA JAGAT

Similar to *Carita Waruga Guru* is the *Kitab Waruga Jagat* manuscript, which was written on twelve sheets of *daluang* paper in Javanese language and Arabic script. According to the colophon, the writing of this manuscript was completed on a Tuesday evening in the year 1117 of the Hejira (A.D. 1706) (fig. 138).

We can surmise from the owner's name (Mas Ngabehi Prana) that the manuscript was written in a heavily Javanese-influenced atmosphere. This is understandable, given that relations between Sumedang and Cirebon, as well as between Sumedang and Mataram, were quite close and continued over a long period. The *Kitab Waruga Jagat* gives the genealogy of the power holders in Sunda and the archipelago and of propagators of Islam.

CARIOSAN PRABU SILIWANGI

The *Cariosan Prabu Siliwangi* (The story of Prabu Siliwangi), is a literary historical work whose language, script, and manner of composition were strongly influenced by Javanese culture. The work, written in *tembang* poetic style, uses Javanese language and script (though some copies of this text use Arabic script). The language is a mixture of Coastal (Cirebon) and Middle Javanese, and shows influences from Old Javanese and Sundanese as well. The oldest copy of this manuscript, now stored at the Pangeran Geusan Ulun Museum in Sumedang, was written in black ink on *daluang*. The composition was finished around the end of the seventeenth century or early eighteenth century.

Cariosan Prabu Siliwangi relates the biography of Prabu Siliwangi—the offspring of Prabu Anggalarang, king of Pakuan Pajajaran, and his consort Umadewi—from childhood until adulthood, when he was recognized as king of Singapore.

The story begins when Siliwangi is nine years of age and still going by the name of Pamanahrasa. He is a handsome lad, possessing superhuman powers, and his father names him crown prince. His physical and personal superiority cause his stepbrother, Parba Menak, to become envious of him; the latter tries to have him killed, but thanks to Pamanahrasa's supernatural powers, the assassination attempt is foiled. Nonetheless, a mixture of resin and soot that was smeared on Pamanahrasa's body blackens his skin and he is subsequently sold as a slave. No longer recognizable to friends and family, he changes his name to Siliwangi, a combination of the words *asilih wawangi*, which means "to become fragrant."

The rest of the tale concerns his travails in captivity, his return to the Pakuan Pajajaran court, and his elevation to sovereign.

While the author of the *Carita Purwaka Caruban Nagari* was well acquainted with the seafaring life, the author of *Cariosan Prabu Siliwangi* knew very little about life at sea. Nonetheless, as is revealed by details in the story, he was very familiar with agrarian life. The story *Carita Ratu Pakuan* is evidently a continuation of the *Cariosan Prabu Siliwangi,* and the complete life of Prabu Siliwangi can be found in the *Babad Pakuan* or *Babad Pajajaran* (fig. 139), which was written in the early nineteenth century in Sumedang.

MODERN TIMES

The middle of the nineteenth century marked a bright turning point for Sundanese, which, after having functioned for so long as a spoken language only, came into use again as a written language (fig. 140). In part this was because of a newly established policy on the part of the colonial government to preserve Sundanese oral texts.

Toward this purpose, numerous heretofore oral tales, both in prose and poetic form, were put into manuscript form. Especially popular were such traditional tales as *Manggung Kusuma, Mundinglaya di Kusuma, Mundingsari Jayamantri, Panggung Karaton, Ciung Wanara,* and *Lutung Kasarung,* which contain stories about the Sunda kingdoms in the pre-Islamic period. These stories recount the magnificence of the kingdoms (Pajajaran, Pasir Batang, and others) and problems of the royal family. The typical hero is a prince who has been sent into exile or who has left the kingdom in order to find experience and knowledge. The story always ends with the return of the hero to the kingdom and his coronation. These tales thus offered not only a nostalgic view of the past but they also served as literary models and educational lessons.

Many Sundanese manuscripts from this period are translations or adaptations of Javanese texts and were usually identified as such by the author, translator, or copyist in the opening section of the text.

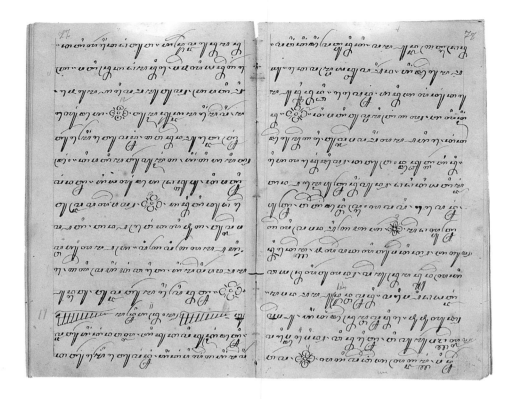

FIGURE 139

Babad Pajajaran, the most complete biography of Prabu Siliwangi, copied in Sumedang in the nineteenth century. Javanese language and script. National Library of Indonesia, Jakarta.

During this period of transition from Javanese to Sundanese, some authors were evidently doubtful about the role and function of Sundanese and used a mixture of the two languages. At the beginning of *Wawacan Suryadimulya*, the anonymous author explains:

> I deliberately wrote,
> in the Asmarandana meter,
> using Sundanese,
> but not completely Sundanese either,
> mixed as it is with Javanese,
> for if in Sundanese alone,
> it seems somewhat less than perfect.

When an author of a text was more sure of his use and the function of Sundanese, the opening explanation was somewhat different:

> These annals are composed,
> deliberately in Sundanese,
> in order to be understood by many,
> —for if they were written in Javanese
> only a few could comprehend—
> because it is the intention,
> that everyone should grasp the meaning herein.

Subsequently, Sundanese manuscripts were based not only on Javanese texts but on Malay tales as well, such as *Carita Perang Istambul* (Annals of the Istambul War) and *Wawacan Ningrum Kusumah* (The story of Ningrum Kusumah).

Numerous *wawacan*, that is, stories in poetic form, appeared during this period of transition. Some were translations, other adaptations, still others were original compositions. The poetic form of the text served as a measure of its literary value. These Sundanese *wawacan* were composed not only to be read but to be sung as well. This could be done by either individuals or by a group of performers (*beluk*). *Wawacan* were thus not only literary works but performance pieces too.

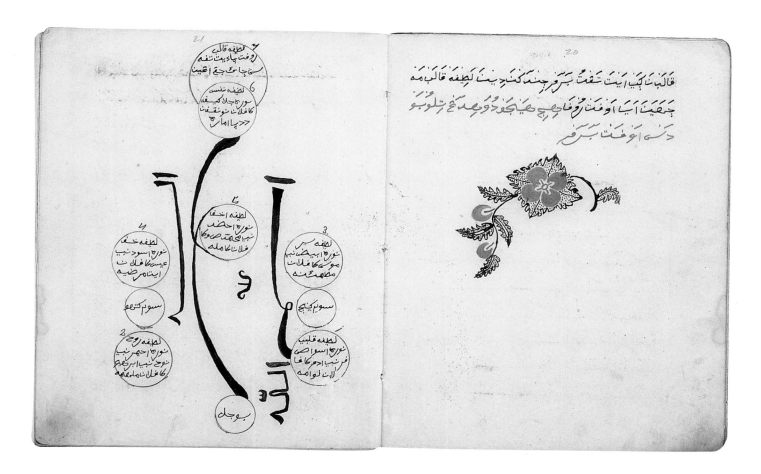

FIGURE 140

Tarekat Satariyah, a manuscript showing the reemergence of Sundanese as a written language. YAPENA, Bandung.

WAWACAN SAJARAH GALUH AND OTHER TRANSITIONAL TEXTS

One of the manuscripts dating from this modern period, *Wawacan Sajarah Galuh* (The history of Galuh), was composed by an anonymous author in Ciamis between 1847 and 1851. One copy of the manuscript, this one in Roman script from the collection of C.M. Pleyte, can be found the collection of the National Library. Another copy, this one in Arabic script from the collection of C. Snouck Hurgronje, can be found in the Leiden University Library. Recently two more copies were discovered in the Ciamis region.

The *Wawacan Sajarah Galuh* relates the origin and development of the kingdom of Galuh, whose seat of power was situated in present-day Ciamis Regency. The text is made up of seven stories that related, in chronological fashion, (1) the story of the family of the Prophet Adam, whose offspring populated the whole earth, (2) the story of the origin and development of the Galuh kingdom, (3) the tale of *Ciung Wanara*, (4) the story of *Tanduran Gagang*, (5) the story of the Mataram court crisis, (6) the story of Dipati Ukur, and (7) the history of Galuh Regency from the first regent, Sangiang Permana, until the fourteenth regent, Dipati Arya Kusumah di Ningrat, who was governing when the *Wawacan Sajarah Galuh* was composed.

The first section of the *Wawacan Sajarah Galuh* is legendary or mythological, while the second part of the text is more historical. Nonetheless, the first part also contains historical elements, but they are presented in a mythological style. In turn, while the second section is historical, it also contains mythological elements. Of historical interest is the fact that the author of this text was familiar with such locations as Turkey, Africa, America, Arabia, China, Jeddah, Penang Island, Bugis, Ambon, Bali, Palembang, Riau, Malacca, Malaya, Sambas, and Java, all of which he cited as places where the descendants of the Prophet Adam had settled.

Historical *wawacan* were created in other areas as well, and we have today copies of the *Sajarah Sukapura* from Tasikmalaya, the *Babad Sumedang* from Sumedang, the *Babad Cikundul* from Cianjur, the *Babad Panjalu* from Ciamis, *Wawacan Carios Munada* from Bandung, and *Babad Cirebon* from Cirebon. There are also such literary-historical texts such as the *Sajarah Bandung* that were written in prose form.

BABAD CIREBON

Copies of the *Babad Cirebon* exist in both Javanese and Sundanese. Both versions of the text were written in poetic form. The Sundanese version of the *Babad Cirebon* appears to be simply an adaptation of the Javanese version, written in Cirebon.

The *Babad Cirebon* was not only translated into Sundanese but numerous adaptations of the text also appear in Sundanese manuscripts. One such adaptation is the manuscript *Carios Lampahing Para Wali* (The story of the Wali's travels).

I maintain that the author of *Babad Cirebon* intended in his tale not just to narrate historical facts. His mission was also to legitimize the role of Sunan Gunung Jati (hero of the *Babad Cirebon*) as the upholder of Muslim rule in West Java, the position of the nine *wali* as rulers of (the rest of) Java, and the authority of the Dutch in their own seat of power, Batavia.

While the above-mentioned *wawacan* originated from and circulated in aristocratic (*menak*) circles, there were also *wawacan* that circulated among the common people. Such texts as *Wawacan Ogin Amarsakti, Wawacan Danumaya, Wawacan Sulanjana,* and *Wawacan Jaka Bayawak* were popular among the Sundanese farming community, while *Wawacan Ahmad Muhamad, Wawacan Nabi Paras, Wawacan Carios Lampahing Para Wali Kabeh,* and *Wawacan Kanjeng Nabi Muhammad* tended to circulate in *santri* circles, among people deeply interested in Islam.

A telling difference between extant manuscripts from artistocratic circles and ones from the general populace is that the former are generally clean and neat in form as well as in writing and spelling, while the latter are somewhat sloppy, in both writing and spelling.

WAWACAN OGIN AMARSAKTI

The *Wawacan Ogin Amarsakti* (fig. 141) was very popular in Sundanese agricultural communities, especially in Bandung Regency. A token of its popularity among the people is that many copies of the text still circulate in the villages and that certain traditional ceremonies make use of this manuscript. This *wawacan* is usually recited in choral (*beluk*) style following a successful harvest. Part of the tale recounts the story of Ogin Amarsakti, an expert farmer, who was able to obtain fantastic yields from whatever crop he chose to plant:

> Ogin liked flowers,
> and in the morning planted some
> that quickly grew and bloomed.
> Ogin planted fruit trees,
> starting with just seeds,
> planting mangosteen in the evening,
> finding ripened fruit in the morning . . .

Rapid growth was seen in the popularity of *tembang* and *dangding* (nonnarrative) poems, especially in the nineteenth century. Because of strict regulations regarding the application and use of poetic meters (*guru gatra, guru lagu, guru wilangan*), one could argue that this trend resulted in the debasement of the literary value of a text; language and meaning were often contorted merely for the

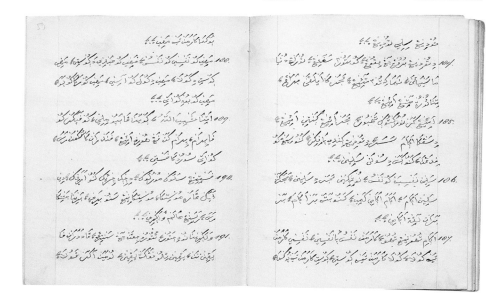

purpose of adhering to poetic norms. And in defense of this argument one can cite numerous examples of poorly written *wawacan* and *dangding* (not in the form of a story).

At the same time, one can also argue the opposite: that the rising popularity of sung poetry enhanced the literary value of texts and ensured their preservation. Here, too, one can cite numerous examples in defense. But one writer, whose output of *dangding* is of unquestionable literary value, both in form and content, is Haji Hasan Mustapa (1852–1930).

As is apparent from the title ("Haji") affixed to his name, this writer spent some time in Mecca. According to his own statements, he was a *penghulu besar* (a prominent Muslim leader) in Aceh (1893–1895) and in Bandung (1895–1918), and began to write *dangding* poetry around 1900, whereafter he produced tens of thousands of verses. Part of his treasury of written work (comprising 3,877 verses) can be found in the Leiden University Library. Another part can be found in the National Library of Indonesia in Jakarta (fig. 142). Yet another remains in the hands of the Sundanese community.

An excerpt from one of Haji Hasan Mustapha's *dangdings*, entitled *Dumuk Suluk Tilas Tepus* (A collection of selected *Suluk*) is as follows:

When the ink is gone, there is still speech;
when speech is gone, there is still writing;
when the writing is finished, the writing material remains,
on which to set for the truths one finds.
For that is, indeed, the contents of the Quran,
all that in books is evident . . .

H. Hasan Mustapa was a writer not only of *dangding* but he also established himself as an essayist on culture, society, and Islamic teachings and thought.

A fairly large percentage of manuscripts from the modern period have been studied and quite a number of those have been published. Nevertheless, a great deal of work remains to be done, and many interesting areas still await investigation.

Edi S. Ekadjati

LEAVES OF PALM: BALINESE *LONTAR*

The Balinese written tradition has a long history that dates back at least a millennium. During this period diverse media have been used as writing material, with *lontar* leaf most common until paper became widespread in the twentieth century. *Lontar* leaf derives from the palmyra species of palm, *Borassus flabellifer*, which grows throughout the Indonesian archipelago. In Balinese the palmyra palm is named *tal* (deriving from *tala*, the Sanskrit name for the talipot palm), and this is reflected in the term *lontar*, which is an inversion of the word *rontal* meaning "leaf" (*ron*) of the "*tal* tree" (*tal*).

Today, although *lontar* leaf is no longer popularly used as writing material, knowledge of the craft of inscribing it survives, and manuscripts made from it continue to be copied, read, and held in high esteem. But despite this, the *lontar* manuscript tradition is endangered. For more than a century it has been going through a transition and has now entered its twilight phase.

This article describes various aspects of the tradition. It moves from an examination of its history to a consideration of such matters as the processing of *lontar* leaf as writing material, the typology of *lontar* manuscripts and the scribal process, to the content of *lontar* texts, reading practices, and the beliefs and ritual behavior that surround manuscripts. The final section concerns their position in contemporary Bali. The documentation of this unique and rich heritage, while it still draws breath and retains many of its customary features, is not only important in its own right but may prove important in furthering our understanding of written traditions in other parts of the Indonesian archipelago.

HISTORY

The practice of writing on *lontar* leaf extends into the distant past, but precisely how far back is not known. No very old *lontar* manuscripts survive because *lontar* leaf is not durable, with the lifespan of manuscripts rarely exceeding a couple of hundred years. They are particularly susceptible to devastation from insect infestations. They are also prey to the ravages of time, which cause them to become fragile and brittle, to split along the grain, and crumble at the edges. Insect infestations, the growth of destructive bacteria and fungi, and breakdown of the leaf structure are exacerbated by Bali's hot and humid climate. The survival of texts written on *lontar* owes a great deal to the popularity that they have enjoyed together with the existence of a vigorous scribal tradition.

Although the origin of writing on *lontar* leaf cannot be pinpointed, it is thought to derive from the ancient Indian practice of writing on the leaf of the talipot palm (*Corypha umbraculifera*), which has been dated to the first century A.D. The present Balinese writing system in fact derives from India's Devanagari script, but it is possible that another writing system that used *lontar* leaf as a medium already existed in Bali prior to its adoption.

Indian influence on Bali has been pervasive and enduring, and information concerning when and how Bali acculturated an Indian worldview and traditions is of value in attempting to establish when the practice of writing on *lontar* leaf might have commenced, assuming that it was instigated by Indian travelers to the island in the distant past. Over the years, considerable speculation has surrounded the Indianization of Bali, and for a long time it was held that Bali was Indianized after and via Java, her politically powerful neighbor who at times exercised political control over Bali. However, recent archeological findings from the

FIGURE 143

Bronze inscription from the village of
Gobleg, North Bali. Gedong Kirtya,
Singaraja.

north Balinese coastal plain at the former site of the village of Sembiran challenge
these hypotheses. They indicate that Bali might have had direct contact with India
as early as between A.D. 1 and 200, earlier than the fifth century West Javanese
inscriptions that are some of the earliest evidence of Indian influence on Java. At
this time Bali was evidently located on a major trade route for spices and fragrant
woods from the Moluccas and the Lesser Sunda Islands to ports in western
Indonesia. Indian traders would have called in at these ports, including Sembiran.
Hence, it is possible that the practice of writing on *lontar* leaf might have commenced at this early stage.

Certainly, there is evidence that *lontar* leaf was already in use as writing material in the ninth century, in the form of Bali's earliest extant texts, most of which
are on bronze (often referred to as "copperplate"), with a few also on stone. They
concern such things as administrative matters relating to religious institutions,
land that constitutes the property of the gods, and taxes for the upkeep of temples. The oldest is dated A.D. 882. These bronze inscriptions generally emulate
incised leaves: they are long and narrow and can accommodate five, or more often
six, lines of writing. From this it has been deduced that the practice of writing on
lontar leaf already existed at the time of the inscriptions and played a role in their
production. Either they were originally composed on *lontar* leaf and were later
transcribed, or else they were engraved by a scribe who was skilled at writing on
lontar leaf (fig. 143).

LONTAR LEAF AS WRITING MATERIAL

The processing of *lontar* leaf as writing material is a "cottage industry," requiring
the use of a variety of tools, presses, clamps, and other instruments (see box on
pages136–137). There are two grades of *lontar* writing material. The superior
product, known as *pepesan*, is reserved for the most important manuscripts. Its
manufacture is a highly specialized craft, both labor intensive and time consum-
ing, that has never been widely practiced.

Pepesan are usually commissioned from a manufacturing household. The
coarser-quality product, sometimes termed *katihan* or *lontar*, is used for more
general writing purposes. It is far less complex to prepare, and is usually made in
the homes of people who employ it as writing material.

It is unlikely that Bali ever managed to sustain more than a small industry for
manufacturing *pepesan*, for it utilizes long, broad leaves. Although *lontar* trees
grow abundantly in dry regions, those bearing such leaves grow in only a few
places. Villages in the easternmost regency of Karangasem, especially Culik,
Kubu, and Tianyar, supply the best leaves. Inferior-quality leaves that are sometimes also processed as *pepesan* are found, among other places, in Karangasem in
the village of Selat and on the slopes of Mount Agung. *Lontar* leaves are not suitable for processing as writing material at all stages of their growth and are only
harvested for this purpose when they reach an appropriate state of maturity, during the dry season, from May until October.

Manufacture of the coarser writing material utilizes inferior-quality leaves,
and involves only drying in the sun, soaking in water for three or four days, and

drying in the sun once more. The leaves are then folded in two along their ribs, which are left intact. The finished product is much less durable than fully processed *pepesan,* which can take up to two years to produce.

Lontar leaf can be fashioned into writing material of varying lengths. In the case of *pepesan,* this is made possible by an assortment of measuring sticks and clamps. The length of leaves used in manuscripts is determined primarily by three factors. First, they can be cut as short as desired, but they can only be as long and broad as mature leaves will permit, that is, no more than, say, 70 by 4.5 centimeters. Second, the length of manuscripts is proportional to the size of the texts they contain. Thus, a short text will rarely be written on very long leaves, or a long text on very short leaves. Finally, the length of manuscripts is usually related to their subject matter, which is also related to their intended use. The longest manuscripts tend to contain important literary texts such as *kekawin* and *parwa.* They are studied by groups of people and are laid flat on a low table or offering tray so that the leaves can be read easily, one by one. Their length is appropriate to this style of reading. Somewhat shorter texts comprising such things as manuals tend to be consulted by individual specialists. They are less cumbersome to handle, for their leaves can be turned over while held in the hand. Some manuscripts are, owing to the brevity of the texts they contain, written on small pieces of leaf. Yet others may be made in special miniature size for portability. An example is the *Pangayam-ayaman,* a manual explaining the characteristics of roosters, that some men carry in their belts to cockfights and consult at the ringside.

TYPOLOGY OF *LONTAR* MANUSCRIPTS

There are four main types of *lontar* manuscripts. The first type lacks a generic name. It typically comprises a single, short piece of leaf—a *pipil*—either of the superior or inferior type. In the case of the superior-quality leaf, both sides may be utilized as a writing surface, while with the inferior product, both outer sides of the folded leaf may be written on. These short pieces of leaf are reserved for recording such things as memoranda, letters, village records, and IOUs (fig. 144). They are also inscribed with magical drawings (*rajahan*), religious formulas (*mantra*) and the names of people for use as charms and amulets, and for use in religious rituals (figs. 145, 146).

_____ FIGURE 144 _____

Above: A nineteenth-century *pipil.* Leiden University Library, Leiden.

_____ FIGURE 145 _____

Below: Details from a *mantra* with *rajahan. Kaputusan Wisnu Ngadeg.* Leiden University Library, Leiden.

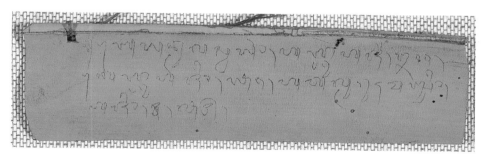

FIGURE 146

The second type, *embat-embatan* or *rencean*, consists of compilations of longer pieces of inferior quality, ribbed leaves whose outer sides provide a writing surface (fig. 147). They are usually reserved for texts whose longevity is not a primary consideration, even though they may be frequently consulted, such as calendars and notes. The leaves of *embat-embatan* are perforated with one hole only, near the top left-hand corner, where the writing commences. A cord made from various materials, among others woven cotton thread or plant fiber, is strung through the holes and tied loosely to keep the leaves in order. *Embat-embatan* may be kept in small cloth bags, usually white or yellow (colors that symbolize divinity), which are closed by means of a drawstring. It is customary to hang *embat-embatan* by their cords or the drawstrings of these bags from a nail protruding from a beam or wall, or from a hook inserted in a plaited bamboo or thatch ceiling, or over kitchen stoves. Because the leaves of *embat-embatan* retain their spines and are not encased by wooden boards, they are prone to warp. If stored suspended without the protection afforded by cloth bags, they rapidly accumulate dirt and dust deposits.

The third and fourth types of *lontar* manuscripts, *lontar cakepan* and *lontar kropakan*, are made from compilations of *pepesan*. As their manufacture is more complex, labor intensive, and costly than that of *pipil* or *embat-embatan*, they are less prone to deterioration and, hence, are usually reserved for important texts.

Both sides of the leaf of *lontar cakepan* and *lontar kropakan* provide a writing surface. As already mentioned, the bundles of leaves that form these types of manuscripts are perforated with a small hole in three places, equidistant from both ends and just off center. (The hole is located slightly off-center so that if any leaves swing around into an upside-down position they can easily be seen. When a *lontar* is picked up by its cord, it should lean to the right; otherwise, it has been picked up upside-down.) The leaves are then sandwiched between two flat boards termed *cakepan*, which have a central hole that corresponds to the central hole in the leaves. *Cakepan* (the root word for which means "close tightly") act like the covers of a book, for they provide the leaves with a degree of protection from dust and dirt and prevent them from warping. They are made from various types of timber or bamboo. They may be elaborately carved or even painted, particularly in the case of special manuscripts in court libraries. A long cord is threaded through the central hole of the boards and leaves. The bottom end is usually knotted and the top end tied to a small round object, such as a *kepeng* (a Chinese coin with a hole in its center) so that it cannot slip through the manuscript. As with the cord in the *embat-embatan*, it keeps the leaves together and in order. When the manuscript is stored, the cord is pulled taut and wound around it several times.

Lontar kropakan are identical to *lontar cakepan* but for one feature: they are stored in wooden, lidded boxes termed *kropak* (fig. 148). The boxes are usually made from fine-quality timbers such as *sawo* (*Mimusops kauki*), teak (*Tectona*

grandis) and *intaran* (*Azadirachta indica*). They may be ornately carved, painted, or even inlaid with, for example, mother-of-pearl, as may occur with important *lontar* kept in libraries owned by wealthy nobility (fig. 149). Short texts are kept in boxes consisting of a single compartment, while long texts may need to be stored in boxes that have a double compartment. The types of texts assigned to *lontar kropakan* are considered to be the most exalted and worthy of preservation, hence the investment of further time and cost involved in the production of the boxes.

INSCRIBING THE LEAVES

Before *lontar* leaves are compiled into book-like form, they are inscribed with an iron stylus known as a *pangutik* or *pangrupak*. Inscribed leaves are termed *lempir*.

Sometimes commentators provide texts—in particular, texts composed in classical languages or those that pose difficulties of interpretation—with interlinear glosses in Balinese or Literary Balinese. The manuscripts containing these texts are known as *lontar marti* (translated *lontar* manuscripts). Each writing surface of *lontar marti* typically contains three lines of writing only. The main text is found on the middle line, and the gloss on the first and third lines (fig. 150). The text and its gloss are connected by means of a line of dots playfully termed *semut sadulur* (row of ants) (fig. 152).

Lontar manuscripts may contain illustrations as well as text. Manuscripts with an abundance of illustrations are termed *prasi* (illustrated *lontar*), and they are inscribed without the aid of preliminary sketches (figs. 151, 153). The illustrations and their accompanying text are customarily inscribed on the same leaf and connected by means of *semut sadulur*. It is uncommon for manuscripts to present text and accompanying illustrations on adjacent leaves (fig. 154).

Once the text and illustrations have been completed, the incisions are blackened by smearing a paste made from a mixture of pulverized, burnt candlenut (*Aleurites moluccana*) and coconut oil onto the surface of the leaves. When the

FIGURE 149
A winged *kropak*. Museum Bali, Denpasar.

excess is wiped off, the blackened incisions stand out sharply against the color of the leaf. If, over a period of time, the incisions lose their blackness, they are reblackened using the paste. Finally, the leaves are cleaned with cut *blingbing buluh,* the small star fruit (*Averrhoa bilimbi*). Its juice not only removes any remaining traces of the black paste and imparts a sheen to the leaves but is also said to deter insects.

SCRIBES

There is no evidence indicating that in the past writing or scribal activity was the exclusive domain of a particular group of people. Men and women of all social groups possessed the skills of literacy; however, it seems that members of the Brahmana descent group were especially disposed to scribal and literary activity, for they alone may train to become high priests (*pedanda*), a process that entails deep and prolonged study of a diverse range of texts, not all of which were available to all members of society.

Before the demise of Bali's courtly culture when *lontar* leaf was popular as writing material, individuals not only copied texts for themselves, but wealthy and powerful courts often maintained scriptoria and amassed vast *lontar* libraries. They employed scribes from all social groups, including commoners. Certain locales were also renowned as scribal or literary centers by virtue of their concentrations of Brahmana, such as the village of Sidemen in the regency of Karangasem.

Today as in the past there are amateur scribes with varying degrees of skill who copy texts for their own use, and professional scribes (*juru tulis*). Some scribes may copy only a few *lontar* texts during their lifetimes, while others may copy hundreds. The latter is exemplified by the *lontar* collection of Ida Pedanda Made Sidemen, Bali's most renowned literary figure of the twentieth century. In 1983, a survey of the library of *lontar* manuscripts that he had acquired through copying revealed 154 *lontar cakepan* and 37 *lontar kropakan*, a total of some 12,500 leaves. In addition, he had copied many *embat-embatan*, several *lontar* that were on loan at the time, and numerous others that had been destroyed by insects.

It takes years of experience to develop a good, even hand, which accounts for the great variation that is found in the legibility of *lontar* manuscripts. Expert scribes usually receive training in their craft. They learn to write the Balinese alphabet, letter by letter, to perfection, and aim to give each letter a distinctive appearance so that it will not be confused with another. Very few people possess the talent to become expert and creative illustrators.

While the preparation of *lontar* leaf as writing material differs from place to place, the following description lists all the steps necessary in the manufacture of superior-quality *pepesan* leaf.

The first step in the production process is the collection and drying of leaves. Bundles of long, broad, superior-quality leaves (still uncut) are dried thoroughly in the sun, a process that causes them to turn a yellowish hue.

The leaves are then soaked either in running water or in a tank whose water is changed daily for a period of three to four days, after which they are rubbed clean in the water with coconut husk or a cloth until smooth.

The drying process is then repeated. This time, however, pairs of leaves with their tips tied together are hung over frames. Alternatively, they may be cut roughly to a size that approximates their final length and spread out on the ground to dry.

The ends of *lontar* leaves taper to a point, and if they have not been previously trimmed, they are now cut off. The central rib is also removed, after which the leaves are cut roughly in accordance with specifications supplied by clients.

After being boiled or cooked in a herbal solution for approximately eight hours, a process that helps both to eliminate dirt in the leaves and to preserve their structure and color, the leaves are then cleaned in water with a cloth. As the leaves are now very fragile, this must be done with extreme care,.

The individual leaves are once again spread out on the ground to dry in the sun. In the early evening the leaves are picked up and the ground beneath the leaves is moistened with

Whole leaves set out to dry.

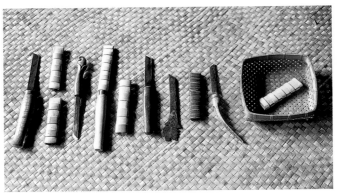

Tools for cutting and inscribing lontar.

A pamlagbagan, *a* lontar *press.*

water. The leaves are laid back down, where they remain for a couple of hours until the moisture of the soil and the cool evening air cause the dried leaves to flatten. The leaves are then wiped clean with a cloth.

Now the leaves are ready for pressing. Bundles of them are clamped in an enormous wooden press (*pamlaghagan*), with a wooden slat placed between each bundle to ensure that they receive uniform pressure. When the press is full, two wedges are inserted between the top slat and the top end of the press by means of a hammer. This increases the pressure applied to the leaves.

After a week in the press, the leaves are removed and cleaned or polished with a cloth, then returned to the press. Thereafter, they are removed and cleaned every two weeks. They remain in the press for a minimum of approximately six (Balinese) months, a calendrical cycle of 210 days, at which stage they should be of suitable quality for sale and further processing as writing material.

After the leaves have been pressed, they are cut with a knife in accordance with the specifications supplied by clients.

The leaves are usually perforated in three places. A piece of wood containing three holes is used as a guide. First, a crude hole is bored in each leaf with a metal pin or nail. The holes are then enlarged and neatened, one by one, with a doubled-bladed implement of needle-like sharpness known as a *pamiritan*.

The leaves are placed in a *panganduhan*, a collapsible clamp whose top and bottom are constructed of thick pieces of wood

Trimming the ends.

Removing the rib.

Drying the roughly cut leaves.

Cooking the leaves.

Flattening the leaves.

Aligning the leaves.

Planing the leaves.

Sanding the edges.

Painting the edges.

Blackening the leaves.

that have three holes corresponding to the perforations in the leaves. The leaves are placed between these two ends, and bamboo pins inserted. Thinner bamboo pins are hammered into the top split ends of these pins, increasing the pressure applied to the leaves until, eventually, they form a compact mass.

It is now possible to plane the long edges of the leaves. This requires extreme care, lest they be nicked in the process. As it is not possible to plane the short ends because a plane cannot grip their surface, they are cut with a cleaver or chopper.

Before the leaves are removed from the clamp, their edges are smoothed with pumice or sandpaper. Usually the long edges are dyed with a mixture of *kincu* (Chinese vermilion), *ancur* (glue made from animal or fish skin), and water.

Before *pepesan* are incised with writing, they are marked with guide lines, which is done by using a *panyipatan*, an implement made from two bamboo sticks joined by threads of equal length. The threads are moistened with Balinese ink and *dlungdung* (*Erythrina*) leaf extract and brought into contact with the leaf. After the script has been incised beneath the lines, they can be wiped off, for the *dlungdung* extract renders the ink nonpermanent.

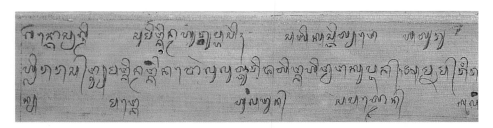

——— FIGURE 150 ———

Above: A section of a *lontar* manuscript showing the original text in the center of the *lempir* with translations above and below. *Smaradahana Marti.* Leiden University Library, Leiden.

——— FIGURE 151 ———

Below: Ambarsari. Sonobudoyo Museum, Yogyakarta.

LONTAR TEXTS

Bali's *lontar* manuscripts are a rich repository of many types of information. They include texts composed in Sanskrit, Kawi (a term designating a linguistic category of interrelated classical idioms, namely Old Javanese, Middle Javanese and Javanese-Balinese), and Modern Balinese, including Literary Balinese. Their diverse subject matter and their circulation throughout society attests to the highly developed nature of Balinese civilization. It also reflects the fact that literacy has not been confined to royalty and the priesthood, as in some other preindustrial societies.

An exhaustive study of Bali's *lontar* texts has never been attempted. In fact, most have been neglected by scholars, with the exception of the corpus, preserved in Bali, of prose and poetic texts composed in the Hindu-Buddhist kingdoms of Central and East Java from the tenth to fifteenth centuries. As previously noted, political and cultural contact had existed between Bali and Java for centuries. After Java's Islamization, these texts were kept alive in Bali through the reading

——— FIGURE 152 ———

Details from *Dampati Lalangon.* Leiden University Library, Leiden.

——— FIGURE 153 ———

Opposite page, above: Bhimaswarga. Sonobudoyo Museum, Yogyakarta.

——— FIGURE 154 ———

Opposite page, Below: Nawaruci. Sonobudoyo Museum, Yogyakarta.

FIGURE 155

Lontar letters—one open, one closed, and
one in its silk wrapper—from the kings of
Bangli, Klungkung, and Gianyar. National
Library of Indonesia, Jakarta.

and scribal traditions that existed there. Western scholarly interest in them commenced in the mid-nineteenth century and has been largely philological to date. This is explicable in terms of philology's historical orientation: the older that texts are, the more authentic and pure they are deemed to be. Since they are earlier than datable texts originating in Bali, they have often been considered to be of superior literary merit.

The tendency to regard Bali as the descendant of a lost, ancient Javanese civilization and a storehouse of its pre-Islamic *lontar* manuscripts has generated a widespread lack of recognition by scholars that the Balinese textual tradition is a discrete and ongoing entity. This, in turn, has had an adverse effect on its study.

This section presents a general overview of the wide-ranging subject of Bali's *lontar* manuscripts rather than a comprehensive coverage. Even such a modest endeavor is complicated by the problem of how to classify Balinese literature. An indigenous concept of genre is elusive, while the Western criterion of genre based on content and form is inadequate for dealing with Balinese literature. Consider, for example, the *Kidung Pamancangah*, which relates Ksatria history during the Gelgel period. It could be classified as a historical-genealogical text, as a narrative poem, or as the text of a musical performance, since it is meant to be sung. Finally, as a text composed in Kawi, it could also be classified according to linguistic criteria. The problem is that none of these classifications alone is able to convey the text's main features.

One important use of *lontar* leaf in writing has been for record keeping. Personal records, such as transactions for goods and memoranda, were made on *lontar* leaf. One nineteenth-century *pipil* records the cost of paint for *wayang* figures. Communal record keeping has also utilized *lontar* leaf, with some villages, for example, keeping *lontar*-leaf records concerning village affairs (*pipil desa*). Typically, they list membership of village councils (*krama desa*), their fulfillment of duties, and related matters. In addition, villages may possess village regulations inscribed on *lontar* leaf (*sima desa* or *awig-awig desa*). *Lontar* leaf has also been used to record supra-village ordinances such as regulations for rice cultivation and irrigation (*sima subak*), and cockfighting. In former times, these and decrees relating to property were customarily issued by rulers or their district heads (*punggawa*). Balinese is the dominant language of these documents. However, there are cases of village regulations and regulations for rice cultivation and irrigation that incorporate Kawi vocabulary, Kawi being an older medium of the chancery than Modern Balinese. Yet others are written wholly in Kawi. Finally, *lontar* leaf has been employed in record keeping at a higher administrative level, between Bali's kingdoms. Formal contracts between kings, for example, were executed on *lontar* leaf.

A second use of *lontar* leaf has been in epistolary matters. Before paper became plentiful and cheap, people from all social groups wrote letters to each other in Balinese on *lontar* (fig. 155).

A third group of texts written on *lontar* comprises the esoteric specialist lore, that is, the corpus of vocational manuals that specialist practitioners must master. These texts are composed in Sanskrit, Kawi, and Balinese, or a mixture of these languages. Most vocations possess their own texts. Brahmana high priests, for example, have liturgical texts that consist of compilations of prayers (*weda*) in Sanskrit interspersed with short explanations of the priest's ritual actions in Kawi. Many other specialist manuals borrow from or are influenced by this liturgy. The litany of temple priests or caretakers (*pamangku*) entitled the *Gagelaran Pemangku* or *Kusuma Dewa* is an example. Some others are the *Purwaka Bhumi*, the litany of Sudra exorcist priests (*sengguhu*), and the *Dharma Pawayangan*, a metaphysical treatise composed in Kawi that is studied by *wayang* puppeteers (*dalang*). Artists (*sangging*) also possess their own text in Kawi, entitled the *Dharma Pasanggingan*. So too do traditional healers (*balian usada*) whose lore is recorded in various medical texts or *usada* (fig. 156) such as the *Usada Kacacar*, which concerns the causes and treatment of smallpox.

There exist other esoteric specialist manuals that have a wider readership than the group just mentioned, even though they too constitute philosophical and religious treatises (*tutur*) of magico-religious import. The *Tutur Aji Saraswati* is an illustration. It concerns the philosophical foundations of alphabet mysticism and the rituals of literacy. As the basic manual on this subject, it is studied by all literate practitioners who are involved in magico-religious vocations. Another subgroup of specialist writings appears to have no specific vocational association today. It includes the above-mentioned *Pangayam-ayaman*, which concerns the characteristics of roosters and is used in betting at cockfights.

A fourth type of information recorded in *lontar* manuscripts is genealogical and historical in character. The term commonly used to designate such writings is *babad*. Most *babad* are composed in a mixture of Kawi and Literary Balinese and are in prose, sometimes interspersed with Sanskrit verses (*sloka*). The *Dwijendratattwa* is an example. It records the biography of Dang Hyang Dwijendra, a legendary Javanese priest who possessed great supernatural powers, migrated to Bali, established a number of temples, instigated many ritual procedures, and took a number of wives of Javanese and Balinese origin. The children of these unions became the ancestors of the various Brahmana subgroups known in Bali today. The Brahmana refer to this text in order to legitimate their title claims and their role as preeminent ritual specialists. A related text, the *Babad Brahmana*, concerns the genealogy of the Brahmana subgroups. Some of these possess their own genealogical texts, such as the *Babad Brahmana Kamenuh*, which focuses on the Kamenuh subgroup.

————— FIGURE 156 —————

A medical manuscript, or *usada*. National Library of Indonesia, Jakarta.

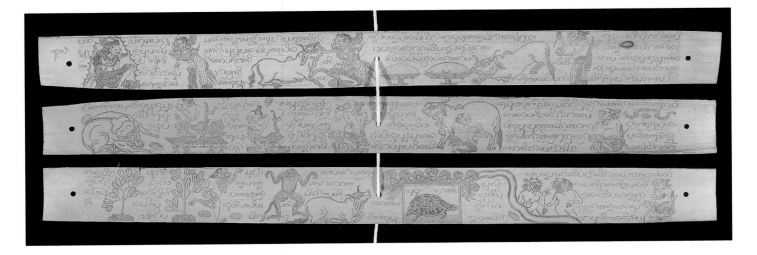

Other social groups besides the Brahmana possess *babad*. The royal house of Klungkung, the former kingdom of highest status in Bali, is often credited with writing the above-mentioned *Kidung Pamancangah*. Some scholars view this text as the first major dynastic genealogy and consider that it set the style for other dynastic genealogies, most of which they believe were composed in the nineteenth century by Brahmana attached to royal houses. On the other hand, they view commoner *babad* as twentieth century constructs compiled by groups trying to assert themselves, largely in response to an initiative of the Dutch colonial administration, which froze the concept of caste on Bali and forged alliances with Balinese ruling groups. The historical-genealogical category of texts also includes texts that relate the collapse of kingdoms, such as the *Rusak Buleleng*, which recounts the Dutch conquest of Bali's northern kingdom of Buleleng.

A fifth distinctive category of *lontar* texts comprises literary works that are often referred to as "belles-lettres." Prose texts composed in Kawi such as the *parwa* fall into this category. The *parwa* are ancient Javanese renditions of the books of the Indian *Mahabharata* epic (fig. 157). Set in a legendary Indic past, they relate the exploits of the five mythical, heroic Pandawa brothers.

One poetic genre that this category encompasses is the *kekawin*, (figs. 158, 159). *Kekawin* are poems composed in Sanskrit meters or indigenous meters modeled on Sanskrit metrical principles. The basis of *kekawin* prosody is a fixed number of syllables and a fixed metrical pattern in each poetic line. Like the *parwa*, many *kekawin* derive their narrative material from Indian epic literature, such as the *Ramayana* and the *Mahabharata*. They relate stories about gods, demons, and legendary heroes, impart religious, ethical, and philosophical teachings, and evoke the Indian source of Balinese culture. The most popular *kekawin* in contemporary Bali are the *Ramayana, Bharatayuddha, Sutasoma, Arjunawiwaha* (fig. 160), and *Bhomakawya* (fig. 161), all of which were composed in ancient Java. In addition, many *kekawin* have been composed in Bali, down to modern times, in the classical Javanese mold.

Kidung poems form another subcategory. They are composed in Middle Javanese in indigenous meters that feature paired stanzas consisting of a fixed number of syllables and a fixed final vowel. Many *kidung* have associations with the pre-Islamic Hindu-Javanese kingdoms of East Java, and are expressive of the court ethos. Others, known as *lulungid,* tend to be mystical and didactic in content. *Kidung* are said to have been composed both in Java and in Bali. One of the best-loved *kidung* reputed to be of Balinese origin is the *Malat*. Like many others, it relates the exploits of the princely hero Panji.

A further subcategory consists of *geguritan* poems. *Geguritan* are written in Literary Balinese and composed in indigenous meters. Their metrical structure is

FIGURE 157

Three leaves from an illustrated manuscript of the *Adiparwa*, the first book of the *Mahabharata*. National Gallery of Australia, Canberra.

FIGURE 158

A detail from the *Adiparwa*. National Gallery of Australia, Canberra.

FIGURE 159

Above: Three leaves from *Smaradahana*, a *kekawin* in praise of Kama, the god of love. *Right:* Two details from the same manuscript. National Gallery of Australia, Canberra.

much simpler than that of *kidung*, consisting of short lines of a fixed number of syllables and a fixed final vowel. *Geguritan* have been composed about all manner of subjects—technical, mystical, religious, historical, and so on.

A final category of texts comprises Balinese didactic tales or *satua*. Traditionally an oral genre narrated to children, they are sometimes committed to writing. Examples are *Siap Badeng* (The black chicken), *Men Tiwas teken Men Sugih* (The poor woman versus the rich woman), and *I Bawang tekan I Kesuna* (Onions and garlic).

READING PRACTICES

In modern postindustrial societies, reading is a silent and private activity, while in preindustrial societies such as Bali, this is not always the case. The reading methods employed in Bali for the study of the esoteric, specialist *lontar* manuals, and belles-lettres illustrate this point.

The esoteric, specialist manuals fall into a unique category, because access to them is restricted to specialists whose vocations depend upon mastery of their teachings. Vocational specialization is tied to religion and locked into a tradition of teachers who pass on textual knowledge to the novice. This knowledge is surrounded by secrecy, and access to the texts is subject to the fulfillment of two conditions that have their origin in religion (fig. 162).

The first condition is ritual purification (*pawintenan*) and initiation into the vocation. This prepares the novice for the receipt of sacred knowledge. The ritual is addressed to Saraswati, goddess of eloquence, knowledge, and literature. There are various types and gradations of religious initiations. They typically involve bathing of the initiate's torso in holy water, beseeching the goddess for her assistance in carrying out the vocation, and writing sacred syllables on various parts of the body. The latter seems intended to transfer the supernatural power of words or letters to the initiate.

The second condition governing access to the esoteric textual tradition prepares the novice both intellectually and spiritually to receive the knowledge that it contains: it must be studied through the mediation of a guru, because it is believed to be imbued with supernatural danger. Study with a guru is essential because if the knowledge is incorrectly acquired, it is believed to produce mental derangement and other dire consequences (fig. 163).

Another style of reading, both alien to this method of acquiring knowledge and to the silent, private style of reading that is common in post industrial societies is termed *pepaosan, mabasan,* or *mabebasan.* It is the favored style for reading *parwa, kekawin,* and *kidung.* It may also be used for reading *geguritan* and *babad* (fig. 164).

FIGURE 161

The *Bhomakawya.* National Library of Indonesia, Jakarta.

Pepaosan typically revolves around a group of people who come together to read texts. The activity centers on two people from the group, one of whom functions as reader, the other as translator. The reader's task is to vocalize the text in accordance with its metrical or prose properties. Thus *kekawin, kidung,* and *geguritan* are sung according to their particular meters, while prose texts are declaimed in the dramatic style termed *palawakia*. The translator's task is to translate the sounded text into Balinese. Other participants form the audience until their turn arrives to act either as translator or reader.

At the commencement of a *pepaosan* session, the first reader always reproduces the initial stanzas or portions of the text that will be read (fig. 164). Only then does the reading and translation proper begin. Now the reader reproduces the text, fragment by fragment, each of which is followed by the translator's interpretation of it. After the pair has read and translated a portion of the text, they retire to the audience and a new pair resumes the reading and translation. At all times the audience is permitted to interrupt to ask questions or challenge the translation. Difficulties in meaning are usually referred to the most authoritative participants. *Pepaosan* is, therefore, as much an opportunity to study texts as it is

FIGURE 164

"A *Bebasan* Reading" by I Gusti Nyoman
Lempad. Private collection.

to savor them. In addition, the oral nature of *pepaosan* enables people who are not literate or who are unfamiliar with Bali's classical languages to participate in text readings through listening.

Even though texts are reproduced orally, *pepaosan* is essentially a text-based activity in that the reader vocalizes the written text. It is never vocalized from memory, for encoded in the written manuscript is vital information concerning the melody, rhythm, and textual phrasing to be applied. In order to fulfill the task of singing or declaiming texts, readers must be knowledgeable about the meaning and syntactic structures of the passages they reproduce. While readers rarely function as translators, aspiring translators usually commence their training as readers.

Translators, on the other hand, must be able to improvise translations of the sounded text. They provide paraphrases rather than literal translations, and never memorize their interpretations, for not only would that be considered a sign of ignorance on their part, but since different readers might reproduce texts in different ways they must be able to render extempore any soundings of them.

There is evidence that *lontar* texts have been performed in the *pepaosan* style in courts (*puri*) and priestly houses (*gria*) at least since the nineteenth century. The practice seems then to have spread throughout the wider community with the establishment of *pepaosan* clubs (*sekaa pepaosan*), commencing in northern Bali in the early twentieth century and southern Bali somewhat later, in the 1930s. It subsequently suffered a decline during the long interlude of political turbulence, violence, and personal trauma that accompanied the Japanese occupation of Bali, the struggle for national independence, the early years of the Republic of Indonesia, and the coup of 1965 and its bloody aftermath. However, since 1969 there have been a number of initiatives by government agencies and private organizations in Bali to stimulate the practice of *pepaosan* as well as interest in *lontar* texts. They include the sponsorship of reading clubs, and regional and island-wide competitions for singing and translating texts, in particular *kekawin* and *kidung*. A number of independent, private study clubs have also formed.

When a club meets to read a text, it customarily reads it in its entirety. Such an enterprise can take months or even years to complete, depending upon the length of the text, the frequency with which sessions are held, and the amount of discussion that the sessions generate. Only upon completion of the text is a new one embarked on.

Pepaosan is not only practiced in courts, priestly houses, and reading clubs, but it may also take place at religious ceremonies. While this is not obligatory, it is said to enhance the occasion. Sometimes a host may even invite a club for this purpose. The practice appears to have commenced in the late 1960s when, after more than two decades of cultural inactivity and the deaths that followed the abortive 1965 coup, hosts could never be sure that sufficient numbers of guests skilled at *pepaosan* would attend ceremonies.

There are five categories of Balinese religious ceremony, and *pepaosan* may accompany four of them: *manusa yadnya* (rites of passage), *dewa yadnya* (ceremonies for gods), *pitra yadnya* (ceremonies for deified ancestors), and *resi yadnya* (ceremonies for priests). During the fifth category, *buta yadnya* (ceremonies for the propitiation of netherworldly forces), *pepaosan* never takes place. In a ceremonial context, an entire text is rarely read as time usually does not permit this. Instead, a passage or a selection of passages from one or more texts are read. Passages with plots or themes relevant to particular ceremonies are commonly selected. For example, at a wake, the passage from the *Ramayana* dealing with Wibhisana's lament upon Rawana's death is often chosen as appropriate, while for a marriage ceremony, the passage from the *Arjunawiwaha* relating Arjuna's marriage may be read. However, there is no prescription regarding which portions of texts should accompany ceremonies or, indeed, that there should even be a connection between what is read and the type of ceremony held. Practical factors such as the availability of texts, the extent of the participants' literary knowledge, and a host's fancy can just as easily determine what is read.

Geguritan and *babad* may also be read in *pepaosan* style. *Babad*, however, are usually only read at ceremonies held by groups whose history and genealogy they relate, such as at the inauguration (*plaspas*) or religious anniversary (*odalan*) of a kin-group temple.

As for other types of texts, such as letters or those related to record keeping, there appears to be no tradition of reading them in this fashion. An exception is provided by some village regulations that have acquired a sacred status, either because they are believed to have been bestowed by the gods, are thought to be their property, or are considered to possess supernatural properties (*pingit*). Owing to the mystique surrounding them, and sometimes because they are difficult to read and cannot be easily understood, particularly in the case of older sets of regulations that are composed in Kawi, they may be read in *pepaosan* style by a group.

Beliefs and Rituals Associated with *Lontar*

The Balinese believe that letters have a divine origin and are charged with an ambiguous, supernatural potency. Therefore, writing not only serves an ordinary communicative function but it can also be manipulated to influence the course of events via magico-religious activity.

The association of writing with magico-religious activity is not uncommon in preindustrial societies. According to Jack Goody, the editor of *Literacy in Traditional Societies,* a number of reasons exist that explain this phenomenon. In some societies, it appears that writing was used as a mode of communicating with supernatural forces because it was considered a means of communication superior to speech—it materialized speech and enabled its transmission and preservation over time. In other cases, where writing was associated with the priesthood, religion legitimized literacy and came to dominate it. Finally, because writing came to traditional societies from cultures with higher levels of technical achievements, it was seen to possess special supernatural powers and became the property of religion. Each of these reasons is applicable to Bali.

The belief that letters are a tool for communicating with supernatural forces has given rise to a highly esoteric and abstruse system of alphabet mysticism in

FIGURE 165

Tutur Aji Saraswati. National Library of
Indonesia, Jakarta.

Bali. Its philosophical foundations are elaborated in specialist texts such as the
Tutur Aji Saraswati (fig. 165) and the *Tutur Swarawyanjana.* Belief in the divine
origin and the supernatural potency of writing has also produced a web of rituals
that surround literate activity including writing, reading, discarding *lontar* texts,
storing *lontar* texts, and paying homage to the Goddess Saraswati, the patroness
of literature, knowledge, and eloquence.

Some of these rituals are prescribed in the *Tutur Aji Saraswati.* For example,
the text lists mantra that must be recited when carrying out the following activities: writing; requesting a boon to write; crossing out consonants (this must first
be recited over the tip of the stylus); crossing out vowels, the mute symbol, and
numbers; opening exalted writings; reading; closing and storing *lontar*; absorbing
knowledge quickly; burning *lontar* (damaged *lontar* cannot be just thrown away
but must be cremated, like the human body); and "adorning" consonants with
vowels. Failure to recite these mantra is said to result in dire consequences. One
manuscript of the *Tutur Aji Saraswati* specifies the unfortunate outcome of crossing out letters without the protection afforded by the recitation of mantra: a short
life-span results should the letter named *cecek* be crossed out; blindness and
headache are the consequences of crossing out the letter *hulu* (*hulu* means
"head"); lameness arises should the letter *suku* (*suku* means "foot" and "leg") be
crossed out; deafness and stomach ailments follow the crossing out of the letter
taleng (*talinga* means "ear").

There are a number of other rituals that complement the writing and reading of *lontar* manuscripts, but these have no textual basis. An example is the conventions associated with writing. They require that the writing in a *lontar* should be bounded by mystic configurations of letters (fig. 166). The initial mystic configuration is always followed by a mantra supplicating the gods, its aim being to ensure that no hindrance or misfortune of supernatural origin will befall the author, scribes or readers. One such typical mantra is: *Ong! Awighnam astu nama siddham!* (Let there be no hindrance! May this offering bear success!).

The ritual performed prior to reading is one that involves the presentation of offerings, burning of incense, and recitation of mantra by a qualified person. For example, C.J. Grader, in an article published in 1969, outlined the ceremony undertaken by the village head (*pasek desa*) of Kubutambahan each time he consulted the village records: he would ask the permission of the village protective deity before opening the basket containing the records, and then present *canang prani* offerings while sprinkling the basket with holy water and reciting mantra.

As far as the handling of *lontar* manuscripts is concerned, custom dictates that they should not be handled by people who are "ritually impure"—for example, by women during menstruation. With regard to storing them, a variety of practices exist. Some methods for storing *embat-embatan* have already been mentioned. Another method of storing this type of manuscript, and *lontar cakepan* and *lontar kropakan* in particular, is in wooden chests, woven baskets, and cupboards. These may then be placed in pure or sacred space: in an "upstream" (*hulu*) rather than a "downstream" (*teben*) position within a room, in a special pavilion (*gedong*), or in the repository in a temple for sacred objects and the property of gods (*panyimpenan*). Individual *lontar* manuscripts are often kept on an offering shelf located high up in the north east corner of a room (*plangkiran*).

The most important community-wide ritual associated with *lontar* manuscripts is *Odalan Saraswati*, the religious anniversary of the goddess Saraswati (fig. 167), when homage is paid to her. Like other anniversaries, it takes place once in each 210-day year. It is observed both by literate and nonliterate people. Each stage of the ritual is prescribed in the *Tutur Aji Saraswati* (fig. 168). The text enjoins that the ritual must be observed before sunset on the day of the *odalan*. For its duration, no letter may be crossed out or any writings destroyed. The transgression of this prohibition is said to bring forth disastrous consequences: "lack of success, and the wrath of the goddess Durga and malevolent supernatural beings." Following the conclusion of the ritual, after the sun has passed its zenith, it is permitted to write, to read texts, and to recite mantra.

To celebrate the anniversary, the *lontar* owned by a household are collected at a central point. During the ritual, they become the symbol of the goddess, who is presented with offerings including, among other things, eighteen Saraswati offerings (fig. 169), one for each of the basic eighteen letters of the Balinese alphabet. Each contains the *ongkara*, the symbol of the single supreme god, made from fried molded rice dough.

FIGURE 166

Nabi Paras, a *pipil* amulet once owned by Anak Agung Gede Ngurah of Karangasam, dating from 1892. Leiden University Library, Leiden.

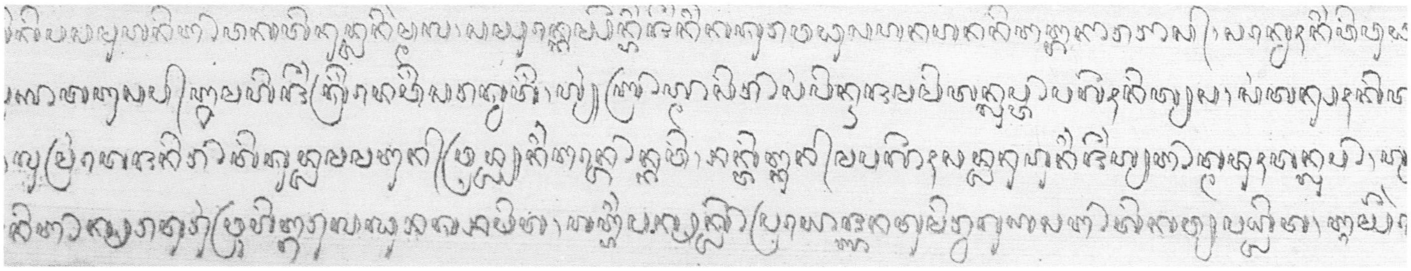

FIGURE 168

Above: Tutur Aji Saraswati, a manuscript made in a very fine hand. Leiden University Library, Leiden.

FIGURE 169

Below: A *sanganan* (rice-dough offering) for the goddess Saraswati. Photo courtesy Leonard Lueras.

FIGURE 167

Opposite: A painting of the goddess Saraswati holding, among other attributes, a *lontar* manuscript, by I Nyoman Mandra of Kamasan of Klungkung, Bali. Photo courtesy Leonard Lueras.

Lontar Manuscripts in Bali Today

Today the *lontar* manuscript tradition is just one of many casualties of the profound social, cultural, and technological changes taking place as Bali becomes involved in the development programs of Indonesia's government, and also succumbs to influences from abroad. However, challenges to the tradition are not a recent phenomenon but commenced centuries ago.

Possibly one of the first serious threats to the tradition's survival came from the alternative writing medium of paper. During the course of the twentieth century, when it had become plentiful and cheap, paper not only usurped the popularity of *lontar* leaf as writing material but also played a role in revolutionizing the traditional method of copying *lontar* manuscripts (fig. 170).

The practice of writing on paper is thought to have been spread by Islam as it made its way throughout the Indonesian archipelago from about the thirteenth century. To what extent the Balinese might have used paper and for what purposes at this early stage remain unknown. About three centuries later, at the end of the sixteenthth century, the Dutch sailor Willem Lodewyckszoon reported that the Balinese were utilizing Chinese paper as a writing medium. Unfortunately, however, he kept no record of what the Balinese wrote on this paper. It was probably in the nineteenth century that the Balinese encountered high-quality paper produced in European mills for the first time. Both Sir Thomas Stamford Raffles and John Crawfurd, members of the British administration of Java who visited Bali in the second decade of the nineteenth century, commissioned copies of *lontar* texts on paper that they would have supplied. Raffles also commissioned a *prasi* on British paper of 1811, which, it has been confirmed, he brought with him to Bali. The Dutch missionary and linguist-lexicographer H.N. van der Tuuk, who lived on the island in the last quarter of the nineteenth century, also had *lontar* texts copied onto paper by his Balinese assistants. In addition, he commissioned paintings on paper, some of which had European watermarks.

It is unlikely that these examples of the use of paper as a writing medium in the nineteenth century were the only instances of its use, for the supply and use of paper increased after the Dutch conquered North and West Bali in 1849 and founded an elementary education system in 1876. Nevertheless, for the duration of the nineteenth century, *lontar* leaf remained the preferred writing medium for traditional texts, and hand copying them onto *lontar* leaf remained the main method of their propagation and dissemination. Although copying onto *lontar* leaf is a labor-intensive, painstaking, and costly undertaking that can be compared to the hand copying of books by monks in European monasteries in the medieval period, paper was still relatively scarce and expensive at the time.

After the Dutch took control of South Bali between 1906 and 1908, the market for European goods, including paper, expanded. In the first half of the twentieth century, "modern-minded" Balinese scribes initiated the practice of hand copying *lontar* texts onto paper for their own consumption. By now, paper was more easily obtained, its use certainly involved a smaller investment of time than *lontar* leaf, and it might even have been cheaper to purchase. Nevertheless, the old method of copying texts onto *lontar* leaf continued in some circles, with

traditionalists even transcribing back onto *lontar* leaf the texts that had been copied onto paper.

The existence of a plentiful and cheap supply of paper in the twentieth century paved the way for a series of technological developments that in turn proved deleterious to the *lontar* manuscript tradition. Perhaps the most serious has come from print technology. On the one hand, it has enabled the production of multiple identical copies of texts that are sold over the counter, making them more widely available than ever before, and for a reasonable financial outlay. On the other hand, it has completely eroded scribal involvement in the copying process. Print technology was introduced into Bali during the period of Dutch colonial rule, and has assumed a variety of forms over the years. In the last decade of the nineteenth century, the Landsdrukkerij or "National Printery," which operated from Batavia and Weltevreden (modern Menteng) in Java, created the first metal typeface of Balinese script. It was first put to use in the publication of a four-volume dictionary compiled by Van der Tuuk (1897–1912). J.B. Wolters, a Dutch competitor with offices in the Netherlands and Batavia, also created a metal typeface of Balinese script somewhat later (fig. 171). Both companies used this technology to produce Balinese-language publications, such as textbooks for use in colonial schools. However, neither made use of it to reproduce *lontar* texts.

The first *lontar* texts to be reproduced in printed form were stenciled, and appeared possibly as late as the 1950s and early 1960s. They included, among other things, a number of popular *kekawin* such as the *Sutasoma, Ramayana,* and *Arjunawiwaha.* The intellectual I Gusti Bagus Sugriwa was the driving force behind

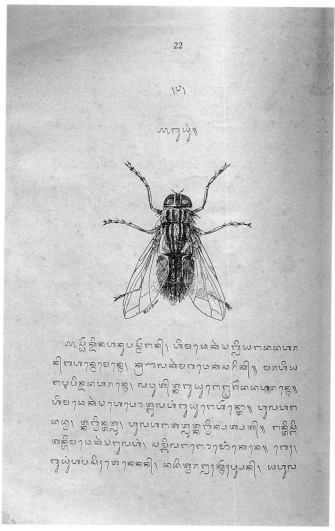

these publications. He wrote these classics by hand in Kawi and Latin script, and provided translations in Balinese and Indonesian. Each text was published as a series of thin volumes by Balimas, a company located in Denpasar.

In the 1970s, photocopying as a means of reproducing *lontar* texts made its appearance, and since the 1980s computer technology has also been utilized, to the detriment of the *lontar* tradition. Nowadays, stenciling machines, photocopying, and computer technology coexist in the publication of *lontar* texts.

The availability of printed texts has in its turn had serious repercussions for Bali's *lontar* culture, by weakening the old reading and study methods. The recitation and group discussion of *lontar* texts, practices that typically accompany the reading and study of handwritten manuscripts in preindustrial societies, are beginning to give way to the silent, private style of reading that is commonplace in postindustrial societies.

Another serious challenge to the *lontar* manuscript tradition derives from the lure of modern popular culture, often of Western origin, and the accompanying breakdown of traditional values. In the 1930s, for example, performing *kekawin* was all the rage among youth in the north of the island. In the 1990s, by contrast, a host of initiatives to keep *pepaosan* alive, sponsored by the government and other institutions, are losing ground to new forms of entertainment, often of foreign origin.

Contemporary Bali is marked by new ways of apprehending the world as well as new modes of behavior, tinged with respect for the past. The *lontar* tradition continues to survive in this environment, albeit in a transitional state, closer to obliteration than to its heyday. Nowadays, traditional texts, including some secret esoteric manuals, continue to circulate, but often as books sold freely over the counter rather than as *lontar* manuscripts accessible only to a restricted readership. And although a watered-down version of *pepaosan* is offered in clubs founded and funded by the provincial and regional governments, their agencies, and other organizations, they are struggling to keep a knowledge of *pepaosan* performance alive, let alone promote a deep understanding of *lontar* texts. Today, one can find evidence of neglect leading to the deterioration and disintegration of heirloom *lontar* manuscripts in private collections. There is also evidence that *lontar* manuscripts are being sold on the tourist market as their owners strive to finance increasingly acquisitive lifestyles. In other cases, manuscripts are moving from the private into the public domain as their owners relinquish them to libraries and other cultural institutions, either for financial gain or simply because family members are no longer interested in or able to read them.

A revival of *lontar* culture seems unlikely. As the revered literary figure Ida Pedanda Made Sidemen once quipped, "There is no salary to be made from studying the *lontar* lore!" However, there is an ironic twist to this tale of a declining tradition. It has experienced one growth area. Since around the late 1970s, *lontar* businesses have sprung up in response to tourism. They supply the burgeoning tourist market with manuscripts, particularly of the *Ramayana*, consisting of a few crudely illustrated and written *lontar* leaves in Balinese, sometimes accompanied by English translations.

Raechelle Rubinstein

OUTPOST OF TRADITIONS:
THE ISLAND OF LOMBOK

The island of Lombok, separated from Bali by a deep strait, is the most easterly of Indonesia's islands to show vast literary influence from Java and more distantly from Malaysia and India, while maintaining a literary tradition of its own. It is the last island in eastern Indonesia where texts from both the Hindu and the Islamic literary traditions are found in great numbers.

The population of Lombok consists of a number of different groups (fig. 172). The most important ones are the indigenous Sasak and the immigrant Balinese who came to the island in waves in the seventeenth and eighteenth centuries. From the seventeenth century onward, after the Balinese conquered much of the island and had an enormous impact on the fate of the Sasak population, the history of the two groups became intertwined (fig. 173). Although the Balinese were extremely influential on the literary scene, in actual numbers they are but a small minority, a mere hundred thousand from a total population of over two million. The Sasak thus constitute the bulk of the population and live all over the island, while the Balinese are mostly found in urbanized western Lombok. The Sasak population can be divided into three separate groups: the Sasak Boda, a small group of about three hundred people who adhere to indigenous traditions and customs; the Sasak Waktu Telu, who adhere to their own culture and customs with an overlay of Islam; and the Sasak Waktu Lima, who practice a traditional Islam. At the present time, the Sasak Waktu Lima form the majority of the Sasak population.

The Sasak and Balinese populations have distinct literary traditions. The Sasak people have produced a wealth of literature in both the Javanese and Sasak languages, largely inspired by, if not actually translated from, texts from the Arabic literary tradition as found in Malay and Javanese. The Balinese share much of the literary tradition of the kingdom of Karangasem on Bali, their place of origin. Thus their literature, both in Balinese and Old Javanese, derives inspiration from a Hindu-Balinese source.

THE LITERARY TRADITION OF THE SASAK IN LOMBOK

Sasak literature was thought to have been brought by Muslim traders from the *pasisir,* the northeastern coastal regions of Java, in the sixteenth and seventeenth centuries. The Javanese came to Lombok either to make their mark in the political field, or as traders who married girls from the local population and disseminated their religion, culture, and literature on the island. And indeed, at first glance their texts are similar in many aspects to the literary products of *pasisir* Java. Many texts share the same titles, and are written in Javanese verse forms in a language that can be identified as the Javanese dialect of the *pasisir.* However, if they are inspected more closely, it becomes clear that the literature of the Sasak has its own characteristics distinct from this Javanese influence.

LITERATURE IN SASAK

Sasak, which is quite distinct from Javanese or Balinese though it shares a number of words with both languages, is used in only a limited number of texts. It would seem that for a long time writing texts in the local vernacular was "not done"—as in the parallel case of Bali, where Old or Middle Javanese were the literary languages, not Balinese. As many texts came to Lombok at the period when Javanese

155

FIGURE 172
A population census and list of taxpayers from Lombok. National Library of Indonesia, Jakarta.

was still considered most fit for literary expression, texts in Javanese are found in considerable numbers, while texts in Sasak are scarce by comparison.

The most famous genuinely Sasak tale is the *Tutur Monyeh*, written in the late nineteenth century. This is also one of the rare texts for which there is a known author: Jero Mikhram, from Pancor, East Lombok. It is a charming story of Prince Witarasari who, disguised as a monkey, manages to win the hand of his beloved princess. Other texts in Sasak are the *Indarjaya, Cilinaya, Cupak,* and *Rengganis,* all of which are Sasak renderings of text material also known in Javanese, Balinese, or Malay. The last text used to be very popular, and present-day Sasak still remember readings of it. It was read at festivities where adolescents gathered to find a partner, using material from the text to make jokes and puns. Manuscripts containing the *Rengganis* in Javanese are found in large numbers, while manuscripts in Sasak are rare.

LITERATURE IN JAVANESE

Though Javanese was not the native tongue of the Sasak, they nevertheless composed original texts in it. The most important text in Javanese is the *Puspakrema*, a tale that is unknown in Java. *Puspakrema* recounts the adventures of a small prince who is taken away by a golden peacock and sent to find a medicine for the royal couple of Sangsyan who have been unable to conceive a child (fig. 174). After a number of adventures, he succeeds in obtaining the medicine and curing the queen. This charming text ends when the prince marries the daughter of the queen and founds his own kingdom. It exists in numerous manuscripts, and it would seem that the Sasak liked the story and were very proud of it.

Other texts originating from the Sasak area contain historical tales of indigenous kingdoms and their downfall at the hands of the Balinese. These texts, such

FIGURE 173
Lombok nobility in traditional court costume. Photograph by Woodbury and Page, c. 1865.

FIGURE 174

Detail from the *Puspakrama*, Leiden
University Library, Leiden.

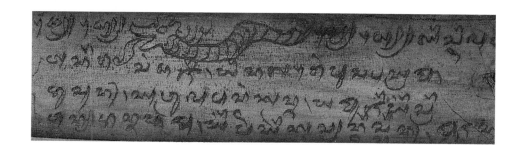

as the *Babad Lombok, Babad Selaparang, Babad Sakra,* to name but a few, provide insight into the way the Sasak people have understood and digested changes in their history.

The introduction of Islam into Lombok is the subject of a number of texts, of which *Kebo Mundar* is the most famous. Other titles are *Hikayat Nabi, Babad Lombok,* and *Sandu Baya.* The Waktu Telu variety of Islam, unique to Lombok, is the subject of the Nursada text, which also explains the arrival in Lombok of Dang Hyang Niratha, who propagated this curious blend of Muslim and indigenous religious practices and customs.

An important part of the literature comprises texts containing translations and adaptations of Arab, Persian, or Islamic texts. The most important group is the *Serat Menak,* or *Amir Hamzah* tales, which relate the adventures of the hero Amir Hamzah and his exploits in the Arab world, conquering kingdoms and spreading Islam. There exists a wealth of texts in innumerable manuscripts testifying to the *Menak's* popularity. Other texts deal with Islamic religion and philosophy, for instance the *Serat Jatiswara,* which tells of Jatiswara, who while traveling in search of his brother Sajati also studies Islam. He meets a number of holy and wise men and engages in dialogue with them on religious subjects, at the same time carrying on romantic adventures with their daughters. Tales of the prophets are also found, as well as texts dealing with Islamic law and religion.

MANUSCRIPTS AND SCRIPT OF THE SASAK

Almost all of the thousands of manuscripts from the Sasak area are written on *lontar,* leaves of the *lontar* palm tree. The leaves are neatly cut and mostly three centimeters wide, while the length of the leaves varies according to the text. Usually each leaf contains four lines, though sometimes a larger or smaller number. The leaves are bound together by a thread through a hole slightly to one side of the middle of the leaf. Wooden end-boards (to protect the leaves from being damaged by use) are common, and these are often nicely decorated. Sasak manuscripts found in collections all over the world are mostly from the late nineteenth or early twentieth centuries. Old manuscripts are rare. We know that paper was introduced a long time ago (though no research has yet been done on this subject), but it has never been used for manuscripts in the Sasak area. The script used on Sasak *lontar* is a variety of Javanese script, but shows influence from both Java and Bali and as such constitutes a unique script.

The most important collection of manuscripts of Sasak provenance is kept in the Museum Nusa Tenggara Barat in Mataram, Lombok. Other collections are found in the Gedong Kirtya in Singaraja, Bali, the National Library of Indonesia in Jakarta, and Leiden University Library.

During ceremonial occasions, the manuscripts are harshly treated. They are bathed in water to provide the ritual water needed for the ceremony, and sometimes the leaves are wet with saliva in order to make reading easier. Many manuscripts are therefore incomplete, damaged, eaten by insects, or otherwise in very poor condition.

———————— FIGURE 175 ————————
Leaves, plus a detail from the *Dampati
Lelangon*. National Library of Indonesia,
Jakarta.

USE OF MANUSCRIPTS

Texts were widely used during numerous ceremonies, particularly during certain rites of passage—for instance, when the hair of a child was cut for the first time, during circumcision ceremonies, and at marriages. Texts were also used at other ceremonial occasions—for instance, when rice was put in the barn, or on other ritual occasions during the agricultural cycle. Texts are also used for educational purposes, to instruct people in religious matters and *adat* (customs), and to explain rules for proper conduct. During reading sessions, one person reads, or rather sings, the text while one or more interpreters explain the contents to the audience. Sometimes these *pepaosan* sessions last the whole night. However, sometimes only sections of a text appropriate to a particular ceremony are used. For instance, during the hair-cutting ceremony of a young boy, the section from the text *Aparas Nabi* describing the cutting of the prophet Muhammad's hair is read. In this instance the relation between the occasion and the choice of text is clear, but this is not always the case.

Nowadays the reading of *lontar* is becoming increasingly rare. Owing to changes in the culture of the island and the different perception its people have of their position in the world, the texts are read less and less often and the tradition is in danger of becoming extinct.

THE LITERARY TRADITION OF THE BALINESE IN LOMBOK

The Balinese literary tradition has much in common with that of Bali proper. The texts owned and used by the Balinese priestly class (*brahmana*) are the same as on Bali, and belles lettres are also similar. However, it seems that some texts in Balinese were composed in Lombok, and not in Bali. For instance, the romance *Megantaka* is said to have been written in Lombok. Of course, texts containing the history of the Balinese in Lombok were composed in Lombok itself—for instance, the history of the downfall of the Lombok house of Kediri, found in the *Babad Rusak Kadiri.*

The most interesting text written in the Balinese community in Lombok is the *Kidung Dampati Lelangon* (fig. 175). This title does not in fact occur in the text but was given to it by Dutch scholars who were amazed by the beauty of the only manuscript known for a long time, which did not contain the text but only its illustrations on *lontar* leaf. The text, which has been translated into Dutch by I Wayan Bhadra and the famous Dutch scholar C. Hooykaas, is unique to Lombok. It describes the journey of a pair of lovers to attain the utmost religious/amorous experience, and that in only 104 verses of the most exquisite Balinese. It is from

FIGURE 176

Kakawin Nagarakertagama. National Library of Indonesia, Jakarta.

the *puri* (palace) Cakranegara and was written by Anak Agung Ketut Karangasem. Unlike the *Puspakrema*, manuscripts are extremely rare. Interestingly enough, the illustrations seem to have been copied almost as often as the text.

Our knowledge of Balinese literature owes much to the collection of manuscripts that the Dutch took with them after they conquered the palace of Cakranegara in 1894. This collection included the famous *Kakawin Nagarakertagama*, written in Old Javanese poetry and telling of the history of the famous Javanese empire of Majapahit (fig. 176). For a long time this was the only manuscript of the text known to exist: it is of such crucial importance to Indonesian history that it was returned to Indonesia in recent times after having been kept in Leiden University Library for generations.

The Balinese are also acquainted with the literature of the Sasak. They use Javanese texts of Sasak provenance during their nocturnal literary sessions, called *mabasan*. Texts from the *Menak Amir Hamzah* cycle are especially popular, but other texts are also known.

Dick van der Meij

TEXTUAL GATEWAYS:
THE JAVANESE MANUSCRIPT TRADITION

The Javanese is the richest written tradition of island Southeast Asia in terms of its great antiquity, the huge numbers of manuscripts produced (and surviving), the scope and variety of subjects addressed on the written page, as well as the sheer number of works created and disseminated over time.

Traditional Javanese literature, meaning that collection of Javanese texts composed and transmitted through written means, flourished within a culture in which most forms of entertainment, knowledge, learning, and wisdom were maintained and transmitted orally. Nevertheless, the manuscript tradition that augmented this oral culture had been in existence for more than a thousand years.

Throughout the entire period of Modern Javanese literature, covering roughly five hundred years from the Islamization of the north coast around the mid-1400s up until the introduction of popular primary education by the Dutch colonial government in the early twentieth century, writing and its products were well known at all levels of Javanese society, though personal literacy was far from universal. In the village sphere, on the one hand, relatively small numbers among the peasant classes had full-fledged literacy in Javanese, and familiarity with most written texts was presumably quite limited. The great works of the Javanese canon were more familiar through theatrical and other presentations. At the courts, by contrast, palace officials cultivated a rich and complex literary heritage, passing it from generation to generation within families of scribes and poets whose copying, composing, and performing of poetic works were carried out at the behest of the sovereign.

In this chapter on the manuscript tradition of Java, I will begin by addressing the basics of the technology of writing and bookmaking. Next, I will briefly survey the sorts of texts that were set down in book form in Java over the past five hundred years, the copyists, and their work. Then I will give an overview of illustration in Javanese manuscripts, and conclude with a short treatment of the illuminating arts that ornament and embellish many traditional manuscripts.

SCRIPTS

The majority of manuscripts copied between the fifteenth and twentieth centuries were written in Javanese script, but a substantial number are in a modified form of Arabic script. A much smaller number were written in Latin script from the end of the nineteenth century. Finally, on rare occasions some form of encrypted writing usually based on antique Javanese forms was used.

Javanese script is a semisyllabary, meaning that the characters (called *aksara*) represent simple syllables (consonant plus vocalization with /a/), not just single sounds or letters. Thus, rather than having letters like "b," "c," "d" as in the Roman alphabet, Javanese has "ba," "ca," "da," and so on. Altogether, there are ninety letters or signs needed to write, as follows: twenty basic *aksara*; twenty conjoined forms (*pasangan*) that serve to cancel the inherent vowel of the preceding *aksara*; eighteen signs tacked on above, below, behind, or in front of the *aksara*, referred to as clothing (*sandhangan*), which change the vowel quality of the *aksara* or make other phonetic modifications within the syllable; eleven capital letters whose forms differ dramatically from their lower-case equivalents; five free-standing vowel characters; at least six characters rigged (*rinéka*) to represent foreign consonants (mostly Arabic); and the ten digits.

As elsewhere in the Indonesian archipelago, writing and script in Java were not just so many arbitrary signs and characters. Rather, the alphabet as a whole and each of its letters were seen as occupying a special position at the meeting point of macrocosm and microcosm, and consequently as being invested with power. The widespread use of letters and writing in cures is evidence of this power, as is the popularity of letter-based forms of prophecy, interpretation, and graphomancy. Individual letters are said to have mystical significance, and there are strains of philosophy that locate each *aksara* in a certain part of the body (fig. 177). The mystical potential involved in writing was such that the work of copying itself was surrounded by rituals, from the preparation of offerings and the burning of incense to the recitation of set prayers and spells associated with various parts of the writing process.

Even the apparently simple act of reciting the alphabet can carry with it a recounting of an exemplary tale from Javanese legend. It goes like this:

ha na ca ra ka	*ana caraka*	There were two messengers
da ta sa wa la	*data sawala*	who came to blows.
pa dha ja ya ña	*padha jaya-ña*	Their prowess was equal,
ma ga ba tha nga	*maga bathanga*	Come, then, let's fight to the death.

The story recounted here concerns the legendary king Ajisaka, who is said to have introduced both civilization and writing to Java. Ajisaka had two loyal retainers, Dora and Sembadra. Dora he entrusted with a priceless magical *kris,* ordering that Dora relinquish it to no one but Ajisaka himself. Later, requiring the weapon, the king sent Sembadra to retrieve it. Neither Dora nor Sembadra would give way, and in the ensuing confrontation each dealt the other a fatal blow. As a result of their unimpeachable behavior, Dora and Sembadra also came to be known as Setya and Tuhu, names meaning "Faithful" and "True."

Javanese script was used over the entire period of Modern Javanese literature, and throughout the island, at a time when there was no easy means of communication between remote areas and no impulse toward standardization. As a result, there is a huge variety in historical and local styles of Javanese writing through the ages. The ability of a person to read a bark-paper manuscript from the town of Demak, say, written around 1700, is no guarantee that that person would also be able to make sense of a palm-leaf manuscript written at the same time only 50 miles away on the slopes of Mount Merapi.

The great difference between regional styles almost makes it seem that "Javanese Script" is in fact the name of a family of scripts, and not just one. Indeed, certain forms or styles of the so-called Balinese, Sasak, and Madurese scripts might be easier for some literate Javanese to read than selected examples of "Javanese" script originating from a distant place or time.

Further complicating matters, from time to time certain scribes, wishing to keep secret the contents of their manuscripts, resorted to inscribing portions of texts, or even entire books, in secret code. This practice was especially popular in Yogyakarta around the second half of the nineteenth century. The Widya Budaya library of the Kraton Kasultanan owns several manuscripts that hold master keys to some of the popular codes of the day, and as recently as the 1930s books were still being published that provided keys to encrypting or decoding writing in the secret Javanese scripts (fig. 178).

With the introduction and spread of Islam along the north coast, and thence to the interior from the fifteenth century onward, it was natural that Arabic script, essential to Muslim observance and scholarship, should also become domesticated in Java. In the Malay world, a modified form of Arabic script, called Jawi, superceded earlier Indic forms of writing, and is the only style of writing found in surviving manuscripts. In Java, by contrast, Arabic-style writing (called *pégon*)

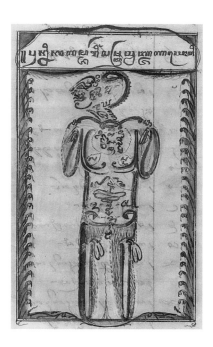

FIGURE 177

An illustration from the *Kridhaksara*, a text on the mystical dimensions of orthography attributed to the nineteenth-century poet Ranggawarsita. Sonobudoyo Museum, Yogyakarta.

FIGURE 178

An ornamental page frame or "textual gateway" containing an encrypted message in a *Serat Suryaraja* manuscript. Copied in Yogyakarta, 1815–1817. National Library of Indonesia, Jakarta.

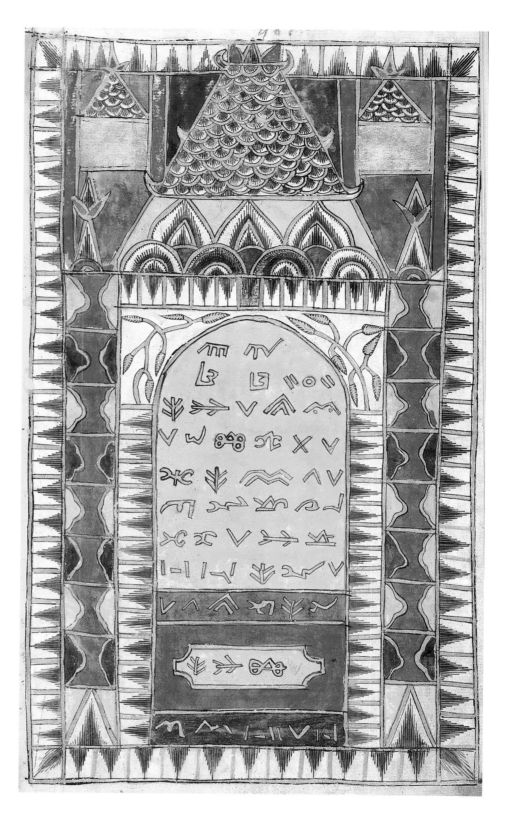

coexisted comfortably beside Javanese script but never displaced it. The varieties of *pégon* used in Java range from the most brilliant styles of calligraphy of the north-coast courts and leading schools to the rudest approximations of backwater villages. All appear to be derived from standard forms of the six styles of Arabic script, particularly Naskhi and Muhaqqaq (figs. 179, 181).

Under normal conditions, vowels are not indicated in Arabic script, which does not fit well with the rich vocalism of Javanese, so that *pégon* was, and is, almost invariably written with complete vowel markings. In the rare cases where it appears unvocalized (called *gundhil* or *gundhul*, meaning bald script), it presents special problems of interpretation.

FIGURE 179

Frontispiece of a *Serat Ambiya* containing
a verse history of the Islamic prophets
from Adam to Muhammad. Copied in
1844 by Ki Ahmad Ngali. Sonobudoyo
Museum, Yogyakarta.

In most areas of Java, Arabic script was reserved for writing texts in the
Arabic language proper, or in Malay—the language in which Islam was largely
propagated and studied throughout the whole of island Southeast Asia. Javanese
texts dealing with law, theology, or mysticism, which commonly incorporated
numerous Arabic quotes or excerpts, were also usually written in Arabic script.
The difficulty of mixing two scripts running in counter directions on the same line
of writing is one factor that certainly encouraged the substitution of Arabic for
Javanese script in such texts (fig. 180).

In some milieux, Arabic script was always the preferred form of writing, especially in the Islamic colleges (*pesantren*) and study houses (*langgar*). Further, in
some regions of the island, particularly in the north-coast courts of Banten and
Cirebon, and in Madura, Javanese works adapted from Arabic and Persian
sources (often through the medium of Malay translations), as well as original
Javanese texts containing Middle Eastern themes—the history of the prophets, for
example, or the adventures of Arabian knights and heroes—were also copied
using modified Arabic script.

Even at the level of small villages far from both courts and schools, the large
numbers of surviving manuscripts written in Arabic script testifies to the central
role that religion played in the acquisition of literacy in rural Java. But despite the
impressive inroads made by Islam in the literary and scribal habits of the Javanese,
the very word referring to Javanese written in Arabic script, *pégon*, means "foreign sounding."

FIGURE 180

Kitab Donga, an Arabic text containing devotional prayers with interlinear Javanese notes. Undated, but very early, possibly sixteenth to seventeenth century. National Library of Indonesia, Jakarta.

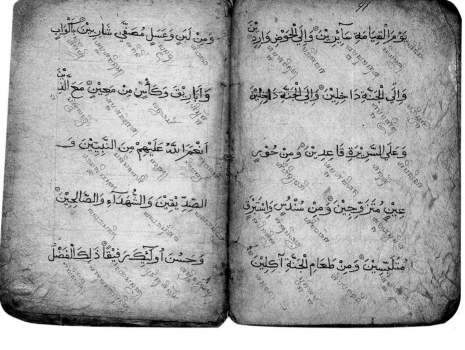

Arabic script was as potentially magical and potent as Javanese script. Amulets and good-luck charms inscribed with Arabic texts—mystical letters or syllables, verses from the Quran, phrases containing praise to Allah—were especially popular, and many cures required an Arabic word of power written on a slip of paper as an indispensable material component. Some oracles in Java speak only in cryptic Arabic syllables that appear mysteriously on leaves supplied for the purpose, as at the grave of Ki Ageng Pengging near Kartasura. Included in the holy regalia of the Yogyakarta palace was a standard, referred to as Kangjeng Kyai Tunggul Wulung ("His Worship Elder Unique Ultramarine"), bearing numerous written repetitions of the word *ayat*, meaning stanza or verse. It was carried in procession around the city as recently as midnight on January 21, 1932, in order to impart its special blessings of health and spiritual well-being to all who lined the streets to view it. In Javanese mysticism, as in Islamic mysticism around the world, the inscribed name of Allah and that of Muhammad bear special significance. Numerous texts expound the secrets and order of creation and salvation on the basis of the string of letters spelling out these two names.

Thus, writing of all sorts in Java, cast in any script, while clearly a technology used to communicate textual content in straightforward narrative ways, was at the same time an important element in the complex spiritualism of the Javanese.

WRITING SUPPORTS

Before rag stock or pulp paper were regularly imported from Europe, there were two types of writing supports commonly used in Javanese manuscripts: prepared palm leaves (usually *lontar* or *nipah*), and sheets formed from the beaten bark of certain trees of the mulberry family.

The making of palm-leaf manuscripts is described in the chapter on Bali. Palm leaves, with their fibrous veins running lengthwise, are well suited to the Indic Javanese and Balinese scripts, but much less so to the undulating, running lines typical of Arabic script. It is extremely rare, therefore, to find palm-leaf books written in *pégon*, even in areas where Islamic influence was pronounced.

Palm leaf is unusually suitable material for the tropics: palm leaves (*lontar*) last a very long time undamaged by insects or climate if they are kept soft and pliable with regular applications of citronella oil. Without this treatment, *lontar* tend to become dry and brittle. Even in this state, though, they may last for hundreds of years under the right conditions.

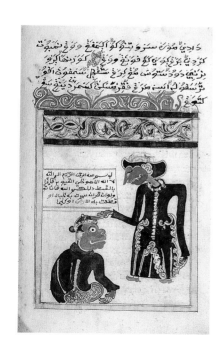

FIGURE 181

A page from the *Serat Ambiya* shown in figure 179.

Beaten-bark paper, variously called *dluwang, gendhong*, or *kemplong* (the production process for which is described in the chapter on the Sundanese manuscript tradition) is likewise a material well suited to bookmaking in the tropics. The rough but supple sheets, manufactured from the inner bark of the *glugu* tree, take ink well and appear to be unsavory to the tropical insects that so universally destroy other papers. Another type of paper, called *téla* by Javanese scholars today, produced a much less satisfactory medium for writing, both because its slick, glossy surface does not absorb ink well, and because it is extremely prone to worm damage.

Tree-bark paper was very commonly used for copying both Arabic and Javanese script texts from at least the sixteenth century onward, both in the courts and *pesantren*. From the late eighteenth century, however, the prosperous courts appear to have begun to prefer European paper, and *dluwang* came to be associated with manuscript production in villages and Islamic schools. Some *pesantren* were centers of the production of tree-bark paper, and it has been suggested that the advent of Islam itself may have been responsible for transforming *dluwang* from a rough fabric used in the hair shirts of mountain eremites (as reported in Old Javanese texts) into a writing medium worthy of the sacred Quran.

As Bernard Arps points out, the role of manuscripts as handbooks or scripts for the public recitation of texts is very old, and has been attested in writing for hundreds of years in descriptive passages of narrative texts. In addition, some scribes or copyists have paused from time to time to inject a bit of advice to future gathered audiences, or to instruct the reciters of the text. Their simple advice still lives on the manuscript page. Listen, for example, to the copyist of the manuscript excerpted below. Although it is more verbose than most, the sentiments expressed and phraseology used are standard for manuscripts from all over the regions under the literary influence of Java. This passage comes from the colophon, or closing inscription from the copyist, of the manuscript Or 5072 in the Leiden University Oriental Manuscript Collection, 377–381. This *lontar* manuscript, which originated from Lombok, is written in a handsome Balinese hand. It probably dates from the early nineteenth century. Although the original text is in verse, my English rendering is in prose form and where necessary paraphrased to make it as readable as possible for a contemporary audience.

> When I finished copying this story I went out through the front door of the mosque and sat down beside the well in Sedeg village. It was the feast of Lebaran, and men, women, and little children had flocked to the mosque, filling it to overflowing, to offer their prayers.
>
> It is a week later now as I add these finishing touches. The day is Friday, the eighth of *Sawal* in the year *Bé*. This is the way of figuring months and years in the Arabic and Javanese fashion. And likewise Malay. So there you have it, three ways of reckoning dates.
>
> I have done this writing at the behest of my lord, who told me to copy out one of his palm-leaf books. I myself am a silly, witless old man, the last of my line, a pitiful character without mother, father, kith, or kin. I have learned from my being here—left behind in the world, all alone without relations, marooned, without respect—that I am in every sense a pitiful creature. I say this about myself by virtue of Allah's munificence to his lowly servant, for He has shown it to me.
>
> I fervently beg the mercy of Allah who rules the universe that His gracious love might be vouchsafed me. May our Lord who rules this world grant his boundless favor; as likewise the Prophet He sent; and the angel Gabriel; and the four companions of Muhammad, their lordships Ali, Umar, Usman, and Abubakar; and all the hosts of angels; and the

saints and prophets; and again, those in the world, the religious leaders, the muezzins, the mosque officials, beadles, and scholars.

Now apart from that, you gentleman, officials, and all others who might read this book of mine, please turn your attention to the following matter: as you are reading, be careful not to let your singing be thrown off track. Please be aware that my writing is sometimes deficient, sometimes excessive: if there is a line with too many syllables, drop one out; or if there are too few, don't forget to add what's needed. With luck you won't trip over the melody if you remember this warning. I am giving you this advice because my writing is like chicken scratchings, and I'm afraid that those listening to a performance from this book—young children, women, old men—whoever hears it, will laugh at it, and I'll become an object of scorn. I should also warn you that I know nothing at all about the proper forms of language, not one wit, not one bit. I beseech Allah, who rules the world, the Almighty God, that He might grant my fervent desire: forgiveness for all the sins I committed while still a youth.

Physical evidence provided by manuscripts collected from the countryside confirms the homey message of the colophon above: rarely does one find a book manuscript without shreds of smoking tobacco or bits of snacks or the smudges of greasy thumbs throughout its pages. For palm-leaf manuscripts, which do not retain such droppings, the care and interest of past readers is still evident in the grass or fiber bookmarks twirled through the leaf perforations marking passages that were read in some long-past recitation.

TYPES OF TEXTS

It is impossible to say with much accuracy how many Javanese manuscripts survive today. Public collections in Europe and Indonesia hold about nineteen thousand. This is only a fraction of all extant manuscripts, though: many tens of thousands more are estimated to remain in private hands and small collections throughout Java.

Javanese literary practice, given the harsh realities of the tropical climate, encouraged the regular recopying and recomposing of older texts; as a result, most surviving manuscripts are eighteenth- or nineteenth-century copies, though their texts may be traced back a further one, two, five, or even ten centuries.

But what exactly did the Javanese write about? The Javanese literary tradition was extremely varied, and there is only space here to review all too briefly a few representative genres, particularly divinatory guides (*primbon*), adventure tales, and historical texts.

PRIMBON: JAVANESE TIME AND PRACTICAL GUIDES TO DIVINATION

The first textual category to be discussed consists of numbers of small, handy works that contain the esoteric wisdom (*ngèlmu*) of essentially Javanist lore enriched by both Hinduism and Islam. *Primbon* are compendia of texts relating to this lore, often compiled by individuals over many years, or by families over the space of several generations (fig. 182). No two *primbon* manuscripts contain precisely the same mix and match of texts. Taken as a whole, this genre represents the largest group of popular (as opposed to courtly) texts in the corpus of Javanese literature; the multifarious works that fall under this rubric played a major role in the formation and maintenance of Javanese tradition in daily life both inside and outside the court circles of traditional Java.

Most numerous, and forming the core of this group of texts, are the guides to the complex systems for measuring time and for dealing with its consequences. Time in Java, as in many other parts of the archipelago, is not perceived exclusively

By and large, traditional Javanese works of literature are poetry rather than prose. They are composed in *tembang*, stanzaic verse forms that encompass not only a particular meter but also melodies. The tunes that are part of the verse forms allow the poems to be sung, and indeed the Javanese term usually translated "to read," *maca,* has the original meaning "to voice." In most regions of Java, the sung recitation of traditional poetry is not accompanied by musical instruments. In a traditional setting, interpreting a poem thus means interpreting it as it is carried by the singing voice. Alongside the form and contents of the text, the voice and the execution of the melody are an important part of the literary experience. This inherent musical quality of Javanese literature means that there are also connections with the orchestral music of the *gamelan*. But when *tembang* poetry is sung with the *gamelan*, the wording is subordinate to the voice, while the voice itself is only one among several sources of musical delight.

There are many *tembang* verse forms. About eleven are best known, and each of these has several tunes. Although there are regional differences between these tunes and between singing styles (ranging from slow and florid to very fast, with one tone to each syllable), the melodic outlines of tunes are remarkably stable over different regions. This is so in spite of the fact that the tunes are largely transmitted without the use of notations. They are picked up from hearing others singing; some are used in lullabies, for instance. Since the late nineteenth century, the tunes have also been taught in primary schools.

It comes as no surprise that the reading of traditional verse often takes place before an audience. Prior to the spread of formal Western-style schooling in the late nineteenth and the present centuries, when many were illiterate, listening to others recite was an important way of becoming acquainted with the Javanese literary classics. But even solitary reading usually means singing or at least humming, in contrast to Western norms. When Javanese literature is read for personal pleasure, part of this pleasure is applying a tune to the text of the manuscript and hearing one's own voice.

Because solitary reading, too, means singing aloud, it can easily develop into an informal reading session as relatives or neighbors are attracted by the singing and sit down to listen. In the past, when men went to the rice fields to work for several days at a stretch, they sometimes took a manuscript along to pass the evenings in their shelters out in the fields. Apart from such casual readings, there are also more formal sessions. These too take place in the evening, and they may continue until dawn. They are hosted by an individual or by a village or government-sponsored institution. They can be held in the context of ritual celebrations, especially on the occasion of a birth, but also for a circumcision, wedding, or the inauguration of a new house, as well as for the commemoration of important events such as the birthdays of wealthy people, the Indonesian declaration of independence, or the annual ritual cleansing of a village. For such occasions, the recital of literature is a cheaper and more contemplative, but also less glamorous, way of entertaining guests than other performing arts. In some parts of Java there are reading associations that meet weekly or every thirty-five days, on the eve of a combination of a day of the seven-day week and a day of the Javanese five-day week.

During such formal readings, the participants sit cross-legged on mats facing the center of the host's reception room or the hall of a public building. Food and drink are served to them in the course of the evening. The recitation itself can take two shapes. The first, which is rare at present but was widespread in the past, was a "staged" performance by a professional reciter. The guests listened or chatted among themselves. Such paid reciters were known in the countryside as *dhalang maca* or "reading *dhalang*," *dhalang* being the usual term for the person who performs puppet theater or, in dance drama, coordinates the dance and music and pronounces the narrations. Another term used in some areas was *bujangga*. In ancient Hindu-

The gamelan *orchestra of the Bupati of Blora, Raden Tumenggung Cakranegara. Photograph by Woodbury and Page, c. 1862.*

OPPOSITE PAGE, TOP
Musical annotation for gamelan, detail from Pakem Wirama. *National Library of Indonesia, Jakarta.*

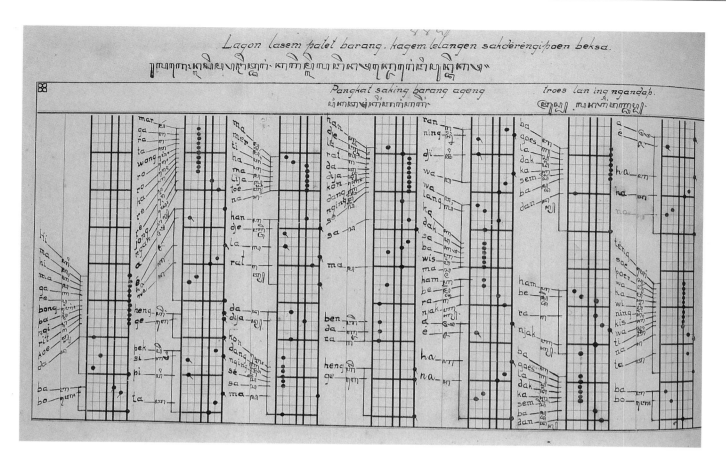

Buddhist times, this was the designation of a religious official and in the later Muslim courts the title of a scholar in charge of the literature department. Aristocratic families often retained a servant especially for reciting to them. In the second type of formal reading session, which is now more common, the performance is shared by the participants, who take turns at singing. The manuscript is passed round the square of reciters on a pillow, or the reciter seats himself behind a low lectern. Each participant recites from a few stanzas to several pages.

Javanese literature was, and is, not read only by the Javanese. Poems written in varieties of the Javanese language are also recited among the Madurese of Madura and East Java, the Balinese of Bali and western Lombok, and the Sasak of central and eastern Lombok, both in staged and shared performances. A special feature here is that the reciter pauses between lines to allow a second performer to provide a translation into the vernacular. This does not happen in Java, even though the poetic language tends to contain many archaic and unfamiliar words and expressions. However, in Central Java some sessions do include group discussion of the work that is being recited.

In the course of the twentieth century, the art of *maca* has died out in most areas. Many factors have played a role in this, among them the desire to modernize society that began around the turn of the century and brought with it Western-inspired kinds of literature (not only in Javanese but also in Indonesian), the disruption of cultural life caused by the Japanese occupation (1942–1945) and the subsequent struggle for independence against the Dutch (1945–1949), as well as the spread of radio, television, and the audiocassette, which have brought alternative ways of spending free evenings. Another factor may be the decline in the production of manuscripts and in the ability to read the Javanese and Arabic scripts in which they are written. Manuscripts are still produced in some places, but only on a very small scale. Printed books and typescripts can of course also be used for reading sessions, and this happens in some places, but on the whole the group recitation of Javanese literature is associated with the use of manuscripts.

In some parts of Java, including the city of Yogyakarta in Central Java and rural Banyuwangi on the eastern tip of the island, reading sessions of traditional literature still take place today. In Yogyakarta the practice was revived in a somewhat modernized form in the late 1960s, after several decades of virtual absence. In Banyuwangi the persistence of reading sessions is mainly due to the ritual importance of the work read: the story of the Islamic prophet Yusup. In neither location can *maca* be said to be a fashionable art form. Its practitioners are small groups of enthusiasts, mostly men in middle age or older. This, however, is nothing new. Javanese literature has always appealed primarily to those who feel a certain detachment from worldly matters, and this feeling tends to surface later in life. But for them, too, its attractiveness has faded.

In other areas where Javanese manuscripts are still in the hands of families rather than museums and libraries, they are kept as *pusaka*, heirlooms, magically powerful legacies from earlier generations. They are wrapped in cloth and incense may be burned near them at auspicious times. This does mean, though, that they are mere material objects that no longer prompt the vocal performance of the texts inscribed on them.

Bernard Arps

as a linear phenomenon. This is not to say that there is no running Javanese calendar: early 1995 falls within the year 1927 *anno javano*. The Javanese year is lunar, meaning it is eleven days shorter than a Western solar year. It shares the twelve months of the Arabic calendar, though it features idiosyncratic intercalation and its starting point is that of the Hindu Çaka era, A.D. 78.

The numbering of years, though, is very much a secondary phenomenon in the overall Javanese view of time. More fundamentally, time is conceived as an interconnected system of repeating cycles of various lengths that mesh together in fixed patterns.

It is useful to picture the network of these temporal cycles turning in tandem as a sort of machine—a large chronometer, if you will—in which gears of different sizes are all interlocked. Each gear corresponds to one of the repeating cyclical units of time: there is a two-day, three-day, four-day week, and so on, up to and including a ten-day week. The number of teeth on a gear is the same as the number of days in the corresponding week. The total possible configurations of the intermeshing teeth of these gears, and therefore the periodicity of the system as a whole, is equal to 10!, or 3,628,800 days. For practical purposes, however, only three of the nine cycles are regularly tracked by the Javanese: that is, the five-, six-, and seven-day weeks, greatly reducing the possible complexity.

The five-day, or market week (*pasaran*, consisting of the days *Pahing, Pon, Wagé, Kliwon, Legi*), intermeshes with the regular seven-day week (*padinan, dina*) to form a month of thirty-five days, called a *salapan*. The *dina-pasaran* combination is the fundamental temporal marker for most purposes in Javanese culture. Even today, many Javanese are fuzzy about the date of their birth (either in the Javanese or Gregorian calendar), but very exact about their *weton*, that is the *dina-pasaran* day of their "coming out" at birth.

By adding the 6-day week (*paringkelan*) to these other two, we arrive at a 210-day cycle, called *pawukon*, that in some respects is similar to an unnumbered, anonymous, ever-repeating year. It consists of thirty 7-day weeks (*wuku*), each of which is named for a character in Javanese legend associated with the king Watu Gunung.

The most import aspect of the *padinan* and *pawukon* systems has to do with divination, the calculus of which is set out in most *primbon*, which provide voluminous tables, charts, guidelines, and prescriptions from which readings of potentially propitious and inauspicious actions may be divined. To begin with, *primbon* indicate that some days are so inherently dangerous that blanket proscriptions have been issued, like standing storm-warnings in a cosmic tornado belt. Tuesday-*Wagé*, Wednesday-*Legi*, Thursday-*Pon*, Saturday-*Kliwon*, and Sunday-*Pahing* are all particularly inauspicious. Major undertakings, journeys, business endeavors, and other risky activities should never be started on these days.

Generally speaking, though, more specific types of taboos and warnings are in effect for the various *padinan*. For example, on Saturday-*Legi* sexual intercourse is categorically forbidden, and couples who ignore this prohibition run the risk of producing a disturbed or mentally handicapped child should conception occur. The *Serat Centhini* offers sympathy but enjoins compliance, pointing out that asceticism always brings rewards.

There is help for unexpected occupations: burglars for instance are advised that operating on Thursday-*Wagé* is likely to lead to being caught and even killed breaking into a house if they enter the target compound from the west, death being almost certain if the break-in takes place between nine and eleven at night. Conversely, making the approach from the east between seven and nine in the evening almost guarantees success. Equitably, other charts instruct those in pursuit of thieves in which direction to chase them, and where to look to reclaim the stolen goods.

Many *primbon* specify Tuesday-*Kliwon* as the day of greatest potential for both good and ill. This is a time of great tidal movement in the realm of spiritual forces, and as such it is an ideal day to perform ascetic acts for accruing preternatural power. Many spells and mantras are only to be uttered on this day, following a period of fasting or abstinence. For example, one spell for gaining popularity with friends, associates, and those in authority calls for three days of white-only abstinence (eating boiled rice, drinking plain water), one day and night of total fasting, a bath and shampoo for ritual cleansing, then the repetition of this formula on the night of Tuesday-*Kliwon* (the italicized lines are in Arabic):

> *In the name of Allah, the merciful, the beneficent,*
> Oh Allah, the gem within our bodies,
> and Muhammad, beloved of Allah,
> created by Allah out of light,
> beloved of all creation
> young and old, male and female, genies,
> spirits and humans,
> and all living things.
> *There is no God but Allah, and Muhammad*
> *is His prophet.*

But Tuesday-*Kliwon* is much more significant than just a good day to pray and make offerings. This is signaled by the fact, among others, that rehearsals and performances of the most sacred heirloom court dance of Surakarta, the *bedhaya ketawang*, are restricted to this one day in each thirty-five-day cycle.

The day is also noteworthy because its absence from a given month of the Javanese year disqualifies that month for the performance of important rituals, including those linked to marriage. This is known as the *Anggara-kasih* rule. As an example, in the current so-called Tuesday calendar, *Jumadilawal* and *Apit* months falling in the octave of *Jimakir* (eighth in an eight-part cycle of years) have no Tuesday-*Kliwon*. Thus, taking the next cycle at the time I write this, no marriages should be entered into during the period September 3 to October 2, 1997, or February 27 to March 28 by adherents of this rule.

An almost endless number of other matters is addressed in Javanese *primbon*. Questions surrounding marriage, compatibility, sexuality, fertility, and pregnancy form a core of concerns that are dealt with at length. The interpretation of omens hidden in dreams, bodily tics, seeing stars, heart palpitations, yawns, ringing in the ears, bird calls, the baying of dogs, shooting stars, earth tremors, and other potential windows into the future are other matters of interest.

In addition to passive divinatory techniques in these and other areas, *primbon* also make potent tools available in the form of mantras, spells, and prayers; mystic symbols for charms and amulets; decoctions, potions, and infusions; liniments, plasters, and unguents.

Apart from divination guides, other text genres that frequently found their way into *primbon* include Islamic catechisms; step-by-step guides to the performance of the five required daily prayers (*pasalatan*); short treatises on issues of Islamic law concerning marriage, fasting, prayer, and the like (*pikih*); textbooks on raising turtledoves, cats, horses (*katuranggan*) and other animals, often containing detailed physiognomic typologies and veterinary pharmacologies; and catalogues of the forms, blade patterns, hilt decorations, and scabbard types of the Javanese dagger, or *kris* (fig. 183, 185). Like the divination texts, these are practical guides dealing with the implementation of principles that have a religious or supernatural significance. Other types of texts often found in *primbon* manuscripts are *piwulang*, or didactic, moralistic treatises, and *suluk*, or mystical discourses of (usually) mixed Islamic and Javanese orientation. Brief sections of certain historical

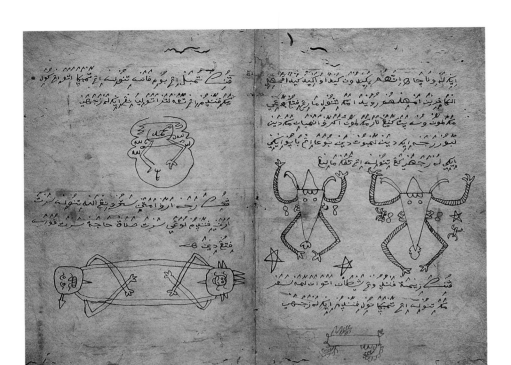

FIGURE 182

A *primbon*. National Library of Indonesia, Jakarta.

chronicles also made their way from time to time into *primbon*. Even more important, the personal histories of the keepers of these manuscripts are sometimes manifest on their end pages and blank spaces. Births, deaths, strange events, unusual or troubling dreams, volcanic eruptions, the succession of rulers and the like are often noted in passing by the owner. Just as the copying of the manuscript was occasionally a matter of several generations' work, so in some cases the accretion of such details occurred over lengthy periods of time, and was recorded in different hands and inks.

BELLES-LETTRES

These works, almost all in the musical meters of *tembang macapat*, fall into the following categories: the multifaceted story cycles based on imported Indian epics; the exploits of Javanese cultural heroes; the martial adventures of Islamic warriors; mystico-picaresque tales of wandering students and mendicant thaumaturges; and marvelous legends borrowed from both indigenous and overseas history.

The Javanese literary tradition did not require poets (the vast majority of whom were anonymous males) to create new stories and characters: their task was much more to hand on the inherited tradition. This they re-presented in the language, style, and poetic manner of the present day and current patron. The result is that there is no single text that can be called the *Ramayana* of Java, for example, or the *Romance of Prince Panji*, but rather a range of recountings of the central tale of Rama and Sita, a plethora of *Panji* texts.

A large number of the works in the literary canon were initially inspired by one of three sources: domestic traditions of storytelling and *wayang* theater, the classical corpus of Old Javanese literature, and foreign texts brought to Java on the tides of South Asian and Middle Eastern religious influence. Perhaps the best-known works are those ultimately derived from the Indian epics *Mahabharata* and *Ramayana*, of which vernacular retellings have been known and loved in Java for more than a thousand years. Their pantheons of deities, galleries of heroes and villains have become so thoroughly domesticated that referring to these stories as imports and adaptations only makes sense in an historically oriented academic context. Indeed, Arjuna, Srikandhi, Gathotkaca, Sembadra, Kresna, Baladewa, and the hundreds of other characters of Indian tradition so well known in Java are

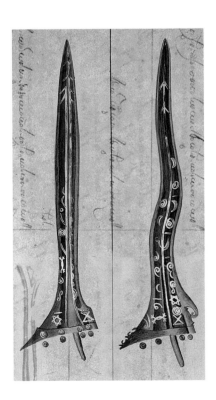

FIGURE 183

Drawings of *kris* from the manuscript *Kawruh Dhuwung*. National Library of Indonesia, Jakarta.

FIGURE 184

A *Serat Yusup* from Palembang. National Library of Indonesia, Jakarta.

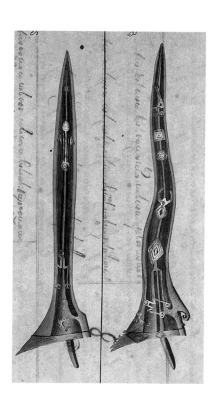

FIGURE 185

More drawings of *kris* from the manuscript *Kawruh Dhuwung*. National Library of Indonesia, Jakarta.

all seen locally to be thoroughly, ineradicably, unequivocally Javanese. This is clear not only from the ubiquitous presence of the epics on the Javanese narrative stage but in their equally strong presence in Javanese history, philosophy, psychology. Royal genealogy, for example, is traced back through Parikesit and the *Pandhawa*; statecraft is analyzed in categories derived from the roles of deities in the epics; even personality types in contemporary Java are understood by analogy to *wayang* characters.

Not only Indian literatures have influenced Javanese, of course. Persian and Arabic tales have also made their way to Java, often via Malay adaptations or translations, and have since been as thoroughly domesticated as the earlier epics. Tales of the prophets, including Joseph, Moses, and of course Muhammad, form a large part of the repertoire of Islamic-oriented literature. So do the adventures of Amir Hamzah (Muhammad's swashbuckling uncle), Iskandar (Alexander the Great of Hellenic antiquity), and countless other figures from the *Arabian Nights,* the Persian *Tuti Nama,* and other sources.

The popularity of the Amir Hamzah stories, known as *Serat Ménak* in Javanese, was particularly great. Indeed, the majority of narrative texts found in manuscripts known to originate from East Javanese villages contain variants of the Amir Hamzah stories or their offshoots. An entire genre of *wayang golèk* plays, as well as minor adaptations within the shadow-puppet theater *(wayang ménak)* further attest to the popularity of the *Ménak.*

The familiar story of Joseph in Egypt is another adaptation of great popularity in Java (fig. 184). Known eponymously as the *Yusup* romance, one version of this tale retains an important place in the cultural life of Banyuwangi district in far-eastern Java, as well as on the nearby island of Lombok. Professor Bernard Arps of Leiden University has written in depth about this literary phenomenon.

Besides the several types of romances adapted from foreign sources detailed above, large numbers of texts also represent poetic renditions of native Javanese legends. Many of these are semihistorical in character and treat of heroes associated with past kingdoms of Java, such as the numerous *Panji* tales already referred to, the adventures of *Damar Wulan,* the *Calon Arang,* and others. Many of these same stories and characters are featured in the oral tradition, especially in the puppet-theater performances known as *wayang gedhog, wayang klithik,* and *wayang madya,* as well as in dance and drama traditions as the *tari golek* of Yogyakarta and *langendriyan* of the Mangkunagaran.

One of the most popular Javanese works of literature is a narrative poem (in *tembang*) about the Islamic prophet Yusuf, known as Yusup in Javanese. Versions of this originally Middle Eastern story are found not only in the Bible and the Quran, but also in literary works in Persian, Arabic, and other languages. It is not known with certainty where and when it was first rendered into Javanese. There are indications that one widespread Javanese version was produced on the north coast of East Java in the early seventeenth century. It is likely that it is adapted from a work in Malay. This particular version is still recited today in East Java and in Lombok.

Some Javanese versions of the story of Yusup cover his whole life, others only up to his ascension of the throne of Egypt. The story is found separately in a work called *Lontar Yusup* or *Serat Yusup*, and as part of compendia of stories about the prophets of Islam, from Adam to Muhammad.

Manuscripts of the story of Yusup are found in many libraries in Indonesia and abroad. Public collections in the Netherlands alone contain almost two hundred copies, which suggests that thousands of Yusup manuscripts are in existence. Many of them are on *lontar* palm leaves and originate from East Java and Madura. These seem to have been written mostly in the second half of the nineteenth and the early decades of the twentieth century. Manuscripts are also known from West Java, the Central Javanese courts, the north coast of Java, Lombok, and other parts of Indonesia. They include not only *lontar* but also paper manuscripts, and some of them are written in Arabic script rather than the Javanese script used with *lontar*.

The story of Yusup begins in Canaan when, at the age of twelve, he sees in a dream how the sun, the moon, and eleven stars bow before him. His father Yakub (Jacob) explains that these represent his parents and his brothers: sometime in the future they will pay obeisance to him. Jealous of Yusup, the brothers attempt to kill him, but thanks to God's intervention they end up throwing him alive into a well, where he is found by an Egyptian merchant. The merchant sells Yusup to the king of Egypt, whose wife, Jaléha or Jaléka, falls in love with him. When she attempts to seduce him, he is greatly tempted, but God sends His messenger, the angel Jabrail (Gabriel). Yusup, realizing that he is about to commit a great sin, flees. The king arrives and Jaléha claims that Yusup has attempted to violate her. Although it becomes clear that Jaléha's version of the story is false, the king has no choice but to imprison Yusup.

Yusup remains incarcerated for many years. At one point Jabrail arrives and gives Yusup a diamond, which he swallows. The diamond signifies the ability to interpret dreams. Yusup gives successful interpretations of several of his fellow prisoners' dreams. Eventually the king himself has a dream, which even his court scholars cannot clarify. He summons Yusup, who explains that it signifies the coming of seven years of plenty followed by seven years of famine. During the years of plenty, the king should store as much rice as possible. The king is greatly impressed by Yusup. A year later he abdicates and declares Yusup his successor. The land of Egypt prospers under Yusup's rule.

Some manuscripts end at his point in the story. Others go on to describe how Jaléha is rejuvenated and married to Yusup.

A Serat Yusuf *of Madurese origin. Sonobudoyo Museum, Yogyakarta.*

During the years of famine, Egypt, which has remained prosperous, is visited by Yusup's brothers who have set out from Canaan to look for food. The king's identity is eventually revealed to them, and as foretold many years before, his relatives pay obeisance to him. Many years later, Yusup passes away.

Scholars have pointed out that in several ways, especially with regard to his physical attractiveness, the character of Yusup parallels non-Islamic Javanese heroes such as Prince Panji and Prince Arjuna, who both feature prominently in literature and theater. While this may have been important for his popularity in Java, Yusup also has another side, and that is his connection with Islam. The motif of his beauty is not a Javanese modification but referred to in the Quran (as well as the Bible) and he is in fact known as the epitome of male beauty throughout the Muslim world. Another point highlighted in the Javanese work is Yusup's closeness to God, who, in what may be a seventeenth-century version of the poem, is named with pre-Islamic Javanese names rather than Allah. There is continual stress on conversion to Islam through Yusup's mediation and on God's ability, again by means of Yusup, to destroy idols. This version of Yusup's story contains numerous asides drawing parallels between events in the narrative and Islamic doctrines, and the reciters and listeners are repeatedly urged to heed the story's message. All of this makes it likely that it was rendered into Javanese to spread and reinforce knowledge of Islam.

The Yusup poem has developed into more than a tool of Islamization. Versions of it are still known and recited in parts of Java, Madura, and Lombok. The hero's closeness to God makes the recitation of his biography eminently suitable for seeking his mediation with God. The abundance of manuscripts from late-nineteenth- to early-twentieth-century East Java may point to a surge of interest in him during this period. As is known from the present situation in Banyuwangi, East Java, as well as from descriptions of earlier practices elsewhere in East and Central Java, a number of ritual acts—frowned upon by those who give a more purist interpretation to Islam—have become attached to the recitation of the Yusup poem. In Banyuwangi, for instance, where it is sung in all-night sessions up to the point where Yusup becomes king of Egypt, the climax of the performance is the preparation of "purifying water" that takes place around midnight. Another example, found in Banyuwangi and elsewhere in East Java, is the practice of *ngugem* (literally "to put one's trust in someone or something"), a kind of bibliomancy in which a solution to pressing questions and problems is derived from the text. When the recitation is complete, the person who wants a question answered places some money in the manuscript without looking where. The manuscript is opened and the passage on which the money is found is interpreted with reference to the problem. This usage may

Page from a Serat Yusup *originating from Pakubuwana IV's royal scriptorium. Sonobudoyo Museum, Yogyakarta.*

have been inspired by the recurring motif of the successful explanation of dreams about future events (done by others, too, but by Yusup in particular). Recitations may even be commissioned to make *ngugem* possible.

The Banyuwangi case shows how important the practice of recitation, especially when it has strong religious connotations, can be for the continuation of a manuscript tradition. In Banyuwangi, new copies of Yusup manuscripts are still produced for use in reading sessions and for practicing recitation privately. They are written on paper and in the Arabic script, as they have been in Banyuwangi for at least a century. But time does not stand still: they are now written with a felt-tip pen rather than pen and ink.

Bernard Arps

One remarkable feature of all the genres mentioned above is that in language, narrative style, plot architecture, and characterization models these texts are barely distinguishable from one another, except for the particularism imparted by the specific names of heroes and kingdoms, the geographical settings, and the iconographic particulars associated with the religious and cultural context of each hero.

CHRONICLING THE JAVANESE PAST

Another family of texts comprises the chronicles, known generally under the name of *babad*, a term referring to the clearing of jungle that accompanied the expansion of human civilization in tropical Java. The *babad* might be divided into four general categories: legendary histories, chronicles of events, chronogram timelines, and genealogies, though many texts incorporate two or three of these elements in a single composition. Royal genealogies, for instance, begin with Adam's issue, work through generations of Judeo-Christian figures including Noah, Moses, Isa (Jesus), and Muhammad on the right-hand line of descent, and through Hindu deities and epic heroes on the left-hand line, before they enter the firmer ground of historical progeniture in the Mataram dynasty of the sixteenth century. The same blend of legend and event is presented in the comprehensive histories of Java and the world, called *Babad Tanah Jawi*, that begin, like Genesis, in the Chaos (*awang-uwung*) preceding Allah's creation of the world *ex nihilo* (or *kun fa yakun* in this Islamic version), proceed with rice myths and other components of indigenous creation stories, the peopling of Java, the Golden Age, and so forth, continue on with early legendary kingdoms of ogres, genies, and men, but eventually refocus on the historical events (often still accompanied by preternatural occurrences) leading up to the establishment of Mataram and its history.

The all-encompassing range of the *Babad Tanah Jawi* is repeated in a few other texts, but most historical texts deal with a more limited time span, such as the period of Islamization and early Muslim kingdoms, the first stages of the Mataram dynasty, the Kartasura period and its bloody end in the wake of the Chinese massacres, the mid-eighteenth-century warfare that led to the division of the realm into the rival courts of Surakarta and Yogyakarta, or the subsequent history of each of those kingdoms, sometimes in overview, sometimes in minute detail. Some noteworthy events—rebellions, wars, uprisings, exilings—have generated highly focused, personalized, historically detailed *babad*, often composed by or about the chief protagonists. In some cases, such as the Java War led by Diponegoro (1825–1830), several independent reports, with different perspectives on the same events, were produced.

The vast majority of historical texts were composed in *tembang* meters until the middle of the nineteenth century. At that time, R. Ng. Ranggawarsita, the court poet of Surakarta, composed in prose a huge, multivolume series that brought together the various threads of Javanese history and mythology, ordering them into a new system of chronology.

In addition to the types of historical texts mentioned above, there existed a parallel tradition of chronogram time lines (*Babad Sengkala*) recording significant events from given years in the Javanese past. Some lists go year by year, others skip dozens or even hundreds of years at the beginning of the time line, but get more detailed as they approach the time of composition. The years on the time line are identified with cryptic ciphers, or chronograms, in which ordinary words that have been assigned a numeric value (often listed in *primbon* manuscripts) are arranged to form a year-date, read from right to left. Words relating to man, god, earth, moon, and ruler (among many others) have the value one; those referring to sight, arms, legs, hearing have the value two; fire, war, knowledge, woman indicate three; and so forth. Thus the chronogram *Destroyed* (0) *Vanished* (0) is the *Prosperity* (4) of the *World* (1) gives the year 1400, the date (*anno javano*) traditionally ascribed to the fall of the great Majapahit empire. The chronogram may refer to events in the encrypted year, as in this case, but they are as often as not neutral or nonsensical if read as text rather than surrogate numerals. The chronogram may list salient occurrences in the indicated years—from grave matters of state to the shenanigans of a young monarch flying kites in the palace forecourt. Both prose and *tembang* versions of these lists are known.

OTHER TYPES OF TEXTS

Many other genres have gone unmentioned: architectural handbooks; compilations of the law; books dedicated to language matters, including lexicons and lists of antiquated words, popular and mystic etymologies, keys to riddles and language puzzles, thesauri of wise sayings, and practical guides to composition and the rules of prosody; music notation and theory; libretti and stage instructions for performances of sacred court dances and dance dramas, often with corrections, emendations, and changes made by a choreographer or dance master; a vast range of *wayang* materials, from technical guides to puppet tooling and the practical concerns of lighting and staging to brief résumés of hundreds of play plots, or expanded presentations of a single play with full expositions on musical accompaniment and puppet movements; allegorical tales and courtly romans à clef, some of which may have been composed as magical tools to circumvent the cosmically determined limitations on the political lifespan of a given court; adaptations in *tembang* meters of classic Chinese tales; animal fables, some of which were written as political allegory; prophecies associated with the Javanese king Jayabaya that extend hundreds of years into the future and are eagerly sought after and quoted—like those of Nostradamus in the West—at every political shudder or tremor today. The list could go on and on. Clearly, the Javanese are a people and a culture within which the book and written forms of knowledge played a central role long before the tardy advent of print technology in the archipelago.

THE ILLUSTRATED MANUSCRIPT

Only a very small number of Javanese manuscripts that survive and can be consulted—that is to say, manuscripts dating from the mid-seventeenth through early twentieth century—are illustrated. To hazard a rough guess, perhaps one in thirty manuscripts containing narrative texts is accompanied by figural drawings depicting scenes out of the story. Given the dominant place of Islam in Java, one might speculate that the well-known Islamic strictures against depicting the human form in art inhibited illustration here as in other arts. But while this may be true in the broadest sense for Java, as a whole, it is nevertheless also a fact that manuscripts containing Islamic stories, including self-consciously pious recountings of the sacred history of the Prophet, are at least as likely to be illustrated as non-Islamic texts.

Representations of human and animal forms have been well known and appreciated throughout Java for many centuries, most familiarly in the form of *wayang kulit*, the flat buffalo-hide shadow puppets. *Wayang* are also known in other forms—three-dimensional carved wooden puppets (*wayang golek*) and flat painted wooden puppets (*wayang krucil, wayang klithik*), for example. Bas-relief *wayang* figures are also a common decorative motif on carved wooden *kris* boards.

Hundreds of characters populate the *wayang* universe, and a highly articulated iconography of dress, stance, facial expression, coloring, attributes, hair styles, even fingernail length was developed to differentiate the individuals and types within this large cast of characters that were usually, though by no means exclusively, observed as flickering black silhouettes on the bright white *kelir* screen.

One particular type of *wayang*, the *wayang beber* theater, attested from at least the year 1416, was not performed with puppets at all, but was delivered in

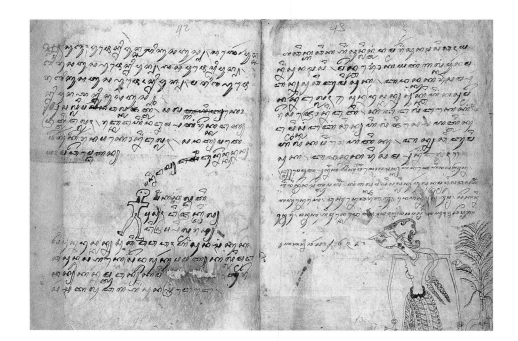

FIGURE 186

Depiction of Bathara Maharesi, the god
associated with the eighth week of the
wuku cycle mentioned in the text as part
of the birthdate of Prince Nalatruna of
Surakarta. Possibly copied in Surakarta,
c. 1766. National Library of Indonesia,
Indonesia.

raconteurial style by a *dhalang* (narrator) explicating pictures on a series of
dluwang scrolls wound out bit by bit as the story developed. The *wayang* characters on these scrolls are illustrated in the same style, and employ the same iconography, as the shadow puppets, and may represent an important link between
wayang art and manuscript illustration.

The first surviving examples of illustrated Javanese manuscripts date from the
eighteenth century. The style of illustration used in them is reminiscent of the
familiar *wayang* style of the *beber* scrolls. This general style continued to dominate
manuscript illustrations until the apparent demise of the tradition about the time
of the Second World War. Within this general style, however, there flourished a
substantial amount of variation in everything from the type of sketching implements used to issues of coloring, outlining, texture, degree of detail, quality of
flatness or naturalness within the *wayang* aesthetic, density of secondary figures
and nonfigural elements, relationship of illustration to narrative, titling and label-
ing of scenes, and just about everything else related to the process of picturing in
recognizable and entertaining form the events described in the flowing text.

One is struck upon first examining Javanese manuscripts by the degree of
variation in the ability and craft of illustrators working at roughly the same time,
often at no great geographical distance from one another. In manuscripts such as
that shown in figure 186 the human forms are flat, dull, and atrophied, mimicking
the rudimentary conventions of puppet tooling but delivering no life in the
process. The relative spiritlessness of the figures is exacerbated by their bare outline form, uncolored and unshaded, and by the lack of background decoration or
enlivening secondary figures, furnishings, and other such visual fill. Structurally,
illustrations of this sort seem to have been lifted directly from the *wayang* screen,
which projects only the central actors of a given scene, providing all other details
of place and mood by the *dhalangs'* narrative, voice, music, and puppetry skills.

A roughly contemporaneous manuscript of a *Serat Rama* from Madura, seen
in figure 187, presents *wayang*-style illustrations reduced to their most primitive
form. One can hardly speak of the conventions of puppet tooling here, since only
the headdresses and elbow articulation of these figures are unmistakably *wayang*-
esque: for the rest, their aesthetic and technique is primitive. In this unusual
example, there is no setting-apart or framing of the scene depicted. One other
anomalous example of primitivist *wayang* illustration is shown in figure 188. Once
again the shapes are *wayang*-esque in only their most fundamental graphic features,

FIGURE 187

Martial audience scene from a Madurese adaptation of part of the *Ramayana*, called *Serat Rama*. Copied in Madura, possibly in the mid-1700s. Sonobudoyo Museum, Yogyakarta.

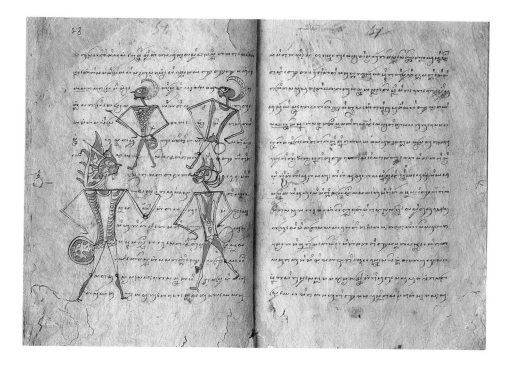

particularly facial profile. This example is particularly noteworthy because it comes not from a manuscript containing text but from a packet of materials that may once have accompanied a *primbon*. It appears to be a sort of planchette or divination board, and might have been used in conjunction with dice for probing the future.

Figure 189 contains a more advanced example of village-style illustration whose merits, despite the obvious artistic effort made by the illustrator, lie elsewhere than in its purely aesthetic accomplishment. Although the battle scenes here are enlivened with some color and the portrayal of action, the figural quality remains quite rudimentary. Even so, the stiff *wayang* style is here rudely transcended by the (unnatural) plasticity of the arms and legs of the *wayang*-esque figures. Captions have been included to inform the reader whom the figures are meant to represent.

The crude and parochial style represented here reflects the distance of the rural literary scene from the centers of culture, art, wealth, and international styles, as well as certain technical limitations and other problems. Paper, even of the local beaten-bark sort, was rare and relatively expensive until the twentieth century, and had always to be used sparingly. The paper shortage was so endemic, in fact, that one of the salient features of village manuscripts is their extremely dense and complex use of the manuscript page. As previously noted, every unfilled space was subsequently crammed with notes recording births, deaths, omens, and other important events, personal reflections on religious and practical matters, jottings of sums, debts, and figures, and even, on occasion, alphanumeric exercises. In addition, large numbers of manuscripts also include rough practice figures, inevitably drawn in *wayang* style, usually of very poor quality. One can almost feel the would-be artists or illustrators struggling with circumstances that made gaining expertise and mastering the medium next to impossible.

Where paper was more plentiful and readily available, however, and access to the currents and stimuli of urban or court life more common, the sophistication of the illustrator rose accordingly. The manuscript shown in figure 191 offers a good example of the north-coastal urban tradition. Copied around 1845 in one of the districts east of Semarang, this manuscript of the *Angling Darma* romance is illustrated with dozens of attractive yet simple pictures. Most maintain the minimalist style of the *wayang* screen, with little or no background or details of place.

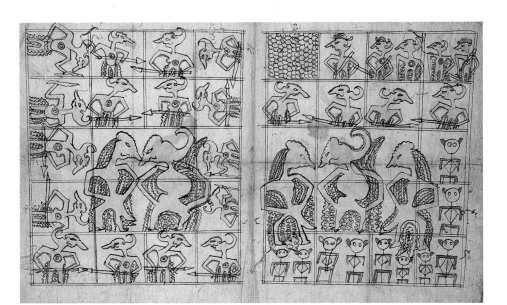

FIGURE 188

Wayang figures drawn in the "fate" squares of a divination board. Possibly copied near Cirebon in the mid-eighteenth century. National Library of Indonesia, Jakarta.

FIGURE 189

A battle scene from the historical romance *Jaransari Jaranpurnama*. West Java; mid-nineteenth century; European paper. National Library of Indonesia, Jakarta.

The characters, though, are carefully executed, and wonderfully colored in bright natural paints and gold leaf. They have the appearance almost of actual *wayang* puppets set down on the page, though with a more fluid line and vigorous presence, since they are freed from the stiffening discipline of the *gapit* grip-stick. One wonders if these are not the products of a professional *wayang* maker, given the careful details of coif, attire, and body ornaments.

A similar style, though considerably less deft, can be observed in figure 190, which contains a story adapted from the *wayang gedhog* called *Panji Déwakusuma Kembar*. Once again, rather vivacious puppet figures engaged in scenes of discourse or battle are placed on the flat page, though here the addition of a floor-like colored platform under the figures hints at the possibility of three dimensions. This manuscript is also less opulently colored and has no gold leaf, suggesting that it came from a less wealthy sphere than the previous example. This is further supported by the interesting details contained in the *mukadimah*, or introduction to the text. This manuscript, with its dozens of vivid illustrations, was made around the year 1850 by one Bagus Sarodin of Sekayu village near Semarang. Sarodin ran a manuscript lending library as a sideline (his main occupation was as foreman in a brickworks), and his intention in making the copy was to rent it out to neighbors and friends at 15 *sen* a night. Illustrations, apparently included to attract more customers than competing libraries, are more common in Javanese manuscripts

FIGURE 190

Semar gives advice to Prabu Tunjung Mirah Kumalawati in *Dewakusuma Kembar*. Copied near Semarang by Bagus Sarodin, c. 1850. National Library of Indonesia, Jakarta.

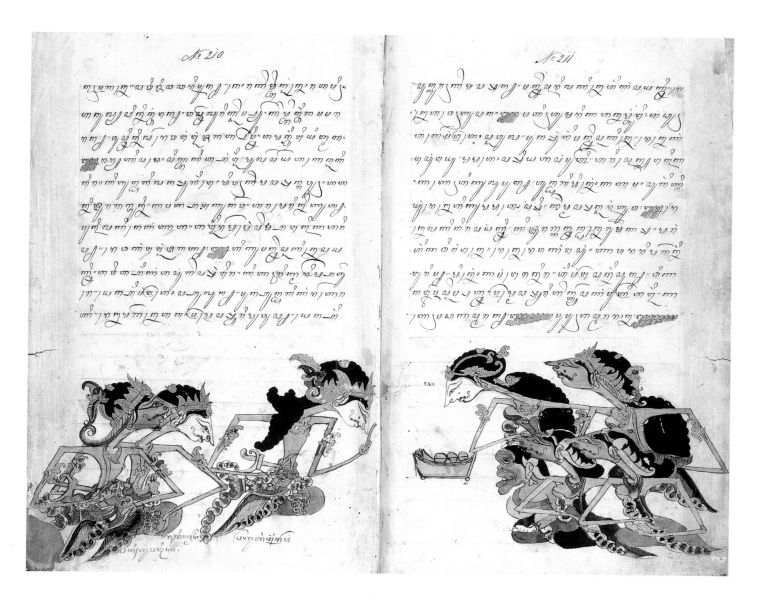

FIGURE 191

A scene from the *Serat Angling Darma* in which the eponymous hero tries to win the hand of Ken Trusilawati. North coast of Central Java, c. 1845. National Library of Indonesia, Jakarta.

known to have been hired out than in other manuscripts. (This is not only true of Javanese manuscripts. Malay manuscripts circulating in lending libraries also used this strategy to boost popularity.)

Lending manuscripts—not for cash, but free, as a neighborly deed—seems to have been a common practice among Javanese everywhere before the advent of the cash economy. Such manuscripts were often disfigured by oil, betel, or cigarette butts, and their readers might even use them for pillows. No wonder Sarodin made the plea in another of his copies that his borrowers take extra care with these lending manuscripts: "My request to those who wish to read this—forgive me for even mentioning it—is that you not read while chewing betel, lest spittle get on it, nor while smoking, to avoid burn marks or worse." While this is very much a standard admonition found in manuscripts throughout the Javanese region, it takes on special force for manuscripts rented out and used to win a family's daily bread.

Not all *wayang*-style illustrations adhered as faithfully to the white-screen aesthetic of the backlit *kelir* as the examples depicted above. Some manuscripts exhibit a real blossoming of the artistic imagination, in which the picture does not simply show puppets as against a *wayang* screen: instead, they depict a fully visualized scene in which the characters just happen to have the form of puppets. Thus the manuscript pictured in figure 192, another midcentury, north-coast example of a *Panji* romance, places its figures in gardens, jungles, seas, and other locales that are sometimes limned with great gusto and exuberance. The figures

themselves, though extremely *wayang*-esque, are notable for the absence of outlining. Normally, a *wayang*-style figure is drawn in outline, then filled in with
appropriate colors, that is, the colors used in the iconography of the character. In
this manuscript, however, the human figures are often free of the ink armature
into which most *wayang* figures are molded, and the colors used for skin tone
often ignore the codes of puppet painting entirely.

The outdoor scene shown here presents a frightened princess of Jenggala in
an overwhelmingly animated jungle seething with botanical life and crawling with
threatening animals like the wild boar and ravenous tiger. The flora and fauna,
being largely free of the stylistic strictures of *wayang* puppetry, are much more
freely drawn than the human figure of the princess. While we do not see real naturalism in these attempts, there is certainly movement in the direction of naturalistic forms. At the same time, the general vividness of the scene strongly recalls the
comparatively rich background textures of the *wayang beber* scrolls mentioned
earlier, and perhaps even of the sinuously animated world of the Candi Panataran
reliefs of eastern Java. In both cases, the styles are purely Javanese.

Not all the illustrations in this manuscript are accomplished with the same
deftness. The quartet of ministers pictured sailing the sea on page 504 of the manuscript, to choose just one example, seems a caricature in which the uncompro-
mising and overlapping stiffness of the figures overwhelms and nearly sinks a
strangely static ship drawn to Lilliputian dimensions in order to fit on a single
page (fig. 194). A twentieth-century trimming of the book for rebinding rendered
the scene even more claustrophobic. Yet even here the slow evolution of the
wayang style is clearly visible as the artist attempts to address the vast potential
offered by paper and paints and to move away from the aesthetic parsimony of the
bare screen.

One inspiration or motivation for stylistic change in manuscript illustration
was the presence of European art and ideas in the Javanese world. Though usually
it is indirect and subtle, a direct and compelling Western influence on artistic
style can be detected in a small number of manuscripts. One striking example is

FIGURE 192

Pages from the richly illuminated manuscript *Serat Panji Jayakusuma*. North coast,
c. 1840. National Library of Indonesia,
Jakarta.

FIGURE 193

Dutch officers receiving a message from the raja of Blambangan. Detail from a historical text. National Library of Indonesia, Jakarta.

FIGURE 194

Another scene from the *Serat Panji Jayakusuma* in figure 192. Copied on the north coast, c. 1840. National Library of Indonesia, Jakarta.

the manuscript shown in figure 193, a *Babad Blambangan* with eight relatively naturalistic illustrations in its pages. The text, copied and/or written in November 1774, recounts the bloody warfare taking place in the easternmost Javanese state, Blambangan. Although the composition of the depicted episodes reminds one clearly of the audience scenes so frequent in *wayang*-style illustration, the figures are portrayed as rounded beings struggling to inhabit three dimensions. The break with tradition is particularly notable in the articulation of limbs, and human portraiture in three-quarter profile. It is unclear who produced this early manuscript, though it seems to show Dutch influence. The illustrator had an especially keen eye—as one would expect in a fine *wayang* stylist—for the garb of his subjects, depicting soldiers, for example, in recognizably French uniforms.

Another possible source of Western influences was through Dutch scholars who collected Javanese manuscripts in search of information on local customs. Where no existing genre covered the area under investigation, new works were commissioned, leading to the creation of new genres. The heyday of such writing was the 1920s and '30s, and information gained in this style would sometimes make its way into government archives and Dutch journals. Often, too, the same reports, or ones similar to them, were published and circulated to a wider readership in the guise of vernacular how-to, instructional, or general-knowledge books.

But this practice began long before the 1920s. From the early nineteenth century, native informants on the fringes of European society and trained to produce materials in line with the needs of Dutch scholars were already active. One of the more productive of these Javanese reporters was Mas Ngabèhi Kramaprawira of Madiun. During the period c. 1868–1885 he produced several compilations of moralistic material, as well as handbooks on geography, agriculture, and other subjects, some of which were later published in Batavia. In addition to his writing talent, Kramaprawira was also an accomplished sketch artist, and his handbooks are liberally illustrated. There is no stylistic clue in the simple naturalism of his sketches that the artist is Javanese. But what if he had been illustrating a traditional narrative tale in *tembang* meters, and not an innovative scientific report in prose? Would his renditions have been so insistently naturalistic? Perhaps Kramaprawira exemplifies one of the routes by which Western techniques of perspective, shading, point of view, and so on from time to time crossed the gap and made an appearance in Javanese illustration.

In some manuscripts a hybrid, three-dimensional style appeared, called by some the *Jaka Tingkir* style of illustration. In this very rare style it is not the flat *wayang kulit* puppets, but the round, wooden *wayang golek* puppets that form the primary figural models. Only a small number of manuscripts has been identified

FIGURE 195

Ki Asmarasupi battles Buta Bégol's gang
of man-eating ogres in this episode from a
Serat Asmarasupi. Copied in Yogyakarta,
1893, by Cakradiharja. National Library of
Indonesia, Jakarta.

in which this style is used, and it is uncertain where it arose, how productive it
was, and why it seems to have died out. When we look at the only example available at the time of this writing, it seems that this style may have represented a min-
gling of Western interest in volume on the one hand with the sensibilities of
wayang iconography and white-screen aesthetic on the other. The scene depicted
in figure 227 shows a style of composition and degree of realism similar to other
mid-nineteenth century *wayang* illustrations described above. The sole difference
between figure 194 and figure 227 lies in the attempted roundness, attributable to
the authority of the *golek* model over the *kulit* in the former.

But the examples above are rare exceptions among the great preponderance
of illustrated manuscripts that continued to employ variations of flat *wayang* styles
until the demise of the manuscript tradition in the second quarter of the twentieth century. Batavia, Cirebon, Semarang, and Yogyakarta each produced numerous examples of illustrated manuscripts in the familiar styles, though with varying
degrees of loosening-up of the *wayang* norms.

The surviving manuscripts seem to suggest that the greatest leeway in this stylistic liberalization existed for noncentral characters. Three types of figures—mon-
sters, ogres, goblins, and the like; the human servants of right-side protagonists;
and assorted forest and domestic animals—were often portrayed with fully developed, somewhat naturalistic limbs, rather than the oddly elongated arms, extruded
fingers, and angular joints characteristic of the central human characters. This feature in itself was a natural outgrowth of the *wayang* tradition in which what
limited naturalism there was found expression in the forms of just those unnatural
creatures mentioned above. Figure 196 shows two ogres routed in battle from a
Batavian *Ménak Jobin* dated 1862 and probably originating in a lending library.
Ignoring the peculiarities of hunched backs and vampire teeth, we see that this pair
has a robust presence on the page as they perform some sort of angry jig of defeat.
The fresh jasmine buds worn in their ears add to the comic but sympathetic effect.

Figure 195 offers a good contrast between the relative naturalism of human
beings and ogres. For all the caricature of these wheel-eyed, tusky nightmares on

"Two Ogres Routed," detail from a manuscript of the *Ménak Jobin.* Copied for Ki Amat Sari in Krukut (Batavia), by Abdullah, 1862. National Library of Indonesia, Jakarta.

A scene from a *Serat Bratayudha* produced in the palace of Sultan Hamengku Buwana VII. Copied in Yogyakarta, 1902–1903. Widya Budaya collection, Kraton Yogyakarta.

the attack, the treatment of their bodies, limbs, coifs, and coloring is much truer to paunchy human naturalism than is the abstracted, heroic figure of Ki Asmarasupi who stands so calmly in their midst. The philosophical attitude underlying this contrast may be that ogres are seen as creatures of the wild, and their dharma includes and demands raw violence. Beasts and growing things partake of untamed nature. Representational naturalism is therefore appropriate for ogres, wild boar, casuarina trees. But humans possess or should possess culture, behavioral norms, and spiritual wisdom that set them apart from nature. The more refined an individual becomes, the more civilized, the wiser, then the more removed she becomes from the givens and strictures of nature. A wise woman will know the hour of her death long before it arrives; a man advanced in spiritual discipline will obtain powers that grant flight through the air. These achievements are the negation of naturalism. In *wayang* iconography, the less formally human a character appears, the more fully human he actually is in moral terms.

This aesthetic, advanced hypothetically, seems to be at work as well in manuscript illustration. Its observance allowed the portrayal of nature, beasts, servants, and physical props to move in the direction of formal realism while delaying, or even denying, development of human realism.

The ultimate expression of this postulated aesthetic, realized with the highest degree of local artistry and the finest materials available, was likely achieved in the palace of the Sultan of Yogyakarta. Between August 7, 1902, and May 14, 1903, under the patronage of the Crown Prince K.G.P.A.A. Mengkunegara II, an illustrated copy of an older manuscript of the *Serat Bratayudha* (a nineteenth-century retelling of the Bharatayuddha tale) was made (fig. 197). The copy was set in elephant-folio sheeves of extra-thick art paper. Text was subordinated to illustration.

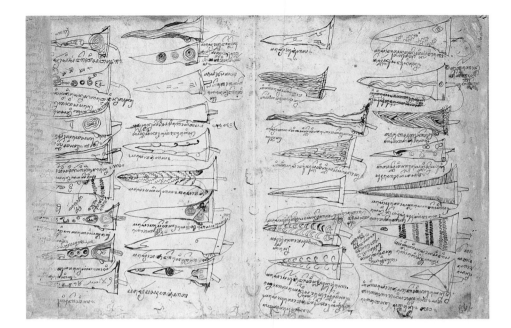

FIGURE 198

Kris blade types and nickeling patterns in
a record belonging to a family from
Surakarta. Central Java, c. 1800. National
Library of Indonesia, Jakarta.

Each page had four to eight lines of text at the top, but around 85 percent of the
writing space was reserved for the pictures: 242 of them altogether, in rich polychrome watercolors and gold leaf, every one spread across an open, double folio
field of approximately 56 x 45 centimeters.

All human and humanoid figures in this manuscript are depicted in an especially detailed and extravagant *wayang* style, prominently outlined, then colored
according to puppet-making conventions. The result is not breathing characters
represented by *wayang*-esque drawings, but rather, puppets, pure and simple,
emphatically flat, intentionally constructed to look like tooled leather with no hint
of living flesh. Yet these remote, classical images of two dimensions are forced by
the inventive skill of the artists to inhabit a fat and lurid three-dimensional world.
In this realm of proportion, depth, and perspective there are dramatic landscapes,
bloodstained fields, falling shadows, scaled and architecturally detailed edifices,
the regalia of legendary kingdoms, droves of realistic, at times almost snapshot-
perfect, animals—in short, a fully realized universe of natural forms, tools, settings. The characters, unnatural by virtue of their civilization, arranged in ascend-
ing ranks of formal abstractness by their degree of moral achievement, insert
themselves into slots in this naturalistic space-time, but remain foreign within it,
expatriates from another plane.

The Javanese aesthetic that served effectively to limit naturalistic illustration
to lesser creatures and inanimate objects was conducive to the development of
several related genres of texts that, in the end, were always illustrated. Most of
these genres, though, are fairly recent, appearing only in the late nineteenth century or early twentieth, and were generally only produced in royal or aristocratic
houses. One, however, is considerably older and had wide general appeal in village as well as city and court: the *Kawruh Dhuwung*, or handbooks concerning the
Javanese dagger (*kris*). The *kris* has an ancient history and complex lore. One
aspect of *kris* lore deals with the technical terminology for blade types and nickeling patterns (*pamor*). At least from the eighteenth century, and probably much
earlier, texts dealing with this terminology frequently incorporated rough diagrams
for clarity's sake. Over the decades, and particularly in the *kraton*, the quality of
illustration improved markedly. Figure 198 shows a simple folk-style compilation
of assorted blades, dated c. 1800, from a Central Javanese village under the juris-
diction of Surakarta; this page is the only section of the manuscript (a *primbon*)
that has such illustrations. Figure 199, by contrast, is one of more than sixty pages
from a manuscript dedicated solely to presenting a systematic typology of *kris*

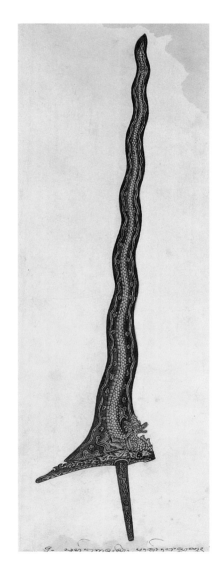

FIGURE 199

Drawing of a *kris* blade from the collection of the Sultan of Yogyakarta. Copied
at the Kraton Yogyakarta, undated. Widya
Budaya collection, Kraton Yogyakarta.

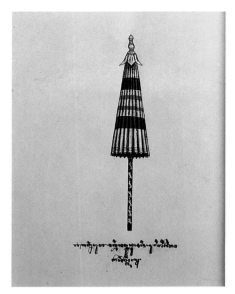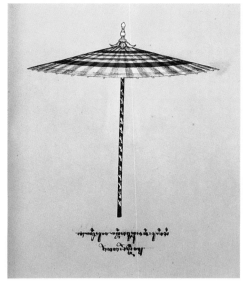

FIGURE 200

Reproductions of the *songsong* style assigned to a high Yogyakarta official. No others were authorized to bear this particular pattern or combination of colors. Copied at the Kraton Yogyakarta, c. 1930. Widya Budaya collection, Kraton Yogyakarta.

FIGURE 201

A *Serat Pawukon*. Sonobudoyo Museum, Yogyakarta.

blades and *pamor* patterns. It originates from the sultan's palace, Yogyakarta, probably late nineteenth century.

The most lavish handbooks on the *kris* originated in the *kraton*, of course. There, in addition to general typologies of *kris*, illustrated inventories were sometimes made of heirloom weapons collected in the royal armoury and treasure rooms. Such an inventory of *kris*, swords, pikes, lances, halberds, arrows, and other *tosan aji*—most of which were considered to be magical, or to have and confer special powers—was made of the Yogyakarta collection on order of Hamengku Buwana V in 1854, though the illustrations to this versified text seem to have gone missing in 1943. Other illustrated lists and inventories were also kept in the palaces. Included among the items thus surveyed are types of umbrellas of rank (*songsong*), (fig. 200), flags and standards, headgear, garments, batik patterns governed by sumptuary laws (*awisan dalem*), and much more.

Finally, several sorts of texts that normally appear in the *primbon* manuscripts discussed earlier are generally furnished with nonnarrative illustrations. Most notable are the *pawukon*, or calendrical charts for the thirty-week *wuku* year used in many types of divination. Each of the thirty *wuku* has a ruling deity, a minor deity, and a number of material attributes associated with it, including a tree, a building, a bird, a drink, a weapon. Manuscripts illustrating these deities and attributes are fairly numerous, and run the spectrum from the simplest tracings in outline form to stunningly sumptuous two- and four-page spreads decorated with exquisite detail and design. The *wayang*-style illustrations found in *pawukon* are exactly cognate to those used in narrative texts (fig. 201).

Many manuscripts also have divinatory tools in the form of tables and charts that are used to address specific situations involving business undertakings, thievery, the recovery of stolen goods, the planning of special events, and so on. Some of these charts, such as the *rajamuka* wheels depicted below (figs. 202, 203), are decorated with small figures representing personified attributes of fate.

Numerological charts frequently provide information on the movements of the *naga* or snake-dragon so that humans can plan their own travels to begin in a direction other than that taken by the *naga*. The example below has the caption "Movement of the Seven-Day Snake," and shows the snake under way (fig. 205). By way of observation, the *naga* is also a frequent character in *wayang*, and its representation on paper is always constrained by the conventions of *wayang* stylistics.

The *naga* also makes an occasional appearance among *rajah*, or figures to be used in spells that require magical drawings. The *primbon* usually have sections of two to five pages containing such drawings, the contexts in which they are to be

 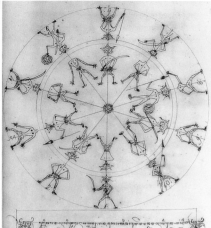

FIGURE 202

Far left: A *rajamuka* wheel, used for reducing complex words and formulas to their basic numeric identity for purposes of divination. National Library of Indonesia, Jakarta.

FIGURE 203

Left: Another *rajamuka* wheel. National Library of Indonesia, Jakarta.

used, and the other components that are required to make efficacious spells. Such figures—which normally have Arabic letters written on them, or may in fact consist entirely of Arabic letters and symbols—may be written on a piece of paper, which is then stuck to, or worn on, some part of the body or clothing. They may also be variously used in other rituals (figs. 204, 206).

ILLUMINATION AND CALLIGRAPHY AS ARTISTIC IMAGE

As already mentioned, illustration of Javanese manuscripts was exceptional: only in certain limited genres (such as *pawukon* texts) was it usual. Illumination, on the other hand, was extremely common, and must be considered a specific trait of the Javanese tradition, since there are almost no manuscripts that do not display at least some illuminatory features. As with illustration, this is an aspect of the Javanese manuscript tradition that has not yet been studied. The short observations that follow, like those that preceded, must therefore be seen as impressionistic and provisional.

By illumination is meant the brightening or enhancing of the page through the use of special lettering techniques, coloring patterns, decorative embellishments, or other devices. In Javanese the words used to refer to the beautification of the written page include *sunggingan* (embellished by painting) or *rerenggan* (decorated, adorned). Taken together, there are five common classes of illuminatory devices that may be found in Javanese manuscripts. I have listed them below in order of my impression of their relative frequency for the manuscript tradition taken as a whole: punctuation, enframing and textual gateways, rubrication, cursive calligraphy, and pictorial calligraphy.

PUNCTUATION

In addition to the nugatory dots, dashes, short lines, quick curves, and other bits and pieces that measure out and manage the running line of text as it moves down a manuscript page, Javanese has developed two special forms of punctuation that boldly stand out and call for attention. Though a variety of names applies to the various forms of each one, together they are known as *pepadan*, or metrical markers. We can distinguish between them here by calling one class the little *pada* and the other the large *pada*. Together they function to mark metrically significant points in the text, thereby helping the reciter keep his melodic place as he sings. A little *pada* marks the end of a stanza of poetry (occurring every thirty-two to eighty-four syllables, depending on the meter), while the large *pada* signifies a change of cantos—and therefore of the meter, melody, and mood of the recitation—and usually appears every five to ten pages, though this may vary considerably, depending on the structure of the text.

FIGURE 204

Magical figures, or *rajah*, to be used as part of certain spells. National Library of Indonesia, Jakarta.

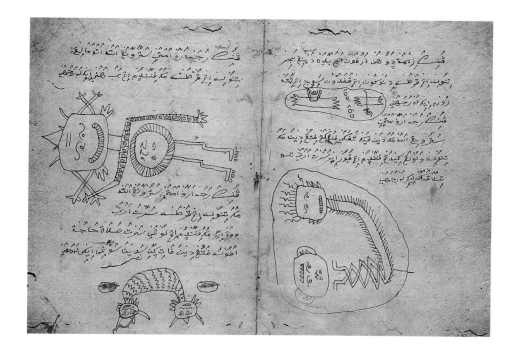

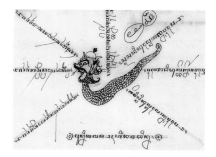

FIGURE 205

Above: A depiction of the *nagadina* ("seven-day snake") and explanations of the directions in which it lurks. Central Java, early twentieth century. National Library of Indonesia, Jakarta.

FIGURE 206

Below: One of hundreds of *rajah* figures from a *primbon* that was probably used by a *dukun*, or magic specialist, as a spell book. National Library of Indonesia, Jakarta.

What I have called little *pada* are in fact biggish when compared with regular letters, usually extending above and below the *aksara* line used for plain text, and taking up more lateral space along its axis. This makes them stand out on the manuscript page and provides a pattern for the eye, however analphabetic in Javanese. Big *pada*, which are often composed in part of several small *pada* strung together with additional marks and signs, can be so long that they fill one or two entire lines of script. The untrained eye easily sees them cutting across a page and dividing it into two parts. Any typical manuscript will have several thousands of small *pada*, and several dozen of the large (see fig. 184).

Pepadan are important for the student of Javanese manuscripts because they required a disproportionate investment of scribal time and energy to produce and because they are highly stylized in typical ways that are easy to identify, thus offering a quick key to dating and region. They are equally important to lovers of Javanese design and art, as they represent rare, deliquescent nodes of linear beauty into which the graphic skill and harmonizing aesthetic of the copyist have been carefully distilled and preserved.

The shapes of little *pada* are most reserved in palm-leaf manuscripts, where they often take the form of a simple double slash mark, a set of two double slashes, or a set of double slashes with a small circle drawn in the center. In *pégon* manuscripts they also tend to show a good deal of reserve, taking the form of a circle with a red dot in the center or of a simple rosette dotted or highlighted in red. By contrast, most book-style, Javanese-script manuscripts use some adaptation of a four-character cluster that reads *ma-nga-ja-pa*, a presumed variation on a word meaning "to long for, wish, or desire," and that has been interpreted by some to mean something like "let your desire lead you on to the next stanza." Others have interpreted it to mean different things, including an injunction to make a wish, presumably of the sort we make when blowing out birthday candles.

nga
ma
ja
pa

The shape of this character cluster varied substantially from place to place and era to era, at times sending a sedate squiggle of tendril high up over the line, at others growing leaves at its base or sending a profusion of spidery-fine gossamer vines climbing and bending in all directions, perhaps sprouting wing-like petals in their ascent. In other places it was not botanical motifs that were used but geometric ones, sometimes spiky, sometimes stepping up like small ladders, sometimes taking on an Islamic tone by employing triple-tittles borrowed from Arabic script. In its most exuberant manifestations, the little *pada* display elaborate, zoo-botanical hybrids in which an elephant head, a swimming fish, a flying bird appear sprouting from a dense patch of tendrils and shoots.

Often colored or highlighted in polychrome paints, each *pada* could become a miniature platform for displaying the illustrator's skill at penning and painting. Sometimes this art contained encoded visual references that related to the cryptic cognomens of the various *tembang* meters. In such cases the shape of the *pada* would change from canto to canto, assuming, for example, the shape of a bird in a *dhandhanggula* passage (*dhandhang* being a literary word for "crow"), then metamorphosing into goldfish for the *maskumambang* meter (the name of which means "gold adrift in the waves"), and so forth.

Figure 207 shows a medley of little *pada* from the past two centuries, mostly from manuscripts of Central Javanese provenance. One can imagine the time that must have been consumed creating the botanically inspired *pepadan* wonders of Pakubuwana IV's royal scriptorium at the turn of the nineteenth century, in Surakarta. The *Serat Yusup* that figure 184 comes from features more than 2,350 filigreed devices of this sort. If it is assumed that a very practiced hand could turn out one of these *pada* in just five minutes, then more than 195 hours, or forty 5-hour days of unbroken artwork would have gone into the stanza markers alone of this 54-canto text.

Another interesting case is that of figure 208, from a Yogyakarta manuscript roughly contemporaneous with the Paku Buwana IV example. In this case, however, the copyist or patron of the manuscript, who by some tantalizing but inconclusive indications may have been a European, initiated the time-saving measure of creating an ink stamp in the form of the little *pada* of the Yogya court of the period. The same patron also created numerous other stamps, including several whole-page-sized ones for large *wadana*, seven small ones bearing the astrological signs for the days of the week (used in a calendrical treatise), and the bulbous-nosed, solar-headed Ngayogyakarta angel.

The forms assumed by large *pada*, which are much longer than the little *pada*, evidence even greater variation, though in every case strong generic traits tie the shape of the large and small *pepadan* together. These canto markers are usually called *madyapada* because of their intermediate (*madya*) positioning between cantos, and often contain a word or phrase at their center that indicates the meter of the new canto. This is particularly the case in *lontar* manuscripts from the east, and in manuscripts originating along the north coast. In the Central Javanese areas under the influence of Surakarta and Yogyakarta, highly stylized letter clusters take the place of meter names, which are hidden instead in literary hints and clues in the text of the final line of the previous canto. Handbooks often distinguish between the proper forms of true *madyapada*, and the large *pada* that appear not between cantos but at the opening and closing pages of a text or manuscript. For most practical purposes, though, they are essentially the same in most parts of Java.

The most beautiful of these *madyapada* may well be those of the Pakualaman, the junior court of Yogyakarta established in 1812. A leading figure in the aesthetic and literary life of that court in the mid-nineteenth century, Prince B.P.H. Suryanagara played a major role in the refinement and elaboration of Yogyakarta manuscript illumination. Among his contributions was an artistic guide in which a finely distinguished typology of *pepadan* and other embellishing features was prescribed for use in illuminated texts.

FIGURE 207

An assortment of little *pada*. *Above:* a Yogyakarta manuscript dated c. 1810. Library of the Faculty of Letters, University of Indonesia, Jakarta; *middle:* a Yogyakarta manuscript dated c. 1815. National Library of Indonesia, Jakarta; *below:* a Kartasura manuscript dated 1717. National Library of Indonesia, Jakarta.

FIGURE 208

Stamped figure of an angel from a *Serat Pawukon*, a treatise on Javanese calendars. Copied in Yogyakarta, c. 1810. Library of the Faculty of Letters, University of Indonesia, Jakarta.

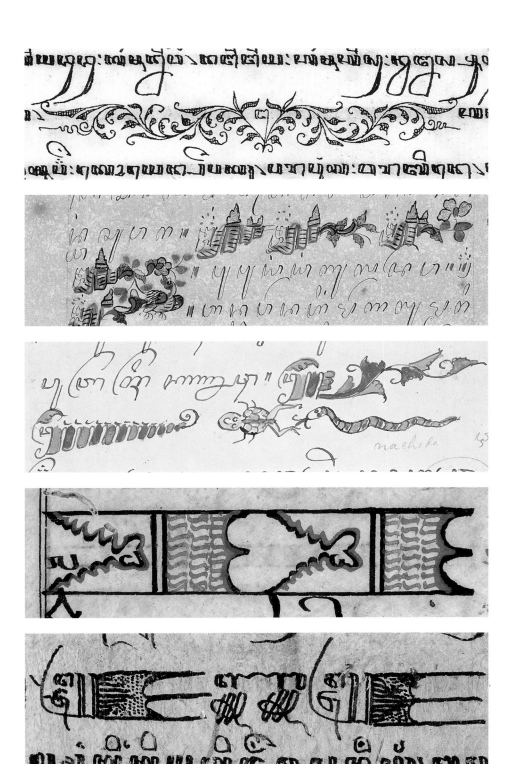

The assortment of *madyapada* arranged in figure 209 represents only a tiny sampling of the multifarious forms encountered. Among the most entertaining of this group are the north-coastal animal friezes incorporated in many *madyapada* decorating lending-library and other urban manuscripts, particularly those copied or circulating in the Chinese community.

ENFRAMING AND TEXTUAL GATEWAYS

From early times, in book-style manuscripts using both Javanese and *pégon* script, simple devices were sometimes used to frame the text on the manuscript page. This helped define and control the writing field, at the same time adding an attractive visual element to the page. At times page frames would be elaborated on the opening and closing pages of a manuscript, becoming ornamental frontispieces, called *wadana*, that acted as monumental gateways giving access to the inner pages

FIGURE 210

Simple frontispiece from a Madurese manuscript, *Sarasilahipun Nabi Adam dumugi
Prabu Watu Gunung*. Copied in Madura,
possibly in the early nineteenth century.
Sonobudoyo Museum, Yogyakarta.

of the text, then leading out of that sacred textual space at the end. It is in these
ornamental gates that Javanese illumination reached its most spectacular heights,
creating page-high patterns of complex, interlocking, geometric designs that mesmerize the eye, or intricate temple-like structures supporting symbols, figures, or
calligraphy that rivet the attention or delight the fancy.

At its simplest, the page frame is just that. It consists of a series of lines—single, double, triple, quadruple—surrounding the writing space on a given page.
Sometimes every page of a manuscript was framed in this way, though more frequently it was only the first few and the last. The lines were sometimes colored
with gilt or paint or filled with a geometric pattern (fig. 211). Figure 210 shows a
page frame elaborately filled with batik-style decorations and studded with round,
leering faces.

In this last case, the faces in the border can trace their genealogy back to the
ancient *kala-makara* faces and figures that are so prominent as guardians on the
gates, doorways, chamber entrances, and sculptural niches of Old Javanese temples
(*candi*) going back to the eighth century. Figure 212 has an even more explicit
replication of the monstrous guardian head flanked by two chthonic entities ready
to frighten away all dangers. At the top of the *wadana,* the *kala* has been replaced
by a crown, while the *makara* are represented by two *naga.* Two ogres repeat the
makara motif on either side of the text box, while a fanged monster and two dogs
fill the same role on the base of the structure. The identification of this *wadana*
with *candi* architecture is made more specific by the silhouette of the figure, by its
prominent base, and by the long vertical patterns containing floral work.

Figure 213 shows a *wadana* in which the *candi* identification is even more
explicitly portrayed by the use of heavy cornices and brickwork patterns in the
base. It should be noted that *kala* heads, or *kala-makara* combinations, are not
restricted to ancient temples: they are also familiar in modern Java in *wayang*
iconography, where they are placed in the headdresses of certain characters, and
above the door to the divine world located at the center of the *kayon* symbol. In
both contexts they are associated with thresholds, liminal margins, the passage by
which one passes from secular to sacred space.

The artistry of the *candi*-like *wadana* was studiously developed and codified
by the same manuscript artists operating under Prince Suryanagara of Yogyakarta
who had created and compiled the typology of *pepadan* mentioned in the previous

FIGURE 211

Frontispiece of a *Serat Ménak Yasadipuran*
manuscript authored by the eighteenth-
century Surakarta court poet, Yasadipura
I. Copied in 1897, north coast.
Sonobudoyo Museum, Yogyakarta.

FIGURE 212

Candi-like *wadana* in a copy of the *Serat Tajusalatin*, a study of behavior and statecraft. Copied in the Jayakusuman household, Pakualaman, Yogyakarta, 1841. Sonobudoyo Museum, Yogyakarta.

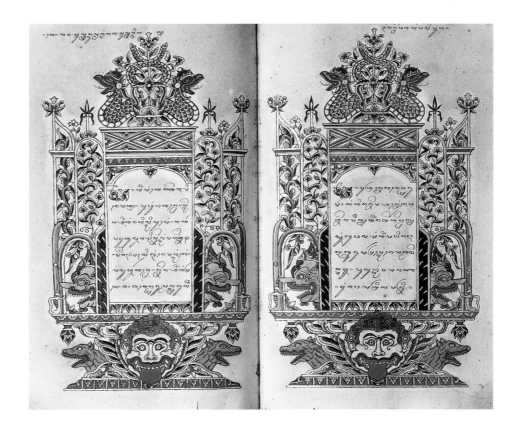

FIGURE 213

Candi-like frontispiece from the story *Srikandhi Meguru Manah*. Copied in Pekalongan, c. 1890. National Library of Indonesia, Jakarta.

section. Under this code, *wadana* styles had descriptive names that reflected the type of decorative fillips added to the basic frame and pattern. Figure 214, with a flattened, oblongish text field squared off in a *wadana* decorated in floral motifs, is called "*parang kusuma* decoration" in the artist's own caption, the name deriving from the floral batik pattern of the same name. Other examples are known that are dedicated to clear themes or images: there are nautical *wadana* equipped with prows, sails, oars, and such; martial *wadana* hung with arsenals of firearms (including huge cannons) or bladed weapons; *wadana* resembling zoological gardens, and so forth. Some have distinctly Western decorative features. One late but interesting example, commissioned by Sultan Hamengku Buwana VIII as a gift to the Royal Batavian Society for Arts and Sciences, is found at the beginning of a book on the *gamelan* music of Yogyakarta copied in parallel pages of Javanese and Latin script. This *wadana* is festooned with musical instruments (fig. 215).

Besides the type of frontispiece described above, there was a second style, probably older and certainly more widespread, whose appearance was far more abstract than the architecturally inspired composition of the *candi*-like Yogyakarta *wadana*. Frames of this style are found not only in Java but as far away as Aceh on Sumatra's northern tip, and are often used to illuminate copies of the Quran.

Among the distinguishing features of this style are its tendency to fill an entire page with decorative motifs, rather than create a distinct outline or image—such as a *candi* or gate—on the page; the use of dense, usually angular, geometric designs built up in series or layers to form a complex rectangular foundation; and the use of secondary designs, usually geometric but often curved rather than angular, that protrude from the four sides of the text box at the center of these patterns. Figure 184 is a beautiful eighteenth-century example of this art at its best. The foundation layer is filled with migrating angular lines that imitate deep-relief carving motifs, but present them in a warped, almost vertiginous, skewing of plumb that leads the viewer in circles trying to find their true square. A minimally bowed rhombus brimming with densely laced vines transects the rectangular base, resting on its outer lines and creating thereby the four protrusions typical of this style. Above this are two smaller rectangles aligned with the base pattern. The

FIGURE 216

Wadana from the allegorical *Serat Suryaraja* of Sultan Hamengku Buwana II, Yogyakarta. Copied in Yogyakarta, 1815–1817. National Library of Indonesia, Jakarta.

FIGURE 214

Opposite page, above: Frontispiece from a compilation of edifying tales entitled *Cariyos Aneh-aneh* (Strange stories). Copied in Yogyakarta, c. 1852. Sonobudoyo Museum, Yogyakarta.

FIGURE 215

Opposite page, below: Musical *wadana* from the *Pakem Wirama* compilation of Yogyakarta traditional *gamelan* pieces. Copied in Yogyakarta, 1932. National Library of Indonesia, Jakarta.

first, lying athwart the parallelogram, is filled with similar vegetative lacework, while the second contains the text in a long, narrow space that reminds one of a lens drawing and magnifying the words from some deep hidden spot.

The manuscript depicted in figure 216, dated 1817 and originating from Yogyakarta, is an unusual example of a book in which there are not one or two sets of *wadana*, but many. Though some are of the *candi* type, most share the abstract attributes pictured here. The pattern is of such a layered, geometric complexity that it cannot easily be described. It carries a sense of having been woven, and in fact resembles a Persian rug. The facing pages of this spread are treated as a single field, so the text boxes are placed right next to each other, almost against the central margin imposed by the gutter, rather than in the centers of the separate pages. The protrusions—in this case rounded and compound—consequently make up one set, rather than two. The somewhat later manuscript pictured in figure 217 is a variation on the themes found in the previous example, but assembled in a much less dense style.

Not all examples of *wadana* come from the courts. Figure 218 exhibits the principal hallmarks of the geometric style, but does so without the density of composition displayed in the palace manuscripts. In place of that hypergeometric density and minutely drawn fill, this manuscript substitutes loosely strung garlands that effectively disguise the relative sparsity of design.

At other times, the need for economy, perhaps, produced truncated versions of *wadana* of both schools. Figure 219 shows frontispieces and endpieces in which

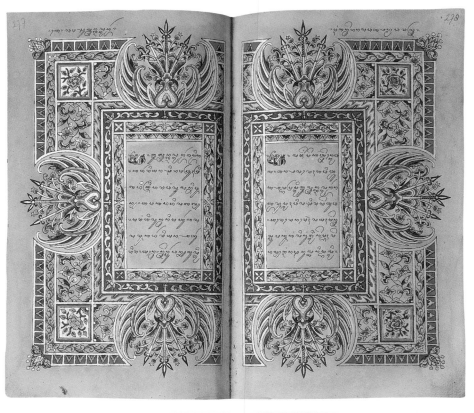

——— FIGURE 217 ———

Above: Wadana from a *Serat Tajusalatin*.
Copied in the Jayakusuman household,
Pakualaman, Yogyakarta, 1841.
Sonobudoyo Museum, Yogyakarta.

——— FIGURE 218 ———

Below: Frontispiece from a manuscript of
the *Ménak Jobin* copied for Ki Amat Sari
in Batavia in 1862. National Library of
Indonesia, Jakarta.

only the relevant portion of the frame remains: the top part for the opening page,
the bottom for the end.

   One last example of the enframing impetus in Javanese manuscript illumination is shown in figure 220. Here, small cartouches or decorated boxes containing
brief notes about the contents are placed in the outer margins of a text. The two
notes in this example respectively introduce section XV of a treatise on statecraft,
and indicate that an example from the life of Sultan Umar is about to be related.
In Javanese manuscripts, these devices are found almost exclusively in the products of the Pakualaman and Suryanagaran schools in mid-nineteenth-century

FIGURE 219

Half-page frames from a manuscript of the
Syarah Al-Iman. National Library of
Indonesia, Jakarta.

FIGURE 220

Marginal box for a subject caption in a
copy of the *Serat Tajusalatin*. Copied in
Yogyakarta, 1841. Sonobudoyo Museum,
Yogyakarta.

Yogyakarta. They are rather more common in Arabic religious texts, and one assumes that the Yogyakartan adaptations were modeled after these exemplars.

RUBRICATION

The original use of the word *rubrication* had to do with the marking in red of letters, words, or titles meant to stand out on the illuminated pages of medieval manuscripts. As used with respect to Javanese manuscripts, rubrication is not restricted to the color red, but to any embellishing of structural elements of letters and devices involving the use of colors, usually by means of gilding, paint, ink, or colored pencils. The round or hollow shapes of certain of the vowel marks and other "clothing" added to basic characters are quite conducive to filling or coloring in this way, particularly the signs for the /i/, /ə/, and /u/ sounds, and for the sound "killer" (*patèn*) for free-standing words ending in consonants. *Pepadan* are also full of curves and curlicues that attract the illuminator's colors. In many cases only the first few pages of a manuscript are rubricated, giving a festive and grand entrée to the text—especially when it is through the gates of a *wadana*—though after five to ten pages it often slacks off or disappears entirely.

The north-coast lending-library manuscripts featured in figures 194 and 196 display the tendency of this family of manuscripts to have full rubrication, usually in red and green or red and yellow, and usually running the full length of the text. *Kraton* manuscripts sometimes are rubricated with rich golden gilding, giving every page extra weight in the turning, and the dull shine of gold (see figs. 29, 30). Once again, the most wonderful examples of rubrication are found in the Yogyakarta and Pakualaman manuscripts decorated in the Suryanagaran style with red, white, blue, and gilt highlights in both *aksara* and *sandhangan*, as well as *pepadan* and *wadana*. One variation on this theme is to go whole hog and make all the writing in a manuscript one vast gilded sea of sinuous golden ink. The results are somewhat disappointing, however, as the low contrast between white page and gold writing makes it difficult to read these texts, and the flaky character of the gold in the ink tends to produce writing that is rather quickly damaged.

Rubrication is also widely used in Islamic texts, and in Arabic script or *pégon* manuscripts generally. In religious works, quotations from the Quran and the Hadith are often rendered in wonderful red inks, while the commentary and interpretation are delivered in staid shades of black. One interesting variation on this theme is a phenomenon observed with most frequency in Yogyakarta, where manuscripts may be copied in Javanese script except for the names of Allah and his prophets, which are reproduced in Arabic script, either using red ink or black. A parallel usage, found exclusively in Yogyakarta, has the names of Allah, prophets, or the clue words that reveal the meter of a new canto, written in cryptics, though the rest of the text is in standard Javanese. In these special uses of both Arabic

script and encrypted Javanese, a distinctive kind of writing, rather than a bright color, creates the same highlighting effect as rubrication or gilding.

CURSIVE CALLIGRAPHY

Javanese manuscripts may be written calligraphically, that is to say, with carefully crafted, fine, and beautiful lettering. However, examples of Javanese-script calligraphy, almost exclusively, tend to originate in the palaces, particularly of Central Java, while Arabic-script examples come from both palace and *pesantren*. In both cases, the fundamental requirement for beautiful writing to arise as an artistic tradition was a cadre of professional scribes, full-time workers in the labor of manuscript copying and adornment. Out of their work easily identifiable stylistic schools of calligraphy arose over time. Only in the large pools of talent available in these institutions was there scope for the exceptional hand to be identified and trained to the required standards, and only in a professionalized scriptorium operating with minimal restraints on time and supplies was there a context for the development and maintenance of the high artistic standards that identify and typify these schools. Arabic-script calligraphy was an import to the region, tuned and adjusted by the passage of materials and experts between Java and other centers of the Islamic world. For Javanese script, on the other hand, the development of the tradition was a purely local phenomenon, though of course the presence of the high Arabic tradition was both an inspiration and source of ideas for Javanese calligraphers.

Despite differences in style and tradition, there are certain hallmarks that generally set apart calligraphic Javanese manuscripts. One such trait is the balanced, uncluttered use of the page, without crowding of lines or pinching of margins. *Wadana* and framing graphics are often used as tools to guide and ensure symmetry. Regular line length is an important aspect of this symmetry as well, and the calligrapher has to carefully manage the flowing line of text by appropriately squeezing or stretching characters and intersticial spaces. It is the appearance of each character and line, and of the page as a whole, that is the ultimate concern of the calligrapher, and so—ideally—there are no smudges, crossouts, overwriting, or formal mistakes apparent in these manuscripts. For the same reason, rubrication and elaborate use of *pepadan* are also common embellishing features for the color and texture they impart to the textual page-as-image.

PICTORIAL CALLIGRAPHY

In Javanese manuscripts it is extremely rare, but always a delight, to come across examples of pictorial calligraphy in which decorative devices or animal figures are created by manipulating and contorting the lettering of a selected text in either Arabic or Javanese script. This impetus is not restricted to manuscripts. Many mosques throughout Java have decorative wood panels, plaques, or cartouches in which the *shahadah, basmallah*, or other Islamic formulas are carved in deep relief. At times the writing is plain to read, but the more rounded or compacted or abstracted it grows, the more difficult the thread of text becomes to follow and interpret. At some point the effort required to decipher the message becomes too great for most viewers, and the geometric or botanic or zoomorphic complexity of the script-motif takes over as the primary visual impression. We know there is a text hidden in there, and can make out a few letters, but the hidden text will only yield to intense, up-close scrutiny. In this situation the very act of distinguishing the textual content from the figural beauty of the design, and of decoding its secret wisdom, becomes a metaphor for the mystic quest of finding Allah amid the display and splendor of creation.

Arabic calligraphy tending in this mystico-metaphorical direction—though still within the bounds of primary textualism and far removed from true abstrac-

tion or pictorialism—is often found in the frontispieces of Quranic and other religious texts copied in Java, as elsewhere. A parallel phenomenon in Javanese script is also seen on rare occasions in the crowns of *wadana*. In both cases the writing may appear in balloon letters set in negative relief (fig. 221).

In Cirebon, however, at least in the early through mid-nineteenth century, there was a full-blown tradition of true figural calligraphy. This is attested not only in a small number of manuscripts, but in numerous ornamental wood carvings and wall panels in the various *kraton* of the city. The favored forms for this calligraphic art are all zoomorphic: birds of various sorts, elephants (recalling the Hindu god Ganesa), tigers, and deer. There does not seem to be a direct connection between the forms created, or even the simple existence of the forms, and the text of the manuscripts in which they appear. Rather, they seem to be the creations of an individual making use of blank space found in preexisting manuscripts. It is not possible to tell how long after the copying of the main text of the manuscripts the calligraphy was added, or who did the work. The identity of the calligrapher, however, may be disguised in the text of his figures (fig. 222).

This introduction to the world of Javanese manuscripts has been necessarily truncated by the limits of space; hampered by the crucial absence of earlier scholarship; and always and in every detail constrained by the availability of photographs and accidents of authorial memory and experience that the explanatory text has been pegged on. Yet despite these challenges and limitations, the images, colors, and lines of the illustrations and illuminations that stand on these pages testify to a bookmaking, text-building aesthetic in which the norms of a creative, sometimes brilliant, tradition reveal themselves. Three intertwining strands of this tradition have been mentioned as being governed by somewhat different principles, or operating under dissimilar circumstances, so that at least three subgroupings of Javanese book arts have been adumbrated: village, urban, and palace or *kraton*. (The place of the *langgar* or *pesantren*, Islamic schools and colleges, in this scheme is somewhere on the cusp between village and urban. Or rather, the *pesantren* continuum stretches from the middle of the village to the middle of the urban, with some schools operating in the isolation of the village, while others functioned with the same urbanity as the international ports of the north-coastal cities whose children they served.)

Each sphere has its own characteristics. Village productions are typified by a lack of technical sophistication in materials and methods, a general artlessness, an overwhelming simplicity of style, and a surprisingly limited range of texts. The focus of the village tradition was local, its orientation popular. It is not surprising that the majority of manuscripts bearing the village mark are of a practical nature, either used to support the pursuit of daily needs in the hard-scrabble, subsistence lifestyle of the peasant—as in the lore-laden compilations of *primbon* wisdom—or to structure the public ritual life of the struggling community—as in the *Serat Yusup* performances with accompanying bibliomantic and other applications.

The urban manuscript tradition, reacting to the same forces that gave rise to the cities themselves, was much more permeable to external influences and developed in part in response to market dynamics. The materials used were of international standard and origin, typically European paper; and the texts recorded in them were also quite frequently of foreign provenance. The cash economy of the cities gave rise to manuscript production and distribution as a purely monetary undertaking as well, and in the process, driven by the engines of competition among lending libraries, saw the most widespread flourishing of Javanese illustrational art of the nineteenth century. A congruent development appears to have occurred in the circles of leading merchant families and other wealthy sophisticates, perhaps as a form of intraclass social competition for the display of wealth.

In the *kraton* all developments of both urban and rural traditions were regularly monitored and, as appropriate, incorporated in the most sophisticated, professionalized, and aesthetically driven of the three traditions. The position of the manuscript, and literature generally, in court society was given special prominence owing to the enabling abundance of wealth, as well as the supporting tradition of artistic and literary patronage as necessary expressions of the sovereign's prestige and power. Outside the palaces there existed little stability, continuity, or articulation of knowledge in the literary arts, with the result that clear trends of stylistic development occurred haphazardly at best. Within the palaces, by contrast, stylistic conventions were much more codified into schools and traditions and styles. Within the royal scriptoria it is possible to observe patterns of evolutionary change rather than the desultory charges ahead, reinventions, and nonproductive individualistic interpretations of the urban sphere. The familial and political ties binding the Javanese *kraton* together, and the regular flow of manuscripts as gifts and dowers among them, also created avenues for the dissemination of styles and changes throughout a system of scribal centers. This contrasts with the chaotic congeries of individual villages—peasants doubling as copyists from time to time as need arose—among whom no large-scale organization, aesthetic tradition, or possibility for wide communication of any sort obtained, and for whom the silent, frozen exemplar was the major representative of canonical standards.

The exploration of these three aspects of the Javanese manuscript tradition has hardly begun. The intellectual and practical challenges that further study holds are numerous. In the meantime, though, this chapter offers readers the simple enjoyment of beholding reproductions taken directly from the manuscripts. And the eloquence of these images speaks for itself.

T.E. Behrend

A LEGACY OF TWO HOMELANDS:
CHINESE MANUSCRIPT LITERATURE

By the sixteenth century in China, popular literature had already begun to achieve wide circulation through xylographic printing, that is, by using carved wooden blocks of pearwood or the like. These books, printed in China, circulated among the Chinese overseas as well. When the Dutch first made contact with Java in 1595–1598, they noticed that Chinese printed books were available there (fig. 223). A copy of the historical romance, *Shuihu zhuan* (Water margin), was brought back to Europe, though only one page of this copy now survives. Chinese settlers naturally sought these books from their home regions. Several bookshops popular fiction are known to have been active in Fujian from the sixteenth century. The circulation of their books among Chinese in Java began a pattern extending into the nineteenth century, when the bulk of Chinese printed books used in Indonesia were imported from the publishing houses in Fujian and Shanghai. For those who could read Chinese, cheap printed literature was readily available.

But in fact, until the late nineteenth century, not many of the Chinese living in Indonesia could read Chinese. The reason for this was noted by Wang Dahai, a Chinese tutor who worked in the Dutch East Indies in the eighteenth century. He observed that:

> When the Chinese remain abroad for several generations without returning to their native land, they frequently cut themselves off from the instructions of the sages; in language, food and dress they imitate the natives and, studying foreign books, they do not scruple to become Javanese. . . .

In other words, established Chinese communities in Indonesia took on a great deal from local cultures. They learned Malay and Javanese (as well as Dutch) and many converted to Islam and married Indonesian women. Chinese communities were small enclaves within the larger regional societies. Indeed, as the process of assimilation progressed, many became native speakers of Javanese and other regional languages.

Chinese links with Indonesia are ancient. A small Chinese community witnessed the decline of the old Javanese kingdom of Majapahit in the fifteenth century, challenged by new Muslim settlements along the north coast of Java. When the Ming government sent admiral Zheng He's expedition to visit Southeast Asia, his secretary, Ma Huan, described rapidly growing Chinese settlements at Tuban, Gresik, Surabaya, and other towns on the north coast of Java.

The Chinese were typically town dwellers, and as time passed, the ubiquitous Chinese temple, or *klenteng*, with its striking and distinctive architectural form and decoration, became a feature of Indonesian cities: a fine old example is found in the once-bustling trade port of Banten, for example, though inland cities also have their *klenteng* (fig. 224).

LITERARY ACCULTURATION

In the coastal towns, a hybrid popular culture flourished. Local-born Chinese, or Peranakan, were important contributors. As early as the sixteenth century, popular Chinese opera was being performed in Batavia in the Malay language (fig. 225), both because the opera had a keen following from townsfolk of other races, who used this lingua franca, and because Malay had become the mother tongue of many Batavian Chinese.

Similarly, Peranakan Chinese read and enjoyed Malay literature. When missionaries distributed tracts and Bibles printed in Malay using the Arabic script, they found the Chinese among those taking an interest. The popular Malay ballads, which were set to simple tunes, were greatly loved by Malay and Peranakan Chinese audiences alike. Particular favorites were the romantic adventure tales set in the port-town environment familiar to Peranakan audiences, such as *Syair Abdul Muluk* (also turned into opera) and *Syair Sitti Zubaidah*.

Peranakan were also devotees of the *pantun*. These sung quatrains of allusive verse were enjoyed in musical soirées by Peranakan Chinese and indigenous Malay speakers alike. A special performance style developed, using violin melodies as accompaniment. The violin was the characteristic instrument of the Portuguese-influenced mestizo culture of Malacca and Batavia. For Chinese it was a substitute for the *erhu*, the two-stringed viol used by Chinese minstrels to accompany the singing of tales. This composite art, with its Malay language and Portuguese-Chinese performance style, reflected the richly hybrid Indies urban culture, which was still marginal to the mainstreams of regional culture.

The urban environment assisted also in the transplanting of another Chinese literary institution, the reading shop. In Indonesia, however, it was not printed books that were stocked for readers to borrow overnight, but Malay manuscripts. There were reading shops in Batavia, Palembang, and probably near Chinese suburbs. They were not necessarily run by Chinese, but were all located in or near Chinese suburbs. Their manuscripts were borrowed by Chinese and non-Chinese

FIGURE 223
A view of Southeast Asia from China's point of view: Jan Huygen van Linschoten's version of East and Southeast Asia published in *Itinerio* in 1596.

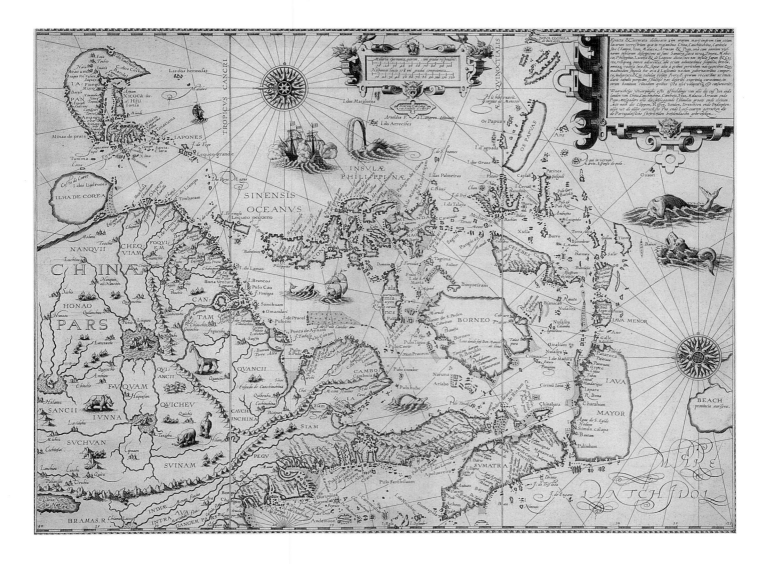

202 ILLUMINATIONS

FIGURE 224
Above: A *klenteng,* a Chinese temple.

FIGURE 225
Below: Malay Chinese Opera performers.

customers alike. Some copyists address their manuscripts to Babah and Nyonya, the Malay terms of address used by Peranakan Chinese, indicating the expected audience.

The full extent of the Chinese contribution to the major literary traditions of Indonesia will never be known. Being town dwellers and often wealthy merchants, the Chinese were well placed to gain entrée to the higher levels of native society. At the height of his power, the Sultan of Banten, for instance, had Chinese in his service as secretaries and interpreters. Around the archipelago, this pattern was

FIGURE 226

repeated, with Chinese acting as commercial agents and even administrators for local rulers. The community was, because of its commercial occupations, more literate than most. Moreover, the man of letters was held in high esteem among the Chinese, as among the Javanese. Even so, the Chinese contribution remains unmarked, for so many literary works are anonymous; and in any case, when Chinese accepted official posts, or converted to Islam, they took Javanese or Muslim names. Very occasionally, an individual is known to us with a name that betrays his Chinese ancestry. One such is Ching Saidullah Muhammad, a Chinese Muslim, who was the most prolific manuscript copyist working in the Dutch Bureau of Native Affairs in the nineteenth century.

Some manuscripts do, of course, deal with specifically Chinese subjects, though their number is rather small. The widest selection is found in the Javanese language.

ORIGINAL COMPOSITIONS

Local Chinese writings on original topics are wonderful sources of social history. The extremes of the moral and social scale are represented by two Malay texts written in the Jawi script. One is an unpretentious manuscript of *Syair Baba Kong Sit*, a ballad about an opium smuggler arrested in Batavia in 1840. This is an early example of the scandal sheets which became increasingly popular with readers as the century progressed. The other is the gorgeous manuscript of *Syair Perkawinan Kapitan Tik Sing*, a celebration in verse of the marriage of the son of the head of the Chinese community in Riau (fig. 226).

A more elaborate literary exercise, though not so brilliant in presentation, are the Javanese memoirs of Ko Ho Sing. They tell the story of a Chinese immigrant family who made good in Yogyakarta. The family made its fortune as licensees under the Dutch opium monopoly, and rose to such prominence that Ko Ho Sing became master of the Masonic Lodge—whose members included Javanese princes. In 1872 the family had their achievements immortalized in Javanese verse (*tembang macapat*). These parvenus thus chose a literary form appreciated by not only the Javanese nobility with whom they ranked themselves, but also by the established Chinese Peranakan families against whom they measured their success in business (figs. 227, 228).

Of course, we cannot be sure that even these texts were actually written by Chinese. They were certainly intended for the edification of Chinese and native audiences alike.

TRANSLATIONS OF CHINESE LITERATURE

So too were the Javanese translations of a very popular Chinese folk romance, "The Butterfly Lovers." The pair are Liang Sanbo and Zhu Yingtai or, using the Hokkien names current in the archipelago, Sam Pik and Eng Tae. Eng Tae is a bright, determined, and passionate young woman who adopts the disguise of a young man in order to attend school, and falls in love with a fellow student, Sam Pik. He is not so quick-witted, and their love remains unfulfilled. Sam Pik dies, and on the day of her wedding to a rich and respected groom chosen by her family, Eng Tae casts herself into the grave of her dead lover. Their souls flutter up from the grave as a pair of butterflies (fig. 229).

This rich mix of tragedy, comedy, and social criticism has appealed to generations of Chinese and Indonesians. In China there are a dozen or more versions of this story in printed form, and it is a favorite of the popular opera. The same is true in Indonesia, where versions of this story have been told in prose and verse. There are manuscript versions from Java and Bali, and many printed versions in Malay and Javanese. The Javanese manuscript versions date from 1878 and from the early twentieth century. This well-loved tale was the first Chinese story to be printed in Javanese, and was also serialized in the first Javanese newspaper. It has

been presented in many forms of folk theater and in popular commercial theater; in the 1980s Javanese *ketoprak* performances of this story were still popular—not to mention its film and audiocassette versions.

REDISCOVERY OF CHINESE ROOTS

This and other translations from Chinese appeared in the latter half of the nineteenth century, a time when the Peranakan communities of Indonesia found their circumstances rapidly changing. This can partly be explained by the influx of new immigrants from China, speaking Chinese and asserting a distinctively Chinese identity with renewed emphasis. In the economic flux of the rapidly developing colonial economy, some of the new immigrants, such as Ko Ho Sing, rose to influential positions. Moreover, the communications revolution of the latter part of the nineteenth century—with regular steamshipping, mails, telegraph, and newspapers—drew all Indonesian Chinese into closer contact with their formerly distant homeland. The result was a new consciousness of being Chinese. In 1863 the Hok Kian Tik Soe, or Hokkien Welfare Association, was founded in Surabaya to aid needy Chinese and to encourage Chinese Peranakan ladies to wear traditional

Chinese dress instead of the customary sarong and *kebaya*. In literature, the same impulse meant a hunger among Javanese- and Malay-speaking Peranakan for translations of the great Chinese historical romances.

Manuscripts of these romances appeared in Javanese from 1857 on. They are substantial works, of up to nine hundred pages: in fact one six-volume manuscript fell just short of three thousand pages. Only the very rich could afford to order manuscripts of this scope. A multi-volume copy of the *Romance of the Three Kingdoms*, for instance, was priced at the enormous sum of fifty guilders. Such vast translation projects sometimes overwhelmed optimistic translators. The first volume (*Fan Tang,* Revolt against the Tang), translated probably in Yogyakarta, ran to 750 pages. With perhaps seven volumes more to follow, it is not surprising that the task was left unfinished.

Most of the Javanese manuscript translations of this kind deal with the early history of the Tang dynasty, the career of its founder Li Shihmin, the redoubtable Empress Wu, and the concubine of peerless beauty, Yang Guifei, who was sacrificed to the ambitions of her Tartar lover. These are culturally definitive works for the southern Chinese, who refer to themselves as the Tang people. The status of these works has been expressed in the Javanese context in various ways. Several of the translations are designated *babad*, applying the term used for Javanese dynastic histories. Furthermore, there was a parallel *wayang* puppet theater, the *wayang titi*, and examples of these puppets can be seen in the Sonobudoyo Museum in Yogyakarta. Quite a number of *pakem* (*dalang's* guides) for these plays survive, all dealing with the Tang cycle. The implication is that, for Indonesian Chinese, these plays were analogous to the Javanese *wayang kulit* as expressions of cultural identity. No doubt for the same reason, these rather intimidating manuscript works were valued by the Javanese courts, and still repose in the court libraries of Surakarta and Yogyakarta.

Two of these manuscripts are particularly interesting, for different reasons. One is the earliest of these translations, entitled *Li Si Bin* (*Li Shihmin*), dating from 1859 (fig. 230). Its 748 pages of Javanese verse are in a clumsy cursive script, which the codicologist T.G. Pigeaud thinks is probably a Chinese hand. It was copied, and perhaps translated, by a Chinese from Kadiri by the name of Babah Tig Og. It must have been well received, for the same copyist made another copy ten years later, and perhaps others that have not survived. The particular interest lies in the Chinese-style drawings at the beginning of the manuscript. They are done in ink, and depict the principal characters of the tale. This was common practice in Chinese printed books, and tells us that the copyist intended this Javanese manuscript to resemble the Chinese printed book from which the translation was made.

The other is the Javanese manuscript of *Lo Thong* (*Luo Tong Sao Bei,* Luo Tong clears the north), which also belongs to the Tang cycle. It is interesting because it was written by a Chinese in Buleleng, Bali, in 1881. It was thus the forerunner of a number of Balinese manuscripts on Chinese folk romances and historical themes, most of which belong to the late nineteenth century or early twentieth century (the earliest to bear a date is from 1915). Like their Javanese counterparts, they also found theatrical expression in the Balinese opera, the Arja.

NEW FORMS

The new commercial opportunities of the second half of the nineteenth century brought the coastal Malay-language mestizo culture into greater prominence. The rapidly expanding economy elevated the importance of Malay as the language of urban and inter-island commerce, and it gained even greater currency among Chinese Peranakan families. Peranakan males, particularly, began to receive schooling in the more economically useful languages of Malay, Dutch, and Chinese.

FIGURE 229

A page from *Sam Pik Ing Tae*, the Chinese tale of the "Butterfly Lovers," popular among both Javanese and Peranakan audiences. Leiden University Library, Leiden.

After 1856 commercial newspapers written in Malay in the Roman (or "Dutch") script circulated from the northern parts of Surabaya, Semarang, and Batavia, feeding commercial intelligence to a multi-ethnic readership. Salmon observes that as Malay translations of Chinese literature began to be published in East and Central Java:

> It shows that a linguistic change was taking place at that time within the Chinese community in these regions, and that Javanese translations of Chinese novels . . . could no longer satisfy the public. (Salmon: 1981, 23.)

A new literacy in printed Roman-script Malay tended to displace literacy in Javanese and in Arabic-script Malay. By about 1890, the increasing numbers of Peranakan Chinese whose literary language of choice was Malay could now read it only in Roman script.

This is why no Malay translations from Chinese can be found in manuscript form. Salmon states that after her exhaustive investigations in libraries and among the Peranakan communities of Indonesia, ". . . we have not been able to find a single translation from the Chinese in Malay manuscript form." For Chinese literature, the Malay counterpart of the Javanese manuscript is the printed book. The first translation into roman-script Malay appeared in 1882, and thus later than its Javanese manuscript counterparts; but within a decade or two there was an extensive and richly varied diet of Malay printed books adapted from Chinese sources. By the end of the century, the primary medium for the reassertion of Chinese identity was the Malay printed word.

It is ironic that the Chinese, who had taken with enthusiasm and creativity to Indonesia's diverse manuscript traditions, were partly instrumental in their demise. The new printing industry was pioneered by Indos, people of mixed Dutch-native ancestry, and quickly taken up by Chinese. It initially concentrated on the printing, publishing, and selling of books and newpapers in Malay in Roman script; but its impact was soon felt in Javanese as well, with presses in Surakarta and Kadiri publishing many Javanese works formerly available only in manuscript form to a limited audience. From this time, cheap versions of many of the texts created a quite different market for the literary tradition.

FIGURE 230

Chinese-style pen-and-ink drawings of the main characters of *Li Si Bin*, a Javanese manuscript described in Pigeaud. Leiden University Library, Leiden.

These changes were very rapid, and not felt evenly by all groups in the Chinese communities, or by different regions across the archipelago. Something of the resulting diversity can be glimpsed through three late-nineteenth-century texts that appeared in differing cultural contexts. All three are translations of Chinese moral texts. They have been made accessible to Indonesian readers in a variety of forms.

Serat Tiyang Gegriya is a short didactic poem on good housekeeping, translated from the Chinese text, *Zhuzi jiaxun* (Master Zhu's family instructions). It is written in Javanese script and in Javanese verse, in the *macapat* meter, and included in an undated and anonymous manuscript. The manuscript contains other short adaptations of Chinese literature, principally a version of the Butterfly Lovers. The juxtaposition of this feminist romance with instruction on housekeeping suggests that this was a manuscript intended for Javanese-speaking Peranakan women.

The *Quran Giok Lek* reflects the older style of Malay-speaking Peranakan community, which retained its Chinese religious beliefs but expressed them in a manner thoroughly acclimatized to the Malayo-Muslim environment in which they lived. The text is a translation by Kwa Tek Yee of *Yuli Baochao* (The precious records to admonish the world), which describes the ten courts of purgatory in the nether world. The facts that it flags its religious nature with the title *Quran*, that it complies with the conventions of Malay manuscripts (and was in fact printed by the same Javanese printers in Singapore who provided the Indies with Muslim literature), and that it uses the Muslim legal term *waqaf* to describe its votive sponsorship—all these are tokens of an older accommodation with local Malayo-Muslim culture. Six years later, this same text would appear in a radically different, modern guise in Batavia: the first of seven editions of this text published by Chinese printers in the Roman script.

Boekoe Peratoeran Beroemah Tangga (*Xiansheng Jiaxun*) was translated by Lim Tjay Tat and printed in Singapore in 1896 for an Indies readership. It deals with the same theme of good housekeeping as the older Javanese manuscript poem, but speaks to the newly educated and consciously Chinese Peranakan who used Malay alongside Hokkien, and read the "Dutch" script. The book has one title page in Chinese characters followed by a second in Malay. Its layout resembles a Chinese book, with the text in vertical columns on the page, and it combines Chinese characters with Hokkien and Malay in the Dutch Roman script. Chinese characters give authority to the text, but the author did not expect his audience to have mastered them, for he provides reading aids: a pronunciation in Hokkien, and running texts in colloquial Hokkien and Malay—all in Dutch script.

The variety of cultural expressions evident in these three texts and the coexistence of printing and manuscripts remind us that the Chinese manuscript traditions of Indonesia have always been highly localized. The manuscript economy is also usually highly personal: manuscripts on Chinese themes were generally owned by the translators or their relatives, who lent them to members of the local Chinese community. Consequently, local circumstances and a personality or two may conspire to create a whole manuscript tradition. This happened in Makasar (Ujung Pandang).

THE TALE OF SIE KONG

The following is a summary of the story of Sie Kong, who was commander-in-chief of the Tang. The first commander-in-chief was his grandfather, Sie Djien Koei. Sie Kong's father, Sie Theng San, was given the crown princess as his bride for having shown great valor and wisdom in defending the Tang kingdom. Unfortunately, Sie Theng San was in love with a commoner, who died of heartbreak upon his marriage to the crown princess. When the princess was pregnant, the spirit of Sie Theng's lover entered the princess's body. Sie Kong was born, and while destined to become a great military leader, he was a drunkard and easily angered.

One day Sie Kong ran amok at the gate of the city and killed the crown prince. As a result he was sentenced to death. In the next war the Tang kingdom was taken over by the Sung, as there was no military leader as brave or as capable as Sie Kong.

Liem Kheng Yong (1817–1938), translator of Sie Kong.

Ten volumes of the Makasarese translation of Sie Kong, *from the collection of the Liem Kheng Yong family.*

WOMEN'S LITERATURE

We have an unusually clear picture of the Chinese manuscript literature of Makasar because it appeared late and ran right through to the modern period. Manuscripts in the Makasarese language written by Chinese authors were produced even after Indonesian independence.

As in Batavia (Jakarta), there was an old Peranakan Chinese community in Makasar that had its own headman as far back as the seventeenth century. Until the end of the nineteenth century, very few Chinese women left their country and immigrants had to marry local women. The result was the development of a community straddling two cultures.

As in Java, the last years of the nineteenth century were characterized by a revival of interest in Chinese culture in Peranakan circles. In the same year that Tiong Hwa Hwee Koan, the Chinese Association, opened its first Chinese school in Batavia, its Makasar branch mobilized merchants to support a Chinese school in Makasar. As elsewhere in the Indies, Malay translations of Chinese historical romances and other literature circulated among Makasar Peranakan Chinese. Two printing companies, one a Dutch-Chinese-Makasarese joint venture and the other a purely Chinese-owned firm, were local publishers of this kind of Malay-language literature. However, this literature was closed to Makasar Peranakan women, for they could not read Malay.

Although the Chinese modernizers favored the promotion of female education, they made little headway in Makasar. Even in the 1930s, most Peranakan women in Makasar still could not read Chinese. A great number of them were, however, literate in Makasarese, and their interest in translations of Chinese works stimulated the production of manuscripts using Makasar script. It is no coincidence that the first translators of Chinese literature were two women: Nona Kakatua ("Miss Cockatoo") and Nona Ua Siok ("Old Spinster Siok"). Both were famous for their ability to retell Chinese stories in Makasarese.

After 1920 this domestic market for Chinese translations in Makasarese was fed by three male translators. One was astonishingly prolific. Liem Kheng Yong came from a wealthy family. He was given a good education in Chinese by private tutors and must have learned at the same time to read and write in the Makasarese script. He was fond of Chinese literature, but at the same time greatly enjoyed composing poems in Makasarese. From the autobiographical notes he sometimes added at the end of his translations, following the common practice of translators, we see Liem as a true intellectual and a prodigious worker, sometimes spending days and nights translating; he was said to be able to complete one fascicle of translation—some hundred pages—in one day. All told, he alone translated more than sixty Chinese works. By the early 1930s he had withdrawn from the family business and lived the life of a scholar, supporting himself on what he could make from lending his manuscript translations to the public. Liem died at the age of sixty-two, after having foretold the date of his death. He was well qualified to do so, for among his translations were Chinese almanacs and horoscopes that he had put into Makasarese.

Interestingly, his manner of writing Makasarese manuscripts reflects this scholarly approach. He wrote them as if he were copying Chinese texts, writing the Makasar script with a brush in the Chinese manner and binding the manuscripts into fascicles in the manner of Chinese books. His text in Makasarese script was, moreover, peppered with Chinese characters indicating the names of the principal actors. When, in 1960, the only one of his translations to be printed appeared, it was done using the old Chinese method of printing from carved woodblocks. (In the wider world, this method of printing had already become a historical curiosity.) Supposedly, the reason for using this technique was that the font for printing Makasarese script had been lost during the Second World War;

but if so, the choice of xylography was fortunate. This method permitted the calligraphy of the manuscript to be reproduced, and the intermingling of Makasarese and Chinese script to be managed.

Through his great energy, Liem had made available in Makasarese a sample of the same translated books that circulated in Malay and Javanese. As expected, the historical romances figure most prominently among his translations. They include the *Romance of the Three Kingdoms* and the Tang cycle. Beyond these were some cloak-and-dagger stories and famous trial cases, such as *Si Poet Tjoan* (*Shi gongan,* The cases of Judge Shi), and novels of manners or fantasy. Of special interest to Chinese in the South Seas was *Sam Po Kong* (*Sanbao taijian xiyang ji,* The voyage of eunuch Sanbao to the Western Sea). And, of course, there was the ever-popular story of the Butterfly Lovers.

This manuscript literature was destined for a female audience. The Peranakan women of Makasar were very fond of these translations of Chinese novels. One, writing in the 1950s, recalled how she and other children used to listen to their grandmothers reading the *Romance of the Three Kingdoms* and the stories of the early Tang dynasty. Today in Makasar there are still old Peranakan women who are able to read these stories. The daughter of Liem Kheng Yong, for instance, knows a great many by heart. However, her father's collection of manuscripts was scattered with the arrival of the Japanese and only about one hundred have been preserved. Moreover, a few attempts launched in the early 1960s to print some of these stories do not seem to have been very successful. Unfortunately the younger generations of Makasarese, as well as young Peranakan Chinese, are no longer able to read the Makasarese script.

Ann Kumar with Ian Proudfoot

A SEPARATE EMPIRE: WRITINGS OF SOUTH SULAWESI

The approximately five million inhabitants of the province of South Sulawesi belong to a variety of ethnic groups. The four major ones are the Bugis (50 percent of the population, mainly located in the east and large parts of the west), the Makasar (30 percent of the population, living in and around the capital, Ujung Pandang, and also in the south), the Saqdan Toraja (5 percent, living in the northern mountain regions) and the Mandar (5 percent, living in the northwest). The rest of the population is made up of people of other ethnic origins such as Malay, Javanese, Chinese, Ambonese, and Manadonese. Of course, both the figures and the geographical locations are necessarily approximations. In urban areas in particular, many people are of mixed descent.

With the exception of the Toraja, all inhabitants of South Sulawesi profess the Islamic faith. More than 80 percent of the population is rural and agrarian, but an important minority of Bugis, Makasar, and Mandar are fishermen and sailors. This latter category has been instrumental in establishing the image of the Bugis, Makasar, and Mandar people as seafaring people and ingenious boat builders (fig. 231). Even today, they play a major role in the interinsular trade of the archipelago. In the past they were renowned throughout Indonesia and Malaysia for their military prowess and political skills, causing them to rise to positions of power in areas such as Trengganu (Malaysia), Riau, Sumbawa, and East Kalimantan. Some also became notorious as mercenaries and pirates.

While these groups are closely related to each other, they differ in their languages and their customs. Each has its own distinct language and traditions—in short, its own cultural identity.

Among the four major ethnic groups, the Saqdan Toraja is exceptional in that it did not have a written tradition. Tales and other traditions were transmitted orally, and no indigenous manuscripts have ever existed. All available Saqdan Toraja texts are from the present century, noted down in Roman script by Dutch missionaries using local informants in the period before the Second World War. Recently quite a number of texts have become available through linguistic and anthropological research in the area, both by Indonesians and by foreigners.

The remaining three groups—Bugis, Makasar, and Mandar—have a written tradition that is at least three centuries old. They also share an indigenous script in which texts were written until recent times. Collections of manuscripts from South Sulawesi are found in a number of major public collections. For geographical and political reasons, data on Mandar texts are still limited. More is known about Makasar, and the written tradition of the Bugis is fairly well documented, although still insufficiently by modern standards. For this reason, more attention will be paid to the Bugis part of the region in the following account.

SCRIPTS

At least four different scripts can be distinguished in the surviving manuscripts from South Sulawesi. Arranged more or less chronologically they are Makasarese (also called Old Makasarese), Bugis (also called Bugis/Makasarese), Arabic, and Roman. Of course there was great overlap in time in the use of these alphabets, and quite often more than one alphabet was used in the same manuscript. In particular, we regularly see the use of Bugis and Arabic side by side in religious

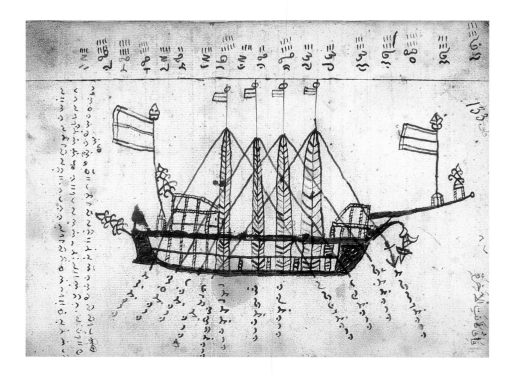

FIGURE 231

Detail from *Kutika*. National Library of
Indonesia, Jakarta.

manuscripts (fig. 232). Also in historiographical manuscripts, personal names and words like *fasal, bab,* and *tammat* are often spelled with Arabic letters, frequently in red ink. This section will not deal with the Arabic and Roman alphabet. Instead, a short survey will be given of the history and peculiarities of the indigenous scripts of South Sulawesi.

Although a common origin from an Indian prototype is beyond doubt, it is very hard to establish the exact historical development of the two scripts of South Sulawesi and their relationship to each other. It is now assumed that Makasarese and Buginese are derived from the same (now extinct) source, which was close to the Kawi alphabet. So, contrary to what has been thought for a long time, the Bugis script is not derived from the Makasarese one. Indeed, both scripts were used side by side at least in the seventeenth century for quite a time. It seems that until the eighteenth century, the Makasarese script was used exclusively for texts in the Makasar language. A famous example is the text of the Bungaya Treaty of 1667 (figs. 233, 234). Very few manuscripts written in the Makasarese script have survived. In the course of the nineteenth century, this script became obsolete and was replaced by the script already in use for Bugis texts. From that time onward, all texts from South Sulawesi (Bugis, Makasarese, and Mandarese) were written in the same indigenous script, here referred to as Bugis script (fig. 237).

When we look at figure 235 and compare the Makasarese alphabet (here called "another form of the Ugi or Mangkasar letters found in old MS") with the Bugis (top and bottom of the illustration), we immediately notice an enormous difference in shape and characteristics. This in itself makes direct derivation of one from the other highly improbable. Whereas there are no dots used in the Makasarese script, they are a prominent and distinctive feature in the Bugis. Furthermore, the Makasarese letters are much more elegantly formed, full of curves, curls, and arches, in contrast to the straight lines and angular impression of the Bugis script. In Bugis, the latter is termed "square" script (*ukiq sulapaq eppaq*), whereas the Makasar script is known as "birds" script (*ukiq manuq-manuq*).

A special type of script seems to have been used in writing on *lontar* leaves. Here the letters make a much stronger vertical impression. It has been argued that this type represents an early phase in the development of Bugis script.

FIGURE 232

Opposite: Pages from *Tafsir al Quran,*
verses in praise of the Prophet. Arabic and
Bugis languages and scripts. National
Library of Indonesia, Jakarta.

أشرق البدر علينا فاختفت
منه البدور مثل حسنك
ما رأينا قط يا وجه السرور

أنت شمس أنت بدر أنت
نور فوق نور أنت البير
وغالي أنت مصباح الصدور

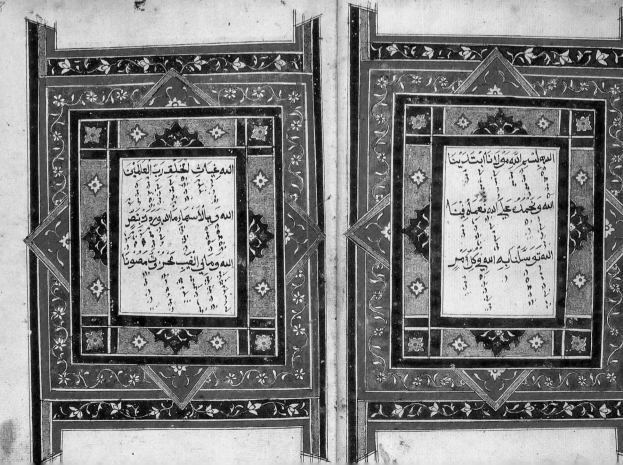

الله غياث لخلق رب العالمين
الله وفي بالأسماء والدعوة ينصر
الله وفي الغيب بحروف مصونا

الله بسم الله مولانا ابتدينا
الله وحمد على الله نعمه فينا
الله توسلنا به الله وكل أمر

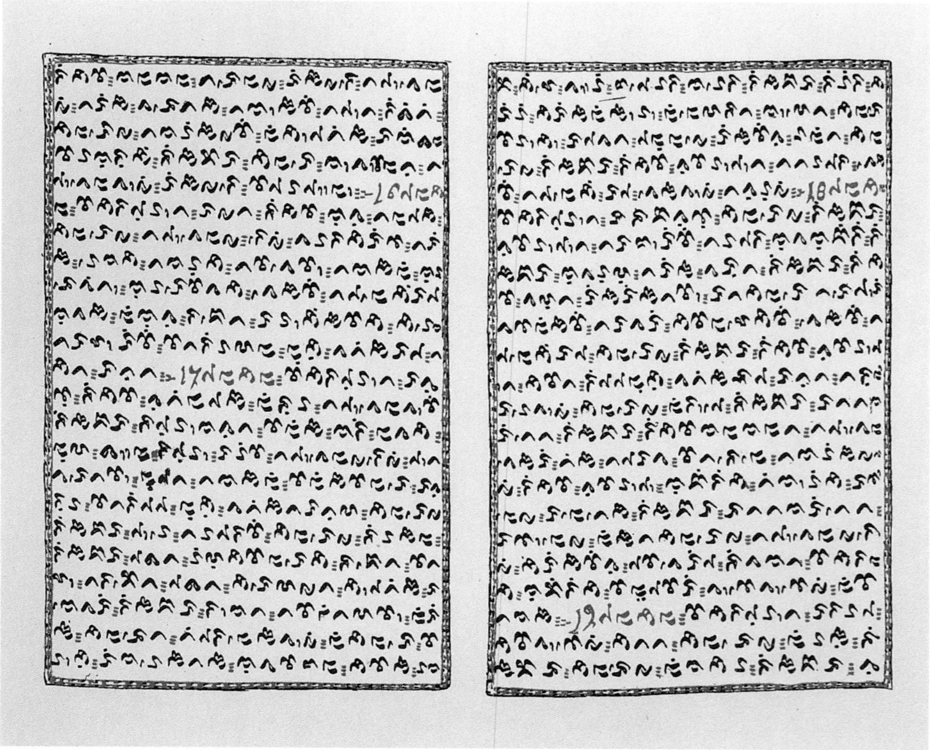

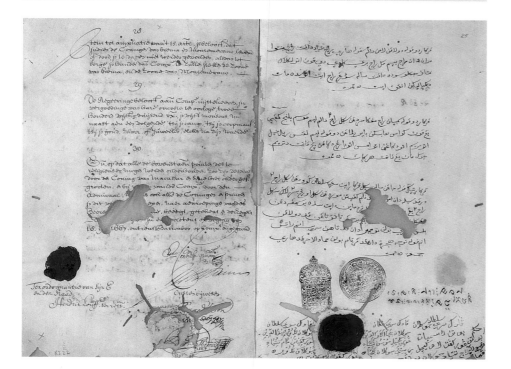

FIGURE 233

Transcription of the Makasarese text of the Bungaya Treaty (1667) in old Makasarese script. KITLV, Leiden.

FIGURE 234

The Bungaya Treaty. National Archives of Indonesia, Jakarta.

The use of the Bugis script was not confined to South Sulawesi. It is also found in regions that were under Bugis or Makasar influence in the past, such as Bima on East Sumbawa and Endé on Flores. Manuscripts of this type are, however, extremely rare. An example of one such manuscript can be seen in the section on Bima on page 75).

The Bugis (and the Makasarese) script is a syllabary. One peculiar feature of the Bugis script is that it is a defective script, that is, not all phonemes are written. Distinctive traits such as geminated consonants ("tt," "ss," etc.), glottal stop ("q"), and final velar nasal ("ng") are never written, and in many cases prenasalation also is not indicated. The script is therefore subject to a variety of interpretations. Theoretically one letter may be interpreted in nine different ways; for instance

——— FIGURE 235 ———

Left: "The Ugi or Mangkasar Alphabet."
From: Raffles, Thomas Stamford (1817).

——— FIGURE 236 ———

Right: "Makassaarsche en Boeginesche
Letters en Zamenstellingen" (The Makasar
language in Bugis script). From: Brink, H.
van den (1943).

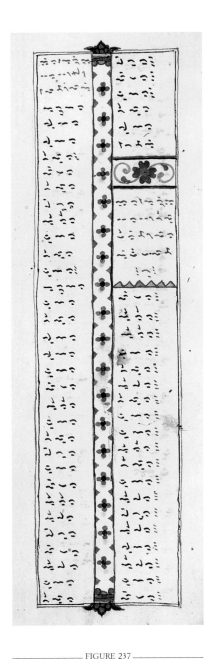

——— FIGURE 237 ———

Daftar Kata-kata, a word list. National
Library of Indonesia, Jakarta.

"Pa," which may be read as "pa," "ppa," "pang," "ppang," "paq," "ppaq," "mpa," "mpang," or "mpaq," though generally the number of legitimate interpretations is smaller. This deficiency sometimes poses huge interpretative problems for the reader. To add to this complexity, separation between the words is not indicated, and only one reading sign (represented by three vertical or diagonal dots) is used, indicating the end of a syntactical unit (fig. 236).

MANUSCRIPTS

The usual word for manuscript in South Sulawesi is *lontaraq.* This word is an evident borrowing from the Javanese or Malay *lontar* and indicates that originally texts were written on leaves of the *lontar* palm. Indeed a small number of highly distinctive palm-leaf manuscripts exist, which may be proof of an old writing tradition.

The shape of these *lontar* manuscripts is unique in that they look like, and are based on the same linear principles as, audio/video cassettes: the text, written in one line on rolled-up narrow *lontar* leaves, can only be read by unwinding the roll. A roll is produced by stitching together a number of ribbons cut from *lontar* leaves. Each ribbon is usually 2 centimeters wide and about 60 centimeters long. These are joined by overlapping the beginning of the next ribbon onto the end of the previous one for a few centimeters and sewing them together with palm fiber. The end of the roll is fixed in a notch of a wooden reel (left). By rotating the reel, the roll is tightly wound onto it. The beginning of the roll is fixed onto another reel (right), the two reels are fastened in a fork, and in order to read the text one has to turn the right reel. The text on the roll moves before the reader's eye from left to right between the two reels (fig. 238). Such a device for reading manuscripts is not known outside South Sulawesi; the same principle, however, is applied in Javanese *wayang beber* performances.

All others manuscripts from South Sulawesi were written on paper, almost exclusively of European make. Very old manuscripts have not survived the tropical climate. The oldest known date from the seventeenth century and are kept in European collections.

Original manuscripts from South Sulawesi are diverse in size and neatness. They range from small and dirty to large double folios in superb condition. Generally there is a relationship between size and content. The small ones contain

FIGURE 238

Sureq Baweng. National Library of
Indonesia, Jakarta.

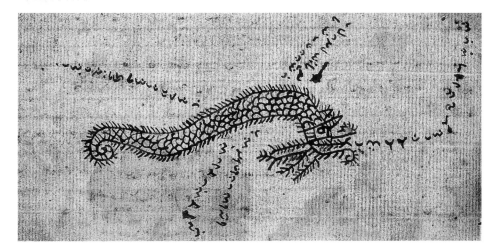

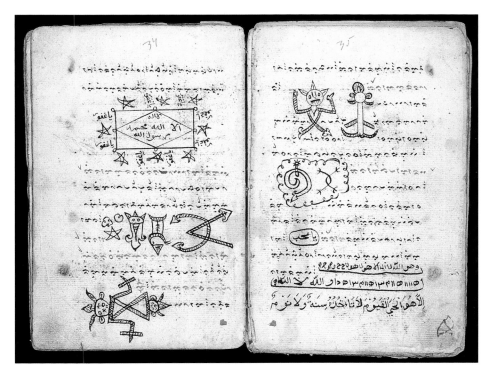

mostly magico-religious texts, such as charms and prayers (figs. 239, 240, 241).
Such manuscripts are very portable. They are particularly likely to be dirty as proof
of heavy use by their owners. Larger manuscripts, usually of folio format, mostly
contain historiographical texts such as chronicles and daily registers.

No general statements can be made on other manuscript formats, except that
anything is possible regarding variety in form and content. Indeed, many manuscripts contain not one "text" but a variety of items: a *toloq* (heroic-historical
poem) or a fragment thereof, some prayers, a sort of agricultural calender, a piece
of a chronicle, a genealogy, some notes on debts, a drawing of a fort, and so on.

Many manuscripts were commissioned by Western scholars. Consequently,
these manuscripts are quite uniform in size and handwriting, mostly folio-sized and
neatly written with wide margins and generous line spacing.

Nowadays the art of manuscript-making is virtually dead. It partially survives
in lithographs that are still produced and seem to be in wide circulation among
the more Islamic-oriented sections of society. These lithographs are usually handwritten in two scripts (Bugis and Arabic), sometimes in three (Bugis, Arabic, and
Roman). They deal exclusively with Islamic matters, such as translations of the
Quran, material on *fiqh* (jurisprudence), *hajj* (pilgrimage) practicalities, and texts
of sermons (fig. 242).

COLLECTIONS

The largest public collections of South Sulawesi manuscripts are found in Leiden, Jakarta, London, and Ujung Pandang. As has been remarked above, almost all these manuscripts were commissioned by Western scholars. The voluminous Leiden collection is the result of active collecting activities by famous scholars such as B.F. Matthes, J.C.G. Jonker, and A.A. Cense between the years 1850 and 1950. Under the aegis of the last in the period 1930–1940 (when he was governmental language officer), about three hundred manuscripts were copied and kept in the Matthes foundation in Makasar. After the war, this foundation with its collection of books and manuscripts became the Yayasan Kebudayaan Sulawesi Selatan, which still exists in the Benteng (Old Fort) of Ujung Pandang. Unfortunately most of these manuscripts now seem to be lost. A recent research project on manuscripts in South Sulawesi disclosed the presence of more than three thousand manuscripts in private hands. These manuscripts have been put on microfilm and catalogued.

Most older manuscripts from South Sulawesi are in the United Kingdom, where they entered public collections through the endeavors of such men as Thomas Stamford Raffles and John Crawfurd in the beginning of the nineteenth century. Many of these manuscripts deal with historiographical matters and are of great importance. The oldest-known manuscript, however, is located in the museum of the Royal Institute for the Tropics in Amsterdam. It contains the Makasarese chronicle of Goa and Talloq, and was written about 1750 in the old Makasarese script (fig. 243).

LITERATURES

The literatures of South Sulawesi were handed down both orally and in written form. This distinction is in fact not tenable, since most texts existed in both oral and written forms, with cross-borrowing. Written texts often bear witness to an oral narrative tradition, while many orally transmitted texts appear to be based on written material. Consequently, there are no clear boundaries between oral and written literature. Let us now turn to the three written traditions of South Sulawesi: Mandar, Makasar, and Bugis.

MANDAR

By comparison with the numerous Bugis and Makasar manuscripts, Mandar manuscripts in public collections are few in number. They consist mainly of historiographical texts, texts on local customs and customary instructions (*pappasang*), collections of poetry in quatrains (*kalindaqdaq*), and traditional love songs (*tipalayo*). Some of these manuscripts are in the form of rolled-up paper sheets about 50 centimeters wide and many meters long. Some sections are illustrated with drawings. Recently there have been reports of the discovery of a basket full of rolled-up *lontar* leafs containing Mandar texts. This find has not been confirmed, though the existence of such manuscripts is not unlikely as they apparently resemble the Bugis *lontar* rolls described above.

MAKASAR

Makasar manuscripts are of varied content. Many have historical relevance, such as chronicles (*patturioloang*) of the well-known Makasar kingdoms of Goa and Talloq, daily registers (*lontaraq bilang*, sometimes referred to as diaries), and genealogies. A vast body of literature consists of Islamic religious texts such as stories from the Quran, some with strong mystical tendencies. There are several works both by and about the great seventeenth-century Makasar mystic Shaikh Yusuf. Other educational texts include *adat* regulations (*rapang*) and codes of law.

More entertaining in nature are the tales of all kinds (*rupama; pau-pau*) and texts known as *sinriliq*. Two types of *sinriliq* exist, one short and lyrical, the other

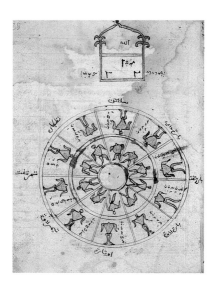

FIGURE 241

Detail from *Kutika*. National Library of Indonesia, Jakarta.

FIGURE 242

Juseq matellu puloé, text and translation of the beginning of *sura* 78. KITLV, Leiden.

FIGURE 243

Two pages from the oldest manuscript from South Sulawesi. Tropical Museum, Royal Institute for the Tropics, Amsterdam.

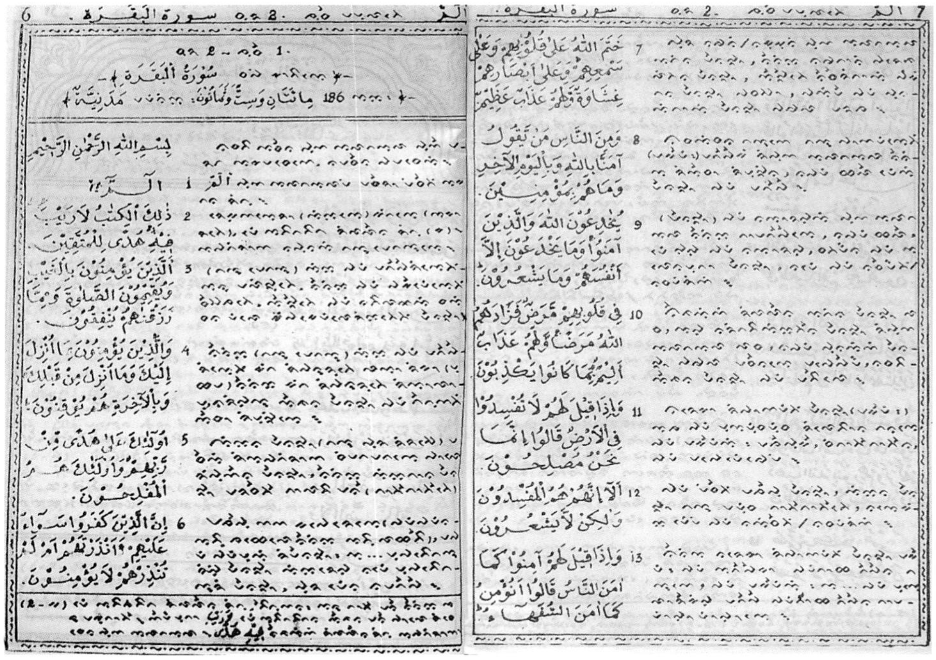

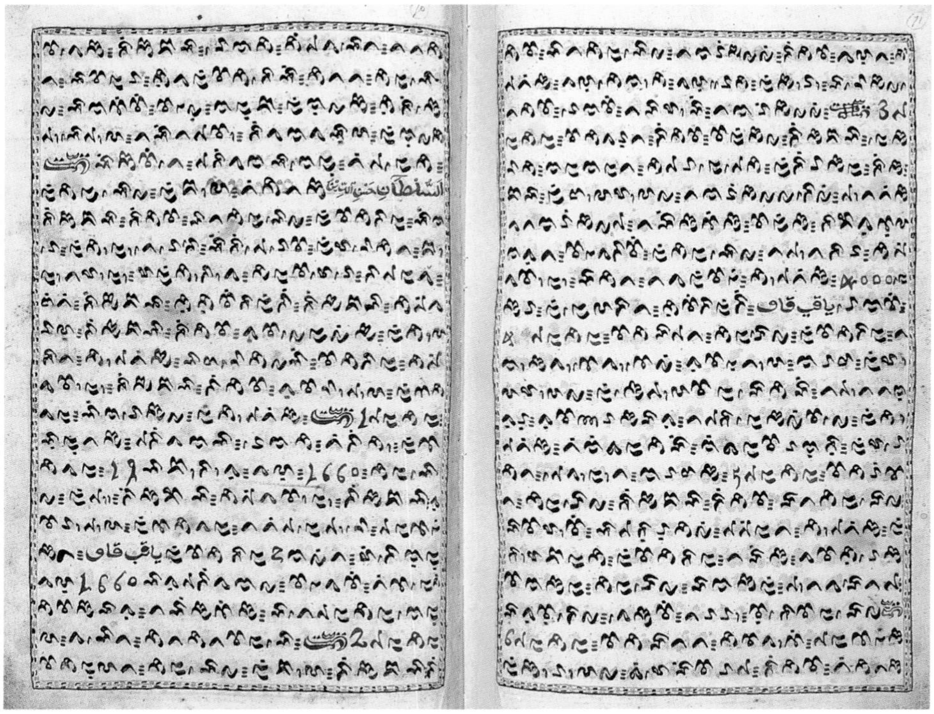

long and heroic-historical. There also exist adaptations from the rich Arabic-Malay-Javanese literary heritage, such as the story of Jayalangkara. This probably entered Makasar literature via a Malay version that was based in turn on a Javanese story. Of the various short poetical texts, mention should be made of *kélong,* or songs, which are quatrains comparable to Malay *pantun* and of oral origin.

BUGIS

As mentioned above, the literature in Bugis is exceptional, both in quality and in quantity. A wide variety of genres is represented in texts, among others, myths, local histories (*attoriolong*), ritual chants, law books, Islamic legends and tracts, daily registers, almanacs (figs. 244, 245, 246), genealogies, wise sayings (*pappaseng*), and folk tales. Special mention should be made of the vast *La Galigo* epic myth, perhaps the most voluminous work in world literature.

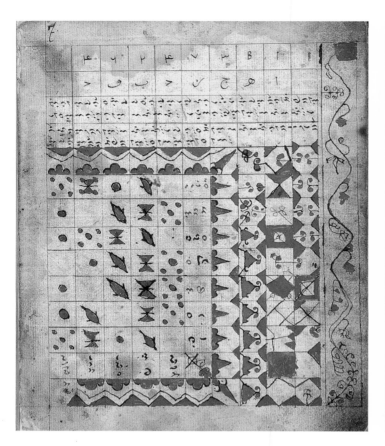

In Bugis poetry, two factors play an important, interrelated role: meter and an archaic vocabulary. These are mutually dependent in that metric texts are always written in "the old language" and texts in this ancient lexicon are always metrical. The meter of Bugis poetry is syllabic; stress is irrelevant. There are three types of meter: five syllabic (as in the *La Galigo* epic myth), eight syllabic (as in other narrative poetic texts), and the so-called *élong* meter, consisting of eight, seven, and six syllables per line. All poetry is distinguished from nonpoetic utterances in its lexicon and in the use of devices such as metaphors, symbols, formulas, and other formal characteristics. This poetic language is highly conventional in character and by some simple devices can be adapted to the meter required by the particular genre.

Most of the surviving Bugis manuscripts cover a combination of the following: the *La Galigo*, Islamic works, and historiographical texts.

LA GALIGO

The vast Bugis epic myth commonly called *La Galigo* (also, *I La Galigo*; Bugis: *Sureq Galigo*), attracted the attention of Western scholars such as John Leyden and Thomas Stamford Raffles from the early nineteenth century onward (fig. 247). Scientific editions of the work have become available only very recently, and a project is now under way to edit twelve major *Galigo* manuscripts kept in the Leiden University Library. The size of the whole work is estimated at approximately six thousand folio pages, making it one of the most voluminous works in world literature. Set in a meter of five and in some cases four syllables, it takes place in pre-Islamic (c. fourteenth century) Luwuq, the kingdom regarded as the cradle of Bugis culture. Though it consists of different episodes, each with its own protagonists, and covers several generations, the work as a whole is still a unity. This unity is evident in the consistency of the complex relationships of the characters, the consistency of the literary conventions, and the use of the techniques of flashback and foreshadowing. The cycle tells the story of the initial residence

——————— FIGURE 244 ———————
Kutika. National Library of Indonesia, Jakarta.

——————— FIGURE 245 ———————
Kutika. National Library of Indonesia, Jakarta.

on earth of the gods and their descendants. It starts with the decision made by the gods of the Upperworld and the Underworld to fill the empty Middleworld by sending their children to live there. From the Upperworld is sent the male Batara Guru and from the Underworld the female Wé Nyiliq Timoq. They marry and become the grandparents of Sawérigading and his twin sister, Wé Tenriabéng. Sawérigading is the main protagonist of the story. He travels extensively and falls deeply in love with his twin sister. This incestuous love is strictly prohibited, and Sawérigading ultimately marries another woman. In the end, the whole divine family gathers in Luwuq and all gods depart from the earth, having lived there for six generations.

Researchers have stressed the high esteem and special sacredness of *Galigo* texts. Their recitation is often accompanied by a ritual involving the sacrifice of a chicken or a goat, the burning of incense, and other spirit-invoking actions. It is also said to help cure diseases and to be potent in averting mischief. (Nowadays, however, it seems that this attitude is extended to all manuscripts, irrespective of their contents.) One reason for the special sacredness of the *Galigo* is the belief that the spirits of the characters reside in the manuscript. When the manuscript is opened, these spirits are present before the audience and they can be approached for help to solve all kinds of difficulties.

The work contains many implicitly or explicitly stated normative rules, according to which the heroes of the story behave, providing an example to the readers. Apart from these normative rules, a wealth of useful information is provided on etiquette and all kinds of ceremonies.

For many Bugis, the events related in the *Galigo* are considered to be real. In this connection, it is interesting to note that the genealogies of nobles in descent-oriented Bugis society are often traced back to the *Galigo* period, preferably to Sawérigading. An indication of the perseverence of this religious reverence is found in incidents that took place in the postwar Darul Islam revolt in South Sulawesi. In its struggle to create an Islamic state, the movement thought it necessary to eliminate all things considered to be non-Islamic. Manuscripts, in particular manuscripts of *La Galigo* texts, were regarded as dangerous, heretical possessions (fig. 248). However, when we read or hear a piece of the *Galigo*, it is not hard to imagine the enjoyment the text provides through the sheer beauty of its wording, repetitions, and parallelisms—the fundamentals of Bugis poetics.

ISLAMIC TEXTS

Many manuscripts or parts of manuscripts deal with Islamic matters, ranging from short magico-mystical formulas to full-fledged tracts on Islamic law. Some contain stories adapted from the Islamic literary heritage—for instance, versions of the story of Lukman al-Hakim. There are also adaptations via Malay, such as versions of the *Bustan as-Salatin* and the *Taj as-Salatin*.

Frequently, one or two pages of a manuscript were used for jottings on Islamic beliefs, be it the profession of faith, a particular prayer, procedures for the prayers, or short magic diagrams and magic formulas (fig. 249).

Even today, lithographed texts on Islamic matters, written in Bugis and Arabic, are very common in Bugis society. It is even fair to say that contemporary Bugis literature deals exclusively with Islamic topics. Of the many works published, one is a translation of the holy Quran into Bugis.

HISTORIOGRAPHICAL TEXTS

Within the framework of indigenous Indonesian historiography, the historiographical works of South Sulawesi seem to be unique. Their objectivity and concern for facts are the main characteristics in which these texts differ from similar

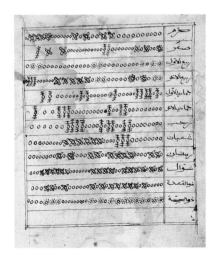

FIGURE 246

Kutika. National Library of Indonesia, Jakarta.

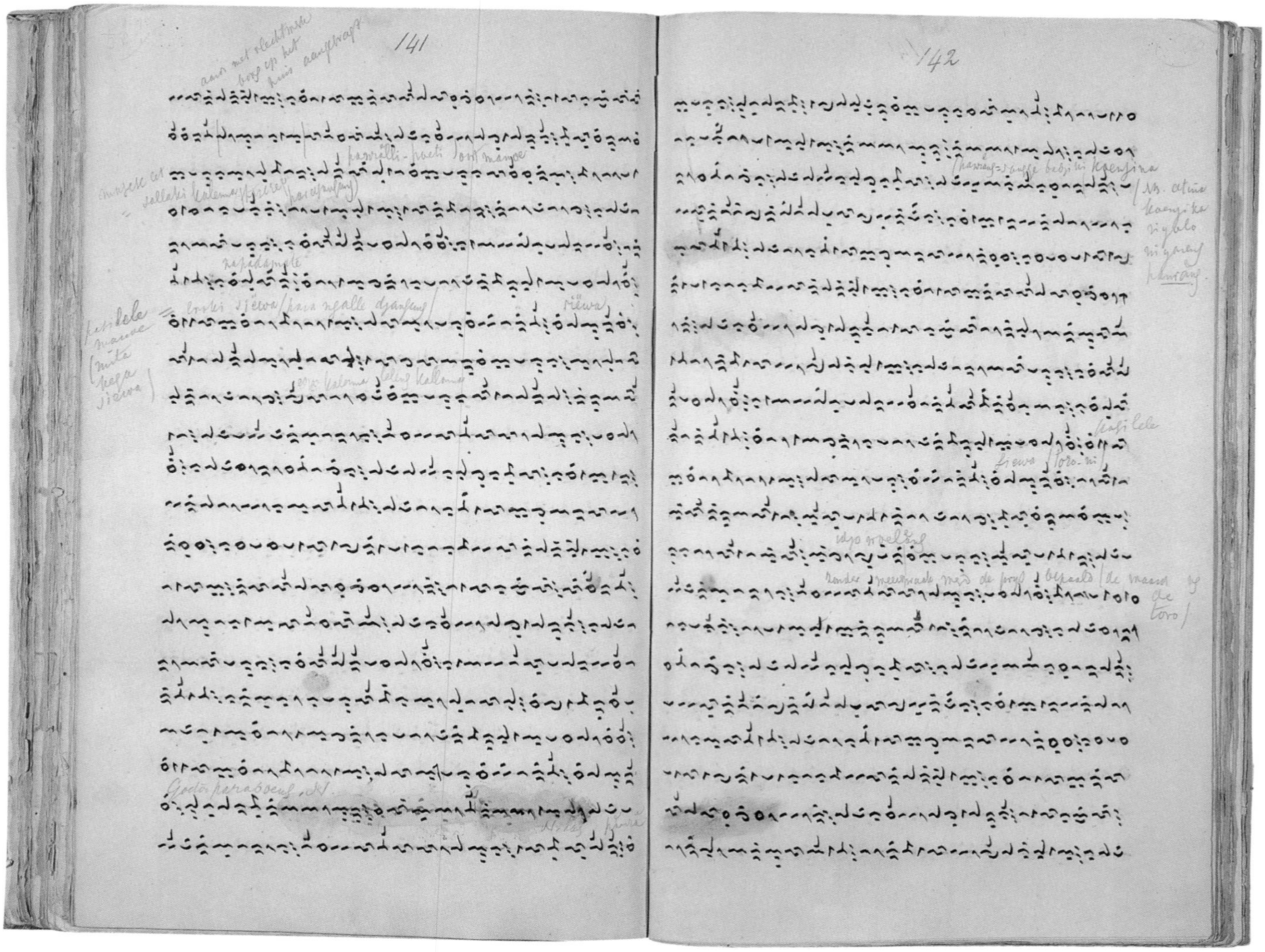

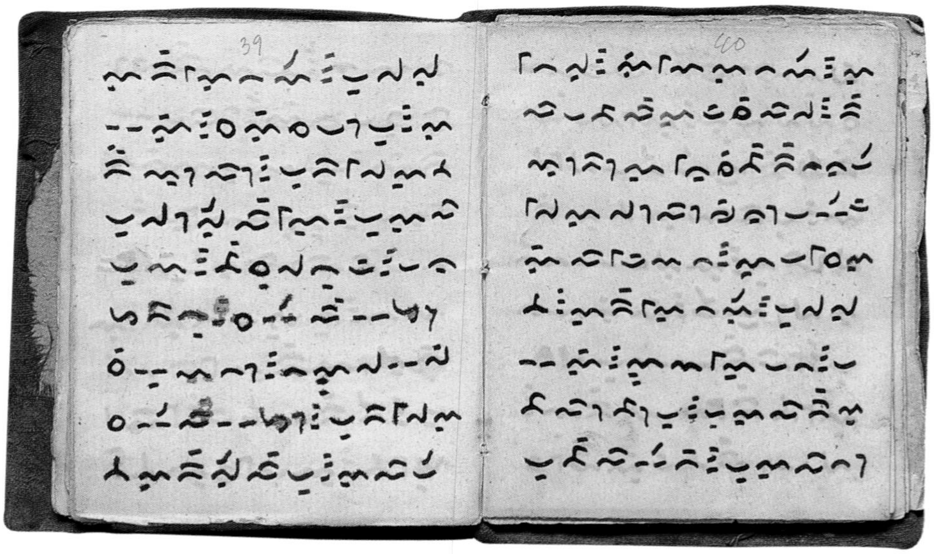

FIGURE 247

Pages from a *La Galigo* manuscript.
Leiden University Library, Leiden.

FIGURE 248

La Galigo. National Library of Indonesia,
Jakarta.

texts from elsewhere in Indonesia. The most important texts in this category
are chronicles (*attoriolong*), daily registers (*lontaraq bilang*), and genealogies
(*lontaraq pangngoriseng*). These different types of text are frequently grouped
together within a single manuscript: chronicles in particular are often interspersed with genealogies. A genre that combines elements from historiographical texts and texts similar to *La Galigo* is called the *toloq*, a type of heroic-
historical poem.

To Appanyompa said: "All you com-moners, go down to bathe and wash your hair, and let the fragrant dirt from your skin flow away in the stream, since we won't return to Aléluwuq."

Sawérigading then spoke: "Brother La Nanrang and cousins, you too go down there and take a bath to let the fragrant dirt from your skin and sweat flow away, since we won't return to Aléluwuq and Watampareq."

Sawérigading stood up and went down to take a bath in the river. Every-body went down to take a bath, the princes who manage the beautiful land, the distinguished princes, pillars of the country, the administrators of justice, children of the rich and the commanders, the conductors of the people's river, the knights accompa-nied by their escorts, made merry by merry-makers.

Sawérigading spoke in tears: "Let us bath in the stream, men, to have our fragrant sweat washed away. Let us bath in the eddies, let us have our fragrant sweat flow away, since we won't return to Aléluwuq."

CHRONICLE OF THE KINGDOM OF WAJOQ

Three days after the Karaéng was beheaded, the people from Boné and Goa concluded a treaty under the mango tree in Caleppaq. This was the treaty they agreed upon: to remember the pact called The Sitting Together of the Suddang Banner and the Téa Ri Duni Banner: the territory to the north of the Tangka River would belong to Boné, the territory to the south of the Tangka River would belong to Goa. Five days after the people from Boné and Goa concluded the treaty, the Makasarese went out together with the king of Boné. They installed Daéng Patoboq as king of Goa. There was no war any more; the lands were completely peaceful. To Udda married Arung Sakuli. They begat one daughter. She mar-ried La Jurangi. They begat one child, called Da Abéng. Wé Tenriateq mar-ried Arung Sékkannasu, called La Pakkanna To Palinrungi. They begat one child called Wé Lompu. Wé Tenriteppoq married To Angkauq, son of Arung Rumpia. They begat one child called Wé Tenriamo. To Kerreq married Wé Tenriukkeq, daughter of Arung Mario, who bore the title Baccoaé. They begat four children: one was called La Pasen-nungeng To Marilauq, one was called To Passakkeq, one was called Wé Tenriabéng, one was called Tenri-wakoreng. An envoy of the Karaéng came to Wajoq and said, "This is the order the Karaéng gave me: call upon the people of Wajoq and tell them to go to Berruq and to bring down for me my wooden posts to the sea." To Maddualeng answered and said, "Envoy, report these words of Wajoq to the Karaéng: even if he wished us to bring down the posts from Temmalaté in Goa, we would go, the more so since it is only in Berruq." The envoy of the Karaéng returned. This king of Wajoq sent an envoy to the king of Boné and he said, "This is the order your brother the king of Wajoq gave me: go and inform my brother that an envoy of the Karaéng called upon me to tell me to go to Berruq in order to bring down posts to the sea."

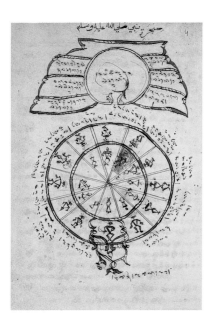

Each Bugis kingdom had its chronicle. They were composed and arranged according to a set of conventions, making use of daily registers, texts of treaties, genealogies, lists of rulers, and other chronicles. Most chronicles were arranged within a framework of reign periods. A fragment of a representative text, shown above, taken from an eighteenth-century chronicle of the kingdom of Wajoq, should give some idea of the contents and style of a chronicle.

This fragment contains the typical idiosyncrasies of a Bugis chronicle. It starts with an example of the notion of relative time ("Three days after"), a manner of referring to the passage of time found in almost any chronicle. Then the renewal of a treaty is mentioned, with the original treaty referred to by its very specific name. Some concise information on kings, wars, and the state of the country is given. A genealogy follows. An envoy arrives and a dialogue is quoted between king and envoy. Let us take a closer look at these features.

Chronicles were primarily based on two main sources, diaries and letter-books. The latter contained correspondence, including drafts and texts of treaties. The dates in the diaries and letter-books were transformed in the chronicles into relative time distances, but retained the chronological order required by the conventions of the genre.

A state history was first and foremost the history of kings and queens and wars with other kings and queens. Treaties formed points of reference in the histories of the different states. They were usually formulated in a symbolic, concise language, often with reference to former treaties. As such, they became an integral part of chronicles and were usually quoted in full.

The genealogy of rulers may be considered as the backbone of a chronicle. In general, the first ruler is described as having been a To Manurung, a person descended from heaven. Consequently, rulers were accorded a divine status that enabled them to lead a respected, privileged life among their people.

Another peculiarity of chronicles is the extensive use of dialogue. Those who speak are from the palace: kings, queens, ministers, wise counselors, and envoys. The scenes in which envoys (*suro*) occur are especially interesting. These *suro*-scenes employ a layered narration technique: the person who gives the order notifies the envoy of the words he should convey, and on each successive occasion these words are repeated in exactly the same wording in direct speech, thus retaining the precise wording of the original order.

The chronicle style is characterically simple and concise. It is simply plain narrative without any lexical embellishments, aimed at lucidity and clarity. Metaphorical language is employed only in the wording of the treaties and wise sayings, obviously as a mnemonic device. Of course a chronicle has its textual conventions too, but they are quite different from the entertaining devices of parallellism, repetition, formulas and meter of *Galigo* texts. Because of the absence of these techniques, the chronicle style is considered to be factual and authoritative.

DIARIES (DAILY REGISTERS)

The phenomenon of diary-keeping seems to be peculiar to the South Sulawesi area (fig. 250). Actually, the term *daily register* is better here, since the texts are not concerned with the private views of the author but rather with the day-to-day registration of events of importance to the state. The keeper of a diary was always a person of high rank, a ruler (*arung*), a prime minister (*to marilaleng*), or the like.

Bugis diaries have a peculiar, chaotic appearance. This is caused by the restrictions of their conventional, rigid layout, which is more or less similar to a condensed form of the modern "executive diary." For each month of the Christian era, there is one (folio) page available with dates already provided, so that the space for one day is limited. On top of the page the year is written in Arabic numerals. In the upper left corner the name of the month is given in Malay written in Arabic script. In a vertical column parallel to the left margin of the page, the dates of the months are written. Each Friday is marked with the word *Jum'at* in red Arabic letters. It is common to find that many dates were not filled in; apparently nothing worth mentioning had occurred on those days. However, there were also days full of events that could not be left unrecorded, so that the space assigned for one day simply was not enough. In order to expand his scribal

FIGURE 250

Ilmu Perbintangan. National Library of Indonesia, Jakarta.

FIGURE 251

A page from a diary. Royal Institute of Linguistics and Anthropology, Leiden.

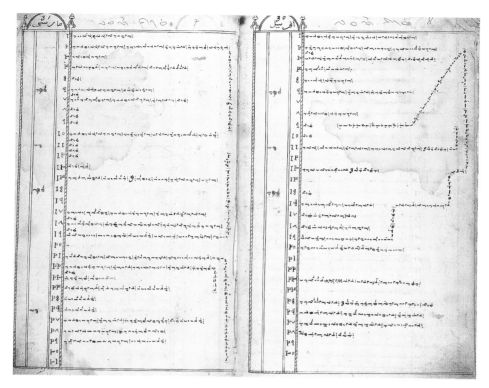

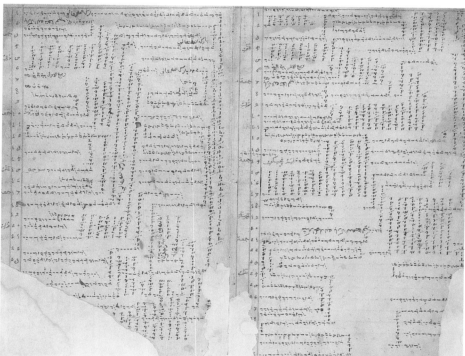

Lebensraum, a writer would start to fill up the free space left on the other days and the margins of the page, rotating the page as he wrote. This produces a chaotic pattern of streams of letters moving across the page, and the reader of such diaries has constantly to turn the diary around in order to be able to understand the message (fig. 251).

Quite a few Bugis daily registers have been identified in at least six collections: the National Library of Indonesia, the British Library, the India Office Library, the School of Oriental and African Studies (SOAS), the Royal Institute of Linguistics and Anthropology (KITLV), and the La Galigo Museum in Ujung Pandang. When we compare the dates from these diaries with each other, we see that all these diaries taken together represent a continuous stream of indigenous historical information on the period 1745 to 1910—almost two centuries. Furthermore, all the diaries seem to stem from one location, the Boné court. Very few diaries from other regions are known to exist.

On closer inspection we also find that the periods 1774–1812, 1818–1819, 1823–1840, and 1876–1893 are continuously covered by at least two different manuscripts. The period 1792–1796 is even represented in diaries from four different collections. It is probably no coincidence that this period of heightened activity almost fully corresponds with the reign of one particular ruler, La Tenritappu Sultan Ahmad Saleh Syamsuddin, posthumously called Matinroéri Rompégading, who ruled from 1775 to 1812. This is exciting for philologists and historians alike, and should make possible the writing of an "inside" history of the Boné court for this period (fig. 252).

TOLOQ

Toloq may be considered the Bugis literary genre par excellence. In these poems, which can run for hundreds of pages, the conventions of chronicles and *Galigo* texts are combined into a coherent whole. Using an eight-syllable meter, they tell of historical events, usually centered on a particular hero, in an archaic language full of parallelisms and formulas.

In the fragment shown on page 229, which also contains an envoy scene, these qualities of *toloq* are evident. The fragment begins with the line *Makkedi La Ménrirana* ("The history relates"), an almost prescriptive formula for beginning *toloq* or marking its main sections. Within the broad framework set by the *ménri-rana*-lines, numerous other formulas typical of Bugis poetic texts are used, almost all of them referring to a notion of time. In the cited fragment, we come across the formulaic time markers *ala maressaq otaé, ala kkédéq pabbojaé* ("faster than betel can be chewed, in the twinkling of an eye") to denote a very short time lapse, *namarété langiqédé, namapappaq bajaé* ("at the break of day, early next morning") and *na llabuqna dettia* ("at sunset"), respectively denoting the beginning and the end of daytime.

Within the formulaic framework, the particular story has to be told. We see a considerable variation among the texts regarding preference for certain formulas

FIGURE 252

An early-twentieth-century photograph of the court of Boné.

The history relates:
At the break of day,
early next morning,
I Lamu respectfully
asked permission to leave.
The request was granted
and he went hurriedly.
Faster than betel can be chewed,
in the twinkling of an eye,
he had left Boné behind,
gone down to the middle of
    Mampu and passed Wélado.
At sunset
he arrived in Pompanua
and entered immediately

the residential palace of
the Commander-in-Chief of Boné.
He made a respectful greeting
and sat down before His Majesty
the commander-in-chief of Boné.
Then spoke
I Lamu:
"I report to you, lord, on
your orders to me.
This is what your father,
Ruler of Boné, has told me:
'It is right if my beloved
son and successor receives
compensation from
the territory of Madello.' "

and their frequency, while "formulaicness" is not always evenly spread within the texts themselves. The fragment cited above, for instance, shows a cumulation of formulas and other poetical clichés, but in the same text there are also long episodes that have only minimal use of such formulas.

Not only formulas but also many of the metaphors are of a highly conventional nature. Even whole scenes in *toloq*, such as battlefield scenes, are mutually exchangeable between different texts. The story of these battles and the preparations for them is often told in terms of a cockfight, the battlefield being the arena and the warriors likened to a variety of glorious fighting cocks with spurs attached, ready to fight. During these battles "guns crack like double thunderclaps" and "bullets rain down like falling berries." The language used is always exalted. Common things are rendered in a special, elevated fashion: a house is called "residential palace," a head, "the carrier of a headdress." To start a war is "to cause a mighty revolt in the arena of lances or the marketplace of shields," attractive young women are "the wearers of red blouses," and sometimes, also, "the pearls of the cookhouse, nightingales of the mid-house, evening stars of the room, torches of the gilded boudoir." And of course these literary devices are furthermore reinforced by means of repetitions and paralellisms.

Obviously the poetic devices used in *toloq* are similar to those used in *Galigo* texts. Yet it is the historical nature of *toloq*, the story that is being told, that distinguishes these texts from all other poetry. These stories of wars and warriors are not fictional tales—all incidents mentioned actually happened and the kings, queens, warriors, and envoys are historical figures.

In *toloq* there is usually an abundance of all kinds of precise enumerations. These can be regarded as reality markers, as is usual in historiographical texts. Exact information is always given on the geographical situation. In the fragment cited above, there is a description of the route that I Lamu took from Boné to Pompanua. Descriptions of this kind are hardly ever lacking when someone is on the move from one place to another. Another convention common in Bugis historiography occurs in the last lines of the fragment. We read how the messenger I Lamu reports to his master the exact words of the ruler of Boné by quoting him in direct speech. In the preceding episode (not cited here), these royal words have already been cited, and indeed, I Lamu repeats them without a flaw. A similar envoy scene—albeit in a quite different setting—occurred in the fragment from the Wajoq chronicle cited earlier.

It is evident that the "unembellished" story of a *toloq* bears a close resemblance to historiographical texts such as are contained in chronicles. There are differences too: for instance, genealogies, so important in chronicles, do not occur in *toloq* texts. However, the similarities in content between *toloq* and chronicle are overwhelming.

To summarize, *toloq* texts can be considered as a merging of two principal categories in Bugis literature: *Galigo* texts and chronicles. They have both an entertaining and a referential function, neither dominating the other. The content of a *toloq* is like that of a chronicle, but narrated in a *Galigo* fashion.

Roger Tol

BARK, BONES, AND BAMBOO:
BATAK TRADITIONS OF SUMATRA

Originally all non-Islamic societies found along the Bukit Barisan mountain chain of what is now the province of North Sumatra were referred to as Batak (fig. 253). This definition of the term "Batak" lost all basis, however, through the Islamization of large areas of the Southern Bataklands (Angkola and Mandailing) following the Padri Wars of the first third of the last century and through the Christianization of all other Batak peoples (Toba, Dairi-Pakpak, Simalungun, and Karo) by missionaries (fig. 254). Today the Mandailing, in particular, avoid referring to themselves as Batak, but in other areas, too, there is an increasing emphasis on belonging to a particular ethnic group. Today only the inhabitants of the district of Tapanuli Utara describe themselves as Batak. In the ethnological literature, they are generally, although not entirely correctly, described as Toba Batak. The six Batak groups mentioned are more or less independent tribal societies that have never formed an overall political unit. Even within the separate ethnic groups, political association was based almost entirely on local considerations and took the form of federations of villages, which, as a rule, belonged to the same clan or subclan.

The different Batak ethnic groups are distinguished not only culturally but also linguistically. The differences between the numerous dialects of Batak are so great that Toba and Karo Batak may practically be considered as two distinct languages. They belong respectively to the Northern and Southern group of Batak dialects. Besides Karo Batak, the Northern group also includes the Alas dialect of southeastern Aceh (a non-Batak people) and Dairi-Pakpak Batak, with the subdialects of Kelasan, Simsim, Pegagan, and the Kata Boang of Upper Singkel. The Southern group are Toba and Angkola-Mandailing. Finally, there is Simalungun Batak, which varies considerably from the Northern and Southern group, but might be regarded as an earlier offspring of the branch of Southern Batak dialects.

Little was known about the language and literature of the Batak until the middle of the nineteenth century. In 1849, the Nederlandsch Bijbelgenootschap (Netherlands Bible Society) assigned the Dutch linguist Hermann Neubronner van der Tuuk to study the Batak language. From 1851 until his return in 1857, he lived mostly in Barus, a small trading port on the west coast of North Sumatra. From there he traveled in 1853 to the interior, where he was the first European to see Lake Toba. Referred to by Braasem as the "Father of Indonesian Philology," Van der Tuuk wrote a comprehensive grammar and a dictionary of the Toba Batak language. After nearly one hundred years, this first modern scientific grammar of an Indonesian language was republished in 1971 in English translation, and the dictionary has remained an important reference for everyone concerned with Batak language and culture. In the four volumes of the *Bataaksch Leesboek* (Batak reader), he published extensive materials on the oral literature of the Toba, Mandailing, and Dairi-Pakpak. Van der Tuuk's legacy is preserved in the Leiden University Library. It consists of numerous folio volumes containing samples of the oral and written literature of the Batak as well as a collection of more than fifty Batak bark books (*pustaha*).

Since 1927 Petrus Voorhoeve has contributed numerous publications to the systematic research on Batak literature. We are particularly indebted to him for a nearly complete inventory of Batak manuscripts in European, American, and

Australian collections. The Batak themselves, however, have also taken a significant part in the study of their language and literature. Liberty Manik has made an inventory of the majority of Batak manuscripts in German collections. According to his comprehensive catalogue, more than five hundred manuscripts can be found in German collections alone. It is difficult to gauge how many are spread throughout the world, but the total may exceed two thousand. To Japorman Edison Saragih, the former assistant of Voorhoeve during his term as *Taalambtenaar* (language officer) in Sumatra, we owe not only the translation of two *pustaha* from the museum of Pematang Siantar (Simalungun) but also a Simalungun Batak-Indonesian dictionary.

THE BATAK SCRIPT

The linguistic differences among Batak languages are also reflected in their script, and have resulted in the development of several variants of Batak script. Depending on dialect, the script (*surat*) consists of nineteen to twenty-one radical signs called *ina ni surat* ("mother of the script") and six to eight diacritical signs called *anak ni surat* ("children of the script"). Inherent to the radicals which, with the exceptions of the radicals /i/ and /u/ are always consonants, is the vowel [a]. The other vowels and several final consonants are indicated by diacritics, which are placed above or to the right of the radical sign. A diacritical in the form of a slash placed after a consonantal radical sign indicates the omission of the *a*-sound. Whereas Javanese script uses a second set of signs (*pasangan*) to indicate consonant clusters, Batak script, like all other non-Javanese scripts of island Southeast Asia, uses only the *pangolet* for consonant sequences. Batak writing is thus more easily learned and is more efficient than other syllabic scripts, since every single variant of Batak script perfectly reproduces the sound composition of each language. The script is written from left to right and from top to bottom. The script signs follow one another without empty spaces, and even signs separating sentences are unknown, except for the decorative signs referred to as *bindu,* which separate paragraphs of text.

There has been much speculation about the origins of the Batak script. Even though the Batak alphabet was already published by William Marsden in 1784 in his *History of Sumatra,* Batak manuscripts were still objects of the most curious speculation in the nineteenth century and were described as Egyptian, old Persian, or old Phoenician writings, or even as a mixture of Arabic and Greek letters written by a Chinese, or as astronomical signs.

According to Batak mythology, there was once a bark book that contained all the knowledge of humankind (fig. 255). Even today there is a widespread belief that the Dutch carried this *pustaha* to Holland, thereby depriving the Batak of access to the source of wisdom. This bark book is referred to as *pustaha tombaga*

FIGURE 253

Early-twentieth-century French map of the Batak lands.

FIGURE 254

Decorative detail from a Batak *pustaha.* Unlike in most parts of Muslim Indonesia, dogs are a common feature in Batak villages. National Library of Indonesia, Jakarta.

FIGURE 255

A *pustaha* containing instruction on a war
divination from the Karo highlands. This
bark book was acquired in 1841 by the
German explorer, Franz Junghuhn.
National Library of Indonesia, Jakarta.

holing. *Pustaha* is a loan word from the Sanskrit, and *holing* (after the Indian region of Kalinga) is the term used to describe the South Indian Tamils. *Tombaga* (copper) brings to mind the inscribed copper tablets that were in use in India, as well as in Java and Bali. So the name of this legendary encyclopedia of knowledge, *pustaha tombaga holing*, suggests that the sources of Batak script should be sought in India or, possibly, Java.

The theory, widely accepted today, that Batak script is derived from the Old Javanese Kawi script is based on the studies of K.F. Holle and H. Kern. There have been attempts to counter this theory, however. Engelbertus E.W. Schröder, in a long but not very convincing treatise, attempted to show a direct connection between the Batak and the Phoenician alphabets. And in an essay by Mangantar Simanjutak entitled "The Batak Script as an Invention of the Austronesian Speaking People," the author, himself a Batak, attempted to demonstrate that Batak script is the medium from which all non-Javanese scripts of island Southeast Asia have developed. His arguments, however, are speculative and cannot withstand scientific investigation.

Most closely related to Batak script are the South Sumatran scripts of Lampung, Kerinci, and Rejang. Kern suspected that the other non-Javanese scripts of island Southeast Asia (the scripts of the Philippines and Sulawesi) developed from the Sumatran scripts. J.G. de Casparis concurs with this view, but cautions that "more research is needed to establish the precise relationships."

The non-Javanese scripts of Southeast Asia are known only in their present forms, since these scripts were never used for inscriptions in stone or other durable materials. Therefore it is not possible—as it is in the case of Javanese script—to follow the historical development of these scripts.

Wolfgang Marschall argues that an Old Javanese inscription from 1286 found in Padang Roco (West Sumatra) represents the link between Kawi script and the South Sumatran scripts. Marschall is mistaken in this, because the Padang Roco inscription is written in contemporary Kawi and shows no close relationship to other Sumatran scripts. Marschall further assumes that the differences between the South Sumatran scripts and Batak script permit the conclusion that "the latter appeared some time after the first formation of the South Sumatran scripts." Marschall's hypothesis builds on the premise that the South Sumatran scripts—probably because of their geographical propinquity to Java—are older than the Batak script. This, however, is in no way certain.

The first inscriptions of Sumatra were written in Indian scripts. They include the Srivijaya inscriptions written in Palawa script in the seventh century and several Tamil inscriptions from the eleventh to the fourteenth century. Inscriptions in Old Javanese script are found between the tenth and the fourteenth century in South and West Sumatra, as well as in the temple complex of Padang Lawas (South Tapanuli, North Sumatra). In his book on Indonesian paleography, de Casparis points out that the inscriptions of Adityawarman (1356–1375, Central Sumatra) cannot be derived from contemporary Javanese script, and suggests that this variant of the later Kawi script may have developed locally over hundreds of years and with its own local tradition. Therefore, it is possible that the Sumatran scripts have developed from the Kawi script as handed down in the inscriptions of Adityawarman. A comparison by H. Parkin of the different variants of the Batak script confirms also that the script spread from south to north. Since Batak manuscripts are never dated, the day of their inclusion in a museum collection becomes the *terminus ante quem* for the age of a particular manuscript. The first Batak manuscript reached the British Museum in 1764. After thorough study, Voorhoeve was unable to detect any differences in form between the script of the oldest and of the most recent manuscripts. Thus the development of Batak script was completed two hundred years ago. Should the hypothesis of the development of the Sumatran scripts from the inscriptions of Adityawarman be confirmed, it would mean that within a period of less than four hundred years the Batak developed a form of writing that in its signs has very few similarities with its script of origin. For this reason, doubts that the scripts mentioned are indeed the prototype of the non-Javanese scripts of island Southeast Asia are very much to the point. It is likely that these scripts developed from the Kawi script at a much earlier time. Only the discovery of additional Sumatran inscriptions can be expected to provide an answer to this question.

WRITING MATERIALS

Bamboo, bones, and tree bark were the principal writing materials. The script was incised into the epidermis of the bamboo (fig. 256) or the shoulder or rib bones of the water buffalo with the point of a knife and was then blackened with soot to improve readability. The bark books of the Batak, however, are even more well known (fig. 257). In the Southern languages they are called *pustaha* and in the northern languages, *pustaka*—a loan word from the Sanskrit that points to the Indian origins of the Batak writing tradition. In Simalungun, these books are called *laklak* (bast). This refers to the bast of the *alim* tree (*Aquilaria Malaccensis*). It is pulled off in long strips which are then cut, beaten, polished, and prepared with rice flour paste. These strips are then folded in the manner of a Leporello Album and glued to two wooden covers which serve as binding (fig. 258).

The bamboo manuscripts, as well as the *pustaha,* vary in size and in degree of elaboration (figs. 259, 260). The largest and most elaborate *pustaha* is without any doubt the one from Van der Tuuk's collection (figs. 261, 262, 263). This contrasts with the *pustaha* in miniature form that only measure a few centimeters, as well as

FIGURE 256
Bamboo *pustaha*. National Library of Indonesia, Jakarta.

FIGURE 257

Bark *pustaha*. National Library of
Indonesia, Jakarta.

FIGURE 258

Bast *pustaha*. National Library of
Indonesia, Jakarta.

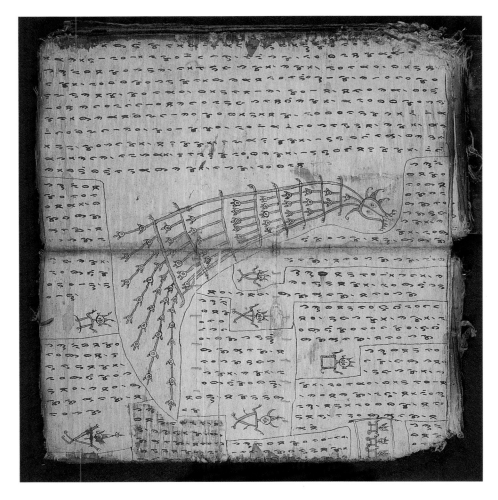

those that were made less elaborately and are often missing even the characteristic wooden cover. There is great variance in the size and quality of *pustaha* (fig. 264).

Betel is a widespread stimulant in Southeast Asia and plays an important role on social and ritual occasions. Not surprisingly, containers for betel and lime (which serves as a fermentation agent and frees the slightly anesthetizing substances of the betel nut) are often beautiful and highly prized objects. On the elaborately

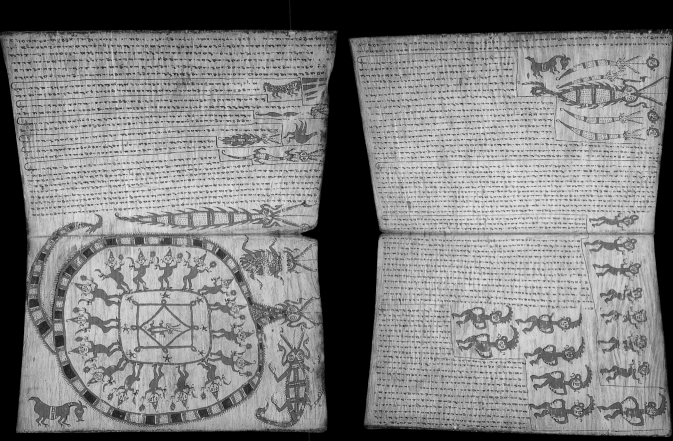

FIGURE 263

Pages from the manuscript shown in
figure 261.

decorated lime container shown here (fig. 265), the text of a Karo lamentation has
been incised in very fine script. The container is closed with a stopper through
which a cloth band is pulled to facilitate easy opening. The bottom of the betel-
lime container is formed by the node of the bamboo. Since the node is marked on
the outside by more or less prominent and irregular swellings, and since these are
evidently viewed as unattractive, they are eliminated with two deep slashes. This
creates a narrow bridge in the middle. The beginning and the end of the text are
separated from each other by a long ornamental strip. The text occupies an area
of only 10 by 10 centimeters. Yet the writer was able to cover this area with an
amazing total of 639 words. This text was written about 1915 by an employee of
the colonial administration in the Karo Batak area of Barusjahe. The same writer
composed thirty-four additional manuscripts that are very similar in form and in
content. In many of his lamentations, the author disapproves of the colonial government and expresses his sympathy for the Karo Batak *raja* of the village of
Batukarang, who in 1904 tried unsuccessfully to prevent the annexation of the
Karo highlands by the colonial army. These manuscripts are the only Batak texts
known to me in which an effort is made to use a traditional medium (Batak script
on bamboo container) to convey modern messages. Other laments of the Karo are
written on equally richly ornamented tobacco containers and occasionally also on
weaving shuttles and bamboo flutes. The laments of the Simalungun, too, were

written on elaborately ornamented bamboo containers such as the container for storing weaving utensils (*parlilian*) that is shown here (fig. 266). The laments of the Mandailing and Angkola however, are always written on plain, thick, and usually long bamboo tubes of several internodes. Items as homely as gourds might also become the slate for inscriptions (fig. 267).

On short but equally plain bamboo pieces are written letters, including threatening ones. The latter are always accompanied by miniature weapons, bamboo rifles, lances, and fire stones intended to reinforce the threat. In the last decades of the nineteenth century, large numbers of these threats were sent by Karo Bataks, who considered themselves cheated out of land or wages, to the administrators of the European plantations in Deli (east coast of Sumatra). Not infrequently these threats were carried out and the tobacco barns of the European entrepreneurs went up in flames.

On the shoulder and rib bones of the water buffalo are found primarily short magic formulas (*tabas*), occasionally also short laments, as well as a number of magic drawings, stars, pentacles, and anthropomorphic figures. Frequently these bones were used as amulets (fig. 268). The amulet shown here is inscribed with an oracle as well as with a fragment of a lament that, according to its text, served to avert illness and bullets. Batak manuscripts, especially the *pustaha,* are usually provided with many illustrations. Figures 262 and 263 show an astrological deity called Pané, which in the course of a year resides three months in each cardinal direction (figs. 269, 270). For military enterprises in particular it is necessary to know where Pané resides at any time. To determine his whereabouts, this oracle is consulted. The eight parts of the text are probably connected to the eight cardinal and subcardinal directions.

Every paragraph refers to a part of the body of Pané and the consequences that result if the enemy's village is located in that direction. Interpretation of the illustrations of a *pustaha* is not always easy, even if the accompanying text is

FIGURE 264

Assorted *pustaha.* Royal Institute for the Tropics, Amsterdam.

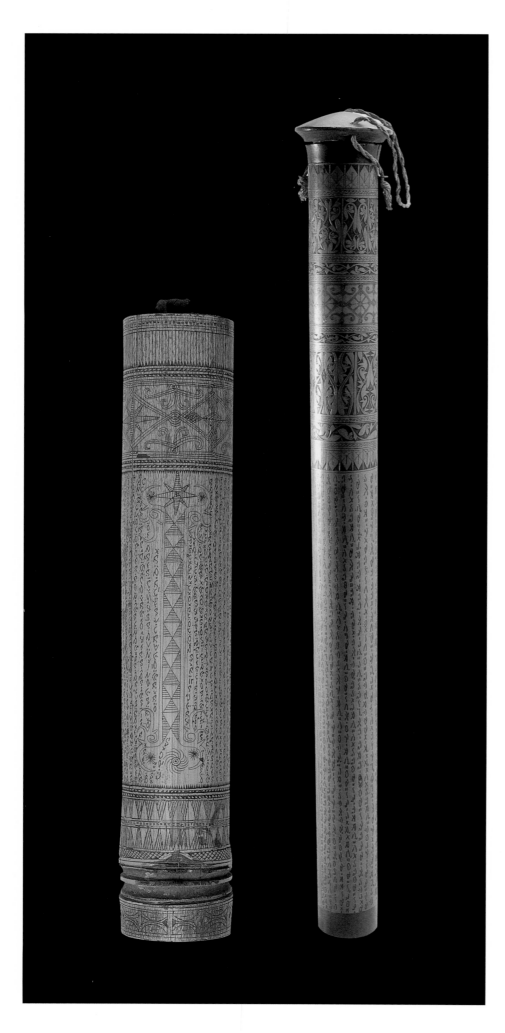

FIGURE 265

A betel-lime container. Museum für
Völkerkunde, Berlin.

FIGURE 266

Parlilian, a container for storing *lili* (small
sticks used in weaving), inscribed with a
lament. Tropical Museum, Royal Institute
for the Tropics, Amsterdam.

known. A comparative study of illustrations in the *pustaha* in the context of their textual reference could throw light on this still largely unknown chapter of Batak literature and illustrative art, thus making it no longer necessary to make do with speculation. Note the comment made by J. Freiherr von Brenner in 1898 on the illustrations of a *pustaha* that he studied:

> Observation of these strange drawings is oddly exciting, like a picture rebus in which a deep truth is hidden and the recurring thought awakens in us that here we have to do with an efflorescence which does not originate in the soil directly before our eyes. We hear the distant roar of the sacred Ganges, the breathing of an old culture sunk into a deep sleep. . . . [One] appears to represent the Buddhist sun wheel, the Cakra. The figures remind us to a greater or lesser extent of the Indian deities.

Some thirty years later, however, Voorhoeve was to add, quite critically, that for this *"wel wat veel fantasie nodig [is],"* that is, a great deal of imagination is required.

LITERATURE: THE SCIENCE OF THE DATU

While the bone and bamboo manuscripts could be made by anyone able to write, the creation of a *pustaha* was the task of specialists. These were the *guru* or *datu*, the magicians and healers of the Batak. The *pustaha* were generally inscribed on both sides. Small sticks were used to apply the ink, which in addition to other ingredients consisted mainly of resin soot and tree sap. The recipes for the manufacture of the ink that were also preserved in the *pustaha* show that this was not an easy task. One of the Simalunguan *pustaha* states: "When the oil is added to the other ingredients, the following signs should be observed. . . . If the oil separates out in the middle, this is a bad omen. There will be unrest. Since this is unavoidable, one should stop the preparation of the ink."

As J. Edison Saragih reports, "To neutralize bad influences a human figure should be carved from a banana trunk in order to avert dangers from the preparer of the ink." The bark books often begin with a chain of transmission that lists the names of the *guru* who have passed on the instructions. A *pustaha* contains almost

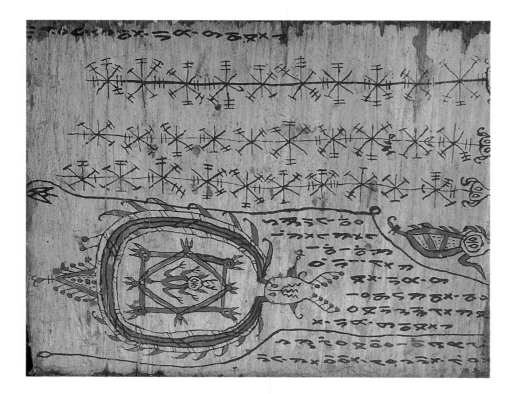

FIGURE 269
A page from a Toba-Batak *pustaha*
showing a Pané, an astrological deity.
Tropical Museum, Royal Institute for the
Tropics, Amsterdam.

exclusively texts on the conduct of rituals, oracles, and recipes for the manufacture of medicines. Myths and legends were handed down orally and reproduced in a *pustaha* only if in the description of a ritual the *guru* considered them necessary for better understanding of the ritual. Thus in a few *pustaha* can be found the legend of the origin of the magic staff. Clan genealogies or historical texts also were not included in the *pustaha*, yet the Batak never used their script for administrative purposes. Apart from letters or love poetry, the script only served the *hadatuan*, the science of the *datu*. The German missionary doctor Johannes Winkler concerned himself intensively with this topic. His publication *Die Toba Batak in gesunden und kranken Tagen* (The Toba Batak in days of health and disease) gives an exhaustive overview of the literature contained in the *pustaha* (figs. 271, 272).

The *pustaha* serve the *guru* and his students as a mnemonic aid. Understanding of the texts therefore presupposes a certain measure of background information. The only ones in a position to understand the texts of the *pustaha* are the *guru* and their students. An additional difficulty encountered in reading a *pustaha* is derived from the fact that the text is composed in the language referred to as *hata poda* (language of instruction) by Van der Tuuk. This is an archaic southern dialect containing many loan words from Malay. This *poda* language was the special language of the *guru* throughout the Batak land. Knowledge of this language simplified communication among *guru* with different mother tongues, but more particularly this language, which was unknown to the layman, served to increase the social status of the *guru*. Depending on the origins of the *guru,* numerous words of their respective linguistic backgrounds flowed into the *pustaha*. The *guru* and their pupils traveled through the region and were often instructed by teachers from other places. This exchange of knowledge among *guru* from different Batak backgrounds resulted in the inclusion in the *pustaha of* expressions from different dialects in addition to the characteristic words of the *poda* language. Because of this difficulty, there has to date been no attempt to publish a critical edition of a *pustaha*. Yet, on the basis of the studies of Voorhoeve and Manik, excellent descriptions and translations of large passages of text from the bark books have been published.

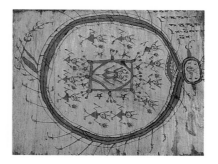
FIGURE 270
Detail from the *Pustaha* in figure 269.

FIGURE 271
Pages from a *pustaha*. National Library of
Indonesia, Jakarta.

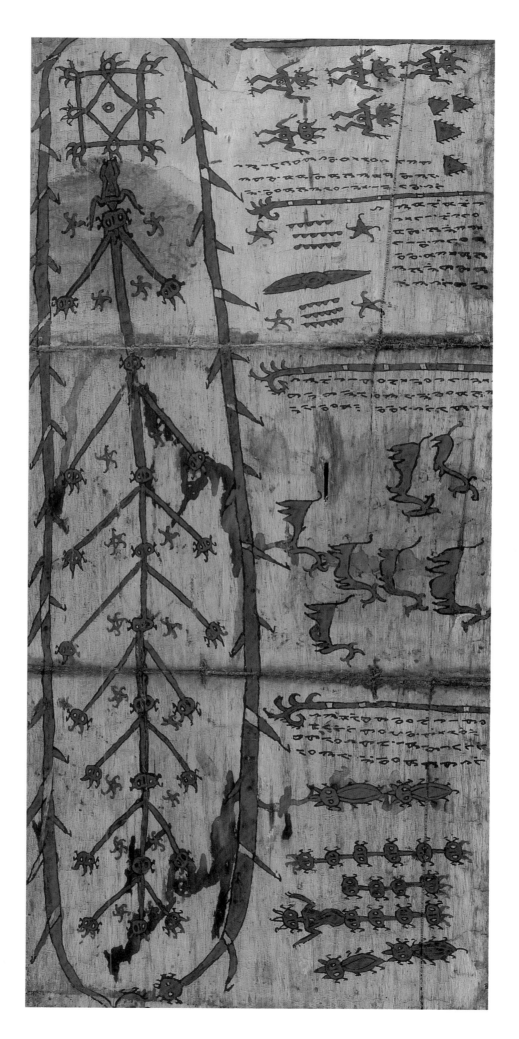

——————— FIGURE 272 ———————

Details from the *pustaha* in figure 271.

THE SPREAD OF LITERACY

The esoteric character of the *pustaha* texts and the specialist nature of their writers as well as the association of the writing with the magico-religious activities of the Batak have again and again led scholars to conclude that the Batak writing tradition itself was the domain of the *guru*. (Raechelle Rubinstein describes the same phenomenon in her chapter on the Balinese writing tradition.) Susan Rodgers connects what she assumes to be the limited spread of literacy in pre-colonial society with the semisyllabic writing system of the Batak. In "Me and Toba: A Childhood World in a Batak Memoir," she writes, "The script was never used as a medium of mass literacy. . . . Only a small elite group could read and write (better, decipher) this syllabic writing system."

In my view, Rodgers is mistaken on two counts. As I will demonstrate below, the literacy of the Batak was not limited to a small group of professional literates and the writing system is extraordinarily easy to learn and simple to read.

Of the approximately 500 Batak manuscripts that Liberty Manik catalogued in German museums and libraries, scarcely half are *pustaha*. Likewise, the majority of the bamboo and bone inscriptions were composed by *guru*. Nevertheless, 122 manuscripts were written by laymen. These include 33 letters, 56 laments, 22 threatening letters, and 11 writing exercises, all written on bamboo or bone. This however, does not permit the conclusion that fewer letters or laments were written than *pustaha*. The attractively made and sometimes elaborately illustrated *pustaha* were preferred by the collectors of curiosities to the pieces of bamboo on which laymen wrote down their letters and love poems, and were guarded by their owners and handed down from generation to generation. It may be the German missionary J.G. Warneck who is responsible for the common assumption of the limited spread of writing literacy among the Batak, for it was he who, in his 1899 study of Toba Batak literature, wrote: "It should be recognized and appreciated that the Batak have shaped their script, which may possibly have come from India, in the most original fashion. But it is not common property of the people and the characteristic literature of the Batak has nothing to do with it."

Warneck wrote this thirty years after the beginning of the Christian mission among the Toba Batak. Similarly, while the Dutch linguist Van der Tuuk was able to acquire a great number of Toba Batak *pustaha* during his five years research in Barus, he writes about a "lack of pigs and *pustaha*" in the Mandailing area, recently Islamized. Evidently, there is a direct relationship between the decline of the writing tradition and the spread of Islam or Christianity.

Together with the "idols," the *pustaha* and other manuscripts were also burnt by overzealous missionaries, as still happened only a few years ago in the Karo highlands. The German explorer Franz Junghuhn wrote in 1847, years before the Christian mission:

> The children are not instructed in anything and the only thing they learn by imitation is writing, that is, scratching characters with the point of their knife onto bamboo and reading what was thus written down. This art of written communication is the only scientific art which they have; it is, however, widespread among them, especially in Tobah [Toba], where young men scarcely fourteen years old usually begin their first literary efforts by sending love letters to young girls, scratched on pieces of bamboo one-and-one-half inches wide and six inches to one foot long. In these letters they praise the full breasts, the shining hair of their beauties, their strong arms when stamping rice, and ask for some evidence of their favor, which happily is generally granted.

In the Karo area where Christianity only slowly established itself after Indonesian independence, the manuscript tradition generally endured the longest.

So the German explorer Freiherr von Brenner writes: "The most important criteria of the entire spiritual development of a people is a script which is not exclusively the property of a privileged class, but which represents the common property of the entire population."

Apart from the fact that Brenner ignored the female half of the population (I have so far found no evidence that in Batak society women have ever been able to write), his statement confirms the results of my own research. In predominantly European ethnographic collections there are about 120 Karo laments. There are many indications that the Karo Batak tradition of the love lament, which was maintained into the second decade of this century, was widespread among young people as part of courting customs. The written tradition of the lament was also known among the Simalungun, Angkola, and Mandailing. The manuscripts of the Angkola and Mandailing can be dated to the 1850s and 1860s. Thereafter, this tradition died out probably as a consequence of Islamic and Christian missions.

In addition to the laments, the numerous letters indicate a general literacy in the pre-Islamic and pre-Christian Batak societies. Only through the influence of, first, the missions and, finally, the introduction of Latin script, an educational system, and modern printing media did indigenous Batak writing begin to be forgotten.

Today Batak script is again taught in the schools. But since the teachers have never read a Batak manuscript, only what is today considered to be Batak script is taught. This is a standardized and simplified form, knowledge of which is not sufficient for reading a manuscript. In any case, a Batak will scarcely have the chance to read a Batak manuscript unless he visits the National Library in Jakarta or travels abroad to Germany and the Netherlands, where the largest collections of Batak manuscripts are found. In the Batak lands themselves, one finds (with the exception of individual, mostly short, manuscripts in the museums of Pematang Siantar and Medan) only *pustaha* manufactured as souvenirs for European and Japanese tourists in the tourist centers of Parapat and Tomok.

A few years ago, an offset printing press was presented to the Batak. Since there are a number of versions of the Batak script, agreement was reached after several seminars and conferences to create a new Batak script only partially based on the old writing, and to create several new signs to facilitate the writing of foreign words. In all this enthusiasm it was forgotten that the printing press would never be able to fulfill its function, because Batak script has not been written down for more than fifty years and this is not likely to change in the future.

Uli Kozok

ANCIENT LINKS: THE MYSTERY
OF SOUTH SUMATRA

Written on bark, bamboo, rattan sticks, copperplates, paper, and buffalo horn, South Sumatran manuscripts represent an important link to the past. They derive from an ancient tradition of Indonesian literature that pre-dates the Islamic presence in Sumatra, and as such they provide important evidence of the cultural development of Indonesia. Yet these manuscripts are rare—there are perhaps no more than four hundred in about twenty public collections throughout the world—and the language they are written in remains poorly documented and relatively inaccessible. What we do know of these manuscripts is due to the work of a handful of Dutch scholars, and above all to Petrus Voorhoeve, who was employed before the Second World War as a government linguist in Sumatra, and who has made this interesting literary tradition far more accessible through cataloguing of South Sumatran manuscripts in public collections, and through his research publications. This account of South Sumatran manuscripts is based primarily on Voorhoeve's published work: even more material is available in the complete collection of his unpublished notes and papers in the Eastern Manuscripts Section in Leiden University Library.

SCRIPTS

The South Sumatra scripts, like the Batak script, were based originally on an Indian model. Voorhoeve postulates an ancestral Sumatran indigenous proto-script from which the Batak and South Sumatran scripts developed. The earliest firm date for a South Sumatran manuscript is 1630, the acquisition date of a bark Lampung manuscript in the Bodleian Library, Oxford. Other manuscripts date from the late eighteenth and the nineteenth centuries. However, it seems clear that a Sumatran proto-script must have been much more ancient, certainly older than any of the attested manuscripts. The Batak and South Sumatran areas in which these scripts are found are separated by the large expanse of central Sumatra (fig. 274), across which Minangkabau and Sumatran Malay are written with an Arabic script (fig. 275). This suggests that the introduction of Arabic script for Malay has restricted the use of Sumatran scripts which were more widely distributed in the past.

The evidence of Malay stone inscriptions, dating from South Sumatra as early as the late seventh century, and from as far north as Pasai at the end of the fourteenth century, points to extensive pre-Islamic use of Indic scripts for Malay throughout Sumatra. However, Voorhoeve suggests that the Sumatran folk scripts have not developed independently from these earlier Sumatran models: rather, they have been deeply influenced by the Javanese script, itself of Indic origin. Voorhoeve produced a model of the origin of the Sumatran folk scripts (fig. 276). This model is somewhat simplified; it has been suggested that there is also some Arabic influence on the South Sumatran scripts (fig. 273).

In describing South Sumatran scripts as Indic, it is important to note that there has been significant simplification from the Devanagari model. First, the letters are simplified to an angular shape (fig. 279) rather than curved strokes to suit them to the medium of bamboo or horn. Indic scripts generally represent consonant combinations with portmanteau consonant letters, based on the form of the first consonant in the cluster, but modified by combination with a reduced sub- or superscript form of the second consonant. This feature has been lost altogether in

South Sumatra. An innovation shared by the South Sumatran and Batak scripts (and also by the Makasarese and Buginese *lontara* palm-leaf syllabary) has been the introduction of a series of letters for prenasalized consonants such as *mba* and *mpa*. The Sumatran scripts still retain the syllabic character of the Indic model: each letter represents a syllable consonant-vowel onset. In the unmarked case the vowel is *a*; other vowels are distinguished by diacritics placed before, after, under, or over the letter.

The area in which the South Sumatran scripts are used stretches over the whole of the southern part of Sumatra. Languages spoken are a great diversity of "Middle Malay" dialects, Rejang, and Lampung. The Kerinci language is of uncertain status; it may be a dialect of Malay, or of Rejang. These languages have their own oral traditions, which have been but little studied.

Existing alongside the vernaculars is a literary or "high" language. This is fundamentally Malay, with Javanese influence, and includes borrowings from the local vernaculars. This register is not regarded as a foreign language—even in the Rejang- and Lampung-speaking areas—but as a more ancient manifestation of the everyday vernacular. This literary language also has a strong oral tradition: texts are passed on from mouth to mouth as well as in written form.

SCRIPT FAMILIES

The South Sumatran scripts vary considerably in their details, but form three main families: Kerinci, Middle Malay (or Rejang *rèncong*), and Lampung.

The use and interpretation of the Kerinci script appears to have died out in the course of the nineteenth century. Early in this century, a text was deciphered by L.C. Westenenk. Only one Kerinci manuscript is known outside of Indonesia.

As for Middle Malay or Rejang *rèncong* scripts, Voorhoeve reports that it seems impossible to distinguish whether the author of a *rèncong* text is a Rejang or a speaker of one of the Middle Malay dialects of the same region. In either case the written language is Malay. A few *rèncong* texts were published by M.A. Jaspan, and a large collection of transliterations can be found in Jaspan's papers at the University of Hull. These transliterations are mostly by Voorhoeve and his wife, M.C.J. Voorhoeve-Bernelot Moens, and are available in the Leiden University Library.

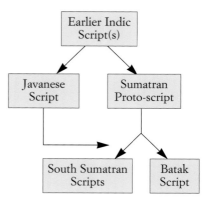

FIGURE 273

Voorhoeve's model of the development of South Sumatran scripts.

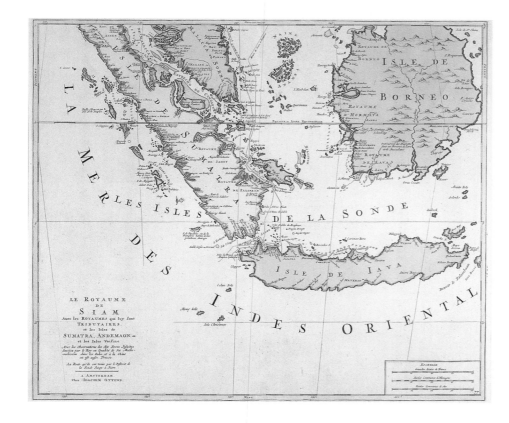

FIGURE 274

A map of Sumatra and Java printed in Amsterdam by Joachim Ottens (1663–1719).

FIGURE 275

Above: Lampung manuscript in Rencong and Arabic scripts. National Library of Indonesia, Jakarta.

FIGURE 276

Right: Bamboo manuscripts from South Sumatra. National Library of Indonesia, Jakarta.

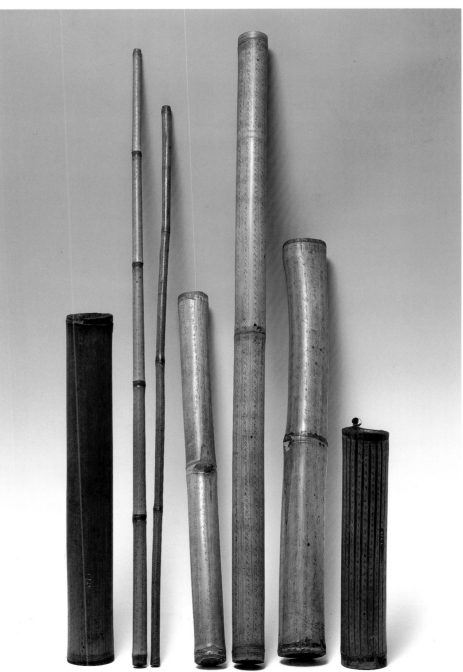

FIGURE 277

Rèncong manuscript from Lampung.
National Library of Indonesia, Jakarta.

Lampung script has many variants. It differs from the *rèncong* scripts in some particularities. The main distinctive features of Lampung script are the existence of a separate symbol for "ə" (fig. 227), and the lack of a set of prenasalized stop letters. Written texts from the Lampung area can also be distinguished by the intrusion of Lampung characteristics into the South Sumatran Malay literary idiom. What we know of the Lampung manuscripts is due first of all to the work of H.N. van der Tuuk, who spent two years in the region. Later Oscar L.Helfrich produced several publications on Lampung, including transcripts of some written texts. Voorhoeve, in his publication entitled *Critical Survey of Studies of the Languages of Sumatra,* provides a critical summary of these and information on possible pitfalls in using them.

CONTENT AND FORM

The many variations in the scripts, the medium itself, missing pages or strips, and the lack of word divisions all make reading South Sumatran manuscripts very difficult. But perhaps the greatest obstacle is the language itself. A prior familiarity with the language is needed to be able to read the manuscripts. For Lampung in particular, but also for the Malay texts, this is very difficult to acquire. Apart from the works of Voorhoeve, there is a dearth of good lexicographic materials for the South Sumatran vernaculars and the Middle Malay literary language.

South Sumatran manuscripts have been collected by many museums and libraries, both in Indonesia and abroad. The largest collection of all is that of the National Library of Indonesia in Jakarta. The Leiden University Library, the National Museum of Ethnography in Leiden, and the Institute for the Tropics in Amsterdam all have substantial collections. A handful of manuscripts are in private collections.

The texts of the South Sumatran manuscripts have rather varied contents. The main categories are traditional epics, legal literature, genealogies (documents to legitimize traditional land ownership rights), Islamic mystic poems, incantations (including charms, magic and medical texts, with intertwined pre-Islamic and Islamic or Arabic elements) (fig. 278), "love" poetry of a kind used in courtship rituals (known as *bandung* or *hiwang* in the Lampung area, and *juarian* in the *rèncong* area), Islamic texts (such as *Saribu Maksa,* Book of a thousand questions), and letters.

The courtship poetry just referred to (*juarian*) is written in a dialogue format with a fixed meter, but no rhyme. The elements of this poetry are traditional, incorporating mythical references. This poetry is mostly written on bamboo tiles

FIGURE 278

"Beschreven rolletje papier," writing on a roll of paper. National Library of Indonesia, Jakarta.

or strips—*gelumpai*—tied together with a string through a hole at one end and numbered alphabetically (figs. 280, 281). It is rare to find complete examples. Inscribed bamboo cylinders are also found (fig. 283). The folding bark books, made from the bark of the *bunut* (*Calophyllum spp.,* Malay: *bintangor*), are mostly magic or religious in nature (Fig. 282).

In a manuscript of the Leiden University Library, a Malay introduction by R. Bangsawan describes the context in which the *juarian* is used:

> According to the customs of the Serawai people, a young man can talk with a girl, and they can also dance opposite each other at a festival, without the relatives and friends of the girl taking offence. However they must follow the rule of exogamy. Thus a youth can himself seek out and select a girl that pleases him.

——————— FIGURE 279 ———————

Lampung manuscript. National Library of Indonesia, Jakarta.

——————— FIGURE 280 ———————

Lower left: Gelumpai. National Library of Indonesia, Jakarta.

——————— FIGURE 281 ———————

Lower right: Lampung manuscript. National Library of Indonesia, Jakarta.

FIGURE 282

Left: Lampung manuscript. National Library of Indonesia, Jakarta.

FIGURE 283

Below: Bamboo cane with *rèncong* script. National Library of Indonesia, Jakarta.

If a girl pleases a boy by her demeanour and behaviour, and if she is well disposed to the boy, he can promise to her: "On such and such a day I will come here to exchange tokens," that is, to exchange tokens in pledge of the betrothal.

On the agreed day the youth comes accompanied by four or five other young men to the house of the girl. She, who is also in company with four or five girl friends of her own age, receives them. The boys are received in the house by the girls, according to custom. Clean mats are spread out for them to sit on, with betel and cigarettes provided for them. They sit down in a row together, with the girls opposite them. Then a conversation begins, each boy addressing a girl in a modest tone, asking pardon for his faults, and praising the girls' attributes. The girl responds in like manner. In the course of the conversation they come finally to the dialogue called *juarian* in the Serawai language. The words of the *juarian* are not spoken by the youth who wishes to exchange tokens, but by one of his fellows, who has mastery of this art: his words are received and answered by one of the friends of the girl who wishes to be betrothed.

Of published examples of South Sumatran manuscript texts, perhaps none is so interesting as Braginsky's preliminary reconstruction of the text of a classical Malay Sufi poem *Sya'ir Perahu* (Poem of the boat). This poem, attested in three much-corrupted South Sumatran manuscripts, contains "a concise but complete course of Sufi knowledge of Sumatran Wujudiyya." It is, Braginsky argues, a work originally composed in Aceh in the first half of the seventeenth century, most probably by one of the Sufi poets of Hamzah Fansuri's circle.

Mark Durie

THE DECLINE OF
THE MANUSCRIPT TRADITION

Printing constituted a communications revolution far more radical even than that which first ushered in the Jawi manuscript tradition in the thirteenth century (figs. 284, 285, 286, 287). In Surabaya, the commercial center of the Dutch East Indies, two events changed the history of the written word in Indonesia. In 1853, the first book printed by a Southeast Asian Muslim appeared. It was *Sharaf al-Anam* (The best of men), the Malay version of a well-loved text in praise of the Prophet Muhammad. This was followed by the first Malay-language newspaper in 1856. The *Soerat Kabar Bahasa Melaijoe* (Newsletter in Malay) conveyed commercial news to an audience of Chinese, Arab, Malay, and Indian traders.

NEW LITERATURES IN PRINT

The *Soerat Kabar Bahasa Melaijoe* was printed in the Roman script (or "Dutch letters"), in the "low Malay" used by the Dutch in administration and for translation of regulations, notices, government service manuals, and so on. This "low Malay" bridged the racial and linguistic diversity of urban society in Java, and was the language of other newspapers that followed in Batavia and Semarang. These newspapers were owned by Dutch and Eurasians, and their presses soon began to print books for the ever-widening reading public.

In 1875 the first Malay translation of a European novel, *Robinson Crusoe,* was published. Others followed, along with popular science, European-style school texts, and reference manuals. During the 1880s, Peranakan Chinese of Java also began publishing both newspapers and books. For these people, whose mother tongue was Malay or Javanese, this coincided with a rediscovery of their Chinese roots. Their numerous books included translations of Chinese popular romances, traditional teachings, and contemporary Chinese tales. Both Eurasian and Peranakan authors wrote a few original stories set in the Indies (in verse and prose). With the exception of a small number of stories adapted from old manuscript texts, these were all new experiences for Indies readers. This printing of Malay in Dutch letters soon became concentrated in Batavia, thereby laying the foundations upon which Balai Pustaka and the government native schools of the next century would be built.

MUSLIM PRINTING

Early Muslim printing followed quite a different path. The second Muslim book was a beautiful edition of the Quran with a Malay introduction published in Palembang in 1854. It sold readily for the huge sum of twenty-five guilders per copy, indicating the strong market for Islamic books. The first aim of Muslim printing was to reproduce religious books and, in general, the earliest Muslim printed books were *kitab*, that is, books of religious knowledge studied in *pesantren* or used for devotional purposes at the mosque. The printing of these bulky editions was sometimes supported by charitable bequests.

This Muslim printing built directly upon the manuscript tradition, as printers strove to reproduce old texts in a style as close as possible to the manuscript original, and of course in the Arabic script. This they could do using the new printing technique of lithography that had been spectacularly successful in Muslim printing in India. Lithographic printing preserved the graceful script and style of the manuscript tradition.

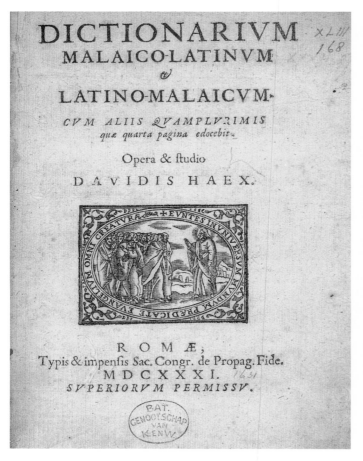

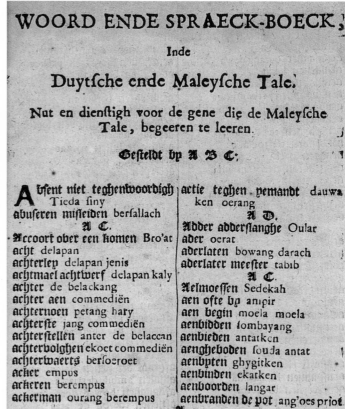

As commercial printing developed, more popular Muslim texts were put into print, including stories of the heroes of early Islam (especially Muhammad Hanafiah), and above all the *syair*, ballads of romantic adventure loved by nineteenth-century audiences. For audiences across the islands, *syair* readings were a common form of entertainment. Listeners reveled in the sweet voice of the singer. A lively and polished recital was rewarded with tokens of appreciation: tea, cigarettes, and sweets.

JAVANESE PRINTERS IN SINGAPORE

By 1860 Singapore had emerged as the center of the region's Muslim publishing activity (fig. 288). Javanese from the Semarang district became Singapore's leading printers. In Singapore they were free of the irksome Dutch press laws, and could sell their books to ever-increasing numbers of pilgrims from the Indies who passed through on the pilgrimage to Mecca. They issued catalogues and sold by mail order to readers in the Indies. Sea traders purchased books in bulk to sell along the native shipping routes to the farthest corners of the archipelago. A Dutch official noted in 1885 that "every year Makasar prows call in at Banda on their way to the Aru islands, bringing a multitude of articles for the native market. Their arrival is awaited with longing, as the natives hope then to be able to make a selection from a stock of *kitab, ceritera* and *syair* all from Singapore." Religious books were sold by Muslim teachers and students as they traveled from place to place.

These developments led to a decline in manuscript production late in the nineteenth century. In 1878 the first president of the Royal Asiatic Society's Straits Settlements Branch delivered his inaugural address. Archbishop Hose had some pretensions as a Malay scholar, and commented on a perception that Malay manuscripts had become "more and more difficult to obtain," asserting that with the advent of printed school books and especially the newspaper press, "the manuscripts (never very numerous) are likely to be less prized, and more rarely copied. . . ." Manuscript copying and printing coexisted for a while. Lithographic printing, favored by Muslim printers, put the handwriting and layout of the manuscript into print. Manuscripts were even copied from printed books. But the cultural setting in which the manuscript tradition thrived had begun to change.

A century and another communications revolution later, the archbishop's prognosis has been fully borne out. Tenas Effendi has reported on the demise of the manuscript tradition in Siak, in east Sumatra. Most of the manuscripts in that community had been in the hands of courtiers, and were dispersed and lost during the turmoil of the Japanese occupation and the period of the independence struggle, during which the sultanate was abolished. To compound matters, succeeding generations lost the ability to read the Jawi script, which was not taught at government schools. In any case, the arrival of national satellite television in 1976 turned the heads of the young. Their eyes are now firmly fixed upon a new future, far beyond the confines of the local traditions in which the old manuscript texts had meaning.

The *pesantren* manuscript tradition suffered a similar fate. Thus the manuscript tradition was already fatally wounded—or dead—when the rise of Roman script impinged upon even the *pesantren*. In a recent survey of Indonesian *pesantren* and their reading materials, van Bruinessen found that modern *pesantren* used locally printed books in Roman script, only the more conservative sticking by Jawi texts. But these were no longer manuscripts, but the so-called *kitab kuning* ("yellow textbooks") named for the distinctive Egyptian paper used by the Cairo press. Printing brought the long drought of written material to an end. Today, the cassette tape conveys the living text more effectively than any written form.

—————— FIGURE 286 ——————

Left: As international trade increased, so too did the need for printed books. *Maleische Woordboek/Collectanea Malaica* is a Malay vocabulary book in Dutch and Latin written by Andries Lambert Loderus and printed in Batavia in 1707. National Library of Indonesia, Jakarta.

—————— FIGURE 287 ——————

Right: Pages from a Dutch-Malay vocabulary book published in 1623. National Library of Indonesia, Jakarta.

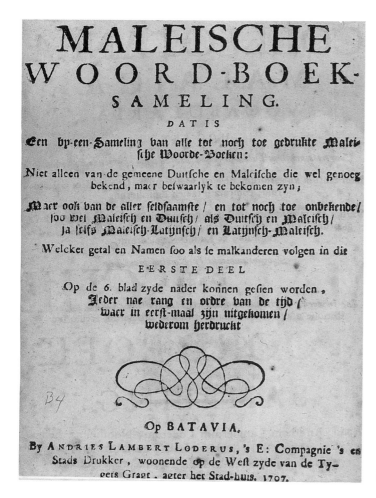

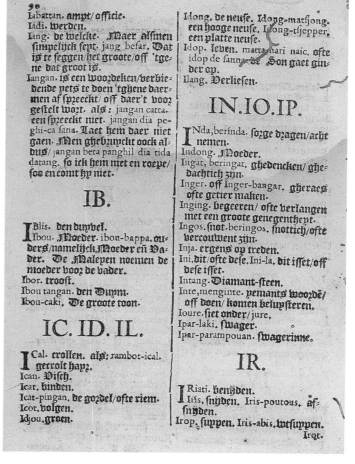

LOOKING BACK

In the 1950s, de Josselin de Jong toured the back blocks of Malaysia seeking out manuscripts in private hands. Those he found were mainly in the hands of old court retainers and a few elderly specialists such as reciters and traditional healers (*bomoh*). The manuscripts were stored away in lofts and cupboards. They were no longer regularly read, but most were still valued as keepsakes and heirlooms. Some of the texts retained sufficient significance in their owners' minds for them to deny de Josselin de Jong access to them, or the opportunity to read them.

Old manuscripts still in the hands of families descended from traditional elites may become the focus of a local history project as individuals, for a variety of reasons, seek to understand and record their past. One example is provided by the descendants of the nineteenth-century scholar and writer Raja Ali Haji, who still live on the island of Penyengat, in Riau, and proudly preserve a considerable collection of Malay manuscripts dating from late last century. They have established a private foundation to study and publish selected texts in Roman script, a project now supported by the Indonesian government.

The modern nation states whose borders now dissect the Malayo-Muslim world are actively collecting old manuscripts. Since independence in Indonesia and Malaysia, there has been a growing interest by political leaders in the artistic and intellectual achievements of their traditional societies, particularly those dating from the precolonial period. Manuscripts have now come to be seen as a precious national heritage. Impressive exhibitions are mounted, opened by ministers, well publicized, and recorded in glossy catalogues. In 1990 a beautiful exhibition of outstanding examples of Malay manuscripts was held in Kuala Lumpur. The exhibition was entitled *Malay Manuscripts*: *Splendour of Malay Civilisation.* The aim of the exhibition was to provide Malays with a sense of pride in their past achievements. In 1991 *Golden Letters,* a traveling photographic exhibition of Indonesian manuscripts, opened in Jakarta at the National Library. Three years later, this exhibition is still touring Indonesia. This volume, *Illuminations: Writing Traditions of Indonesia*, is itself a contribution to this theme, reflecting the pride Indonesians feel in the manuscript traditions of their nation, unified in its diversity.

Ian Proudfoot

FIGURE 288

Hikayat Abdullah bin Abdul Kadir Munsyi, the story of Abdullah, lithographed in Singapore at the Mission Press in 1849. British Library, London.

THE PRESERVATION OF
MANUSCRIPTS IN INDONESIA

Indonesia, with a tropical climate in which the natural enemies of book materials thrive, faces a daunting challenge in preserving its book collections. In addition to the range of animals, insects, microorganisms (for example, molds, fungi, bacteria), and the effects of chemical reactions brought about by light, heat, and humidity, human beings must also be counted as potential enemies: uninformed collectors and readers often unintentionally destroy books by mistreating them or storing them improperly. And as a developing nation with other equally pressing economic and social problems to deal with, Indonesia has very limited resources to bear upon preserving its books for posterity and making them available to a geographically dispersed readership. The nation's literary and historical record is thus seriously at risk.

Manuscripts by their very nature are unique; multiple handwritten copies of a single text are never exactly identical, and the survival of variant copies is essential to the task of reconstructing a text's history and significance. The great bulk of Indonesian indigenous literature, historiography, religious custom, traditional medicine—to mention only a few branches of knowledge—exists only in manuscript form. With written traditions in the many languages of the archipelago stretching back a millennium or more, the number and importance of such manuscripts are considerable. Though most Indonesian manuscripts, with the exception of inscriptions on durable material like stone or metal, do not last for more than a few hundred years under ideal conditions, the often-ancient texts conveyed in them were passed along from generation to generation by a tradition of copying and recopying. With the enormous social and intellectual changes that have occurred over the last century, the copyist tradition is almost extinct. To those manuscripts must be added the tens of thousands of vernacular and foreign-language books printed in Indonesia that survive in unique copies. Public and private libraries with origins in the eighteenth and nineteenth centuries (for example, the royal libraries of the sultans of Central Java, mosque libraries in Sumatra, *pesantren* libraries in Java, and colonial libraries in Bali, Ujung Pandang, Bogor, and Jakarta) hold numerous unique copies of printed books and periodicals, often printed on the machine-made paper of low quality that we call "newsprint," so notoriously difficult to preserve under the best of circumstances. The result of the waning of the copyist tradition and the poor state of so many unique printed materials is the distinct possibility that a part of the world's intellectual heritage could disappear without a trace when the surviving manuscripts and books have decayed beyond legibility, unless their contents are transferred to a more durable medium such as microfilm.

These dire prospects of loss have not gone unnoticed by scholars, librarians, or bibliophiles in Indonesia and abroad, though attempts to avoid them have only really been made in the last ten to fifteen years. These include programs to systematically record rare materials on archival microfilm, to upgrade expertise in restoring items of historic or artifactual value, and to prevent further deterioration by improving storage conditions. But first, how important are Indonesian manuscripts, and should they be preserved?

It is important to note that there were and still are many Indonesian societies that either did not know writing or chose not to use it for storing certain categories of information. For those ethnic groups, such as the many so-called Dayak groups in Kalimantan, for numerous groups in Irian Jaya, Maluku, and East Nusa Tenggara, knowledge was transferred by means of oral/aural media. Even in societies like the Javanese, Malay or Balinese, which have ancient writing traditions, the oral media for transmitting certain kinds of knowledge have always coexisted with written media. These oral traditions are as fragile as, if not more so than, the moldering pages of ancient *lontar* or paper codices, and it is as crucial that efforts be made to document them, and more important, support their continuation as living traditions, as it is to preserve the texts of threatened physical documents.

Amin Sweeney has pointed out that the notion of physical preservation of manuscripts was in general a foreign one in the archipelago, since the climate dictated that manuscripts were essentially disposable items to be preserved more by copying than by physical conservation. Sweeney is doubtless correct to argue that Malay (and other Indonesian) written texts are as evanescent and transitory as orally transmitted genres. However, on the one hand, recent technological innovations allow the extension of the life of the manuscript-as-object (or of the text-as-information) in ways that were not available before; on the other hand, the extinction of the copyist tradition means that the traditional method of preservation is no longer possible.

Sweeney and Behrend point out that many extant Malay and Javanese manuscript copies were not produced according to "traditional" norms (in which the copyist had considerable freedom to interpret or even recreate the text being copied), but rather commissioned by Europeans and produced according to foreign criteria of philological correctness. Paradoxically "corrupt" in their philological "purity" as they may thus be, they are still an invaluable record, at the very least of the interaction of colonial and indigenous sensibilities.

I will give a brief description of some recent programs undertaken so far, including a discussion of the scope of the challenge (with huge numbers of materials at risk and disproportionately minuscule resources brought to bear to preserve them), and end with a plea for a concerted effort to educate the public in Indonesia about these issues. I will divide the programs into the general categories of *salvaging* materials at risk so that they may still be used by future generations, even if in only limited ways; *restoring* materials as nearly as possible to their original conditions; and *preventing* deterioration of library materials.

Inventorying and Cataloguing

In order to set priorities to attack a problem, it is essential to gather information about its scope. These first steps are only now being taken with respect to preserving books and manuscripts in Indonesia. Librarians and conservators need to work closely together to determine (a) what is "rare" and what is at risk; (b) where rare and fragile materials are kept and under what conditions; and (c) what can be done to preserve them. These may seem straightforward tasks, but they very often turn out not to be so simple.

For instance, just what is a "rare book" in the Indonesian context? A book in a public or private collection, regardless of how old or fragile looking it seems, may, in fact, not be rare at all. It could be held in hundreds of other libraries in equally good or better condition; the text in it may have been reprinted or republished; it may have been reissued as a facsimile edition; it may have been microfilmed by a commercial dealer or by another library. To know for sure, a librarian or book collector needs access to bibliographic reference tools: holdings lists, accessions lists, catalogues of microfilm dealers, rare-book dealers' lists, to mention a few that are normally published in hard copy, or, more common in the 1990s, through access to on-line computer catalogues, or constantly upgraded catalogues on CD-ROM or microfiche. Or, in the absence of such tools—as in

Damage due to infestation: *Keagamaan*, a
religious treatise. National Library of
Indonesia, Jakarta.

Indonesia where finding aids do not exist or accessions budgets do not allow purchase of them—librarians need to be in touch with each other on a regular basis.

I mentioned above the unique value of all manuscripts: they automatically fall into the "rare" category. But their value is severely limited unless we know where they are kept, where they came from, and what is in them. Again, librarians and conservators use bibliographic tools to aid in that process. Unfortunately, in Indonesia at present there is no equivalent to the United States Library of Congress's *National Union Catalog of Manuscript Collections*, a continually updated series begun in 1959, or Canada's *Union List of Manuscripts in Canadian Repositories*, to name two national-level reference works. The sad fact is that very few Indonesian libraries have systematically listed or described their manuscripts. Several of the projects to preserve manuscript or rare-book collections on microfilm carried out so far in Indonesia (see below) have included an inventorying and cataloguing as a preliminary or corollary component.

Those projects can be divided into two major categories—public or quasi-public libraries on the one hand, and private or personal collections on the other. The inventorying of heterogeneous public collections containing materials in various languages and scripts in various states of disrepair is a difficult and painstaking task. More arduous still is the task of uncovering and preserving manuscripts in private hands. A Makassarese farmer in South Sulawesi may keep a handful of manuscripts in his attic; a Balinese priest may be the custodian of ten or more *lontar* kept in a village temple; the heirs of a Javanese aristocrat may have inherited books on divination or astrology or religious lore or musical notation. It is a continuing challenge to the would-be inventarist, book lover, or government librarian to discover where such manuscripts are kept and to persuade the owners or guardians to let an outsider examine them. The outsider can play a crucial role, too, in suggesting how to conserve the objects or in suggesting where to donate them in cases where the owners are no longer interested or capable of keeping them. Several efforts are noteworthy:

• The late scholar of Balinese literature, religion, and culture, C. Hooykaas, initiated the so-called Proyek Tik to uncover *lontar* manuscripts in Bali and then to transliterate them (see below).

• The Center for Documentation of Balinese Culture (Pusat Dokumentasi Bali) under the office of the provincial governor, has been gathering manuscripts and has added to its own collection of materials in Denpasar and Singaraja (at the former Kirtya Liefrinck van der Tuuk Library founded in 1928).

• Edi Ekadjati and colleagues from Padjadjaran University, Bandung, have attempted over a period of several years to discover, inventory, describe, and, finally, microfilm manuscripts in public and private collections in the province of West Java.

• Taking Ekadjati's project as inspiration, Dr. Mukhlis and colleagues from Hasanuddin University, Ujung Pandang, have carried out a similar undertaking in South and Central Sulawesi and have shown that there were thousands of manuscripts in private hands where previously there were supposed to have been few.

In the course of their research, many scholars report in articles or books on private collections of manuscripts they have come across, thus helping to draw a more detailed picture of what is extant. For example:

• Virginia Matheson and Vivianne Wee on manuscripts they investigated (and photographed with ordinary 35mm cameras) in Riau;

• Henri Chambert-Loir and Mark Durie on collections they visited in Aceh;

• Timothy Behrend on the importance of small private collections of Javanese manuscripts and suggestions on how individual manuscripts discovered in the field by scholars should be described in a systematic and comprehensive way.

• An important pilot project undertaken by Th. C. van der Meij and colleagues from the West Nusa Tenggara Provincial Museum in Mataram in 1994 to find a method for assessing the extent of private ownership of manuscripts in Lombok. Enlightened collectors play an important role by donating or bequeathing their holdings to a public library or by allowing them to be investigated, described, and photographed.

Finally, since any sort of salvage or preservation effort must be preceded by knowledge of the physical condition of items designated as "rare," trained experts in paper and book conservation have been attempting to advise book owners, both individual and institutional, on (a) how to keep the item in optimal condition, (b) or how to return it to as flawless a condition as possible, or, (c) in extreme cases, how to salvage what is legible or otherwise valuable in it. An international team of library preservation experts was convened in 1989 by the National Library of Indonesia with assistance from several international donor agencies to advise the Library on the necessary elements of a national preservation policy, to outline a preservation program, and to identify the education and training required to support those policies and programs. Several of the suggestions put forward by the International Review Team have since been put into practice by the Library, while others will require additional funds and other resources that are not as yet forthcoming. The International Review Team report underlined the importance of an extended staff-training program and of upgrading equipment at the National Library, as the premier national-level institution in the country. Some staff have since been trained abroad, and the Japanese government has donated a large amount of paper-conservation equipment to the Library as well as helped them to carry out workshops and training exercises in-country. A small number of trained Indonesian museum and library conservators has been trying to educate their junior colleagues, other professionals, and the public at large, and to influence public policy. But on the national level, only the very first tentative steps have been taken toward developing a meaningful cadre of book conservators with easy and regular access to the necessary sophisticated equipment and materials of their trade.

MICROFILM

According to Norman Shaeffer, a member of the International Review Team and at the time head of photo duplication at the Library of Congress, Washington, in countries with well-developed preservation programs, total expenditures for microforms usually exceed expenditures for the conservation treatment of items whether or not the microfilms are created in-house or are purchased from institutions or commercial firms. Although advances in digitization of images and text point to digital storage as the probable wave of the future, microforms are still considered by library conservators and librarians to be the preferred archival medium and the cheapest and most efficient format to preserve and distribute information. Filming is clearly less costly than physical restoration, too. As Shaeffer writes,

> The cost ratio of physical treatment versus conversion to microfilm is at least 5:1 in many countries, and frequently much higher. In other words, a 300-page book that can be converted to microform for about US$40 including the production of negative and positive copies could be expected to require approximately US$300 to US$400 if it received full conservation treatment. While these figures may not strictly apply in Indonesia, it is nevertheless unquestionable that when dealing with large quantities of deteriorated materials the cost and time involved in physical treatment far exceeds the cost of microfilming.

FIGURE 290

Damage due to humidity and mold: *Babad Balambangan Purwasastran*. National Library of Indonesia, Jakarta.

Although many of the thousands of Indonesian manuscripts in local collections should properly be given the kind of conservation treatment Shaeffer refers to, many are in such a state of deterioration that it is a race against time and the elements merely to preserve the intellectual contents of the item, postponing the restoring of the physical artifact to some indeterminate future time when expertise, equipment, materials, time, and money allow it.

In our earlier article, Timothy Behrend and I laid out a review of past and current projects involving the microfilming of Indonesian manuscripts. Here I will only provide a brief summary:

• The first effort does not actually involve microfilm, but the project's aim of transferring the intellectual contents of fragile manuscript to more durable media is certainly comparable. Christiaan Hooykaas, as a Dutch colonial language officer, started a project with Balinese colleagues in 1939 that was interrupted by the Japanese invasion. Hooykaas and his Balinese assistant I Gusti Ngurah Ketut Sangka recommenced the work in 1972, and, after Hooykaas's untimely death in 1979, his student, H.I.R. Hinzler, carried on as informal supervisor. The Proyek Tik, or Balinese Manuscript Project, involves the Romanized transliteration of Balinese *lontar* in public and private collections throughout the island and has resulted in upward of six thousand typed transliterations. Hooykaas and Hinzler arranged to have copies deposited with various "subscribing" libraries, in Singaraja, Denpasar, Jakarta, Leiden, Berlin, London, Paris, Ithaca, Sydney, Auckland, and elsewhere.

• In the early 1970s, Cornell University donated a microfilm camera to the Central Museum Library (now the National Library of Indonesia) to film rare books and newspapers. The Library filmed several manuscripts in its collection—though by no means all. Inadequate storage facilities for the master negatives has resulted in many of the films being of less than archival quality.

• In the 1970s, too, the Royal Institute of Linguistics and Anthropology (KITLV) in the Netherlands provided microform copies of thousands of Indonesian manuscripts in Dutch collections to the Central Museum Library. It also helped to film literary and lexicographical manuscripts at the Faculty of Letters, University of Indonesia. Unfortunately, inadequate and improper storage of the master negatives and duplicate copies have caused many of the films to be unusable.

• A project initiated in 1980 by Nancy Florida, then a graduate student at Cornell University, enabled the cataloguing and microfilming of three major libraries in Surakarta (Solo): those of the Istana Mangkunagaran, of the Kraton Surakarta, and of the Radyapustaka Museum. Some two thousand manuscripts (about six hundred thousand handwritten pages) were recorded on 250 reels of film. Florida, with the help of young Indonesian scholars and librarians, later created author, title, and subject card catalogues of two of the three collections, and has since published the first of a multi-volume series, *Javanese Literature in Surakarta Manuscripts*.

• A similar project, inspired by Florida's example, was initiated in 1985 by Jennifer Lindsay, then of Sydney University, to film two collections of the Kraton Yogyakarta. Some seven hundred manuscripts were filmed on 121 reels of microfilm, several of them in color. The Indonesian-language version of the catalogue Lindsay and her collaborators produced, the second volume of a multi-volume union catalogue of manuscripts in Indonesian collections, is now available from the Indonesian publisher, Yayasan Obor Indonesia (Obor).

• A third cataloguing and microfilming project was begun in 1987 with major funding from the Ford Foundation (which also helped with Florida's card catalogues and with partial funding of the Kraton Yogyakarta project). The museum's 1,150 manuscripts were described in considerable detail by a team led first by

Alan Feinstein and then by Timothy Behrend: a six-volume, 3,800-page catalogue and 162 microfilm reels were the result. That preliminary catalogue was later published in shorter form as the first volume of the above-mentioned union catalogue.

• The projects carried out by Edi S. Ekadjati and colleagues at Padjadjaran University in Bandung and Mukhlis and colleagues at Hasanuddin University in Ujung Pandang have already been mentioned. The difficulties faced by such field teams trying to uncover, describe, and film manuscripts *in situ* (in both cases using portable microfilm cameras provided by the Genealogical Society of Utah to the National Archives of Indonesia) were considerable. The Pajajaran team filmed more than a thousand manuscripts, and their descriptive catalogue is expected to be published eventually. The Hasanuddin team is still carrying out its work, but has already uncovered more than a thousand manuscripts, and will eventually prepare an indexed catalogue. Both these catalogues are to be part of the union catalogue published by Obor.

• Library staff of the Faculty of Letters of the University of Indonesia (UI) inherited a valuable collection of mostly Javanese manuscripts that is kept in the Faculty's library in Depok near Jakarta. Under the coordination of Edi Sedyawati, T.E. Behrend, and later Titiek Pudjiastuti, a team of faculty and students has described the manuscripts and sent them to the National Library for filming. The project is nearing completion and yet another volume of the union catalogue should be the result.

• Finally, a large ongoing project is taking place at the National Library of Indonesia itself. Following up on recommendations by the 1989 International Review on Conservation mentioned above, the Library is in the process of listing, briefly describing, and filming manuscripts in its very large collection (about seven to eight thousand items in various languages and scripts). Behrend was also a coordinator of and consultant to this project. Although the vast number and diversity of materials preclude the sort of detailed descriptions that were possible in the earlier Kraton Yogyakarta or Sonobudoyo projects, the compilation of an updated indexed list is extremely valuable, and of course the texts themselves will in future be accessible on film.

Two important outgrowths of the National Library project are: (1) the development of a large database, dubbed DANATARA, of all known Indonesian manuscripts in the world. DANATARA already comprises seventeen thousand items (though it should be stressed that many of the entries are still very sketchy or incomplete) and will no doubt grow over the years; (2) the growth of the Library's collection of microform copies of manuscripts from other libraries. Thus, the National Library, with microfilm facsimiles of manuscripts from Leiden, London, Yogyakarta, Surakarta, West Java, South Sulawesi, Bali, and from other libraries in Jakarta promises to become the premier center for the study of Indonesian manuscripts.

For readers wishing to consult the microfilms mentioned or for those interested in ordering copies (only for scholarly or research purposes), the situation is somewhat complex: (1) For the Kraton Solo, Mangkunagaran, Museum Radyapustaka, copies of the microfilms can be consulted at the three depository libraries and at Cornell, and copies can be ordered from either the National Archives of Indonesia in Jakarta or from Cornell University. Such copies can be made, however, only upon presentation of written permission from the depository library. Permission is, unfortunately, sometimes difficult to arrange through the mails. (2) The master negatives of the Kraton Yogyakarta films are stored at the National Archives in Jakarta, while positive copies can be consulted at the Sonobudoyo Museum in Yogyakarta, the National Library of Indonesia in Jakarta, the Fisher Library of the University of Sydney, the Menzies Library of the Australian National University (Canberra), and the Center for Research Libraries

FIGURE 291

Damage due to the use of cellophane tape: *Hikayat Purasara*. National Library of Indonesia, Jakarta.

in Chicago. The late Sultan Hamengkubuwono IX, in the spirit of his legacy as a hero of Indonesian nationalism, turned over limited copyright authority to the National Archives, thus allowing patrons to request copies from the Archives without first gaining permission from the palace in Yogyakarta. (3) The master negatives of the Museum Sonobudoyo films are stored at the National Library, and positive duplicates can be read at the museum, the National Library of Indonesia, the Center for Research Libraries in Chicago, and at the Menzies Library of Australian National University, Canberra. (4) The master negatives of the Unpad project in West Java are stored at the National Library. Copies are on deposit at Pajajaran University, the National Library, the Center for Research Libraries (Chicago), and the Ecole Française d'Extrême-Orient (Paris). (5) The Hasanuddin University, University of Indonesia, and National Library projects are still ongoing, but eventually the master negatives of all will be stored at the National Library, with copies at the depository, the National Library, and at the Center for Research Libraries.

RESTORATION

Although transferring a book's contents to another medium such as silver-halide film can be said to "preserve" them, much information about the text and about the people who produced it and used it is also conveyed by the myriad details of the object itself—the paper, the bindings, the covering materials—which cannot easily be recorded on film. It would be ideal, of course, to restore the original as well as to copy the book's contents. But, as I mentioned above, quoting Shaeffer, the costs and time involved make that dream impracticable except for only the most valuable of originals (for example, the original copies of Indonesia's procla-mation of independence on August 17, 1945, the so-called Giyanti Treaty between the warring princes of Central Java in 1757, or the earliest *lontar* manuscript of the fourteenth-century *Nagarakertagama*, to name three famous items in Indonesian collections).

Restoration is the "process of returning a book, document, or other archival material as nearly as possible to its original condition." This can involve the repair of a torn leaf, or the removal of a stain, or much more extensive work, which may include deacidification, alkaline buffering, resizing, filling in missing parts, resewing, replacement of end papers or boards, recovering or restoration of the original covering material, and rebinding in a way appropriate to the historical period. Lack of funds for requisite equipment, the general lack of archival mate-rials locally, and the dearth of trained conservators with technical skills necessary to carry out the more sophisticated treatments make it relatively unusual for Indonesian libraries to be able to carry out such treatments. The National Archives and the National Library are the main exceptions, but even there full restorations are rarely attempted. Simple repairs are routinely carried out in major Indonesian libraries, but for rare books or manuscripts requiring treatment, most libraries do not have the facilities for even the simplest of procedures. Unfortunately, some well-meaning collectors or librarians do proceed with "restoration" procedures even in the absence of proper materials, equipment, or expertise. Very often, such "common-sense" repairs (using adhesive tape to repair torn leaves or pages, for instance) have disastrous consequences over time.

PREVENTION

One of the major themes of the advice of outside experts called in by Indonesian institutions has been the need for a "phased" conservation program, in which items at risk are not given restoration treatment, but are prevented from further deterioration. Thus, a Japanese-government-funded two-month workshop at the National Library, led by a Japanese book conservator, emphasized the construc-tion of simple boxes of acid-free cardboard to house individual *lontar* and paper codices. Similarly, although Nancy Florida and colleagues in Solo did attempt to deacidify books and to repair torn leaves with heat-set tissue, one of the most important "interventions" that her team accomplished was to clean the manuscripts, the bookcases, and the rooms of the library itself and to house each book in a simple cotton slipcover.

Improving or maintaining the environment in which manuscripts, books, and microfilms are stored is probably the most important and yet often the simplest and least expensive means of caring for them. Although it cannot be denied that an environment with a constant low temperature and low humidity is the best for book storage, the continual reiteration of this truism by foreign experts may have had the effect of leading Indonesian collectors or librarians to believe that (a) installing an air conditioner is *sufficient* for a good environment, or, conversely, that (b) since it is prohibitively costly to maintain twenty-four-hour-a-day regulation of humidity and temperature, it is hopeless to attempt to create a "proper" storage environment in the tropics at all. Actually, even basic manuals on book storage stress that two of the most important factors are an even climate, changing as slowly as can be managed, throughout the room, and the free circulation of air. Thus, installing an air conditioner in a dank and moldy room that is rarely cleaned, or in a room exposed to high levels of light, or only turning it on for part of the day are all well-intentioned attempts at prevention but potentially disastrous in their effects. Simple housekeeping procedures, like regular dusting and cleaning, or providing for adequate air circulation and avoiding high levels of light, are far preferable. Boxing or housing in protective enclosures (as long as the materials used are not acidic or potentially chemically harmful) is another simple preventive measure already mentioned. Such basic advice is practical and relatively simple to pass on to individual book collectors or to volunteers looking after books in small libraries.

Most of the problems that face owners of books and manuscripts in Indonesia are universal, and some of them are much harder to address than by merely adopting sound housekeeping techniques. Libraries throughout the world, for instance, are full of books printed on mechanically produced "groundwood" paper, or "woodpulp" paper, a mid-nineteenth-century innovation that revolutionized the production of books, but the side-effect of which was a "time bomb" of staggering proportions: such paper is made from a base of ground wood pulp; the wood leaves a residue of lignin that in turn absorbs chemicals in the air (such as sulfur), creating acids that result in brittleness. This brittleness becomes extreme over time, until finally the paper disintegrates into fragments. From the mid-nineteenth century on, Indonesian manuscripts and books were inscribed or printed on such paper and their sorry state of disintegration can be seen in libraries throughout the country. (Heat and light accelerate the acidification process, so Indonesian books stored in cooler and darker environments, as in libraries in Europe or America, are in somewhat less perilous condition.) Although many countries have recognized the danger of using paper with high lignin content and have set up standards of permanence in paper manufacture, Indonesia (and other developing nations) have not yet paid much attention to this problem: lignin-free or acid-free paper is almost completely unavailable, so of Indonesia's books are printed on paper that has little hope of surviving beyond about fifty years. The corrosive effects of acidic inks in Indonesian manuscripts are also a common problem, and there are sadly many examples of manuscripts with paper that has literally been eaten away by the ink.

Clearly, concerted efforts by librarians and book conservators to lobby the paper and book industries about the necessity for printing on nonacidic papers are essential. Government policy-makers and those who decide on budgets for public libraries, archives, and universities need to be made aware of the issues of

library conservation in general. Too often there is a complacent attitude that the mere erection of a building to house a library and a minimal acquisitions budget to fill it with books is sufficient: unfortunately, little planning goes into the effects of the architectural design on the storage of books and book materials, and precious little is budgeted for the practical prevention of book deterioration. Unfortunately, too, there are many examples of spending what limited funds there are on misguided efforts to repair books (rebinding old and rare materials in such a way that the original bindings are destroyed or discarded, often with textual contents obscured in the process) or on mistaken notions of how to prevent deterioration (for example, in trying to prevent insect infestations by wholesale chemical fumigation of the materials). Also, as several examples stated above make manifest, there should be no easy satisfaction felt upon the production of a microfilm copy of a rare text if the resultant film is not produced and stored under strict archival conditions.

It is fairly safe to say that the public awareness of the problems of conserving Indonesia's written heritage is very low. In a country with a rising but still low per capita income, a country that must deal with such crucial issues as population control, high infant mortality, or grave environmental problems, this is probably understandable. I would, of course, not argue that book preservation is on a par with those more pressing issues. But Indonesia is also committed, rightly, to ensuring its continued existence as a nation and to educating its people: to achieve those ends, preserving its historical, literary, and cultural record is essential.

Those in Indonesia who have warned of these problems and those from abroad who have advised how best to set about addressing them must ultimately depend on the interest of Indonesians in these materials: if no one cares about reading them, after all, there is little point in conserving them. Much of the preservation effort so far in Indonesia has depended heavily on foreign assistance. That other more prosperous nations (and those in a formerly exploitative political relationship) should accept a responsibility to help Indonesia to preserve cultural materials as part of a worldwide effort is not surprising. But Indonesia faces several challenges that it will inevitably have to meet on its own. First, it must eventually decrease its dependence on foreign funding and foreign expertise in its efforts to preserve the nation's written heritage. To that end, funds will have to be budgeted for increased staff training, and for purchasing, upgrading, and maintaining expensive equipment and supplies. Second, because conservation of cultural property for its own sake is ultimately fruitless, efforts should be stepped up to increase public and especially scholarly interest in the *contents* of the nation's rich written heritage. The cultural, literary, social, political, and economic history of Indonesia remains to be fully explored and interpreted by *Indonesians* themselves. I cannot help agreeing with Hooykaas who pointed in 1973 to what he saw as an alarming decrease in interest among Indonesians in their written and orally transmitted heritage, and stated, "There are numerous disasters that threaten to destroy the treasures of ancient cultures. Fires, floods, and the ravages of war cause considerable losses, but what is even more disastrous is indifference because the result of it is disappearance once and for all." Of course to so agree with Hooykaas's grave warning is not to deny that many Indonesians are very much concerned about these and other related issues of cultural conservation and are working hard to educate a wider public about them. This book, one hopes, will be a useful tool in aiding such efforts to enhance appreciation for Indonesia's rich cultural heritage.

Alan Feinstein

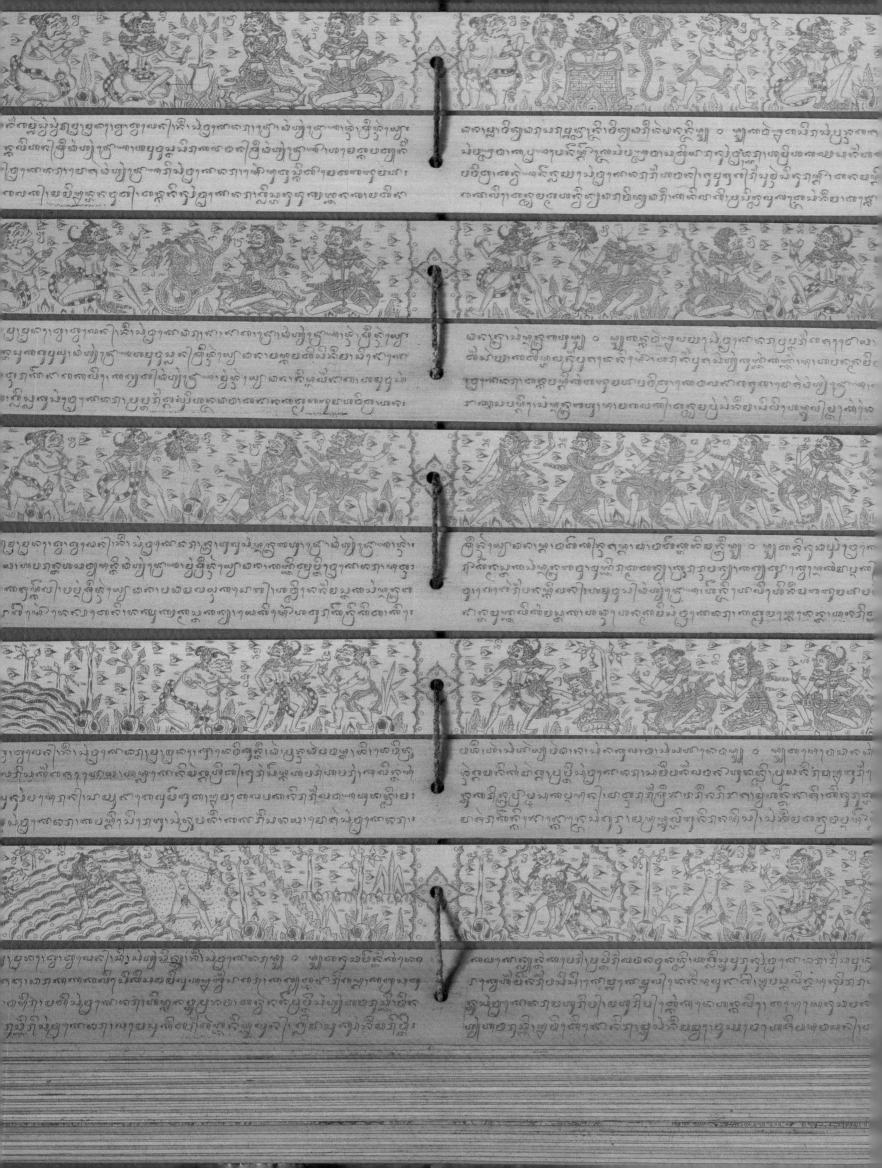

Bibliography

Abbreviations

BGKW	Bataviaasch Genootschap van Kunsten en Wetenschappen
BI	Bibliotheca Indonesica
BKI	*Bijdragen tot de Taal-, Land- en Volkenkunde*, published by the KITLV
BSOAS	*Bulletin of the School of Oriental and African Studies*
HKS	Hooykaas-Ketut Sangka Collection
IAIC	International Academy of Indian Culture
JMBRAS	*Journal of the Malay Branch of Royal Asiatic Studies*
KITLV	Koninklijk Instituut voor Taal-, Land- en Volkenkunde
MK	*Mededeelingen van de Kirtya Liefrinck-van der Tuuk*
RIMA	*Review of Indonesian and Malayan Affairs*
SOAS	School of Oriental and African Studies
TBG	*Tijdschrift Bataviaasch Genootschap voor Kunsten en Wetenschappen*
VBGKW	*Verhandelingen van het Bataviaasch Genootschap van Kunsten en Wetenschappen*
VKI	*Verhandelingen van het KITLV*, published by the KITLV
VKNAWL	*Verhandelingen der Nederlandse Akademie van Wetenschappen, Afdeling Letterkunde*

Chapter 1
Ancient Beginnings: The Spread of Indic Scripts

Behrend, T.E., and W. van der Molen. "Manuscripts of Indonesia." *BKI* 149.3 (1993).

Bellwood, P. *Prehistory of the Indo-Malaysian Archipelago*. Sydney, London, New York: Academic Press, 1985.

Bernet Kempers, A.J. *Monumental Bali*. Singapore: Periplus Editions, 1991.

Brandes, J.L.A. *Beschrijving van Tjandi Singosari*. 1909.

——. "Oud-Javaansce Oorkonden." *VBGKW* 60.2 (1918).

Casparis, J.G. de. *Indonesian Palaeography: A History of Writing in Indonesia from the Beginnings to c. A.D. 1500*. Leiden, Koln: E.J. Brill, 1975.

——. *Indonesian Chronology*. Leiden, Koln: E.J. Brill, 1978.

Chabbra, B.Ch. *Expansion of Indo-Aryan Culture during Pallava Rule*. 2nd ed. Delhi: Munshi Ram Manohar Lal, 1965.

Chattopadhyaya, A. "*Atisha and Tibet: Life and Works of Dipangkara Shrijnana in Relation to the History and Religion of Tibet.*" In *Indian Studies: Past and Present*. Calcutta, 1967.

Fontein, Jan. *The Sculpture of Indonesia*. Washington: National Gallery of Art, 1990.

Holle, K.F. *Oud- en- Neeuw- Indische Alphabetten: Bijdrage tot de Palaeographie van Nederlandsch-Indie*. Batavia: W. Bruining; The Hague: M. Nijhoff, 1882.

I Wayan Ardika and P. Bellwood. "Sembiran: The Beginnings of Indian Contact with Bali." *Antiquity* 65: 221-32, (1991).

Jaspan, M.A. *Folk Literature of South Sumatra (Redjang Ka-Ga-Nga Texts)*. Canberra: Australian National University, 1964.

Kern, H. *Verspreide Geschriften*, 7. 1917.

Noorduyn, J. "Variation in the Bugis/Makasarese Script." *BKI* 149.3: 533–570 (1993).

Pleyte, C.M. "Het Jaartal op den Batoe-toelis nabij Buitenzorgin." *TBG* 53: 155–220 (1911).

——. "De Patapaan Adjar Soeka Resi." *TBG* 55: 280–428 (1913).

Proyek Pengembangan Museum Nasional. *Prasasti Koleksi Museum Nasional, Jilid 1*. Jakarta: Museum Nasional, 1985–1986.

Reid, A. *Southeast Asia in the Age of Commerce 1450–1680. Volume 1: The Lands Below the Winds*. New Haven and London: Yale University Press, 1988.

Saleh Danusasmita. *Masalah Transkripsi Prasasti Batutulis (Bogor) dan Tradisi Megalitiknya*. Bandung: Lembaga Kebudayaan Universitas Pajajaran, 1975.

Stutterheim, W.F. *Cultuurgeschiedenis van Java in Beeld*. 1926.

van Stein Callenfels, F.V. "Epigraphica Balica." In *VBGKW* 66.3. 1926.

Vogel, J.Pa. "The Yupa Inscriptions of King Mulavarman, from Koetei (East Borneo)." *BKI* 74: 167–232, Plates 1–3. 1918.

Zurbuchen, M. S. *The Language of Balinese Shadow Theater*. Princeton: Princeton University Press. 1987.

CHAPTER 2
THE SOVEREIGNTY OF BEAUTY: CLASSICAL JAVANESE WRITINGS

Ando, M. "Krsnantaka: An Old Javanese *Kakawin*." Ph.D. diss., Australian National University. 1991.

Berg, C.C. "De Arjunawiwaha, Er-langga's levensloop en bruiloftslied?" *BKI* 97: 19–94. 1938.

——. "Herkomst, vorm en functie der Middeljavaansche rijksdelingstheorie". *VKNAWL* 59.1. Amsterdam: Noord-Hollandsche Uitgevers. 1953.

Bernet Kempers, A.J. "The Reliefs and the Buddhist texts." In *Proceedings of the International Symposium on Chandi Borobudur*, 92–105. Tokyo: Executive Committee for the International Symposium on Chandi Borobudur. 1980.

Brandes, J.L.A. "Pararaton (Ken Arok), of het Boek der Koningen van Toemaplen van Majapahit." *VBG* 49. Batavia: Albrecht & Rusche. 1896.

Casparis, J.G. de. *Prasasti Indonesia II: Selected Inscriptions from the 7th to the 9th Century*. Bandung: N.V. Masa Baru. 1956.

——. "Some Notes on the Oldest Inscriptions in Indonesia." In *A Man of Indonesian Letters: Essays in Honour of Professor Teeuw*. Edited by C.M.S. Hellwig and S.O. Robson, 242–256. Dordrecht-Holland: Floris. 1986.

Chhabra, B.Ch. *Expansion of Indo-Aryan Culture During Pallava Rule (as evidenced by inscriptions)*. Delhi: Munshi Ram Manohan Lal. 1965.

Coedès, G. *The Indianized States of Southeast Asia*. Canberra: Australian National University Press. 1968.

Creese, H.M. "*Subhadrawiwaha*: An Old Javanese *Kakawin*." Ph.D. diss., Australian National University. 1981.

——. "Sri Surawirya, Dewa Agung of Klungkung (c. 1722–1736): The Historical Context for Dating the *Kakawin* Parthayana." *BKI* 147: 402–419. 1991.

——. *The Parthayana — The Journeying of Partha: An Eighteenth-Century Balinese Kakawin*. KITLV. Forthcoming.

Damais, L.C. "Études d'épigraphie Indonésienne, 4. Discussion de la date des inscriptions." *Bulletin de l'École Francaise d'Éxtrême Orient* 47: 7–290. 1955.

Drewes, G.W.J. "The Struggle between Javanism and Islam as Illustrated by the *Serat Dermagandul*." *BKI* 122: 309–365. 1966.

Gonda, J. *Het Oud-Javaansche Brahmanda-Purana: Prozatekst en Kakawin*. Bibliotheca Javanica 5. Bandoeng: A.C. Nix. 1932.

——. "Agastyaparwa, uitgegeven, gecommenteerd en vertaald door." *BKI* 190: 329–419; 92: 389–458; 94: 223–85. 1933–1936.

Goris, R. *Prasasti Bali: Inscripties voor Anak Wungsu*. 2 vols. Bandung: Masa Baru. 1954.

Hooykaas, C. "The Old Javanese *Ramayana Kakawin*: With Special Reference to the Problem of Interpolation in *Kakawin*." *VKI* 16. The Hague: KITLV/ Martinus Nijhoff. 1955.

——. "The Old Javanese *Ramayana*: An Exemplary *Kakawin* as to Form and Content." *VKNAWL* 65.1. Amsterdam: Noord-Hollandsche Uitgevers. 1958.

I Made Suastika. *Kakawin* Dimbhiwicitra: Suntingan Naskah, Analisis Struktur dan Fungsi. Denpasar: Fakultas Sastra, Universitas Udayana. 1986.

I Kuntara Wiryamartana. *Arjunawiwaha: Transformasi Teks Jawa Kuna lewat Tanggapan dan Penciptaan di Lingkungan Sastra Jawa*. Yogyakarta: Duta Wacana University Press. 1990.

Juynboll, H.H. *Wirataparwa: Oudjavaans prozageschrift*. 's-Gravenhage: KITLV/ Martinus Nijhoff. 1912.

Karandikar, M.A., and S.K. Karandikar. *Bhatti-kavyam: Edited with an English Translation*. Delhi: Motilal Banarsidass. 1982.

Kats, J. *Sang Hyang Kamahayanikan: Oud-Javaansche tekst met inleiding, vertaling en aanteekeningen*. 's-Gravenhage: KITLV/ Martinus Nijhoff. 1910.

Khanna, V., and M. Saran. "The *Ramayana Kakawin*: A Product of Sanskrit Scholarship and Independent Literary Genius." *BKI* 149: 226–249. 1993.

Lohuizen-de Leeuw, J.E. van. "The Beginning of Old Javanese Historical Literature". *BKI* 112: 383–394. 1956.

Partini Sardjono-Pradotokusumo. *Kakawin Gadjah Mada: Sebuah Karya Sastra Kakawin Abad ke-20*. Bandung: Bina Cipta. 1986.

Pigeaud, Th.G.Th. *De Tantu Panggelaran: Oud Javaansch Pprozageschrift*. 's-Gravenhage. 1924.

———. *Java in the Fourteenth Century: A Study in Cultural History*. 5 vols. The Hague: KITLV/ Martinus Nijhoff. 1960–1963.

———. *Literature of Java: Catalogue Raisonné of Javanese Manuscripts in the Library of the University of Leiden and Other Public Collections in the Netherlands*. 3 vols. The Hague: KITLV/ Martinus Nijhoff. 1967–1970.

Poerbatjaraka, R. Ng. "Het Oud-Javaansche Ramayana." *TBG* 72: 151–214. 1932.

———. *Kapustakan Djawi*. Djakarta/Amsterdam: Djambatan. 1952.

Pulsalkar, A.D. *Studies in the Epics and Puranas*. Bombay: Bharatiya Vidya Bhavan. 1955.

Raghu Vira. *Sara-Samuccaya: A Classical Indonesian Compendium of High Ideals*. Sata Pittaka 24. New Delhi: IAIC. 1962.

———. *The Virataparvan, Being the Fourth Book of the Mahabharata*. Poona: Bhandarkar Oriental Research Institute. 1936.

Robson, S.O. "The Kawi Classics in Bali." *BKI* 128: 308–329. 1972.

———. "Notes on the Early Kidung Literature." *BKI* 135: 300–322. 1979.

———. "The Ramayana in Early Java". *South East Asian Review* 5: 5–19. 1980.

———. "*Kakawin* Reconsidered: Toward a Theory of Old Javanese Poetics." *BKI* 139: 291–319. 1983.

S. Supomo. "Kama di dalam Kekawin." In *Bahasa, Sastra, Budaya*. Edited by Sulastien Sutrisno, et al., 383–414. Yogyakarta: Gadjah Mada University Press. 1985.

———. "On the Date of the Old Javanese Wirataparwa". In *Studies in Indo-Asian Art and Culture*. Edited by Perala Ratnam. *Sata-Pittaka* 95: 261–266. New Delhi: IAIC. 1972.

———. "The Dating of the Old Javanese Uttarakanda". *The Journal of the Oriental Society of Australia* 8: 59-67. 1971.

———. "Arjunawijaya: A Kakawin of Mpu Tantular." *BI* 14. 1977.

———. *The Bharatayuddha: An Old Javanese Poem and Its Indian Sources*. Sata-Pittaka 373. New Delhi: IAIC, Aditya Prakashan. 1993.

Sarkar, H.B. *Corpus of the Inscriptions of Java*. 2 vols. Calcutta: Firma K.L. Mukhopadhyay. 1971–1972.

Sharada Rani. *Slokantara: An Old Javanese Didactic Text*. Sata-Pittaka 1 (2). New Delhi: IAIC. 1957.

Soewito-Santoso. *Ramayana Kakawin*. Sata-Pittaka 251. New Delhi: IAIC. 1980.

———. *Sutasoma: A Study in Javanese Wajrayana*. Sata-Pittaka 213. New Delhi: IAIC. 1975.

Srinivas, M.N. "A Note on Sanskritization and Westernization." *The Far Eastern Quarterly* 15: 485. 1956.

———. *The Cohesive Role of Sanskritization and Other Essays*. Delhi: Oxford University Press. 1989.

Stutterheim, W. *Rama-Legends and Rama-Reliefs in Indonesia*. New Delhi: Indira Gandhi National Centre for the Arts, Abhinav Publications [translation of 1925]. 1989.

Sutjipto Wirjosuparto, R.M. "*Kakawin* Ghatotkacaçraya: Tjeritera Lakon dalam Bahasa Kawi." Ph.D. diss., Universitas Indonesia. 1960.

Swellengrebel, J.L. *Korawaçrama: een Oud-Javaansch Proza-geschrift*. Santpoort. 1936.

Teeuw, A., and Th.P. Galestin, S.O. Robson, P.J. Worsley, P.J. Zoetmulder. "Siwaratrikalpa of Mpu Tanakung.". *BI* 3. 1969.

Teeuw, A., and S.O. Robson. "Kunjarakarna Dharmakathana: Liberation Through the Law of Buddha. An Old Javanese Poem by Mpu Dusun." *BI* 15. 1981.

Vickers, A.H. "The Writing of *Kakawin* and *Kidung* on Bali." *BKI* 138: 493–495. 1982.

Warder, A.K. *Indian Kavya Literature*. Vol. 1. Delhi: Motilal Banarsidass. 1972.

Wolters, O.W. *History, Culture, and Region in Southeast Asian Perspectives*. Singapore: Institute of Southeast Asian Studies. 1982.

Zoetmulder, P.J. *Kalangwan: A Survey of Old Javanese Literature*. The Hague: KITLV/ Martinus Nijhoff. 1974.

——. *Old Javanese-English Dictionary*. 's-Gravenhage: KITLV/Martinus Nijhoff. 1982.

CHAPTER 3

IN THE LANGUAGE OF THE DIVINE: THE CONTRIBUTION OF ARABIC

Beg, Muhammad Abdul Jabbar. *Arabic Loan-Words in Malay: A Comparative Study*. 3rd ed. Kuala Lumpur: University of Malaya Press. 1883.

Berg, L.W.C. van den. *Codicum Arabicum in Bibliotheca Societatis Artium et Scientiarum quae Bataviae Floret Asservatorum Catalogus*. Batavia and The Hague: M[artinus] Nijhoff 1873.

Drewes, G.W.J. "The Study of Arabic Grammar in Indonesia." In *Acta Orientalia Neerlandica Proceedings of the Congress of the Dutch Oriental Society held in Leiden on the Occasion of its 50th Anniversary, 8th–9th May 1970*. Edited by P.W. Pestman, 61–70. Leiden: E.J. Brill. 1971.

Drewes, G.W.J. "Directions for Travellers on the Mystic Path." *VKI* 81. 1977.

Matheson, M.B., and Virginia Hooker. "Jawi Literature in Patani: The Maintenance of an Islamic Tradition." *JMBRAS*, 61. 1. 1988.

Muhammad Radjab. *Semasa Ketjil diKampung*. Jakarta: Balai Pustaka. 1950.

Nieuwenhuijze, C.A.O. van. *Shamsu'l-Din van Pasai Bijdrage tot de Kennis der Sumatraansche Mystiek*. Leiden: E.J. Brill. 1945.

Rida, Rashid. "Tafsir al-Manar". In *Etudes Arabes, Dossiers* No. 65. pt. 2. Arabic text and French translation. Pontificio Istituto di Studi Arabi e Islamici Rome, 81–95. 1983.

Ronkel, Ph. S. van. *Supplement to the Catalogue of the Arabic Manuscripts Preserved in the Museum of the Batavia Society of Arts and Sciences*. Batavia: Albrecht. 1913.

Voorhoeve, P. *Handlist of Arabic Manuscripts in the Library of the University of Leiden and other Collections in the Netherlands*. Leiden. 1957.

CHAPTER 4

MEDIATING TIME AND SPACE: THE MALAY WRITING TRADITION

Braginsky, V.I. *The System of Classical Malay Literature*. Working Paper 11. Leiden: KITLV. 1993.

Chambert-Loir, H. "Malay Literature in the 19th Century: The Fadli Connection." In *Variation, Transformation and Meaning: Studies on Indonesian Literatures in Honour of A. Teeuw*. Edited by J.J. Ras and S.O. Robson. Leiden: KITLV. 1991.

Ding Choo Ming. "Access to Malay Manuscripts.". *BKI* 143: 425–451. 1987.

Gallop, A.T., with Bernard Arps. *Golden Letters: Writing Traditions of Indonesia/Surat Emas: Budaya Tulis di Indonesia*. London: The British Library; Jakarta: The Lontar Foundation. 1991.

Gallop, A.T., with an essay by E. Ulrich Kratz. *The Legacy of the Malay Letter/Warisan Warkah Melayu*. London: The British Library. 1994.

Hussainmiya, B.A. *Orang Rejimen. The Malays of the Ceylon Rifle Regiment*. Bangi: Universiti Kebangsaan Malaysia. 1990.

Jones, R. "The Origins of the Malay Manuscript Tradition." In *Cultural Contact and Textual Interpretation*. Edited by C.D. Grijns and S.O. Robson. Dordrecht: Foris. 1986.

Josselin de Jong, P.E. de. "Privately Owned Malay Manuscripts in Malaya." *Indonesia Circle* 21. 1980.

Kratz, E.U. "Running a Lending Library in Palembang in 1886." *Indonesia Circle* 14: 3–12. 1977.

Matheson, V. "Questions Arising from a Nineteenth Century Riau *Syair*." *RIMA* 17: 1–61. 1983.

Overbeck, H. "Malay Animal and Flower Shaers". *JMBRAS* 12.2: 108–148. 1934.

Sweeney, Amin. *Authors and Audiences in Traditional Malay Literature*. Monograph no. 20. Berkeley: Center for South and Southeast Asian Studies, University of California. 1980.

Voorhoeve, P. "A Malay Scriptorium." In *Malayan and Indonesian Studies: Essays presented to Sir Richard Winstedt on his Eighty-fifth Birthday.* Edited by J. Bastin and R. Roolvink, 256–266. Oxford: Clarendon. 1964.

Wilkinson, R.J., ed. "Malay Literature." In *Papers on Malay Subjects*. Kuala Lumpur: FMS Government Press. 1907.

Winstedt, R.O. *A History of Classical Malay Literature*. 2nd ed. *JMBRAS* 31.3 (1958). Reprint. Kuala Lumpur: Oxford University Press. 1969.

CHAPTER 5

POETRY AND WORSHIP: MANUSCRIPTS FROM ACEH

Damsté, H. T. "Hikayat Prang Sabi." *BKI* 84: 545–609. 1928.

Hamidy, U.U. *Anzib Lamnyong: Gudang Karya Sastra Aceh*. Kertas Karya No.5. Pusat Latihan Penelitian Ilmu-Ilmu Sosial, Banda Aceh. 1974

Langen, K.F.H. van. *Handleiding voor de beoefening der Atjehsche taal.* 's Gravenhage: Nijhoff. 1889,

——. *Woordenboek der Atjehsche Taal*. 's Gravenhage: Nijhoff. 1889.

Snouck Hurgronje, C. "Studiën over Atjèhsche klank- en schiftleer." *TBG* 35: 346–442. 1892

——. *De Atjèhers*. 2 vols. Batavia-Leiden. 1893–1894.

——. *The Achehnese*. Translated by A.W.S. O'Sullivan. 2 vols. Leiden: Brill. 1906.

Voorhoeve, P. *Catalogus van de Atjèhse handschriften van het Koninklijk Bataviaasch Genootschap en Beschrijving van de Atjèhse handschriften in bruikleen afgestaan door Prof. Dr. P.A.H. Djajadiningrat*. Typescript. 1949.

——. *Catalogus van de Atjèhse handschriften in de Universiteitsbibliotheek te Leiden, ten behoeve van het Instituut voor Taal- en Cultuuronderzoek van de Universiteit van Indonesië samengesteld*. Typescript. 1949.

——. "Three Old Achehnese Manuscripts." *BSOAS* 14: 335–45. 1952.

Voorhoeve, P., T. Iskandar, and M. Durie. *Catalogue of Acehnese Manuscripts in the Library of the University of Leiden and Other Collections Outside Aceh*. Leiden: E.J. Brill and Leiden University Press. Forthcoming.

Wamad Abdullah, ed. *Katalog Manuskrip Perpustakaan Pesantren Tanoh Abee Aceh Besar*. Banda Aceh: PDIA.

CHAPTER 6

CULTURAL PLURALITY: THE SUNDANESE OF WEST JAVA

Abdurahman and Ayatrohaedi. *Wawacan Ogin Amarsakti.* Jakarta: Departemen Pendidikan dan Kebudayaan. 1991.

Atja and Ayatrohaedi. *Nagarakretabumi*. Bandung: Bagian Proyek Penelitian dan Pengkajian Kebudayaan Sunda (Sundanologi), Departemen Pendidikan dan Kebudayaan. 1986.

Atja and Saleh Danasasmita. *Amanat dari Galunggung.* Bandung: Proyek Pengembangan Permuseuman Jawa Barat, Departemen Pendidikan dan Kebudayaan. 1981.

——. *Carita Parahiyangan.* Bandung: Proyek Pengembangan Permuseuman Jawa Barat, Departemen Pendidikan dan Kebudayaan. 1981.

——. *Sanghiyang Siksakandang Karesian.* Bandung: Proyek Pengembangan Permuseuman Jawa Barat, Departemen Pendidikan dan Kebudayaan. 1981.

Atja. *Carita Purwaka Caruban Nagari.* Bandung: Proyek Pengembangan Permuseuman Jawa Barat, Departemen Pendidikan dan Kebudayaan. 1986.

——. *Kitab Waruga Jagat.* Bandung: Lembaga Kebudajaan Universitas Padjadjaran. 1972.

——. *Ratu Pakuan: Tjerita Sunda Kuno dari Lereng Gunung Tjikurai.* Bandung: Lembaga Bahasa dan Sedjarah. 1970.

——. *Tepatkah Metoda Epigrafi Diterapkan dalam Penelitian Manuskrip?* Makalah pada Seminar Akademis di Fakultas Sastra Universitas Padjadjaran. 1988.

——. *Tjarita Parahijangan.* Bandung: Jajasan Kebudajaan Nusalarang. 1968.

Ayatrohaedi. "Kerajaan Tarumanagara: Pertemuan Kebudayaan." BA thesis, Jakarta: Fakultas Sastra, Universitas Indonesia. 1964.

——. *Tarumanagara: Sejarah Jawa Barat Dari Pra Sejarah Sampai Penyebaran Agama Islam.* Bandung: Pemerintah Daerah Tingkat 1 Propinsi Jawa Barat. 1975.

Brandes, J.L.A. *Babad Tjêrbon. TBG* 59: 1–144. 1911.

Cortesao, A. *The Suma Oriental of Tome Pires.* London: The Hakluyt Society. 1944.

Dam, H. Ten. *Verkenningen Rondom Padjadjaran. Indonesië* 10e. 1957.

Edi S. Ekadjati. *Babad Cerbon Edisi Brandes: Tinjauan Sastra dan Sejarah.* Bandung: Fakultas Sastra Universitas Padjadjaran. 1978.

——. *Cerita Dipati Ukur: Karya Sastra Sejarah Sunda.* Jakarta: Pustaka Jaya. 1982.

——. *Cerita Dipati Ukur: Karya Satra Sejarah Sunda.* Jakarta: Pustaka Jaya. 1982.

——. *Naskah Sunda: Inventarisasi dan Pencatatan.* Bandung: Universitas Padjadjaran–The Toyota Foundation. 1988.

——. "Penyebaran Agama Islam di Jawa Barat." In *Sejarah Jawa Barat dari Prasejarah hingga Penyebaran Agama Islam.* Bandung: Proyek Penunjang Peningkatan Kebudayaan Nasional Propinsi Jawa Barat. 1975.

——. *Priangan Historiography.* Paper on Indonesia-Netherland Historical Congress in Lage Vuursche. 1980.

——. *Wawacan Carios Munada.* Jakarta: Departemen Pendidikan dan Kebudayaan. 1993.

——. *Wawacan Sajarah Galuh.* Jakarta-Bandung: Lembaga Penelitian Perancis untuk Timur Jauh (EFEO). 1981.

Edi S. Ekadjati et al. *Naskah Sunda Lama Kelompok Cerita.* Jakarta: Departemen Pendidikan dan Kebudayaan. 1983.

——. *Naskah Sunda Lama.* Jakarta: Pusat Pembinaan dan Pengembangan Bahasa, Departemen Pendidikan dan Kebudayaan. 1980.

——. *Naskah Sunda: Inventarisasi dan Pencatatan.* Bandung: Lembaga Penelitian Universitas Padjadjaran/The Toyota Foundation. 1988.

Eringa, F.S. "*Loetoeng Kasaroeng: Een Mythologisch Verhaal uit West Java.*" *VKI* 8. 1949.

——. *Soendaas-Nederlands Woordenboek.* KITLV. Dordrecht: Foris Publications. 1984.

Ginting, A. "Sistem Penanggalan (Parhalaan) Batak Toba; Sebuah Kajian Filologi". MA thesis, Universitas Padjadjaran. 1990.

Graaf, H. H., and Th. G. Th. Pigeaud. "*De Eerste Muslimse Vorstendommen van Java.*" *VKI* 69. 1974.

Haan, F. De. *Priangan: De Preanger-Regentschappen onder Nederlandsch Bestuur tot 1811.* Vols. 2 & 3. BGKW. Batavia: G. Kolff. 1912.

Hageman J. Cz., J. "*Geschiedenis der Soenda-landen*". *TBG* 16: 193–251. 1867.

Hasan Djapar. "*Prasasti-prasasti dari Masa Kerajaan-kerajaan Sunda.*" Makalah pada Seminar Nasional Sastra dan Sejarah Pakuan Pajajaran, Bogor. 1992.

Hermansoemantri et al. *Babad Cirebon: Edisi Teks dan Terjemahan.* Bandung: Bagian Proyek Penelitian dan Pengkajian Kebudayaan Sunda (Sundanologi), Departemen Pendidikan dan Kebudayaan. 1985.

Hoesein Djajadiningrat. *Critische Beschouwing van de Sadjarah Banten.* Haarlem: Enschede en Zonen. 1913.

Holle, K.F. "*Pijagem van den Vorst van Mataram.*" *TBG* 13: 492–496. 1864.

——. "*Vlugtig Berigt omtrent Eenige Lontar Handschriften Afkomstig uit de Soendalanden.*" *TBG* 15. 1867.

——. "*Bijdragen tot de Geschiedenis der Preanger-Regentschappen.*" *TBG* 17: 316–367. 1869.

Kartodirdjo, et al. *Sejarah Nasional Indonesia.* Vol. 2. Jakarta: Balai Pustaka, Departemen Pendidikan dan Kebudayaan. 1975.

Krom, N.J. *Oudheidkundige Rapporten van Java.* Batavia. 1914.

Moh. Amir Sutaarga. *Prabu Siliwangi.* 2nd ed. Jakarta: Pustaka Jaya. 1984.

Mohamad Kosasih. "*Pamidjahan en zijn heiligdommen.*" *Djawa* 18: 121–144. 1938.

Noorduyn, J. *"Het Begin Gedeelte van den Tjarita Parahijangan: Tekst, Vertaling, Commentaar."* BKI 118: 405–432. 1962.

——. *"Over het Eerste Gedeelte van de Oud Sundanese Tjarita Parahijangan".* BKI 118: 374–383. 1962.

——. *"Eenige Nadere Gegevens over Tekst en Inhoud van de Tjarita Parahijangan."* BKI 122: 366–367. 1965.

——. "Traces of an Old Sundanese Ramajana Tradition." *Indonesia* 12: 151–157. 1972.

——. "Bujangga Manik Journey Through Java: Topographical Data from an Old Sundanese Source." BKI 138: 4. 413–442. 1982.

——. "The Making of Bark-paper in West Java." BKI 121: 472–473. 1965.

Panitia Kamus LBSS. *Kamus Umum Basa Sunda.* Bandung: Tarate. 1975.

Pleyte, C.M. *"Het Jaartal op den Batoe Toelis nabij Buitenzorg."* TBG 53: 155–220. 1911.

——. *"De Patapan Adjar Soeka Resi, Andersgezegd: De Kluizenarij op den Goenoeng Padang."* TBG 55: 321–428. 1913.

——. *"Poernawidjaja's Heelevart op de Volledige Verlossing."* TBG 59: 380–418. 1914.

R.H. Moehamad Moesa. *Dongeng-dongeng Pieunteungen.* Batavia: Landsdrukkerij. 1867.

Ricklefs, M.C. *A History of Modern Indonesia.* London and Basingstoke: MacMillan. 1981.

Rinkes, D.A. *"De heiligen van Java, I. De maqam van Sjec Abdoelmoehji."* TBG 18: 121–144. 1910.

Saleh Danasasmita. "Latar Belakang Sosial Sejarah Kuno Jawa Barat dan Hubungan antara Galuh dengan Pajajaran." In *Sejarah Jawa Barat dari Prasejarah hingga Penyebaran Agama Islam.* Bandung: Proyek Penunjang Peningkatan Kebudayaan Nasional Propinsi Jawa Barat. 1975.

Saleh Danasasmita et al. *Babad Pakuan atau Babad Pajajaran.* Jakarta: Proyek Pengembangan Media Kebudayaan, Departemen Pendidikan dan Kebudayaan. 1977.

——. *Masyarakat Kanekes.* Bandung: Bagian Proyek Penelitian dan Pengkajian Kebudayaan Sunda (Sundanologi), Departemen Pendidikan dan Kebudayaan. 1986.

——. *Sewaka Darma, Sanghiyang Siksakandang Karesian, dan Amanat dari Galunggung.* Bandung: Bagian Proyek Penelitian dan Pengkajian Kebudayaan Sunda (Sundanologi), Departemen Pendidikan dan Kebudayaan. 1987.

Sasadara. *Dalancang Panaraga/Penaraga Paper.* Translated by Alan Feinstein. 1900.

Suhamir. *"Tjatetan Sadjarah Sunda."* Kudjang 276. 6. 1961.

Sunarto H. and V. Sukanda-Tessier. *Cariosan Prabu Siliwangi.* Jakarta, Bandung: Lembaga Penelitian Perancis untuk Timur Jauh (EFEO). 1983.

CHAPTER 7

LEAVES OF PALM: BALINESE LONTAR

Ando, M. *"Krsnantaka*: An Old Javanese *Kakawin."* Ph.D. diss., Australian National University. 1991.

Bernet Kempers, A.J. *Monumental Bali: Introduction to Balinese Archaeology & Guide to the Monuments.* Berkeley/Singapore: Periplus Editions. 1991.

Clercq, F.S.A. de. *Nieuw Plantkundig Woordenboek voor Nederlandsch Indië.* Amsterdam: J.H. de Bussy. 1909.

Creese, H. M. *"Subhadrawiwaha*: An Old Javanese *Kakawin."* Ph.D. diss., Australian National University. 1981.

——. *The Parthayana — The Journeying of Partha: An Eighteenth-Century Balinese Kakawin.* KITLV. Forthcoming.

Eck, R. van. *Beknopte Handleiding Bij de Beoefening van de Balineesche Taal ten dienste van Zendelingen en Ambtenaren.* Utrecht: Kemink. 1874.

Ensink, J. *"Rekhacarmma*: On the Indonesian Shadow-Play with Special Reference to the Island of Bali." In the *Adyar Library Bulletin* (Dr. V. Raghavan Felicitation volume) 31–32: 412–441. 1967–1968.

Forge, A. "Balinese Painting: Revival or Reaction?" In *Modernity in Asian Art.* Edited by J. Clark. Sydney: Wild Peony. 1993.

Goody, J. "Introduction." In *Literacy in Traditional Societies*. Edited by J. Goody, 1–26. Cambridge: Cambridge University Press. 1968.

——. "Restricted Literacy in Northern Ghana." In *Literacy in Traditional Societies*. Edited by J. Goody, 198–264. Cambridge: Cambridge University Press. 1968.

Goris, R. *Prasasti Bali: Inscripties voor Anak Wungsu*. 2 vols. Lembaga Bahasa dan Budaja (Fakultas Sastra dan Filsafat), Universitet Indonesia. Bandung: Masa Baru. 1954.

Grader, C.J. "De Vervaardiging." In Grader, C.J., and C. Hooykaas. "*Lontar* als Schrijfmateriaal." *MK* 13:23–29. 1941.

——. "Pura Meduwe Karang at Kubutambahan." In *Bali: Further Studies in Life, Thought and Ritual*. J. van Baal et al. eds. The Hague: W. van Hoeve, 131–174. 1969 [1940].

Guy, J. *Palm-Leaf and Paper: Illustrated Manuscripts of India and Southeast Asia*. Melbourne: National Gallery of Victoria. 1982.

Hinzler, H.I.R. "Catalogue of Balinese Manuscripts in the Library of the University of Leiden and Other Collections in the Netherlands." Vol. 3 of "Manuscripts from the Van der Tuuk Collection," Bibliotheca Universitatis Leidensis, Codices Manuscripti."

——. "Balinese Palm Leaf Manuscripts: Manufacture, Manipulation and Magic. Writing Materials, Writing and Scribes." Paper presented at the Workshop on Southeast Asian Manuscripts. KITLV. Leiden. 1992.

——. "Het Gebruik." In Grader, C.J., and C. Hooykaas. "*Lontar* als schrijfmateriaal." *MK* 13:26–29. 1941.

——. *Surya-Sevana: The Way to God of a Balinese Siva Priest*. Nieuwe Reeks 72. 3. Amsterdam: Noord-Hollandsche Uitgevers Maatschappij. 1966.

——. *Bagus Umbara: Prince of Koripan*. London: Trustees of the British Museum. 1968.

——. *Balinese Bauddha Brahmins*. VKNAWL, Nieuwe Reeks 80. Amsterdam: North-Holland Publishing Company. 1973.

——. *Kama and Kala: Materials for the Study of Shadow Theatre in Bali*. VKNAWL, Nieuwe Reeks 79. Amsterdam: North-Holland Publishing Company. 1973.

——. "A Balinese Temple Festival". BI 15. The Hague: Martinus Nijhoff. 1977.

——. "Introduction à la littérature Balinaise." *Archipel* 8. 1979.

I Gusti Bagus Sugriwa. *Kakawin Bharata Yuddha*. 15 vols. Denpasar: Balimas. 1958.

——. *Kakawin Ramayana. Ditulis dengan huruf Bali dan Latin. Diberi arti dengan bahasa Bali dan bahasa Indonesia*. Denpasar: Balimas. 1959.

——. *Kekawin Ardjuna Wiwaha. Ditulis dengan huruf Bali dan Latin. Diberi arti dengan bahasa Bali dan bahasa Indonesia*. Denpasar: Balimas. 1961.

——. *Poerwa Sastera 3. Wawaosan Alit-alit Kelas 2 ring Sekolahan Bali*. Groningen, The Hague, Batavia: J.B. Wolters. 1936.

——. *Sutasoma. Ditulis dengan huruf Bali dan Latin. Diberi arti dengan bahasa Bali dan bahasa Indonesia*. Denpasar: Balimas. 1959.

I Ketut Ginarsa. "The *Lontar* (Palmyra Palm)." *RIMA* 91: 90–103. 1976.

——. *Sepintas Tentang Sejarah Aksara Bali*. Singaraja (Bali): Balai Penelitian Bahasa. 1980.

I Ketut Nasa and I Gusti Putu Djlantik. *Balineesch Leesboekje*, 2. Weltevreden: Landsdrukkerij. 1931.

I Made Suastika. "Kakawin Dimbhi Wicitra: Analisis Struktur dan Fungsi." M.A. thesis, Universitas Gadjah Mada. 1985.

I Wayan Ardika and P. Bellwood. "Sembiran: The Beginnings of Indian Contact with Bali." *Antiquity* 65: 221–232. 1991.

I Wayan Bhadra. "Het 'Mabasan' of de Beoefening van het Oud-Javaansch op Bali." *MK* 5. 1937.

I Wayan Warna, I Bagus Gede Murdha, I Nyoman Sujana et al. *Kekawin Ramayana*. 2 vols. Denpasar: Dinas Pendidikan Dasar Propinsi Dati I Bali. 1987.

——. *Kekawin Arjuna Wiwaha*. Denpasar: Dinas Pendidikan Dasar Propinsi Daerah Tingkat I Bali. 1988.

——. *Kekawin Bharatayuddha*. Denpasar: Dinas Pendidikan Dasar Propinsi Daerah Tingkat I Bali. 1990.

Jean, Georges. *Writing: The Story of Alphabets and Script*. London: Thames & Hudson. 1992.

Jones, R. "European and Asian Papers in Malay Manuscripts. A Provisional Assessment." *BKI* 149 3: 474–502. 1993.

Kat Angelino, P. "Over de Smeden en Eenige Andere Ambachtslieden op Bali". *TBG* 61: 370–424. 1922.

Liefrinck, F.A. *Nog eenige Verordeningen en Overeenkomsten van Balische Vorsten*. KITLV van Ned.-Indië. The Hague: Martinus Nijhoff. 1921.

——. "Noord-Balische désa-monographieën 1882-1889." In *Adatrechtbundels 37: Bali en Lombok*, 1–345. 1934.

Lovric, B.J.A. "Rhetoric and Reality: The Hidden Nightmare. Myth and Magic as Reverberations of Morbid Realities." Ph.D. diss., University of Sydney. 1987.

Monier-Williams, M. *A Sanskrit-English Dictionary*. Delhi, Varanasi, Patna: Motilal Banarsidass. 1976 [1899].

Ong, W.J. *Orality and Literacy: The Technologizing of the Word*. London, New York: Methuen. 1982.

Partini Sardjono-Pradotokusumo. "Kakawin Gajah Mada: Sebuah Karya Sastra Kakawin Abad ke-20. Suntingan Naskah Serta Telaah Struktur, Tokoh dan Hubungan Antarteks." Ph.D. diss., Universitas Indonesia. 1984.

Pigeaud, Th.G.Th. *Literature of Java: Catalogue Raisonné of Javanese Manuscripts in the Library of the University of Leiden and Other Publications in the Netherlands*. 3 vols. The Hague: Martinus Nijhoff. 1967–1970.

——. *Codices Manuscripti-20. Literature of Java: Catalogue Raisonné of Javanese Manuscripts in the Library of the University of Leiden and Other Public Collections in The Netherlands*. Vol. 4. *Supplement*. Leiden: Leiden University Press. 1980.

Reid, A. *Southeast Asia in the Age of Commerce: 1450–1680*. Vol. 1, *The Lands Below the Winds*. New Haven: Yale University Press. 1988.

Robson, S.O. "Wangbang Wideya: A Javanese Panji Romance." BI 6. The Hague: Martinus Nijhoff. 1971.

——. "The Kawi Classics in Bali." *BKI* 128: 308–329. 1972.

Rubinstein, R. "Beyond the Realm of the Senses: The Balinese Ritual of *Kekawin* Composition." Ph.D diss., University of Sydney. 1988.

——. "*Pepaosan*: Challenges and Change." In *Balinese Music in Context: A Sixty-fifth Birthday Tribute to Hans Oesch*. Edited by D.H. Schaareman. Basler, Winterthur: Amadäus Verlag: 85–113. 1993.

Tuuk, H.N. van der. *Kawi-Balineesch-Nederlandsch Woordenboek*. 4 vols. Batavia: Landsdrukkerij. 1897–1912.

Vickers, A.H. "The Desiring Prince: A Study of the Kidung Malat as Text." Ph.D. diss., University of Sydney. 1986.

——. *Bali: A Paradise Created*. Ringwood (Victoria): Penguin. 1989.

Wallis, R.H. "The Voice as a Mode of Cultural Expression in Bali." Ph.D. diss., University of Michigan. 1980.

Weck, Wolfgang. *Heilkunde und Volkstum auf Bali*. Jakarta: PT Bap Bali, PT Intermasa. 1976 [1937].

Worsley, P.J. "Babad Buleleng: A Balinese Dynastic Genealogy." BI 8. 1972.

Zurbuchen, M.S. *The Language of Balinese Shadow Theater*. Princeton: Princeton University Press. 1987.

CHAPTER 8
THE LITERARY TRADITION OF LOMBOK

Behrend, T.E. *The Serat Jatiswara. Structure and Change in a Javanese Poem, 1600–1930*. Ph.D. diss. Australian National University. 1987.

Departemen Pendidikan Dan Kebudayaan Wilayah Propinsi Nusa Tenggara Barat. *Puspakrama*. 1981–1982.

Eck, R. van. "*Tekst en vertaling van de Megantaka, Balineesche-gagoeritan, voorafgegaan door eenige algemeene opmerkingen over de Balineesche Kidoeng.*" TBG 38. 1875.

Eerde, J.C. van. "*De toetoer Monyeh op Lombok.*" BKI 59: 17–109. 1906.

——. "*Tutur Cilinaya op Lombok.*" BKI 67: 22–58. 1913.

I Wayan Bhadra and C. Hooykaas. "*Dampati Lalangon, Balisch Gedicht van West-Lombok.*" TBG 82: 1. 1942.

Marrison, G.E. "Modern Balinese: A Regional Literature of Indonesia." *BKI* 143/4: 468–498. 1987.

Pigeaud, Th.G.Th. *The Nagara-kertagama by Rakawi Prapanca of Majapahit, 1365 A.D.* 5 vols. The Hague: Martinus Nijhoff, 1963.

V.J. Herman, et al. *Bunga Rampai. Kutipan Naskah Lama dan Aspek Pengetahuannya.* Departemen Pendidikan dan Kebudayaan, Direktorat Jenderal Kebudayaan, Museum Negeri Nusa Tenggara Barat. 1990.

CHAPTER 9
TEXTUAL GATEWAYS: THE EVOLUTION OF JAVANESE MANUSCRIPTS

Arps, B. *Tembang in Two Traditions. Performance and Interpretation of Javanese Literature.* London: SOAS, University of London. 1992.

Crucq, K.C. "Houtsnijwerk met inscripties in den Kraton Kasepoehan te Cheribon." *Djawa* 12: 8–10, plus 4 plates. 1932.

Day, A. "Islam and Literature in South-East Asia. Some Pre-modern, Mainly Javanese Perspectives." In *Islam in South-East Asia* (2nd impression) Edited by M.B. Hooker, 30–159. Leiden etc.: E.J. Brill. 1988.

Florida, N. K. *Javanese Literature in Surakarta Manuscripts.* Vol. 1, *Introduction and Manuscripts of the Karaton Surakarta.* Ithaca: Cornell University Press. 1993.

Guillot, C. "*Le dluwang ou Papier Javanais.*" *Archipel:* 26: 105–115. 1984.

Kamajaya, ed. *Serat Centhini Latin.* 12 vols. Yogyakarta: Yayasan Centhini. 1985–1991.

Poerbatjaraka, R.M.Ng. *Beschrijving der Handschriften: Menak.* Bandung: A.C. Nix & Co. 1959.

Poerbatjaraka, R.M.Ng., P. Voorhoeve, and C. Hooykaas. *Indonesische Handschriften.* Bandung: A.C. Nix & Co. 1959.

Soemodidjojo Mahadewa, ed. *Kitab Primbon Betaljemur Adammakna,* 43rd ed. Yogyakarta: Soemodidjojo Mahadewa. 1979.

Vreede, A.C. *Catalogus van de Javaansche en Madoereesche handschriften der Leidsche Universiteits-bibliotheek.* Leiden: E.J. Brill. 1892.

CHAPTER 10
A LEGACY OF TWO HOMELANDS: CHINESE MANUSCRIPT LITERATURE

Pigeaud, T.G. Th. *Literature of Java: Catalogue Raisonné of Javanese Manuscripts in the Library of the University of Leiden and Other Public Collections in the Netherlands.* 4 vols. The Hague: Martinus Nijhoff. 1968.

Salmon, C. *Literature in Malay by the Chinese of Indonesia: A Provisional Annotated Bibliography. Archipel* 3. 1981.

Salmon, C., ed. *Literary Migrations: Traditional Chinese Fiction in Asia (17th to 20th centuries).* Beijing: International Culture Publishing Corporation. 1987.

CHAPTER 11
A SEPARATE EMPIRE: WRITINGS OF SOUTH SULAWESI

Abdul Muthalib, et al. *Transliterasi dan Terjemahan Pappasang dan Kalindaqdaq Naskah Lontar Mandar.* Ujung Pandang: Proyek Penelitian dan Pengkajian Kebudayaan Sulawesi Selatan La Galigo. 1986.

Andaya, L.Y. *The Heritage of Arung Palakka; A History of South Sulawesi (Celebes) in the Seventeenth Century. VKI* 91. 1981.

Brink, H. van den. *Dr. Benjamin Frederik Matthes; Zijn leven en arbeid in dienst van het Nederlandsch Bijbelgenootschap.* Amsterdam: Nederlandsch Bijbelgenootschap 1943.

Cense, A.A. *"Beknopte beschrijving van de Boeginese en Makassaarse handschriften van de Lembaga Kebudajaan Indonesia 'Kon. Bataviaasch Genootschap van Kunsten en Wetenschappen."* Carbon copy kept in the Leiden University Library (O.L.G. C 2440). [1950].

Cense, A.A. *"Enige aantekeningen over Makassaars-Boeginese Geschiedschrijving."* BKI 107: 42–60. 1951.

———. "Old Buginese and Macassarese Diaries." *BKI* 122: 416–28. 1966.

Cense, A.A., with Abdoerrahim. *Makassaars-Nederlands woordenboek; Met Nederlands-Makassaars register en voorwoord door J. Noorduyn.* 's Gravenhage: Nijhoff. 1979.

Daud Ismail (trans.). *Tarjumah wa tafsir al-juz' al-thalathuna = Tarejumanna nennia tapessrna juseq amma.* Ujung Pandang: Bintang Selatan. 1982.

Fachruddin Ambo Enre. "Ritumpanna Wlenrnng: Telaah Filologis sebuah Episoda Bugis Klasik Galigo." Ph.D. diss., Universitas Indonesia. 1983.

Jumsari Jusuf et al. *Katalog Naskah Aneka Bahasa Koleksi Museum Nasional.* Jakarta: Departemen Pendidikan dan Kebudayaan, Direktorat Jenderal Kebudayaan, Museum Nasional. 1983.

Kern, R.A. *Catalogus van de Boegineesche, tot den I La Galigo-cyclus behoorende handschriften der Leidsche Universiteitsbibliotheek alsmede van die in andere Europeesche bibliotheken.* Leiden: Universiteitsbibliotheek. 1939.

———. *Catalogus van de Boeginese, tot de I La Galigo-cyclus behorende handschriften van Jajasan Matthes (Matthesstichting) te Makasar (Indonesië).* Makasar: Jajasan Matthes. 1954.

Matthes, B.F. *Kort verslag aangaande alle mij in Europa bekende Makassaarsche en Boeginesche handschriften, vooral die van het Nederlandsch Bijbelgenootschap te Amsterdam.* 's Gravenhage: Nijhoff. 1875.

Millar, Susan Bolyard. *Bugis Weddings: Rituals of Social Location in Modern Indonesia.* Center for South and Southeast Asia Studies Monograph Series No. 29. Berkeley: University of California. 1989.

Noorduyn, J. *Een Achttiende-eeuwse Kroniek van Wadjo: Buginese historiografie.* 's-Gravenhage: Smits. 1955.

———. *A Critical Survey of Studies on the Languages of Sulawesi.* Bibliographical Series 18. Leiden: KITLV Press. 1991.

———. "The Manuscripts of the Makasarese Chronicle of Goa and Talloq: An Evaluation." *BKI* 147: 454–484. 1991.

———. "Variation in the Bugis and Makasarese Scripts." Paper presented at the Seventh International Workshop on Indonesian Studies, Leiden, December 14–18, 1992.

P. Parawansa, et al. *Sastra sinrilik Makassar.* Jakarta: Pusat Pembinaan dan Pengembangan Bahasa. 1992.

Rachmah, et al. *Monografi kebudayaan Makassar di Sulawesi Selatan.* Ujung Pandang: Pemerintah Daerah Tingkat I Sulawesi Selatan. 1984.

Raffles, T.S. *The History of Java.* London: Black, Parbury and Allen. 1817.

Ricklefs, M.C., and P. Voorhoeve. *Indonesian Manuscripts in Great Britain: A Catalogue of Manuscripts in Indonesian Languages in British Public Collections.* London: Oxford University Press. 1977.

S.W.R. Mulyadi and H.S. Maryam R. Salahuddin. *Katalogus naskah Melayu Bima.* Bima: Yayasan Museum Kebudayaan "Samparaja." 1990.

Stapel, F. *"De oprichting der Vereenigde Oostindische Compagnie; De Nederl. Oostindische Compagnie in de zeventiende eeuw."* In *Geschiedenis van Nederlandsch Indië,* Vol. 3. Edited by F. Stapel. Amsterdam: Joost van den Vondel. 1939.

Tol, R. *Een haan in oorlog: Toloqna Arung Labuaja, een twintigste-eeuws Buginees heldendicht van de hand van I Mallaq Daéng Mab,la Arung Manajéng. VKI* 141. 1990.

———. "Fish Food on a Tree Branch; Hidden Meanings in Bugis Poetry." *BKI* 148: 82–102. 1992.

———. "A Royal Collection of Bugis Manuscripts." Paper presented at the Seventh International Workshop on Indonesian Studies, Leiden, December 14–18, 1992.

———. "Indonesia." In *Islamic Manuscripts in the World.* London: Al-Furqan Foundation. 1993.

Braasem, W.A. "H.N. Van der Tuuk: Bij het 60ste Sterfjaar van de Vader der Indonesische Filologie." *Cultureel Nieuws-Indonesië* 39: 46–52. 1955.

Brenner, J. Freiherr von. *Besuch bei den Kannibalen Sumatras: Erste Durchquerung der unabhängigen Batak-Lande.* Würzburg. 1894.

Holle, K.F. *Tabel van Oud- en Nieuw- Indische Alphabetten.* Bijdrage tot de Palaeographie van Nederlandsch-Indië. BGKW. Batavia: W. Bruining & Co., 's Hage: M.Nijhoff. 1882.

J.E. Saragih and A.A. Dalimunte. *Pustaha Laklak No.252 Museum Simalungun & Pustaha Laklak Mandailing.* Jakarta: Proyek Pengembangan Media Kebudayaan, Direktor Jenderal Kebudayaan, Departemen Pendidikan dan Kebudayaan. [circa 1984], n.d.

J.E. Saragih. *Kamus Simalungun-Indonesia.* Pematang Siantar: Kolportase GKPS. 1989.

Junghuhn, F. *Die Battaländer auf Sumatra.* 2 Vols. Berlin: G. Reimer. 1847.

Kern, H. Over de Sanskrit-opschriften van (Muara Kaman, in) Kutei (Borneo) (±A.D. 400). In Verband met de geschiedenis van het schrift in den Indischen Archipel. *Verslagen en Mededeelingen der Koninklijken Akademie van Wetenschappen, afd. Letterkunde,* 2e Reeks, dl. 11. Amsterdam: van der Post. 1882.

———. Eene bijdrage tot de palaeographie van Nederlandsch-Indië. *Verspreide Geschriften 6. Bijdragen tot de Taal-Land- en Volkenkunde van Nederlandsch-Indië, 4e Volgreeks, dl. 6.* 's Gravenhage: Martinus Nijhoff. 1882.

Kozok, U. "Aksara Batak: Antara Mesin Tik dan Komputer." *Sinar Indonesia Baru* 27: 9. 1990.

———. "Batak Script and Literature." In *Living with Ancestors. Batak: Peoples of the Island of Sumatra.* Edited by Achim Sibeth, 100–114. New York: Thames and Hudson. 1991.

———. "Lamentations of the Karo-Batak, North Sumatra." *Indonesian Circle* 59, 60: 57–61. 1992–1993.

———. *Die Klageliedtradition der Batak Nordsumatras.* Ph.D. diss., University of Hamburg. 1994.

Liberty Manik. *Batak Handschriften. Verzeichnis der orientalischen Handschriften in Deutschland.* Bd.28. Wiesbaden. 1973.

Mangantar Simanjuntak. "The Batak Script as an Invention of the Austronesian-speaking People." *Akademika* 9: 59–76. Kuala Lumpur. July 1976.

Marschall, W. "*Die indonesischen Handschriften von Sumatra.*" *Studium Generale.* Jg.20, Heft 9: 559–564. 1967.

Marsden, W.E. *The History of Sumatra: Containing an Account of the Government, Laws, Customs, and Manners of the Native Inhabitants, with a Description of the Natural Productions, and a Relation of the Ancient Political State of the Island.* London: Author. 1783.

Parkin, H. *Batak Fruit of Hindu Thought.* Madras. 1978.

Pigeaud, Th. G.Th., and P. Voorhoeve. *Handschriften aus Indonesien: Bali, Java und Sumatra. Verzeichnis der orientalischen Handschriften in Deutschland.* Edited by Dieter George. Stuttgart: Franz Steiner Verlag; Wiesbaden: GmbH. 1985.

Pleyte, C.M. *De Verkenning der Bataklanden. Een Bijdrage tot de Geschiedenis der Ontdekking van het Toba-meer.* 1. Periode van 1772-1872, 2. Periode van 1873-1893. *Tijdschrift van het Koninklijk Nederlandsch Aardrijkkundig Genootschap* 2: 71–96; 12: 727–739. Amsterdam: Stemler 1895.

———. *Hoe de Bataks over Wijlen Dr H.N. Van der Tuuk dachten. Tijdschrift voor indische Taal-, Land- en Volkenkunde.* BGKW 47: 468–470. 1904.

Rodgers, S. "Me and Toba: A Childhood World in a Batak Memoir." *Indonesia* 45. Cornell. April 1988.

Schröder, E.E.Gs. *Über die semitischen und nicht indischen Grundlagen der malaiisch-polynesischen Kultur.* 3 vols. Medan: Köhler & Co. 1928.

Tuuk, H.N. van der. *Bataksch-Nederduitsch Woordenboek.* Amsterdam: F. Muller. 1861.

———. *Bataksch Leesboek.* (1) *Stukken in het Tobasch,* (2) *Stukken in het Mandailingsch,* (3) *Stukken in het Dairisch,* (4) *Taalkundige aantekeningen en bladwijzer, vertaalde stukken en inhoudsopgave tot de drie stukken van het Bataksche Leesboek*. Amsterdam: Frederik Muller. 1861–1862.

———. *A Grammer of Toba Batak.* Edited by A. Teeuw and R. Roolvink. KITLV Translation Series 13. The Hague: Martinus Nijhoff. 1971.

Voorhoeve, P. *Overzicht van de volksverhalen der Bataks.* Ph.D. diss. Rijksuniversiteit te Leiden. 1927.

———. *A Catalogue of the Batak Manuscripts in the Chester Beatty Library.* Dublin: Hodges Figgis & Co. Ltd. 1961.

———. *Catalogue of Indonesian Manuscripts.* Part 1, Batak M. Copenhagen: The Royal Library. 1975.

———. *Supplement to the Batak Catalogue.* The Chester Beatty Library. *BKI* 124. 3. 1968.

———. *Codices Batacici.* Codices Manuscripti 19. Leiden: Universitaire Pers. 1977.

Warneck, J.G. Studien über die Literatur der Toba-Batak. *Mittheilungen des Seminars für Orientalische Sprachen zu Berlin.* Erste Abtheilung. Ostasiatische Studien. Berlin und Stuttgart: Commissionsverlag von W. Spemann. S.101–139. 1899.

Winkler, J. *Die Toba-Batak auf Sumatra in gesunden und kranken Tagen.* Ein Beitrag zur Kenntnis des animistischen Heidentums. Stuttgart: Chr. Belser. 1925.

CHAPTER 13
ANCIENT LINKS: THE MYSTERY OF SOUTH SUMATRA

Braginsky, V. "A Preliminary Reconstruction of the Rencong version of the "Poem of the Boat." *Bulletin de l' École Française d' Extrême Orient.* 77: 263–310. 1988.

Damais, L.C. "Études soumatranaises I: La date de l'inscription de Hujung Langit (Bawang)." *Bulletin de l' École Française d' Extrême Orient.* 50.2: 276–310. 1962.

Jaspan, M.A. *Redjang Ka-ga-nga Texts.* Folk Literature of South Sumatra, Part I. Canberra: Australia National University. 1964.

Marrison, G. *A Catalogue of the South-East Asian Collections of Professor M.A. Jaspan in the Brynmoor Jones Library, University of Hull.* Bibliography and Literature No. 6. University of Hull, Centre for South-East Asian Studies. 1989.

Voorhoeve, P. *Critical Survey of Studies of the Languages of Sumatra.* Bibliographical Series 1. KITLV. The Hague: Martinus Njihoff. 1955.

———. "Kerintji documents." *BKI* 127: 369–399. 1970.

———. *Südsumatranische Handschriften.* Verzeichnis der Orientalischen Handschriften in Deutschland. Bnd 29. Wiesbaden: Franz Steiner Verlag GMBH. 1971.

Voorhoeve, P., ed. *Materials for a Rejang-Indonesian-English Dictionary.* Canberra: Australia National University. 1984.

Westenenk, L.C. *Rèntjong-schrift. II. "Beschreven hoorns in het landschap Krintji.* Tijdschrift voor Indische Taal-, Land-, en Volkenkunde. 61: 95–110. 1922.

CHAPTER 15
PRESERVATION OF MANUSCRIPTS IN INDONESIA

Agrawal, O. P. "The Care and Conservation of Palm-leaf and Paper Illustrated Manuscripts." In *Palm-leaf and Paper: Illustrated Manuscripts of India and Southeast Asia.* Edited by J. Guy. Melbourne: National Gallery of Victoria. 1982.

Agrawal, O. P. *Conservation of Manuscripts and Paintings of Southeast Asia.* London: Butterworths. 1984.

Baynes-Cope, A. D. *Caring for Books and Documents.* London: British Museum. 1981.

Behrend, T.E. "Javanese Manuscripts in Indonesia: The Problem of Uncatalogued Collections." *Caraka* 9: 9–18. 1986.

———. "The Serat Jatiswara: Structure and Change in a Javanese Poem, 1600–1930." Ph.D. diss., Australian National University. 1987.

———. "Small Collections of Javanese Manuscripts in Indonesia." *Archipel* 35: 23–33. 1988.

Behrend, T.E., et al. *Katalog Induk Naskah-naskah Nusantara, Jilid 1: Museum Sonobudoyo Yogyakarta.* Jakarta: Djambatan. 1990.

Behrend, T.E., and A. Feinstein. "Preservation of Manuscripts on Microfilm in Indonesia: Notes on Past, Current and Future Projects." *Southeast Asia Microfilms Newsletter* 20: 1–6. 1991.

Chambert-Loir, H. "Rapport de mission à Aceh, avril-mai 1976." *Bulletin de l'Ecole Française d'Extrême-Orient* 64: 306–309. 1977.

———. "Catalogue des catalogues de manuscrits Malais." *Archipel* 20: 45–69. 1980.

Cohen Stuart, A.B. "Catalogus van de Javaansche handschriften in het bezit van het Batavaiaasch Genootschap." *BGKW* 1: 260–268. 1872.

Florida, N.K. *Javanese Literature in Surakarta Manuscripts,* Vol. 1, *Introduction and Manuscripts of the Karaton Surakarta.* Ithaca: Southeast Asia Program, Cornell University. 1993.

Gordon, R. S. and E. Grace Maurice, eds. *Union List of Manuscripts in Canadian Repositories: Joint Project of the Public Archives of Canada and the Humanities Research Council of Canada.* Rev. ed., 2 vols. Ottawa: Public Archives Canada. 1975.

Hinzler, H.I.R. "The Balinese Manuscript Project." *South-East Asia Library Group Newsletter* 25: 7. 1983.

Hooykaas, C. "La conservation des manuscrits et de la parole parlée en Indonésie." *Archipel* 6: 33–41. 1973.

International Review Team. *Conservation and Preservation at the National Library of Indonesia: A Report by the International Review Team for Conservation and Preservation.* Jakarta: National Library of Indonesia. 1989.

Library of Congress. *The National Union Catalog of Manuscript Collections: Based on Reports from American Repositories of Manuscripts.* Compiled by the Library of Congress with the advice of the Advisory Committee on the National Union Catalog of Manuscript Collections. Ann Arbor, Michigan: Edwards. 1959.

Lindsay, J., R.M. Soetanto and A. Feinstein, eds. *Katalog Induk Naskah-naskah Nusantara,* Jilid 2, *Kraton Yogyakarta.* Jakarta: Obor. 1994.

Molen, W. van der. "A Catalogue of Catalogues of Javanese Manuscripts." *Caraka* 4: 12-49. 1984.

Muhammadin Razak, Retno Anggarini and Supriyanto, eds. *Pelestarian Bahan Pustaka dan Arsip.* Jakarta: Program Pelestarian Bahan Pustaka dan Arsip, Perspustakaan Nasional. 1992.

Poerbatjaraka, R.Ng. "Lijst der Javaansche handschriften in de boekerij van het Kon. Bat. Genootschap". BGKW 1: 269–376. 1933.

Poerbatjaraka, R.Ng., P. Voorhoeve and C. Hooykaas. *Indonesische Handschriften.* Bandung: A.C. Nix. 1950.

Roberts, M., and D. Etherington. *Bookbinding and the Conservation of Books: A Dictionary of Descriptive Terminology.* Washington, D.C.: Library of Congress. 1982.

Ronkel, P. van. *Catalogus der Maleische Handschriften in het Museum van het Bataviaasch Genootschap van Kunsten en Wetenschappen.* VBGKW No. 57. 1909.

S.W.R. Mulyadi, and H.S. Maryam R. Salahuddin. *Katalogus Naskah Melayu Bima.* 2 vols. Bima: Yayasan Museum Kebudayaan "Samparaja" Bima. 1990–1992.

Supriyanto, Retno Anggarini and Muhammadin Razak, eds. *Prosedur Perbaikan Buku,* Jakarta: Program Pelestarian Bahan Pustaka dan Arsip, Perpustakaan Nasional. 1991.

Sweeney, Amin. *A Full Hearing: Orality and Literacy in the Malay World.* Berkeley: University of Caifornia Press. 1987.

———. "Malay Sufi Poetics and European Norms." *Journal of the American Oriental Society* 112/1: 88–102. 1992.

Wahjudi Pantja Sunjata. *Katalog Naskah Kuna dan Buku Lama Koleksi Perpustakaan Balai Kajian Sejarah dan Nilai Tradisional, Yogyakarta.* Yogyakarta: Balai Kajian Sejarah dan Nilai Tradisional, Direktorat Sejarah dan Nilai Tradisional, Direktorat Jenderal Kebudayaan, Departemen Pendidikan dan Kebudayaan. [1993].

Wyatt, D.K. "The Surakarta Manuscript Project." *Indonesia* 34: 75–88. 1982.

LIST OF ILLUSTRATIONS

In preparation for the publication of *Illuminations* Lontar obtained illustrational materials from numerous lending institutions, both public and private, as well as from individuals. For reasons of brevity this List of Illustrations, which is arranged by the illustrations' order of appearance, incorporates abbreviations for the names of certain collections. These abbreviations as well as translations of the names of institutions that appear are as follows:

Behrend	T.E. Behrend Private Collection
FSUI	Faculty of Letters, University of Indonesia (Fakultas Sastra Universitas Indonesia), Jakarta
KIT	Royal Tropical Institute (Koninklijk Instituut voor de Tropen)
KITLV	Koninklijk Instituut voor Taal-, Land- en Volkendunde
Leiden University Library	Bibliotheek Rijksuniversiteit te Leiden
Lontar	The Lontar Foundation (Yayasan Lontar), Jakarta
MNJB	Sri Baduga State Museum of West Java (Museum Negeri Jawa Barat Sri Baduga), Bandung
National Archives	National Archives of Indonesia (Arsip Nasional Republik Indonesia), Jakarta
National Archives of Portugal	Arquivos Nacionais Torre do Tombo Gavetas, Lisboa
National Library	National Library of Indonesia (Perpustakaan Nasional Republik Indonesia)
National Museum	Museum Nasional, Jakarta
Royal Library of The Hague	Koninklijke Bibliotheek Den Haag
Samparaja Museum	Museum Kebudayaan Samparaja, Sumbawa
SOAS	School of Oriental and African Studies, London
Sonobudoyo	Sonobudoyo Museum (Museum Sonobudoyo), Yogyakarta
Tropical Museum	Tropenmuseum (of the Royal Institute for the Tropics), Amsterdam
Widya Budaya	Widya Budaya Collection of the Palace of Yogyakarta (Perpustakaan Widya Budaya, Kraton Kasultanan Ngayogyakarta Hadiningrat)
YAPENA	Foundation for the Preservation of Manuscripts (Yayasan Pemeliharaan Naskah), Bandung.

Please note that neither measurements nor folio numbers of the manuscripts featured in this book are given below. This shortcoming was unavoidable because a substantial percentage of the manuscripts have not been properly measured or foliated. For reasons of consistency, therefore, we chose not to include any measurements or folio numbers. Also note that in the list that follows all illustrations are manuscripts or details thereof unless otherwise indicated.

INDEX

The "weathermark" identifies this book as a production of Weatherhill, Inc., publishers of fine books on Asia and the Pacific. Editorial supervision: Meg Taylor. Typography, book and cover design: Liz Trovato and Mariana Canelo. Production supervision: Bill Rose. Printed and bound by Oceanic Graphic Press, Hong Kong. The typeface used is Simoncini Garamond.